The English Actor

From Medieval to Modern

Peter Ackroyd

REAKTION BOOKS

Published by
REAKTION BOOKS LTD
Unit 32, Waterside
44–48 Wharf Road
London N1 7UX, UK
www.reaktionbooks.co.uk

First published 2023
Paperback edition first published 2024
Copyright © Peter Ackroyd 2023

Printed and bound in Great Britain
by CPI Group (UK) Ltd, Croydon CRO 4YY

A catalogue record for this book is available from the British Library

ISBN 978 1 78914 839 8

Contents

The English actor has always striven to bind the two, sometimes contending, imperatives of the familiar and the far away.

Richardson, in common with many English actors, had felt the allure of other arts. He had wanted to be a painter. Realizing that he lacked the skill, he nursed the hope that 'one day I could "illustrate literature".' This is the glory and perhaps limitation of the native approach. The text is the English actor's guide and master in a way that still seems strange to his or her Continental counterparts, and it is impossible to consider the English actor without reference to the English play. 'My springboard is always the script,' said John Hurt. As a result, the English actor tends to savour and taste the words, not disguise them or replace them with his or her own. Improvisation, although often employed in training, is in origin a Continental practice. The written word lies at the heart of the English drama and therefore at the centre of the English actor's craft, in the pauses of Pinter as much as in the verbosity of Ben Jonson. It is not, then, surprising to learn that, for many centuries, the English actor was more orator than dancer. The body was never neglected – fitness, vocal flexibility and the arts of dance and fencing were all considered vital – but, compared with that of other cultures, it was rarely central to the English actor's art.

Hamlet himself has much to say about acting. One speech, his address to the players, has acquired almost canonical status. 'Speak the speech, I pray you, as I pronounced it to you, trippingly on the tongue . . . Nor do not saw the air too much, thus, but use all gently; for in the very torrent, tempest, and as I may say, the whirlwind of passion, you must acquire and beget a temperance that may give it smoothness . . . Let your own discretion be your tutor.' It is not quite a summons to tea in the drawing room, and indeed Hamlet makes a point of emphasizing the importance of 'passion', yet it cannot be denied that restraint or 'discretion' is the watchword. Here, then, is the English actor that many would recognize: restrained, discreet, even polite. If a masterclass in technique, Hamlet's speech says little of any inner life in the actors and offers no hint as to how, in the cause of verisimilitude, the springs of the spirit might be tapped. What, then, of this inner life? How can we probe something so inevitably intimate? We must go back to childhood.

A play begins in play, in the playing of a child. Sooner rather than later, the child's play takes the form of 'make-believe'. And once that deeply English expression is considered, it will soon become clear that it need not be the same as pretending. For the actor, this 'make-believe' must make belief. The resulting belief is not easy to classify. It is not the concession that two and two make four, nor, at the other extreme, a faith in the existence of fairies. It is rather the belief, however ephemeral, in a different reality of which one is part. And this belief must be enacted if it is to live; that is its peculiarity. The more one acts on the assumption that the alternative reality is the true one, the truer it becomes. It is in no sense pathological, although it might seem so to many. It begins in the play instinct. Acting may thus be considered the play instinct come to flower.

The English actor understands this. Unlike the American or Continental actor, perhaps, the English actor tends to regard his or her profession playfully. Thus an actor cannot afford to put aside childish things; they represent a livelihood. It is no accident that 'player' was for so long the preferred term to 'actor'. That great seventeenth-century anti-theatricalist William Prynne understood perhaps more than he knew when he asked how actors could demand payment for enjoying themselves.

It was in the miracle plays of the late medieval period that the distinctive qualities of the English actor emerged, above all, a gestural vocabulary that is clean, bright, extrovert and directed towards the audience. And it was in these plays, where private faith and public spectacle were one, that this vocabulary was wedded with rapture. Without access to rapture, the energy to play Christ or

Adam or Herod before an audience awaiting the coming of God to their city would have been impossible. Those actors called the deity into their hearts and saw him in the marketplace. We see something of this spirit in Michael Redgrave's description of 'feeling the god descend' as he acted.

In the Elizabethan period, the status of the actor was transformed. From being little better than an outlaw, the player became in turn a respected citizen and then an idol. 'A sound magician is a demigod,' as Faustus puts it at the beginning of Marlowe's drama, and the man who played him, Edward Alleyn, was considered semi-divine. For the actor to acquire this status, it appears that the style had to be both 'great', large in address and even in inches, and, in a phrase used again and again, 'to the life'. But, we may ask, whose life? And, for that matter, what kind of life? Naturalism in the twentieth-century sense was not to be sought. Just as the miniatures of Anglo-Saxon England showed not reality copied but reality transfigured, so the actors of the time, at least before Richard Burbage, offered man magnified. Then, as now, it was believed that there were actors who swelled a progress and actors who simply swelled: actors and great actors. This distinction, however, is increasingly in question. The director Bill Gaskill once told Simon Callow that 'the conditions for great acting no longer exist.' Steven Berkoff, the actor and playwright, put it more bluntly when he asked, 'Where are the Albert Finneys, the Scofields, the O'Tooles? Ain't here mate.'

What was, or is, great acting? Great acting is daring. And it dares, above all, to fail. Anyone who wishes to scale Olympus must accept the bruises and the breaks. Present conditions, it may be argued, do not permit the actor to fall or fail. But perhaps it is too early to say. In any event, the conditions for great acting are the same as those for any great endeavour. There must be virgin territory to conquer and the will to conquer it. What in turn creates the will to conquer is another question. It is not always born of desperate need; as these pages will suggest, happenstance or even whimsy can be enough.

Habitually, at least, the English actor tends to stress the element of control – control of self and control of the audience. The most constant, if fractious, relationship has been with the audience and constant labour is needed to tame it. Edith Evans, peering hard at students at Royal Central School with her familiar emphasis (for it was not really intensity), put the matter beyond doubt. 'You must *govern* the audience,' she said. 'You must never let the audience run away with the play . . . I always listen at the side to know what they're up to . . . You've got to be able to manage a lot of human beings.' Simon Callow, too, has warned of the danger of the audience 'directing' the play. The result is a performance weakened and impoverished.

The English actor is innately suspicious of what Callow has called 'directocracy'. In other words, the English actor does not like to be told what to do. This must be qualified: particularly in rep, many actors can be strikingly passive in relation to the director. But it remains true that the auteur tradition, where the director is the actor's tutor and the playwright's master, has yet to put down native roots.

The English actor has a great sense of acting as artifice, unapologetic in its love for the cosmetic. On one occasion, Ian McKellen teased Antony Sher about his desire to delve into real emotion. 'Oh you're such a Method actor, darling,' he said. 'It's very simple.' And he spat on his fingertips, and rubbed them under his eyes, to mimic tears. Edith Evans, asked by an earnest interviewer from Oxford, 'Tell me, Dame Edith, how do you go about it? What do you do? Do you research it? How do you get into them?', responded with a puckish, 'I pretend, dear boy.' But if that were so, why was there quite so vivid an impression of a soul at work in her acting?

This notion of pretence, or rather of control, persists. 'You are giving the *impression* of feeling,' Noël Coward declared. 'Feeling . . .

is not acting.' That is why the English actor glories in theatricality, in the vocal and physical adjustments to suit the character. Laurence Olivier summed it up for many when he spoke of working 'from the outside in'. The highest compliment you can pay to American actors is that they seem not to be acting; the English actor does not necessarily court that compliment. The English actor is as much performer as transformer. The shadow, or perhaps the sunbeam, of the orator is still present.

All this manifests the English actor's fraught but lively relationship with the notion of 'becoming' the part. It is one replete with paradox. John Philip Kemble used to scoff at David Garrick's claim to 'become' the character, yet he himself studied the characters he was to portray with exhaustive assiduity. And we may recall Olivier's famous, or notorious, advice to Dustin Hoffman when he saw him working himself up into a fury to attain an inner truth in the Method style. 'My dear boy,' Olivier asked him smoothly, 'why don't you just try acting?' But this has been taken far too seriously as a mark of the English approach. In all likelihood, Olivier was being mischievous.

The notion that you must feel the character's feelings was described by Coward as a 'modern' one, but in reality it is very ancient. The monks and nuns of the ninth century were almost certainly 'feeling' their roles when they enacted the parts of the women who met the risen Christ, and the scop before the king would have felt what he spoke or he could not have persuaded him. But ignorance of the ancient is an infallible mark of the old-fashioned, and Coward, for all his brilliance and modernity, was prone to orthodox prescriptions. His central objection, however, was practical. Such a degree of emotional investment cannot, he said, be sustained over many performances.

It is to the stage actor that the present narrative confines itself. On rare occasions it has been necessary to infer or extrapolate an actor's style from a film performance, but the stage work remains the object of study. Questions of brevity and convenience have played their part, but the main reason lies elsewhere. It is not possible to recognize of what actors are capable until they are seen on the stage. To preserve in purity the truth of a character and the reality of their impulses, while engaged in the highly coloured and artificial business of projecting the voice and altering the body, has always been the test of the actor. The camera, so unforgiving in many respects, simply requires less. Indeed, 'less' is precisely the requirement.

The camera can distort in more ways than one. It was once received wisdom that the English actor is best suited to the suit, to the cigarette holder and antimacassar, to the suppression of feeling rather than to its exposure. But this is a legacy from early film, and one that can be misleading. The 'drawing room' actor, so typically English in the popular mind, is in fact an anomaly; on stage, the English actor tends to be big, expansive, even crude.

Another definition must be added here. What were the constituents of modern 'acting'? It was based on the work of Konstantin Stanislavski, the great Russian practitioner of the early twentieth century. His contention, to put it very simply, was that if actors were to imitate human feeling or behaviour, it was not enough to mimic it; they were obliged to reproduce it. To do this, in turn, they had to locate it in themselves, in their own passions and motives. Emotional truth was held to be indispensable. Scenes were broken down into 'units' and 'beats'. Actors were told to cast off the script altogether and improvise scenes. They would then return to the script with true, practised insight into the characters' hinterland and motives. It was the opposite of 'trial and error'. You had to learn what you as a character were doing and the reasons for it. The director 'blocked' the scenes (placing the actors where they needed to be) very little, since actors should be allowed as much latitude as their characters demanded, and lines sank into the memory as the actors went along. They were never formally 'learned', particularly not at the outset.

This system, sometimes refracted through what has become known as the American Method, was adopted throughout the drama schools of England. It has been suggested that the object of this approach was a 'naturalistic' style, but that is misleading. In fact, the system proved startlingly adaptable, responding as well to Shakespeare as to Chekhov, and the vast majority of actors under the age of sixty have received a training based upon it.

It could never be said that English theatre received this foreign dignitary with flags waving and open arms. But its benefits were soon felt, and are indeed to be seen on most stages in the country. The English actor, so instinctively theatrical, learned to look inwards, how to do no more than was convincing, how to cope with stage fright, how to engage with fellow actors rather than the audience. Above all, perhaps, the player learned that which had for so long been forgotten: how to be a priest in a timeless ritual and an ageless space. The approach brought by the great Russian was nothing if not sacred.

At almost the same time, but with far older roots, the regional or repertory theatre was born. At the heart of repertory theatre lies a seeming paradox. The actors form a touring troupe that is also an in-house company. You stayed but then moved on before you stayed again. It was, and is, a realm with constantly shifting boundaries, and this is part of its nature and a great part of its glory. An anecdote from the rep runs as follows. An actor has 'dried' or forgotten his lines and so, naturally enough, asks the prompter, 'What's the line?' After a worryingly long pause, he hears the plaintive riposte, 'What's the play?'

The story is untraceable, which alone suggests that it is probably a legend. But that heightens rather than diminishes its significance: the tale has become totemic. That should be no surprise. Repertory theatre is a world that can turn swiftly into a blur.

The schedule alone is unforgiving. As soon as one play is scheduled for the evening, the company begins rehearsing its successor during the day. This assumes a twelve-hour day, six days a week. During those twelve hours the actor's body and mind are stretched to an extent inconceivable to most members of an audience. This may seem extravagant, but it should be kept in mind that acting involves the whole person, the whole exhausting human composite.

There is often far more to repertory than acting. At least in its golden age in the 1950s and 1960s, every participant was ready to take on additional responsibilities. An actor could find him- or herself stage-managing, building props, accounting, repairing costumes and directing. While working for the West of England Touring Company, Joan Plowright made rugs on the bus. Men of the company would assemble the sets, for example, and the women would iron the costumes. Or vice versa. How did they learn their lines? That is the question often asked of actors. But far more often than not, that is the least of their problems. For the players in repertory the answer is simple: it was their professional obligation.

In the heyday of rep the director was, not infrequently, considered to be in a higher realm. It may be that, what with 'blocking' and planning, there was no time to be a mere human being. A common practice was to use the Samuel French acting editions, which were transcripts of the prompt copy of West End productions. Accordingly, a director in a hurry (as was generally the case) could find all the necessary moves as well as the script itself. We tend to take for granted now the role of director as pedagogue, but in truth there was little scope for this. When one actor asked the director Peter Dews about motive and subtext, he was given the curt, ironic answer, 'your salary at the end of the week, love'. This, of course, was a theatrical commonplace; Alfred Hitchcock took it to America with him. It reveals an unmistakably English approach.

For the most part, the actor had to be content with the rather broad advice quoted by Richard Pasco: 'Learn the lines and don't bump into the furniture.' This is another commonplace of the English theatre. The highest accolade the actor often received was that of 'adequate'. It became a joke, but one with a quite serious root. The director in rep, therefore, was indeed a deity, but a disengaged one – in no way as immanent or involved as his counterparts in other theatres. In the golden era he was architect, not builder. Above all, repertory was for the actor an apprenticeship, a hard if exhilarating period in which their craft was honed, skill was acquired, mistakes were made and learned from.

But from whom did you learn? Rosemary Harris, who worked at the Roof Garden Theatre in Bognor Regis, was in no doubt: 'One was taught by one's elders and betters, that's who you learned from.' And what, in turn, was taught? Most markedly, you were taught 'professionalism', the basic courtesies of the stage, whether in rehearsal or performance. To 'corpse', to let yourself collapse in giggles, was inexcusable, an insult to the audience and to your fellow actors. To be 'off' – to miss your cue to be on the stage or to be late for rehearsal – was likewise a cardinal sin. You had to be smart, you had to be prepared and you had to be willing. Above all, you had to be kind: consideration for others was no less than a professional obligation. There are innumerable anecdotes about actors helping one another out in a difficult moment or in the teeth of all odds. Many actors attribute the high quality of much rep acting to this collegiate and comradely spirit.

You were also taught 'the tricks of the trade', and tricks they often were. Alec McCowen recalled how to get 'a round', which means 'a round of applause':

> I played an ordinary little man in some post at the ministry and he turned out to be a German spy and I was shot in the arm at the end and had a rather grand exit, and the audience seemed very impressed but quiet and I remember Geoffrey Staines saying to me, 'Would you like to get an

exit round?' and I said, 'Ooh, yes, how do I do it?' and he
said, 'You just pat your arm where you've been shot as you
go out of the door and you'll get a round.' I didn't believe
it, but I did it that night and I did get a round and I did for
the rest of that week. He knew things like that.

McCowen, and others of his generation, would also have learned
how to get a laugh and how to prolong that laugh, and how to provoke a gasp or a yelp. It is suggestive that we hear less now about
how to 'get' a tear or a sob.

As an actor in rep, you were obliged to take on the most unlikely
roles. Part of the joy of this training lay in exploring an age, a gender
or simply a type that you would never have the opportunity of
playing again. This was only one of the many benefits of miscasting.
McCowen remembers how

> part of the fun for the audience lay in watching an actor in
> his twenties play a character aged sixty or more . . . At York
> my biggest claim to fame was on the week of my nineteenth
> birthday. I played a character who was a hundred years old
> and it was the leading role. There was a character actor in
> the company who was seventy-six who had to play my son.
> He went into a terrible sulk. The director thought it would
> be a good selling point, to have me, aged nineteen, playing
> the hundred-year-old man.

It is perhaps in its relationship with the audience that repertory
differs most sharply from other forms of English theatre. Simply
put, it is your primary relationship to which all others must give
way. Audience members knew you and might even bump into
you on the street. Stephen Hancock, who acquired most fame as
a television actor, remembered how

at Ipswich there was a theatre club that met every fortnight to discuss the play. We were part of the community definitely, not as now, where you go to a so-called repertory company for one show. That means nothing to the community; it's a touring show as far as they're concerned. You were seen about and people came to see you.

In that sense the theatre became once more a form of religious ritual, in which the actors are bound in communion with the spectators.

From all this it should be apparent that repertory is a vital corrective to the more extreme proponents of internal or naturalistic acting, for whom the audience is something to forget. A branch of rep was known as 'fit-up'. This involved, if possible, a still more testing routine. Charles Simon, who remained on the stage for almost eighty years, remembered his experience at Dorothy Grafton's company in 1930. 'You played three different sections on the bill,' he said. 'First off was variety and everyone in the cast had to do something, sing a song, do a bit of conjuring, recite a poem, something. Then you did the play itself; then in the old custom of the Theatres Royal at Drury Lane and Covent Garden years ago, you played a farce.' 'Fit-up' had a supreme virtue, therefore, which Simon described: 'doing fit-up you just touch with your fingertips the continuous line going back to Burbage, of the actor-manager with his company barnstorming round the country.'

From the 1970s onwards, repertory went into decline, and indeed for a while its very future was uncertain. As ever, many factors contributed to this, but the salient one was not so much the competition offered by television itself as the kind of acting seen on television. The camera is a bleak, unsparing judge of excess and mannerism, and it cannot be denied that these qualities were nurtured rather than corrected by repertory. But perhaps McCowen spoke for the majority when he remarked that 'doing rep meant that you learned to get on and do it, you were not fazed by anything, whatever happened you made a go of it, you had to . . . I don't think it [rep] made you a good actor but it did stretch you.'

It is not reductive or glib to suggest that while drama school gives you a bag of tools, repertory gives you a box of tricks. Drama school exists to turn performers into actors, and in that process mannerism is an inevitable casualty. In rep, mannerism can be a virtue. On the other hand, rep offered, unambiguously, a training. You emerged toughened, speedy, adaptable, unsentimental about your own abilities, considerate and, above all, versatile. John Perry, assistant head of drama at the Arts Educational Schools, observed tersely that rep was 'a good antidote to places like this'. As we are beginning to see, the dramatic demands of the twentieth century were different. It would no longer be enough to get a clap or a laugh from the audience; the business now was to steal its heart.

In the pages that follow, the English actor emerges as mage, as fool, as prophet, as activist, as worldling and as simple entertainer. Yet it is never quite simply entertainment; some nimbus will always cling to this art, ennobling the frivolous and humanizing the epic. A note must be added on the scope of this study. It includes certain actors who were born outside England but within the British Isles; they include some who learned their trade or fashioned their style on the English stage, as well as those who found distinction and even identity upon it.

One

In the beginning

The English actor is born, like so many aspects of English cultural history, from diverse and sometimes disputed origins. Like the figure of the porter in *Macbeth*, he steps out of the mist and opens the gate. But from where did his fellows, Macbeth, and Duncan, and the witches, originally come? There is one theory that the variety of players reflects the emergence of polyphonic music between the thirteenth and fifteenth centuries, when one individual melody is combined with others. We might see an analogy between the language and the music of the period. It is a theory, at least, and theories can rarely do harm.

Yet the commentator must always embrace the notion of continuity rather than of change in English cultural history, and might, for example, find the Anglo-Saxon predecessors of the drama and the performer. The 'thyle' who recited battles past has been interpreted as a *histrio* or performer. He was both custodian and spokesman of authority, whether liturgical or secular, who characteristically engaged in 'flyting' or exchanging provocative remarks with another *histrio*. Perhaps we may call them some of the first English actors.

They were contemporary, however, with the 'scop' or bard whose primary function was that of a storyteller in verse in which acting, voice and gesture were intrinsic elements. The word 'scoff' has been derived from scop. Nor should this surprise us, since a tradition of mockery lies close to the heart of English acting. These actors are also related to the ancient rhapsodists who first recited the sagas. They were associated, too, with the 'gleeman' who characteristically accompanied his recitals with music and was often associated with a troupe of entertainers. It may be that the recital of the scop was followed by the music of the gleeman. Some lines from *Beowulf* suggest this: 'When the bard had finished his song, the sound/ of talk and laughter began.' This was the festive occasion when various mimes or performers might enter the proceedings, with jugglers and dancers and fire-eaters who earned their living by going from town to town.

THE APPETITE FOR imitation is not in doubt, from the earliest tribal rites to the latest stage play. The dialogue of the stage, however oblique or unkempt, is an imitation of conversation; most plots are an imitation of human activity and behaviour. But the actual nature of imitation changes continually. In its preliminary phases it might be used to inspire or console a community, or to re-enact passions that were in danger of being forgotten. The scop could be called upon to clothe disaster in the mantle of victory. Often, he had to persuade his audience that, in spite of all appearances, any present darkness was only a tattered shroud and that beyond it lay the sun. For this, pretence would not have served. He had to act.

This is not a great leap from the instinct of the modern theatre. The early drama was also a useful palliative at times of social transition. In an expanding commercial world, for example, a gradual atrophy of faith might have been tempered by the advent of the Resurrection Play in the tenth century.

Many scholars locate a specific provenance for the drama in the sacred rituals and figures, in the prayers and responses, that first took place in the parish church, so that the 'parish play' may have been the first manifestation of English drama. By the eleventh century it had spilled out into its precincts. The first liturgical dramas were performed in the previous century, followed by 'miracle plays' of the same era and the 'morality plays' of the fifteenth and sixteenth centuries. The first players in any formal sense were the clerics (and, at Barking Abbey, for example, the nuns), and it is worth noting that the task of the priest was to adopt a role complete with costume and script; he is in essence an actor rather than a specific individual. It may be, as many scholars suggest, that the rise, or resurrection, of drama in England began in a specific text known as the *Visitatio*. It consisted of little more than a minor, but perhaps crucial, addition to a festive service. The priests took on the roles of the angels who greeted Christ's handmaidens at his tomb. '*Quem quaeritis?*' asked the angels. Whom do you seek?

The questions and answers were repeated in antiphon, with some of the priests themselves dressed in the robes of women. In this they might have been performing a role far older than Christianity itself; it could be argued, in fact, that it was shamanic in character. And what else is the actor but one who channels the spirit of another? 'Whom do you seek?' is the question that every actor must ask and heed, for all acting is composed of action and all action proceeds from desire.

By the eleventh century episodes beyond the formal liturgical cycle were employed for the benefit of those assembled outside the church. Fragments of the relevant parts have survived: for the third shepherd in 'the shepherds' play', for the third Mary in the 'resurrection play' and for Cleopas in 'the pilgrims' plays'. Cues were provided by the iteration of a phrase or sentence, while it seems that rough plots were drawn up not dissimilar to the 'plats' nailed or pasted on the wall of the Elizabethan stage. We have here a theatrical world in miniature, focused on the parish church, but the growth of urban life and mercantile activity wrought a necessary transition. It was perhaps inevitable that the role of the priests was taken over by the city and the city guilds who directed and administered civic activity.

The guilds themselves were at the centre of the town's dramatic activities, and several were closely identified with the mechanics and appurtenances of the pageants. The people flocked from neighbouring towns and villages, no doubt spending their money in the process, in a festive atmosphere that was both a celebration and an advertisement for York and Chester, Norwich and Wakefield, as well as other centres.

As the participation of the guilds and people of the towns increased, so the interest in their proceedings naturally grew. In the eastern quarters of England the performances were enacted in an open space beside the church; in Cornwall the dramas were performed 'in the round', where the 'playing place' might be an amphitheatre of some antiquity; in London certain areas, such as Finsbury Fields and Clerkenwell Green, were the natural site for productions; in northern England, as in York or Wakefield, the 'pageant wagons' trundled across the cobbled stage with each guild performing one episode of sacred history in each wagon. They may be considered as living tapestries representing the sacred world. The wagons, approximately 7 metres (24 ft) in height, moved from 'station' to 'station' in a pre-ordained route as the crowds assembled to watch them. They were not ramshackle devices, as the name might suggest. They were often of considerable value, mounted at great expense and stored for safekeeping. Documents survive detailing their costumes and props. The York Cycle of Mystery Plays, known as the York Corpus Christi plays, were performed annually from the late fourteenth century to the late 1560s. They were well executed, proficiently played and enormously popular. They were composed by several hands, and were enlarged by revision and addition, so that they can be understood as genuinely communal exercises. Many of the early dramatists, such as Marlowe and Shakespeare, would have been intimately acquainted with them. They would have experienced the close connection between actors and audience.

While we cannot know exactly how the actors in these performances played, we may glean much from what they were given to speak. There was no room for individual interpretation. The scripts have many virtues, but psychological subtlety is not among them. It would in fact be a fault if this quality were present; a broad space often requires broad strokes. In the texts, we see Hebrew priests quarrelling like spinsters, Christ as a homely confessor, Mary not a spotless statue but a human mother, and Herod ranting and blaspheming. The writing is couched in a medley of styles, from low humour to the peaks of piety, and it was the task of the actors to follow these variations. Perhaps what distinguishes such 'streaky bacon' from that of Shakespeare is that here the clashes of style would not have been smoothed over but emphasized and dramatized. Endless shifts of tone would have kept the audience alert. That was part of their purpose.

It should not be forgotten that the actor fulfils the interpretations of the audience. When God himself, at his most homely, says of Adam and Eve, 'Alle likes me wele, but this the beste,' we may imagine the actor patting the pair on the head in the manner of a father. The blessing that ends the scene confirms this. Here was a world in which every gesture held an understood significance, where a blessing was the fixed ritual of a touch on the head and a bend of the knee.

The actor playing Adam had perhaps a more testing task. He had to switch from an entirely conventional address, full of pious gratitude, to a mode altogether more urgent. When Eve entreats him not to blame her for the eating of the apple, Adam replies with bitter sarcasm, 'Do wey, lefe Eue, whame than?' The modern equivalent would be 'Come off it, Eve love, who then?' Since the script dictated the delivery, only real and recognizable anger would have sufficed.

It was sometimes assumed that the mystery plays and pageants 'evolved' from sacred drama, but it seems more likely that the guild dramas and the parish plays, together with other forms of liturgical performance, existed contemporaneously. The aptitude for performance is deep and continuous. In all areas of human activity, in fact, we find variety and superfluity rather than, as the Victorians suggested, an inevitable convergence into uniformity. The players worked in the same sphere as jugglers, dancers, mimes and musicians. Actors were also needed for such folk dramas as the 'Robin Hood plays'. In 1535 'playing laddes' from the village of Towton, some 20 kilometres (12 mi.) from York, toured the surrounding countryside with what must have been a mixed routine to attract their audiences.

In another context, dramatic variety was maintained by the 'college plays' and the dramas staged by the various Inns of Court. Where young men were assembled in large numbers and bound together by a common identity, drama seemed to spring up naturally and even instinctively. Their dramatic training often began at an early age, and boys were soon to be found in dramatic troupes such as the Children of the Chapel and the Children of Paul's. What began as an educational exercise had by the 1580s become a financial speculation. They were not hired for show or for sexual titillation – although they were no doubt used as such in a homo-erotic culture – but they often played females old or young, and if they were not convincing, they would not have lasted so long. They could be funny, pathetic, athletic, seductive. The boys were in turn 'bound' as apprentices to professional actors for a term of approximately seven years, generally from the ages of fourteen to twenty-one.

The boys who stayed in the grammar schools of England performed plays and also participated in staged debates by assuming contrary positions on the principle of 'sic et non'. This may help to explain the prevalence of debate in the drama of the time, but it also exemplifies the manner in which the children, advancing an argument, might tend to forget themselves in the heat of the contest. Certain boys, however, would come forward and address the audience directly. This eventually came to be known as 'breaking the fourth wall', although, given the nature of the plays and the structure of the stage at that time, it might better be described as 'opening the gate'. 'A delivery and sweet action', it was written, 'is the gloss and beauty of any discourse that belongs to a scholar.'

In the life of Thomas More it is recorded that when he was a boy of twelve or thirteen in Archbishop Morton's household at Lambeth Palace, he watched, and participated in, the theatrical and oratorical diversions following dinner in the Great Hall. His son-in-law records that 'thoughe he was younge of yeares, yet wold he at Christmas tyde sodenly sometimes steppe in among the players', and would then improvise his part so skilfully that he excelled over all the others. His dramatic skill was also greatly extended at Oxford University, where he wrote and performed in comedies or comic sketches. It was a theatrical world, oral, communal, spectacular and ritualistic.

By the fifteenth century, records document payments to *histriones* and *lusores* from university colleges and from the universities themselves. The colleges might put on 'disguisings' with costumes, sets, scripts and incidental music. Interlude players as well as players from Bury St Edmunds, Saffron Walden and elsewhere visited King's College, Cambridge, in 1467. The audience was made up of academics, collegians, visiting notables and selected townspeople. Each college kept its own collection of costumes, as well as beards, wigs and armour. The queen's visits to Cambridge and Oxford in 1564 and 1566 set the seal upon the importance of the college plays. The young actors themselves were praised for 'elegance and graceful action and much command of voice'. They are not to be confused, however, with the professional actors who began to emerge in the 1560s.

There was a communal exercise in another sense, since at York, for example, the spiritual history of humankind from Creation to the Last Judgement had to be apportioned between fifty separate guilds, from potters to plasterers. A cleric was sometimes hired to choose and rehearse the players, and so it would be anachronistic to describe them as 'professional'; some of them may have had a reputation in their neighbourhoods for their skill in festive rituals, while others were no doubt chosen for their evident sincerity in taking on sacred parts. A local cleric might have noticed someone who entered the role with enthusiasm as well as piety. The pageant masters, who combined the roles of director and producer, may have come to rely upon well-established and trusted performers who played the same part, for example, at each of the twelve stations of the York Cycle. This would have required endurance as well as memory. The actors could in turn instruct one another in gesture, speech and movement; they would rehearse and perhaps even learn how to improvise skilfully. The art of gesture was of supreme importance, and some of its most prominent effects were taken from the Roman stage. A handbook of the art, for example, notes that 'the middle joynt of the left Index apprehended, intends more earnestness.' If you wish to seem old, or anxious, or jealous, you must adopt this action. The hands were of the greatest importance, down to the position of the little finger.

The *histriones* often performed in the street, where Herod might rage and Joseph might lament. Visors or masks were worn by those who played creatures of supernatural origin, and costumes were often also of symbolic significance. The masks were crucial for those enacting a supernatural role; the performer was in a sense separated from himself, and allowed the possibility of freedom from the restrictions of ordinary human life. Thus for the actor, as for the audience, it was understood that drama existed as much to conceal as to reveal.

By the sixteenth century the players had grown in skill and importance, and were required to be 'well arrayed and openly speaking' with a proficiency in 'cunning, voice and person'. We should note that while 'cunning' in this context meant primarily interpretative skill, it also had wider connotations of craft or magic, an association that lingers. It has been suggested that in the crowded streets of the larger towns the players would rely on bombastic attitudinizing and loud formal rhetoric, but that is most unlikely. The audience wept as well as laughed, and preserved a reverent silence at moments of solemn drama.

The performer was aided by music to instil such passions. The blaring of the trumpets that announced his arrival would have stirred the audience greatly, but they might also have put the actor playing Herod in the appropriate mood to bully or cajole. The strains of the 'Coventry Carol' would have quickened the actors' hearts as they lamented the massacre of the innocents. We may suppose that some performers were well known for the ability to provoke sorrow, while others played the fool. The cast varied from two to twenty, the narrative itself derived from a variety of sources knitted together by consistent stanzaic forms. There was even an alliterative master to provoke echoes of the Anglo-Saxon dispensation.

The church performances were often accompanied by the puppets or wooden dolls also to be seen at fairs or markets, but, like so many aspects of popular religion or folk religion, they lost favour at a later date and the mass itself was denounced in 1548 as a 'puppet play'. Their decline was one part of a larger transition in which private devotion began to replace the public re-enactment of spiritual practice. The complaints against plays and players increased as the power of the Church was challenged by certain priests and eventually overturned by the secular authorities. 'Playing' was believed to diminish the spiritual world and turn the power of God into a caricature. In *The Treatise of Miraclis Pleyinge*, written at the beginning of the fifteenth century, the dramas were condemned for stirring the populace 'to lechery and disputes'. The character and, by extension, the actor were identified with 'evil behaviour' passing from player to audience. Entertainment in itself was not necessarily harmful, but entertainment disguised as devotional activity was truly wicked. For a priest to act in a miracle or mystery, as some were supposed to do, was anathema.

The decline and demise of the civic cycles were provoked by a range of causes historical, religious, financial and social. The economic difficulties of the late fifteenth and early sixteenth centuries adversely affected the towns and their guilds, and the general decline was compounded by the advent of the Reformation, which affected Church property, land rights and guild monopolies. Gate receipts were down, sponsors were scarcer and the civic authorities had fewer resources. Bitter controversy was also aroused by the dissolution of the monasteries and the promotion of Protestantism during the reign of Edward VI. Given this combination of circumstances it is not surprising that the great pageants of the past were diminished and eventually discarded. One chapter is closed.

But another opens. Now that God had been ejected from the theatre, his children could play among themselves. Indeed, the author of the *Treatise* had prophesied as much when he put these words into the mouth of a scornful Deity: 'Do not play with me. Go play with your peer[s].' In the succeeding centuries, this demand was at last obeyed.

Two

The first playhouses

The last Mystery Play in Chester was performed in 1547, and Nicholas Udall's *Ralph Roister Doister* followed four or five years later. It has some claim to be the first English comedy. William Stevenson's comedy, *Gammer Gurton's Needle,* was staged in 1553, while *Jack Juggler*, a secular comedy of anonymous composition, was played in the same period. The transition from religious to secular drama is clearly marked, but that transformation was irregular and various.

There were, for example, three levels of what might be called academic acting at various levels of achievement in the schools, the universities and the Inns of Court. Interlude players had already visited the colleges. The interlude, as its name suggests, was in origin a short entertainment placed between more serious – which is to say more overtly spiritual – performances. Soon it became the accepted term for morality plays, and indeed for plays in general. The first classical drama, a comedy by the Roman playwright Terence, was staged at King's Hall, Cambridge, in 1511. The practice of playing was firmly established by the 1520s, with some of the dramas composed by contemporaries. Lists of the original actors survive, but their identities are in a mist.

The colleges gained credit from their productions, and Elizabeth I's visits to Cambridge and Oxford in 1564 and 1566 set the seal of eminence on university drama. This was exemplified in the three Parnassus plays written at St John's College, Cambridge, between 1598 and 1602. As the influence of piety and devotion waned with the decline of religious drama, the scholars learned what was known as 'audaciousness'. The 'disguisings' of King's College were recorded in the latter half of the sixteenth century, and the college plays or *ludi* continued into the early part of the seventeenth century.

But the palm for drama should really be awarded to the Inns of Court. *Gorboduc*, the first English tragedy in blank verse, was performed in 1561 at the Inner Temple. It might be claimed in fact that English drama began at Gray's Inn, Lincoln's Inn, the Middle Temple and the Inner Temple in an atmosphere of high spirits, mock learning, satire and parody. Another element played its part. The 'moots' or mock trials, as well as the legal debates and dialogues of this rhetorical world, were also forms of performance that would have afforded room for theatricality. It is arguably in this world, avowedly pious but innately theatrical, that the development of secular drama can be found. The members of the Inns were later known as 'Afternoon's Men' for their habit of frequenting the playhouses at those hours.

But as early as 1526 theatrical performances were being given by residents of, or visitors to, certain noble households. Many of the successful travelling companies had been obliged to separate themselves from the guilds that had originally sponsored them, and came under the direct control of powerful or wealthy noblemen who were happy to be associated with this most popular form of entertainment which was also the pastime of the queen. The first of these groups was the Earl of Leicester's Men. They were followed by the Queen's Men in the 1580s and then by the two great companies of the Lord Admiral and the Lord Chamberlain. When Leicester's Men visited the court of Denmark they were described as singers and dancers who took part in 'medley' or 'gallimaufry' plays; they could vault and tumble, jig and juggle. The early drama was intimately associated with all forms of entertainment. The English players were known all over Europe, perhaps because they did not follow the orthodox formulae of French or Italian drama.

These players, therefore, had changed their allegiance from clerics and guildsmen to less precarious patrons. During the reign of Queen Mary, as John Strype recorded in his *Ecclesiatical Memorials,* published in 1721, 'certain lewd persons, naming themselves to be the servants of Sir Francis Lake, and wearing his livery or badge on their sleeves, travelled through the north performing plays and interludes.' They may represent one of the origins of such touring companies, which eventually included Lord Strange's Men, the Earl of Pembroke's Men, Sussex's Men, Worcester's Men and Oxford's Men. Players sometimes switched allegiance, collaborated in informal groups, parodied one another, copied one another, stole individual players and generally added to the atmosphere of merriment and melancholy that characterized mid-sixteenth-century drama. By 1558 there were 334 'playing troupes', a fact that testifies, if nothing else, to the intense appetite for plays and players in the towns and cities. Where companies once accommodated some seven or eight players, their numbers rose to twenty or more. England was described as 'a nest of singing birds' in the Elizabethan period, but the players were the song.

The lodestar had now become London. It was in most respects a youthful city, in which half of the population was under the age of twenty. But with the evidence of disease and mortality in every quarter, the young were often condemned to a short burst of existence, and their expression of life may as a result have been more vital and intense. That may in part explain the popularity of the boys' companies. There was also a rapidly expanding audience. A population of approximately fifty thousand had reached two hundred thousand by 1620, so there grew up a unique form of self-awareness among Londoners that in turn prompted the growing interest in new plays and new players. Merchants and usurers were copied from the street and put on the stage, and by the early seventeenth century the vogue was established for 'citizen comedies'.

The powerhouse of the drama was of course the novel and flourishing theatre. The London playhouse was a new kind of building, erected for the first time in this period. The first theatres were the inns or, rather, large rooms within inns that would otherwise have been used for meetings and assemblies. The plays guaranteed more ale and more revenue. It used to be supposed that inn yards, with covered galleries around them, were the first public theatres, but these were really venues for horses, wagons and passing travellers. The Black Bull Inn of Bishopsgate owned an extra yard that could hold five hundred people, but this was an exception.

The Cross Keys and the Bell Inn were both in Gracechurch Street; the Belsavage was on Ludgate Hill; and the Boar's Head was on the north side of Whitechapel Street beyond Aldgate. For the actors these were more amenable surroundings than the pageant wagons, but the popularity of the new drama was such that larger and sturdier venues were soon required. The first of them recorded in London documents, the Red Lion at Mile End, was constructed in 1567. Its stage was 12 metres (40 ft) wide and 9 metres (30 ft) deep; there was a trapdoor for special effects and a 5.5-metre (18 ft) wooden turret for dramatic ascents and descents. Its coherent architecture suggests that it was based on lost originals. The actor experienced a sea change in style; he had better acoustics with which to work, a formal space upon which to elaborate his action, and a stage that propelled him into the heart of the audience. He was the centre of all eyes and had no need to vie for attention. The high walls were in part an echo chamber, too, for increasing the attentiveness of the audience. The emergence of the secular drama had required, and obtained, a new kind of space.

The second known public theatre, constructed in Shoreditch, outside the city walls, in 1576, was simply called the Theatre. It was a large building, established by James Burbage, and was advertised as the first public building devoted to theatrical activities. It had capacity for some fifteen hundred people seated in three levels of galleries around an open yard; the yard was also used by members of the audience and the stage was set back against one side. The fixed stage had a roof supported by pillars, with a 'tiring house' at the back that was used for exits, entrances and quick changes of costume.

People watched the actors in order to learn how to behave, how to speak and even how to bow. The dominant theme was no longer the world as it had been, or as it might be, but the world as it is. The new form of blank verse, as opposed to formal stanzas or the alliterative line, allowed a more conversational idiom. Under the aegis of James Burbage and his son Richard, the Theatre also became a kind of dramatic academy with informal lessons in elocution, language, dancing, deportment, manners and music. The drama had come of age with remarkable speed. Richard Tarlton, a comedian or jester, reported how 'I would needs to the Theatre to a play.' It was a highly successful venture.

The Theatre was itself rivalled by the Rose, established by Edward Alleyn, a formidable actor, and Philip Henslowe, an entrepreneur of the Elizabethan kind who ranged from usury to starch-making and pawnbroking. The Rose, south of the river, was outside the concourse of the other playhouses, but it soon became the centre of much theatrical activity. By 1572 the number of players had so increased that they had to present licences on pain of being treated as rogues or vagabonds. In 1586 two hundred players were reported in or near London. Three years before that, it was reported that the new players had 'grown [so] very skilful and exquisite actors for all matters that they were entertained into the service of divers great lords'.

In 1577 the Curtain playhouse was opened in Shoreditch, on the same model as the Theatre. There were no theatrical curtains then in use, and it was named after a wall that offered some protection from wind and weather. It cost a penny to stand in the yard, a further penny to sit in the gallery, and threepence for seats with cushions. The new playhouses were decorated and gilded; the wooden pillars were painted to resemble gold and marble, while carvings and murals completed the ensemble. This was where Romeo and Juliet 'won Curtain plaudities'. Other theatres rose on the south bank of the Thames: the playhouse at Newington Butts in 1575, close to Southwark High Street, and the Globe in Southwark in late 1598. The last had the distinction of being the first playhouse built for the sole purpose of staging drama rather than such rough spectacles as bear-baiting. Alleyn and Henslowe erected the Hope playhouse close to the Globe, no doubt in an attempt to steal its glory.

Another venture succeeded. A 'private theatre' was opened at Blackfriars in 1599; it was an indoor space, conveniently sheltered by a roof, and designed for the more affluent spectators. It was almost too popular, since, according to contemporary complaints, 'there is so great multitude of coaches, whereof many more are hackney coaches, bringing people of all sorts, that sometimes all the streets cannot contain them.'

These early theatres owed something to the intimacy of the pageants. It might be supposed that actor and audience were sep-arated, as at a later date, but in fact the spectators were as close as they could conveniently assemble. The passions and agonies of the players charged the audience with sympathetic feeling so that they might weep with compassion or howl with rage. The players were not amateur enthusiasts, nor did they rely on the gestures of formal ritual; they played to the very life, as it was then understood to be. Such was the wealth of drama, too, that they were obliged to become more skilled in the art and technique of memory.

By the later part of the sixteenth century acting was a profession in which it was customary for the aspiring actor to become informally 'apprenticed' to a senior actor, who would pass on his inherited expertise. Certainly it required an intense and specific training in the arts of deportment, dancing and vocal technique, as well as swordsmanship; many of the younger players were trained at the fencing school of Rocco Bonetti in Blackfriars.

The popularity of the drama, therefore, was not in doubt, and trumpets and flags were used to announce the oncoming play. By the late 1580s theatrical companies were performing six days a week, with a different play each day and a completely new drama each week. The players had 'scrolls' of their own parts but no complete script; they would gather before rehearsals in order to resolve problems of casting and 'doubling' as well as to add jokes or stage action. Improvisation was known as 'thribbling'. Problems of plot and dialogue were also addressed by the company. The general business of the day was rehearsals in the morning, playing in the afternoon and the learning of innumerable lines in the evening. The play began at two o'clock in the winter and three o'clock in the summer.

The actors' effect on the audience had the freshness of first things. One adult recalled of a touring company playing *The Cradle of Security* that 'this sight took such impression in me that, when I came to man's estate, it was as fresh in my memory as if I had seen it newly acted.' Many companies engaged in touring, while others remained at their base in London. So the new drama spread across the country. But the established companies were often obliged to leave their familiar venues at times of plague, when the London playhouses were closed. At this juncture, like their predecessors, they went on tour. There is evidence of more than three hundred travelling troupes before 1558, each with a cast of four or five. They might travel in a wagon, or mount their horses with their packs on their backs, carrying with them a document allowing them to perform. At one time of pestilence, for example, the Lord Chamberlain's Men visited some eighty towns and thirty noble households. They took with them trumpets and drums to announce their arrival.

Three

The art of playing

When Shakespeare travelled to London, in 1586 or 1587, he arrived at the opportune moment when the drama of Thomas Kyd and Christopher Marlowe was just emerging. There was a change in temperature. The 1570s and 1580s were the decades of the comic performers, while the 1590s witnessed the rise of the tragic actor. The chronicle or history plays had already found an audience eager to discover how historical events might bring illumination to a confused present, and they were gradually accompanied by revenge tragedy and citizen comedy. On these foundations the seventeenth-century drama, and part of the theatre of Shakespeare, was laid.

The basic elements were in place. The theatres had been erected, the players were prepared and the audience was, as ever, ready. It is clear that there was a variable and sometimes hesitant transition from formal to more naturalistic acting, even if 'nature' was ill-defined. It gave way to the significance of what came to be known as 'personation'. It was understood of the sixteenth-century actor that he must 'frame each person' so that 'you may his nature rightly know'. From this practice came the art of soliloquy and the direct address to the audience, as well as the self-revelation of certain characters in whispered asides. There was in any case more interest in the fate of the individual lost in a turbulent world. 'By his action,' one textbook advises, 'he fortifies moral precepts with example, for what we see him personate, we thinke truly done before us.'

The gradual change in the style and manner of the actors is documented in a pamphlet of 1612 by the playwright and actor Thomas Heywood entitled *An Apology for Actors*. It was essential for the actor to abandon all formal tricks 'as if the Personater were the man Personated, so bewitching a thing is liuely and well spirited action, that it hath power to new mold the harts of the spectators and fashion them to the shape of any noble and notable attempt'. In that manner 'the wisdome of the Poet, as supported by the worth of the Actors, wrought such impression in the hearts of the plebe.' The player must 'obserue his commas, colons, & full poynts, his parentheses, his breathing spaces, and distinctions'. This was perhaps the most important weapon in the player's arsenal, emphasizing once more the importance of speech and language, as opposed to plot, in the unfolding of the play. It is the speech and soliloquy that have survived the centuries, just as continual exercise and testing of the voice was the principal routine for any actor. Only thus was 'the most rude and vnpolisht tongue . . . growne to a most perfect and composed language'.

Heywood also dismissed the techniques or tricks of earlier drama. The actor should not 'stare with his eies, draw awry his mouth, confound his voice in the hollow of his throat, or teare his words hastily betwixt his teeth, neither to buffet his deske like a mad-man, nor stand in his place like a liuelesse Image, demurely plodding, and without any smooth and formal motion'. It may be assumed that these inelegant devices were commonplace in the public theatres. What is required instead is 'a comely and elegant gesture, a gratious and a bewitching kinde of action, a naturall and a familiar motion of the head, the hand, the body, and a moderate and fit countenance suitable to all the rest'. Avoid 'any impudent or forced motion in any part of the body, no rough, or other violent gesture, nor, on the contrary, to stand like a stiffe starcht man, but to qualifie euery thing according to the nature of the person personated'. Anything else amounts to 'over-acting tricks' that become 'violent absurdities'. This is as good a manual as any for seventeenth-century acting. Heywood knew of what he spoke. He asserted that he had had 'either an entire hand, or at least a main finger' in 220 plays, and he specialized in domestic dramas, adventures, romances and adventure-romances. The range of his invention may have been bolstered by the contribution of the actors to sustain both plot and character. It would also have been swayed by the reaction of the audience. His was in part a communal endeavour, in which the play was always in the process of becoming. But in a sense his abundance was his undoing. Even by the standards of the seventeenth century Heywood wrote too much, and most of his work has been forgotten.

The Elizabethan and Jacobean actors were not, in any case, bound in a straitjacket of style. There was no director to manage the proceedings. The player knew the approved and familiar gestures; he had the voice, he had the natural talent that had brought him on to the stage, he had served an apprenticeship, and he was surrounded by his fellow actors, who might cajole or encourage as well as instruct him.

The actors would have known that speeches, in which meditation or melancholy were often the predominant notes, were performed centre stage and towards the audience. There was also much leaping and jumping and falling; a dragon appears to Faustus and then in a quick change turns into a Franciscan friar. It was characteristic of Marlowe's drama in particular that actors often simply appeared, as if unconsciously summoned by the previous speaker, and brought a new scene with them. Stagecraft, as such, had not been invented. Some plays resembled moving pageants rather than dramatized tales. The actors might address one another directly before retiring to the back of the stage, and their battle of wits or boasts may owe something to the legal origins of the English drama, or indeed to the 'flyting' practised by their Anglo-Saxon forebears. But there is no one continuous or continuing style; it might change with every speech or every scene.

The theatrical traditions of the previous decades could encompass human life only as comic; tragedy belonged to the Deity, and the broken covenant between God and humanity. But the actors now had to express grief or joy in fundamentally different ways that in theory required them to tap inner springs of feeling. Although still dominant, iambic verse was increasingly marbled with passages of prose, thus allowing a still more conversational style. The stage was bare; the players needed to pay precise attention to imagery in order to convince and enchant the audience. That is why the language they used is richer than that of succeeding centuries. Language was all the dramatist could offer, but it was all the actor required.

Thomas Nashe was perhaps the first and most unfortunate dramatist of the era. He was essentially a pamphleteer, but in 1592 he composed *Pleesant Comedie Called Summers Last Will and Testament* for the Children of Paul's and the Children of the Chapel. But he also used a fool, Will Summers (based on the Tudor clown Will Somers), who was intended to 'flout the actors' and recite Nashe's highly elaborate and glittering prose. It was part masque and part farce, during which Summers mocks the playwright as well as the audience; he interrupts the narrative and directly addresses the audience. It was called a 'shewe', but its parodic and satiric thrusts were suited to the children.

The boys were at the centre of theatrical proceedings at this time. Alexander Cooke, originally a child actor with the Children of the Chapel before joining the King's Men, played Shakespeare's great heroines, while another boy player, Joseph Taylor, progressed to Hamlet and Othello. Ralph Radcliffe, a schoolmaster in Hitchin, made his pupils act in plays 'to remove useless modesty', and Richard Mulcaster of Merchant Taylors' School used drama to teach 'good behaviour and audacity'. So the boys were, or were meant to be, bold and assertive. We can imagine them, with their piping voices and brash manner, capturing the attention of a good-humoured audience. They had a licence to be free, and often obscene, with the excuse that they did not really understand what they were saying. But of course they did.

The Children of Paul's and the Merchant Taylors' boys leased rooms at Blackfriars, part of a former Dominican priory, which became, to the annoyance of neighbours, 'a Continual house for plays'. They were competing with the 'Chapel Children', who played dramas by Ben Jonson, George Chapman, John Marston, Thomas Middleton and others. The Children of the Chapel Royal were first introduced to court but were soon also established at Blackfriars, where they became a highly successful commercial enterprise. Like their juvenile contemporaries, they excelled in satirical comedy. They played three times a week over a period of six months. In 1599 the choristers of St Paul's were gathered into an acting troupe, and with other young players removed to a second Blackfriars theatre, modelled on the first and erected under the guidance of Richard Burbage. That theatre and another indoor one, the Cockpit, charged more for their entrance fees than the public theatre. The cheapest seats cost twopence, double the price of the public theatres.

Everything worked together to create the profligacy of composition. Nashe was considered one of the 'university wits', together with Marlowe and Robert Greene, and his name appears with that of Marlowe on a 1594 edition of *Dido Queene of Carthage*. It has also been suggested that he played a part in an unauthorized quarto of *Romeo and Juliet*. Nashe's misfortune, after his success with the boys, arose in 1597 from his collaboration with Ben Jonson in a comedy entitled *The Isle of Dogs*, which was denounced by the Privy Council as 'lewd . . . seditious and slanderous'. Jonson was dispatched to the Marshalsea prison, while Nashe left the city.

Significantly, three of the actors in that drama were also confined to the Marshalsea, a fact that testifies to the extent to which the players were identified with the play.

This confirms, also, that the players may have deserved their reputation for being unruly and violent. A representative list of players from the Lord Admiral's Men refers to lawsuits, fights, 'trespasses and contempts', bankruptcy, the purchase of stolen goods, the receipt of stolen clothing, theft, serious assault with robbery, and inflicting injury. One player, Gabriel Spencer, killed James Feakes with a rapier in 1596 and was in turned killed by Jonson two years later. It was a brutal world in which the drama of life often rivalled events on stage.

Marlowe was also a member of the Lord Admiral's Company, and knew at first hand the turmoil and violence of his profession. In Hog Lane, the players' quarter, he was engaged in a duel with the son of a local landlord, whom he killed; he was discharged on the plea of self-defence. He was in any case known for his quick temper and pugnacity, and we may see this riotous world as a background to his magniloquent and violent drama. He was himself murdered in Deptford.

Marlowe and his fellow actors could not have existed without Edward Alleyn, who, as leader of the Admiral's Men, played a role for Marlowe similar to that of Burbage for Shakespeare. Alleyn's company was inevitably dominated by Alleyn, who took for himself all the major roles for which he was supremely fitted. We may suppose that Shakespeare, with a sterling company in the Lord Chamberlain's Men, was too occupied and perhaps too modest to steal the most prominent parts. For six years from 1594 the Admiral's and Lord Chamberlain's were in direct competition. Their competitiveness was stimulated by another company under the guidance of the earls of Worcester and Oxford, which played at the Boar's Head and was eventually granted the title Queen Anne's Men. In addition, two boys' companies were revived, at St Paul's and Blackfriars. London now had three adult troupes and two groups of boys, and as a result the plays kept coming, still a fresh one every day and a new one every week. With a relatively small cast and a vast number of plays, the technique of 'quick change disguises' seems to have delighted the audience, who appreciated any novelty in the fast-moving world of the theatre. It was also invaluable for players who appeared each day and were easily recognized. Spectacles and dumbshow increased the diversity.

Under the guidance of Alleyn, the Admiral's Men staged some 161 plays at their playhouses, the Rose and the Fortune. One clown in a forgotten play remarks of his mistress that 'will I confound her with compliments drawn from the Plaies I see at the Fortune and Red Bull where I learne all the words I speake and understand not.' Alleyn also possessed the advantage of Marlowe's plays, whose magniloquent heroes, Tamburlaine and Faustus among them, he adopted to great acclaim. It is recorded in one anecdote that one player 'had a head of hair like one of my Divells in Doctor Faustus, when the old Theatre crackt and frighted the Audience'. The magic and superstition that Marlowe exploited were living phenomena.

Edward Alleyn himself was a large man who was the virtuoso of the mighty line. He was born in 1566 in the parish of Bishopsgate, a Londoner as were most of his colleagues. According to Thomas Fuller, in *The Worthies of England*, published posthumously in 1662, 'he was bred a stage-player' and 'made any part (especially a majestic one) to become him'. Alleyn also possessed considerable financial acumen, and in 1599 he decided to invest in a new theatre, the Fortune in St Giles, Cripplegate, to accommodate the Admiral's Men; it was designed to rival the Globe with its plays and players, and was in business by 1600. Alleyn himself was in one sense a typical Elizabethan actor, playing often and variously. Nashe wrote that 'not *Roscius* or *Aesope* . . . could ever performe more in action than famous *Ned Allen*.' Alleyn began early, at the age of fourteen, but so mastered his craft that in the summer of 1594, at the age of about twenty-eight, he played seven different parts in fourteen days. On another occasion he played four different parts in the same play. This was not really a matter for amazement at the time; the player was worked until, sometimes, he dropped.

Yet Alleyn was exceptional. He performed in the plays of Jonson and John Webster as well as in those of Marlowe. He was very tall, over 1.8 metres (6 ft), and excelled in what were known as 'majesticall' parts. He might be described as an actor of the old school. He was an exponent of what was known as passionate acting, and, in the phrase of the period, could tear a cat upon the stage. He stalked rather than walked before the spectators, strutted and bellowed in the familiar style, and even laughed at himself as 'the fustian king'. At his apogee, however, he must have been stirring indeed.

It has been related that the force Alleyn commanded in his role as Doctor Faustus was so potent that the devil himself appeared during one performance at Exeter, when the players themselves 'were all perswaded there was one devell too many amongst them; and so after a little pause desired the people to pardon them, they could go no further with this matter: the people also understanding the thing as it was, every man hastened to be first out of dores.' Sooner or later, perhaps, the English actor summons what he portrays.

In his eagerness to acquire tokens of status, Alleyn was typical of the English actor in every age. From his diary it is clear that his expenditure on clothes was very high, and his agate ring was three times the size of any other; but he also paid for the shoes and clothes of the boys at Dulwich, the school he had founded from his profitable theatrical ventures. He spent a great deal on his various doctors, but nevertheless would often go to London to drink beer with his fellow actors.

The Admiral's and the Chamberlain's men were engaged in a 'war' of wit as well as popularity; they caricatured each other's productions and parodied their players. Alleyn, for example, was satirized as Bottom. At the same time they were happy to introduce catchphrases that echoed one another. It can be surmised that the London audience attended the performances of this 'duopoly', and the Admiral's Men continued the tradition of the comedy of 'humours' even as they introduced one important innovation: comedies set in contemporary London. This was the next step forward in the theatrical world. It was perhaps balanced, metaphysically speaking, by the new fashion for biblical episodes and stories on the stage.

Thomas Kyd was a playwright for the Queen's Men, who had dominated the London theatre in the 1580s, but his early work has not survived. His most significant drama, *The Spanish Tragedy* (1592), can be noted as the first revenge tragedy in English, and was the begetter of what became a fashionable genre. In the process it was responsible for a heightened form of melodrama. The new form accommodated murder, madness and cannibalism among other enticing themes, and would have attracted a style of acting closer to Alleyn than Shakespeare. One actor, rehearsing a scene for Thomas Rawlins's *The Rebellion*, boasts, 'mark it if I do not gape wider than the widest mouth's Fowler of them all.' The reference was to a player at the Fortune, Richard Fowler, who as Hieronimo in *The Spanish Tragedy* continued Alleyn's tradition of stalking and roaring, and was associated with his colleagues at the Fortune known as 'terrible tear-throats'. The new mode of 'personation' or the more naturalistic mode of acting never did succeed in supplanting the old styles.

A lighter note was struck by John Lyly, whose first published work was a prose extravaganza. *Euphues* or the *Anatomy of Wit* (1578) was an immediate success for its fanciful and extravagant prose, together with the plentiful use of metaphor and simile,

allusion and alliteration, periphrasis and antithesis. It is an indication of the fascination for rhetoric and highly mannered prose in
a world largely dependent on the uses of language. Lyly became
the great success of his time, but after *Euphues* he turned his
attention to drama and became attached to the private theatre of
Blackfriars, the indoor setting of which offered an alternative to
the raucous surroundings of the public theatres and the best possible context for his mellifluous dialogue. This was the setting in
which he could train a body of children known as 'Oxford's Boys',
who acted in two of his early plays, *Campaspe* and *Sappho and
Phao*, classical entertainments enlivened by Lyly's delicate wit
and the skilful acting of the boys. He learned much from courtly
entertainment, with its mythological interludes and pageant-like
spectacle, but enlivened it with his wit, his sparkling dialogue and
his inventive staging.

Four

The early actors

Of what quality was this new breed of actor who emerged in the late sixteenth century? Aside from their comic roles, they were meant to be 'handsome and well shaped'. They dressed well and, when finances permitted, elegantly; they were sometimes mocked for their costumes as the second-hand clothes of nobles or nobles' servants, but there are suggestions that they were inclined to pride because of their appearance as well as their popularity. The actors themselves were sometimes identified as 'Mr', which meant that they were shareholders in the company and therefore highly considered and almost as highly rewarded. Others were given an initial followed by a surname or by an abbreviated form of the Christian name. It was a question of rank and degree. Some were simply known as 'fool', as if they were partially detached from the play itself.

But the new men came flooding in, searching for fortune and fame. Two aspiring actors from Cambridge were told, 'be merry, my lads, you have happened upon the most excellent vocation in the world for money: they come North and South to bring it to our playhouses.' Gabriel Harvey wrote to Edmund Spenser of the 'freshe starteupp comedanties' with 'sum new devised interlude' which might be 'natural' and 'to the life'. This was once again intended to be in contrast to the actors of a previous era, who stamped on the stage, lifted their arms in the air, interrupted their speeches with sighs and rolled their eyes to signify fear. The old mode of walking across the stage was strutting, and the word 'ham' to convey bad acting came from the visibility of the hamstring of the leg. Thomas Nashe described it as 'ruff raff roaring, with thwick, thwac, thirlery bouncing'. This mode of acting did not disappear altogether, and it is likely that the actors even of the eighteenth century continued to employ some of the mannerisms. Perhaps certain modern actors still do. There were also some players who used the old style of recitation just at a time when a more conversational idiom was beginning to take its place. As late as the eighteenth century a Frenchman noted that an actor in English tragedy sounded like the night-watchman who wailed 'past twelve o'clock and a cloudy morning'.

But the rise of the professional actor and playwright, together with that of secular drama and a contemporary urban audience, altered the nature of performance. There were no more clerks on the green or pageants in the street. There are as many ways of acting as there are actors, but they were guided in the sixteenth century by certain accepted conventions. There were orthodox ways of signalling love or hate, jealousy or distrust, and this was known as 'visible eloquence'. Much of the crowded audience would not be able to see the actor's face in full, so he was obliged to perform with his body. To lower the head was a form of modesty, and to strike the forehead was a sign either of shame or of admiration. Dejection of spirit was noted by the pulling down of the hat over the eyes. There were textbooks devoted to the gestures of the hands.

The player would find it perfectly natural to address the audience in an aside or soliloquy, and the great set speeches were declaimed rather than recited. The only general lighting effect was daylight, so facial expressions would have been exaggerated and deliberate. The actor was advised 'to look directly in his fellowes face' without ever turning his back on the audience. It was said of Desdemona, in a letter from a spectator who had seen a performance of *Othello* by the King's Men at Oxford in 1610, that 'she implored the pity of the spectators in her death with the face alone'.

It is salutary to remember that Burbage and many other actors of the time began their careers in boyhood, when they played women. Their training therefore consisted of what any actor would agree is the most challenging transformation of all in the change of gender. These boy actors were not engaging in 'female imperson- ation', 'gender-subversion' or, except occasionally, even winks to the audience. Shakespeare's texts alone give the lie to that notion; Cordelia, Desdemona, Lady Macbeth, Imogen, Hermione and Olivia do not offer themselves as figures of fun. The boy actor had to adopt and assimilate the voice, the gait, the rhythms, the mannerisms, the poses and even the inner life of a woman. He had to transform, not merely impersonate. And we have the com- pound witness of contemporaries, approving and hostile, that he succeeded. Indeed, the boy who played Desdemona was no tyro. So austere an apprenticeship forged remarkable actors.

In an age of great actors, who was the most admirable? It is an impossible question, with Edward Alleyn of the Admiral's and Richard Burbage of the Chamberlain's vying for suprem- acy. Shakespeare might have been seen as the shining star of the new theatre, but there are intimations that he was not as good an actor as playwright. The historian John Aubrey later reported that Shakespeare 'did act exceeding well', but, having been born ten years after Shakespeare's death, he could never have seen him on stage. Meanwhile the dramatist Henry Chettle described Shakespeare as 'excellent in the quality he professes', which is equivocal. To perform as skilfully as he wrote is beyond the bounds of human possibility, and it is often supposed that he preferred to impersonate old men and royalty. We may think of Alonso, King of Naples, rather than King Lear; he had too much to do to undertake lengthy parts. It was believed that one of his best performances was as the Ghost in *Hamlet*.

Yet by the chemistry of fame Shakespeare has spread his lustre over the actors with whom he played and for whom he wrote. The most conspicuous example can be found in his colleague Richard Burbage. Richard's father, James, had also been an actor in the old tradition of performance that runs from father to son, and it has already been noted that the senior Burbage had also been the builder of the Theatre and the Blackfriars Theatre, which was perhaps the most luxurious of its time. James had taken fortune by the ears. Richard himself was widely understood to be the pre-eminent artist of Shakespeare's ultimate company, the Lord Chamberlain's Men. It was he who played the first Lear, the first Hamlet and the first Othello. It is also likely that he introduced Romeo and Macbeth to the world, as well as Prospero and Henry v.

Burbage was the Proteus of the Elizabethan stage, as the phrase went, and it is very likely that Shakespeare created certain characters with him in mind. It was reported that 'what we see him personate we think truly done before us'. Like many great actors he was short in stature; this is an anomaly only when you consider that the actor projects himself physically as well as temperamentally. When his character was angry he gnawed his lower lip. His delivery may have been rhythmical or musical, distinctly at odds with contemporary speech, but that is what the audience expected. The dramatist Richard Flecknoe may have been considering Burbage when he wrote that 'there is as much difference betwixt him and a common Actor as betwixt a Ballad-singer and an excellent Musician . . . his Auditors being never more delighted than when he speaks; no more sorry than when he holds his peace. Yet even then he is an excellent Actor still, not failing in his part when he has done his speech but with his looks and gestures maintaining it still unto the heighth.' By this Flecknoe meant that the actor was unusual in staying in his part until the conclusion of the play.

The published reports of Richard Burbage's acting tend to emphasize his naturalness and fluency, with the ability of projecting individual characters 'to the life' or 'with lively action'. There is no question of formality or restraint except as the plot warranted it. The emphasis had begun to move from representing the outlines of passion, as in the religious drama, to the attempt of the actor to display or express that passion. It may well be that some new art of emotive or emotional action, employed by Burbage and his colleagues, would help to explain the impact of Shakespeare's plays upon his contemporaries.

The Lord Chamberlain's Men were so closely knit that many players had worked together for twenty years, an arrangement that would now be inconceivable. They knew one another's strengths and weaknesses, their tricks and quiddities. More importantly, they were well known to Shakespeare, who could tailor his cast accordingly. Such cross-pollination may be considered typical of this mixed and motley age. We may wonder who, given the vast but unacknowledged contribution of the actors, were the other spirits behind the plays.

Burbage had the reputation of a 'tough fellow', and he would have needed a rough edge to deal with all the landowners, profiteers and rivals of the city to cope with the new business of entertainment. He, like Shakespeare, came from the hard-earning and hard-working section of Elizabethan society that provided its initiative and energy. He was also accustomed early to the hard labour of touring, when he was one of Leicester's Men; curiously enough, the company visited Stratford-upon-Avon when Shakespeare was nine and quite capable of joining the audience. Burbage's career was one of incessant labour and, in the words of Flecknoe, his life 'was nothing else but action'. He died at the age of fifty.

The other members of the Lord Chamberlain's Men deserve consideration. Augustine Phillips emerges as an actor of great repute, although the course of his career is not altogether clear. When he was cast as Sardanapalus in *The Seven Deadly Sins*, with Lord Strange's Men, he was one of two players who were not obliged to play more than one part. He toured the provinces in 1593, his reputation boosted by *The Seven Deadly Sins*, and in the following year joined the Lord Chamberlain's Men. Phillips became a stalwart of the company, performing first at the Theatre and then at the Globe. His acting career is not well documented, but in a folio edition of Ben Jonson's *Workes* he is named third among 'principall Comoedians'. It seems likely that he sang and danced in the jig that concluded the plays. He finally took off his sock and buskin – the two ancient symbols of comedy and tragedy – in 1605. (The tragic buskin was a boot and the comic sock a thin-soled shoe. The tragedian might then rise above the comedian.)

There were actors for all occasions. William Robbins, for example, was a 'lean fool' (Sir Andrew Aguecheek?) and was sometimes paired with a player known as 'the fat clown' (Toby Belch?). The number of actors had in any case been increased by the passing in 1572 of the Vagabonds Act, which decreed that 'all common players . . . who wander about and have not a licence shall be taken, adjudged and deemed rogues, vagabonds and sturdy beggars.' So their numbers swelled as they sought protection from the authorities. It became in their vital interest to attach themselves to a lord's retinue. There were already a large number of itinerant players who were able, directly or indirectly, to take advantage of the emergence of secular drama. The two monarchs after Mary, Elizabeth and James, far from condemning the theatre, loved plays and play-acting, and this encouraged a new sense of freedom. The Lord Chamberlain's Men had one outdoor and one indoor playhouse, the Globe and Blackfriars, while Alleyn's Men possessed two outdoor theatres only with the Rose and the Fortune. Whether this affected the quality of their respective skills is open to question.

There are many players who survive only by association with the Lord Chamberlain's Men. Henry Condell was an actor who also had the distinction of helping to edit Shakespeare's first folio. Condell was part of the company when he played in Jonson's *Every Man in His Humour* and *Every Man Out of His Humour*. He also acted in four other plays by Jonson, *Sejanus*, *Volpone*, *The Alchemist* and *Catiline*. As one of the Chamberlain's Men he may be presumed to have taken part in Shakespeare's drama. He also performed the Cardinal in John Webster's *The Duchess of Malfi*. In common with the majority of his colleagues in the Chamberlain's Men, he prospered and followed the pattern of dramatic success by buying a country house in Fulham.

John Heminges was the principal editor of Shakespeare's first folio. He began stage life with Lord Strange's Men at a time of plague, but when the disease abated he joined the Lord Chamberlain's Men, where he acted primarily in Jonson's plays. Like other players he soon found his true gift in the more technical skills of managing company business and supervising theatrical accounts. That is no doubt why he was given the task of editing the folio.

Reports of John Lowin's acting emerge in 1602, soon after he had completed his apprenticeship as a goldsmith. Lowin began with Henslowe of the Rose, who lent him five shillings 'when he went into the country with the company to play', but in 1604, after an outbreak of plague that lasted intermittently for more than a year, Lowin joined the newly named King's Men (formerly the Lord Chamberlain's Men), with whom he remained for the rest of his career. He looked the part of command and authority. He played Falstaff 'with mighty applause' and took on the Jonsonian roles of Volpone and Sir Epicure Mammon. He acted Belleur, a man 'of a stout blunt humour', in Fletcher's *The Wild Goose Chase*, but was also Bosola in Webster's *The Duchess of Malfi* and the title character of John Clavell's *The Soddered Citizen*, 'of great beard and bulk'. It is clear that some parts were made expressly for him. It has been said that he was chosen for Shakespeare's *Henry VIII* in 1611, and in fact 'had his instructions from Mr Shakespeare himself'. In 1635 he remarked that he had 'laboured herein buskins and in socks this thirty year'. The theatres were closed by administrative fiat in 1642 and did not reopen until after his death. There are some reports of his participating in illegal playgoing in a city starved of drama, and of being briefly arrested, but who could blame him after a lifetime of acting? He retired, turned innkeeper, and died in 1653.

Nat Field, or Nathan Field, entered the profession under duress. He was 'impressed' in the manner of a sailor, although no doubt in gentler fashion, and was granted to the Children of the Chapel Royal at Blackfriars. It was not uncommon for boys of promising appearance or voice to be taken up and enlisted, and it is possible that some of them enjoyed the experience of being removed from Elizabethan street life into quieter or at least more comfortable surroundings. At Blackfriars Field worked on new plays by Jonson, including *Cynthia's Revels* in 1600, as well as dramas by Fletcher, John Marston and Thomas Kyd. In 1609 he played the title role in Jonson's *Epicoene* with the Children of the Queen's Revels at the Whitefriars Theatre.

Field 'personated' many different parts, and was summoned to play at court on eleven occasions. His popularity showed his worth, which he may have suspected all along. He then continued work with the Children of the Queen's Revels, for whom he displayed his skill as a writer rather than player; he composed *Amends for Ladies* and *A Woman Is a Weathercocke*, which, like most productions of the time, have been forgotten. He stayed with the Revels Children until they were amalgamated with the Lady Elizabeth's Men, managed by Shakespeare's colleague Philip Henslowe. The combined company worked at the Hope and Swan theatres, where they played Thomas Middleton's *A Chaste Maid in Cheapside* and

Jonson's *Bartholomew Fair*. But by 1616, after much of the internal wrangling that seems endemic to theatrical politics, he joined the King's Men, which was bereft after the death of Shakespeare. In part because of Shakespeare's absence, Field became one of the leading players of the company, playing Face in Jonson's *Alchemist* and Voltore in *Volpone*. He was in essence the 'second lead'. He collaborated with Fletcher and Philip Massinger in certain of the newly fashionable 'tragicomedies', one of which was Massinger's *The Fatal Dowry*, to which Field himself contributed. The title tells the tale, and this is one of the plays that, according to Fletcher, 'want [lack] death but bring some near to it'. It came to Field sooner than he may have wished; he died in the late summer of 1620 at the age of thirty-three.

John Sincler or 'Sinklo' had joined the Lord Chamberlain's Men by 1597, having previously been part of Lord Strange's Men, Pembroke's Men and Sussex's Men; he was short and thin, a physique that might sometimes work to his advantage and sometimes not. Shakespeare mentions him by name three times, which suggests that he was a familiar and valuable member of the company. He was so notably lean that Doll Tearsheet called him a 'nut-hook' and Mistress Quickly a 'starved bloodhound'; we can surmise that his appearance allowed him to play a multitude of parts, but he refused to sit between the legs of one actor in John Marston's *The Malcontent* for fear of being mistaken for a viola da gamba. He may have played Slender in *Merry Wives of Windsor* and Starveling in *A Midsummer Night's Dream*, together with a score of other emaciated parts.

Christopher Beeston is first recorded as part of the Lord Chamberlain's Company, where he was apprenticed to Augustine Phillips. He eventually moved on in 1602 to Worcester's Men (which became Queen Anne's Men the following year), where he remained for the next fifteen years. He was best known for playing in *Every Man in His Humour*, but he acted in many works by James Shirley, who composed some thirty plays of variable quality, and John Ford, whose most notable production was *'Tis Pity She's a Whore*.

Richard Cowley entered the dramatic world as one of Lord Strange's Men, before leaving with others for the newly established Lord Chamberlain's Men. He played several different parts in *Seven Deadly Sins*, but he was skilful enough to play Verges opposite Will Kemp's Dogberry in *Much Ado About Nothing*. Nevertheless he was listed last on the licence that created the new King's Men, so he might not have proved outstanding. But at this late date who can tell? He may have been a victim of the professional jealousy that was rife among the players, or he may just have been unlucky.

Other players deserve attention. In 1584 William Knell became one of the members of the newly established Queen's Men, where he seems to have specialized in the 'heroic' roles for which there was always more room. He is described as playing the title role in *The Famous Victories of Henry V*. A short while later his heroic career came to an end when a fellow actor pierced his neck with a sword.

Nicholas Tooley was an apprentice to Richard Burbage, but no record of his acting remains. Instead there is a letter he wrote at the age of seventeen to the doctor Simon Forman, complaining of 'melancholy . . . much gnawing in his stomak & stuffing in his Lungs'. He did not have the vigour or resilience of the born actor, and died at the age of forty. He seems not to have been very cheerful, either, but that is an occupational hazard. The picture of the Lord Chamberlain's Men is reinforced as a tightly knit and often interrelated group of actors who played together, toured together and drank together. They even lived in close proximity to one another: Hog Lane in Shoreditch was known as the actors' street.

There were also shared fashions in the style of play-writing, with dramas of domestic murder, Roman plays, political satires, historical epics, city plays, pastoral dramas, Greek plays, biblical plays and all the rest. It can be surmised that the London audience attended the performances of diverse players, and compared them with some enthusiasm.

The adult companies were united, however, by their use of the fool or clown to enliven the proceedings of a serious historical or tragical drama. There were certain eminent, or resourceful, adult comedians, of whom Richard Tarlton was one of the first. It was rumoured that he earned his living keeping pigs until reports of his droll manner and his 'happy unhappy answers' persuaded the Earl of Leicester's Men to enrol him in their troupe. His performance on the stage transformed him into the most popular comedian of the age, and perhaps the first great English clown. He took questions principally from the audience, which he answered with improvised rhymes or jokes.

As a fellow actor put it, 'there will never come his like, while the earth can corn. O passing fine Tarlton!' Tarlton's date of birth is unknown, but he died in 1588. It was said that the sight of his face peeping from the side of the stage reduced the audience to hysterics. His costume was a suit of russet and a buttoned cap; he carried a great bag by his side, and wielded a large bat, no doubt to use against his fellow players. He played on the tabor and the pipe, which were invaluable for the jig, and he had a moustache, a flat nose and a squint eye that made him unmistakable. Many alehouses were named after him, complete with his swinging portrait as a sign. He was for a while the queen's favourite clown, and one contemporary wrote that 'Tarlton could undumpish her at his pleasure. He told her more of her faults than many of her chaplains, and cured her of her melancholy better than all her physicians.' As a result he became the leading comic of the Queen's Men in 1583. The writer and antiquary John Stow described Tarlton as 'a man of wondrous plentifull pleasant extemporal wit', so that he became 'the wonder of his time'. For Edmund Spenser he embodied 'all joy and jolly merriment'.

Tarlton may not have been the favourite, however, of play-wrights and other actors. It is said that Hamlet's 'poor Yorick' was based on him. The problem for his colleagues is that he was more famous than any of the roles he played. He was meant to take the part of an innocent countryman in the city, but Tarlton would break off from this performance to engage in improvised or vulgar repartee with the spectators. It is true of many eminent actors, even in our own time, that they so outstrip their characters that it is unclear whether the audience has come to see the play or certain players. Tarlton might suddenly spring into a dance or introduce comic 'business' into the action. It is likely that some people attended simply to enjoy his jigs at the close of each performance.

Tarlton's successor in the comic mode, Will Kemp, also had his own 'act', like that of a modern comedian. 'I will lay myself open to you', he said, 'like an oyster.' But he was a more skilful performer, closer than Tarlton to Shakespeare's ideal clown. He played Dogberry as well as Launcelot Gobbo, Touchstone as well as the First Gravedigger in *Hamlet*. His vitality and enterprise are registered in such items as 'Kemp's Pleasant New Jig of the Broom Man', 'Master Kemp's New Jig of the Kitchen-Stuff Woman' and 'Master Kemp's new jygge betwixt a soldiour, a Miser and Sym the clown'. One of his most popular routines was to heave his leg over his staff and pretend to urinate like a dog. No detail was too small. The architect Inigo Jones records that when Kemp played Falstaff he appeared with 'a roabe of russet Girt low . . . a great belley . . . greate heade and balde' and 'buskins to shew a great swollen leg'. It is reported that he watched and studied real simpletons so as to copy their speech and behaviour perfectly. Would that allow him to be called the first 'method actor'? It is in fact a familiar stratagem: David Garrick played the mad Lear after very carefully observing a real lunatic. Kemp's exploits were not confined to the stage; he performed a Morris dance from London to Norwich – no doubt with various pauses for refreshment – and published a pamphlet boasting of his exploits. He also managed by some mysterious means to walk backwards to Berwick. His skill as tumbler, acrobat, mime and musician also earned him an international reputation, but his primary identification came with the general citizenry of London, for whom he became an emblem and representative until his death in 1603.

Kemp's place as resident fool with the Lord Chamberlain's Men was taken over by Robert Armin. Armin would also join forces with those who were managing the newly completed Globe playhouse, and so he was associated, among others, with Burbage, Heminges, Shakespeare and Thomas Pope as fellows and colleagues. He was quite different from Kemp or Tarlton, being said to resemble a pixie or, rather, a pixie with a brain. He began the world as an apprentice to a goldsmith but soon found his vocation as a dramatist and writer of ballads. He wrote popular plays such as *A Nest of Ninnies* and *The History of Two Maids of More-clacke*, but acquired his real fame as a performer. It is significant that Shakespeare wrote parts for fools only after Armin had joined the company.

Armin also had a strong singing voice, and Shakespeare wrote many songs for him. It even became fashionable for fools to break into song. He was melancholic and whimsical, witty and philosophical, learned and satirical, a mixture of characteristics different from that of earlier clowns. He did not extemporize or improvise as his predecessors did, but studied each part with great care. It has been claimed that the introduction of Armin was an indirect means of curbing the folly or foolery of other actors. He was Touchstone and Feste, the Fool in *King Lear* and, more surprisingly, the scabrous Thersites in *Troilus and Cressida*. Improvisation on the model of Kemp or Tarlton would have destroyed the tone and atmosphere of such drama.

William Rowley was a clown in the London mode. He was a dramatist as well as an actor, but in his playing he specialized in 'fat clown' roles such as the Fat Bishop in Middleton's *A Game at Chess* and Plumporridge in the *Inner Temple Masque* by the same author. He was originally one of the Queen's Men, and no doubt found an appreciative audience in the raucous surroundings of the Curtain or the Red Bull. There was always space on the stage for a fat clown, and he can be classified as a London type or a male version of the pig woman in *Bartholomew Fair*. In 1624 he joined the King's Men, where he stayed until his death two years later. He was buried in the churchyard of St James, Clerkenwell, in the company of many other actors. It had become the necropolis of the theatrical profession.

Standing behind these eminent comedians was a more shadowy and ancient figure in the shape of Vice. It is likely that in early Tudor drama all actors might have wanted to play the Vice, since it offered so many possibilities. The stagehand known as 'the whiffler' might clear a space for him before his arrival; he was not simply the begetter of mischief and mayhem but often also the compere of the proceedings. He had a direct communication with the audience and might comment on the plays and players. He might provoke hissing, laughter, shouts or whistles. He was the centre of the action, which was why his position was a coveted one. His deviousness and hypocrisy might act as a subliminal reminder that the theatre was the work of the devil, as the preachers insisted, but that may simply have increased the fun. He sings and jokes and plays the gittern; he dances, jumps and tumbles. He cleans his nails with a wooden dagger. His origins lie too far back to identify, but the comedians and fools of sixteenth-century drama, as well as comic characters of the present day, owe much to him.

Tarlton, Kemp and Armin were, like Vice, facing an audience of mixed and multifarious characters. Playgoers were drawn from all classes except the very poorest, who would beg outside the doors; common sense suggests that the majority were of the 'middling' group of people together with the 'gentry' and their consorts.

Among them were 'all Martial men . . . all Students of Artes and Sciences, and by our English custome, all Innes of Court men, professors of the Law'. To this heterogeneous list may be added courtiers, merchants and assorted travellers, who paid a penny for the pit and another penny for a seat; those in the yard, the 'understanders', might find room to sit upon rushes on the ground.

The playhouse was in many respects an egalitarian place where 'every lewd person thinks himself (for his penny) worthy of the chief and most commodious place.' The audience could be very noisy in their displeasure, with 'mew, blirt, ha, ha' often orches-trated by the 'Apple-wives and Chimney-boyes'. But the flow of the crowd aroused the electricity of the actor. Actors have always depended on the audience for their own energy and invention. Plato defined it as *theatrokratia*, the dictatorship of the spectator. The audiences would stand up during a particularly exciting duel or battle, urging on the participants. They would applaud indi-vidual speeches. There were hisses and shouts, tears and applause, but contrary to received wisdom they did not hurl apples or oranges at the stage. That was a later development; in these early days, the play was too exciting to interrupt.

By 1582 there were six or eight 'playing places' in London, which suggests that the municipal officers had little luck in expel-ling 'vagabonds' and strolling players. The city itself had become a form of theatre by the time of Elizabeth, with parades, pageants, fairs and executions complementing the growth of playhouses. As the churches became desacralized, their candles and images removed, so urban society became more profoundly ritualistic and spectacular. This was the world that Shakespeare and his contemporaries inhabited.

scribes who abridged, amended and generally patched up the newly written plays.

Jonson's own first play, *The Case Is Altered*, was composed for the Children of the Blackfriars in 1597, but he seems already to have involved himself with the Lord Chamberlain's Men, for whom in 1598 he wrote *Every Man in His Humour*. Anything to do with that company, of course, borrows Shakespeare's reputation, and it has been suggested that he himself chose the play. However that may be, Shakespeare was certainly one of the principal actors in the production, together with Richard Burbage. It was performed at the Curtain and was set in the London streets that Jonson knew so well; in its prologue he invoked 'deeds and language such as men do use' so that the play became 'an image of the times'. This was the fundamental and vital spirit of Jonsonian drama. When Jonson said he wished to employ 'language such as men do use', we may take his word for it that he copied the patter and banter of the Londoner. Londoners always talked and walked very quickly, so there would have been a marked acceleration of speech and action.

Jonson's next play, *Every Man Out of His Humour*, was played by the Lord Chamberlain's Men at the Globe in 1599. His comedies of 'humour' were designed to illustrate or caricature the dominant temperament of the individual character: melancholic, choleric, sanguine or phlegmatic. It was not to be expected that the actors would necessarily display any elusive subtlety in their emotional range; the broader brush was the better. It was, in essence, a further development of English drama as a mirror of contemporary life. A later play by Jonson, *Bartholomew Fair* (1614), begins and ends with mayhem and confusion, business and activity, as substitutes for a single or concentrated plot. His was the art of the crowd, full of squabbles, fights, insults and misunderstandings. It afforded the players the opportunity to be scurrilous and even shocking. Improvisation may have been required, as well as squeals and grunts, shrieks and guffaws. If we can imagine this conducted at a rapid pace, we may have an inkling both of Jonsonian urban drama and of the actors who participated in its joyful frenzy. *Bartholomew Fair* is Jonson's hymn to London, and it creates a new form of incessant business and contention, with the variously contrasting characters all using their own tricks, games and subterfuges. The pig woman, who shouts and drinks and bawds, can be taken, in Jonson's terminology, as typical. The actor will always have a point of reference that will never fail him and the prospect of contention as his guide. This is London. A quiet monologue turns to a discussion, a discussion to a contention, and a contention to a fight. Everyone in the audience will be aware of this chain of consequences, and it would probably need Londoners to enact it.

Their style of performance was guided by Jonson's predilection for activity and for the instinctive manifestations of greed and assertion. But the point of Jonson's text, and perhaps direction, is that, like his human characters, he was inspired by types. Where Shakespeare preferred to guide his actor by means of imagery, cadence and even metre, Jonson used names, repetition, and verbal and physical 'tics' to identify his players. The actors' skill was to transform these 'types' into living individuals. Their world is London, and the city is living material with a stage filled with objects and gimcracks fit for their purposes. Jonson never used a bare stage in the old manner, and this made for a different style of acting. Shakespeare can be played in mime at certain moments, and often has been, where Jonson cannot. Mime is the antithesis of his art.

Jonson's principal characters were in fact sometimes named after animals, perhaps an atavistic echo of much earlier and more primitive ceremonies. One of the most evocative parts in *Volpone* (beside Volpone himself as 'fox' and Corvino as 'crow') is that of Voltore, vulture, the bird of prey tearing at the entrails of the weak. The actor would have been trained to imitate the style of that voracious animal as far as humanly possible, cracking his knuckles, rippling his fingers, stretching out his arms and darting his mobile, piercing eyes. It is also possible that, like other members of the cast, he wore a mask or half-mask to accentuate his features, but this is uncertain. Masks had become unfamiliar on the English stage. Those who did wear them were accustomed to look long and hard at them before putting them on; this was intended to assist the actor in understanding and assimilating the character. But it was not a common practice. Corvino would in any case have been familiar to the audience since the crow, like its fellow raptor the kite, was a denizen of the London streets, picking up what food it could find. If the part was acted with some agility and verve, it might earn a round of 'plaudits'. Mosca, or fly, might have provoked less enthusiastic recognition.

Jonson's actors seem to have been largely informed by Shakespeare's dramaturgy. Burbage, John Lowin and Nathan Field had Shakespeare in their blood. But that made Jonson even harder to play. In *The Alchemist* of 1610, for example, they must play their part with sincere deception. They do not wear a mask but a face. Face is in fact the name of one of the characters. And the actors must be aware of this face; they cannot seem but must be, and they must mean every word they utter, otherwise the play would collapse under the weight of its own artifice.

JOHN WEBSTER'S *The Duchess of Malfi* was first performed in 1614 and was the defining drama of the period. One of a number of plays that have been collectively and conveniently classified as 'Jacobean tragedy', it was performed by the King's Men at the theatre in Blackfriars, in front of a fashionable audience, and also at the more public Globe. It is a dramatic representation of melancholy, morbidity, restlessness, brooding anger, impatience, disdain and resentment. It embodies the horror of life, and gives the actors the opportunity to accentuate and exaggerate. They are measured and conspiratorial; their words drop from their mouths like overripe fruit. They are in danger of suffocation from a syllabub of syllables. Yet the narrative insists that they are possessed by a wild and frantic energy as they run towards darkness. When the players expressed despair, they would let their hands droop downwards, and in moments of grief they would strike the breast with the hand.

Webster's *The White Devil*, staged two years before, had been a comparative failure; Webster blamed that on a dull and uneducated audience at the Red Bull, and there may be some truth to this. It is more likely, however, that the Queen's Men were not quite up to the task of conveying the Websterian quiddities. The style is as cerebral as it is visceral, and to play it in the manner of Kyd or Marlowe – as no doubt they did – would not have been a success. The verse is loose and there is an abundance of prose. There is wit, but it is not Shakespearean or Jonsonian wit; it is wit within wit, just as the Jacobean player knew how to act within acting. He needed to play different roles within each part. He cannot confess too much; he cannot give away too much.

The title role of Webster's *Duchess of Malfi* was in fact a case study in complexity. The audience was used to monsters and angels, but here they were in the presence of a difficult, demanding and inconsistent woman. It would have been a hard task for the boy who played her, requiring all the skill of a subtle actor. Bosola of the same play is a figure that only the Jacobeans could have conceived, an aspiring courtier who resorts to murder. The actor needs great suppleness of style and behaviour, by turns brusque and ingratiating, fierce and seductive. The Jacobean theatre places layer upon layer, with the whole weight of world-weariness and startled reaction, upon the actor. Real passion also emerges in the boys and boy-women; through dint of training and experience they had become quicker and more observant. They seem more resourceful. They are more human.

But where was the new Burbage or the new Tarlton? One actor stands out in the Jacobean and Caroline periods, stretching from 1603 to 1649, although his name and reputation have been all but forgotten. Richard Perkins is first recorded as a member of Worcester's Men, and remained with them until they changed their allegiance to become Queen Anne's Men in 1603, when he was in his early twenties. It is likely that he played in the first production of Webster's *The White Devil* at the Red Bull; Webster praised him highly for his performance, despite the failure of the play. 'In particular,' he wrote, 'I must remember the well-approved industry of my friend Master Perkins, and confess the worth of his action did crown both the beginning and the end.' By common consent Perkins's greatest achievement was as Barabas in Marlowe's *The Jew of Malta*, in which his skill was compared to that of Edward Alleyn. He was believed to be the greatest tragedian of his time. Perkins moved for a short while to the Cockpit, the theatre created by Christopher Beeston, then joined the King's Men before renewing his allegiance with Beeston. Beeston himself had been a child actor and an adult player before turning to the more profitable tasks of management; it was a familiar trajectory in the London theatre. As the impresario's principal actor, Perkins played in dramas by Marlowe, Thomas Heywood, James Shirley and John Ford. Eventually he took lodgings in Clerkenwell, which had become the theatrical quarter of London, and where he died in 1650.

The comic tradition in London was inexhaustible. Thomas Greene had succeeded Robert Armin as the city's principal comedian by 1611, when a play entitled *Greene's Tu Quoque* was presented at Court; it was performed at the Red Bull the following year. 'Tu quoque', meaning 'you as well', was his favourite catchphrase. Greene was a member of the Queen's Men, where he was known as 'Bubble', wore a hat with two large feathers and was described as 'one of the principall and chief persons of the said Companie' until his death. The range and extent of his jokes and repartee cannot be recovered, but Heywood, the company's playwright, wrote that 'there was not an Actor of his nature in his time of better ability in performance of what he undertooke; more applauded by the Audience, of greater grace at the Court, or of more general love in the Citty.'

Joseph Taylor was of slightly later growth. He is first recorded as playing at the age of twenty-four as a member of the Duke of York's Men, but his reputation was such that he was taken up by the King's Men in 1619 on the death of Richard Burbage, at which time he adopted most of Burbage's familiar roles. For the sake of the audience, there was always a continuity of parts, and in any case there were not enough good or complex roles to squander among the second rank of players. Taylor had left the Duke of York's Men in 1611 to join Lady Elizabeth's Men, a joint company of Princess Elizabeth's and Prince Charles's Men. Taylor was perhaps the most important living actor to maintain the tradition of Shakespeare and Jonson until the closure of the theatres by parliamentary edict in 1642.

The refurbished company of the Admiral's Men, ready to play in the newly erected Fortune Playhouse, was formed in 1600 on the birth of the future Charles I, under the management of Edward Alleyn, but little is known of it. We can only assume that Alleyn employed those actors whom he already knew, and as a result certain actors can be identified. Among them were Robert Benfield, Joseph Taylor, Michael Bowyer, William Ostler, John Underwood, Stephen Hammerton and Eliard Swanston.

The paths of their careers were broadly similar. Ostler was a reputable boy actor who at a suitable age joined the King's Men, where he played in Jonson and Webster; such was his skill that he became known as 'the Roscius of these times' before his early death in 1614. Premature death seems to have been a familiar fate of the theatrical profession. Underwood followed Ostler in proceeding from the Children of the Chapel to the King's Men, and appeared in what had become the familiar but still popular works of Jonson and Webster, as well as eighteen dramas by Beaumont and Fletcher. Hammerton also made the transition from female to male after changing from boy to man; he was known as 'a most noted and beautiful woman-actor', but in male dress he became something of a favourite among the women in the audience. It was said that if 'Stephen misses the Wench . . . that alone is enough to spoil the Play'. It is a mark of his popularity that he was known simply by his first name.

Benfield joined the King's Men after a suitable spell with Lady Elizabeth's Men, and is mentioned eighteen times in the cast lists. Bowyer was also hired by the King's Men and soon became 'of principal note' and one of the troupe's 'eminent actors'; it is pertinent that the acting profession was so little regarded by the chroniclers of the age that, as with his contemporaries, very little is known of him. There is a paradox in this, for the age was one in which actors first began to acquire both wealth and, more significant, prestige. It has been suggested that certain actors took on the same Shakespearean character, such as 'the devoted lover' or 'the smooth-faced villain', but the evidence for such type-casting is not necessarily convincing.

The dearth of pre-eminent plays does not mean that no new work was being created. Plays were in abundance, even if they were not of the highest quality. An 'indoors' playhouse, 'new' and 'fair', was established near St Bride's, on the north bank of the Thames, in 1629, and was called the Salisbury Court Theatre. It was erected and maintained by Richard Gunnell, one of the actors who has escaped the maw of oblivion. After an unsuccessful attempt to reintroduce the Children of the Revels in 1629, he brought with him Prince Charles's Men to the new venue. One of the most eminent of their company was Andrew Cane, who had already played at the Cockpit, Fortune and Red Bull. He specialized in the role of clown or fool, and was known for his jigs and impromptu entertainments as well as more formal theatrical parts. We can perceive a pattern of young actors completing an apprenticeship or early training before being taken up by the major companies. Much of their work was devoted to renewing the favoured plays of Shakespeare, Webster, Marlowe and Jonson, but there were recent dramas by Beaumont and Fletcher, Philip Massinger, James Shirley and others whose skill was perhaps less in evidence than was that of their predecessors.

There was a receptive audience, however, for Shirley's elaborate and confusing romances in which boy meets girls after false identities, mistaken assumptions, confused intentions and vindictive parents. They depended, as did much of the drama, on the use of stock types, and the actors would have presented not people so much as popular traits. Old men are greedy and ladies are witty; servants are clever and their employers gullible. Clowns and fools abound. One comic performer, Timothy Reade, was well-known for his nimble-footed dancing, and under the name of Light became a success with the London audience. One Caroline dramatist, Richard Brome, extolled his skill: 'I never saw Reade peeping through the curtain,/ But ravishing joy entered my heart.' Peeping through the curtain – or, more precisely, the rear hangings that disguised the tiring house – had become a device of the principal comedian. As we have seen, William Robbins was another popular favourite who came under the type of the 'lean fool' with all the parts that appertained to it. The list of celebrated players is long. The style of the actors was to a certain extent pre-ordained, and any extravagant or eccentric interpretation would divert the flow of the drama. Works 'of low life and roguery' relied on melodrama, sensation and adventure. The audience of the Red Bull, for example, would not take kindly to highly individualistic performances. Those would come later.

Six

The female actor

I n the autumn of 1642, after the success of the Puritan cause, the theatres were closed by parliamentary order. In these 'times of humiliation', all 'public stage-plays' were believed to represent 'lascivious Mirth and Levity'. A further measure of 1648 condemned actors as rogues and vagabonds, while at the same time ordering that the interiors of the theatres be demolished. Occasional plays were performed in defiance of the edict, but the official policy was strengthened by the arrest that year of players from the King's Men in the middle of a performance of *Rollo, Duke of Normandy* at the Cockpit Theatre.

The fates of the expelled players were various. Some took up employment that bore some relation to their theatrical experience, becoming jewellers, tailors, clothiers and goldsmiths. Others joined the Royalist cause, even after the death of Charles I, while others simply faded into obscurity and earned a living where they could. Certain actors staged private plays in the houses of sympathetic citizens. One of them, Alexander Gough, had been a boy actor and in the times of repression became what was known as a 'jackal', who helped to collect audiences for these clandestine performances. Bills advertising plays were thrown into the coaches of likely citizens.

But the purge continued. One contemporary wrote that 'the Soldiers have routed the Players. They have beaten them out of their *Cock-pit*, baited them at the *Bull*, and overthrown their *Fortune*.' The Globe was pulled to the ground in 1644. The popularity of the plays, and the vitality of the players, however, ensured that some performances were arranged in clandestine places or outside the bounds of the city. In the absence of proper plays it became necessary to put on hastily contrived playlets, which were known as 'drolls'; some of these were performed at the Red Bull in semi-secrecy. They consisted of six or seven extracts from well-known and well-favoured plays, with interludes of song and dance. The actors were not about to surrender to the authorities without a struggle.

They kept up their discreet activities with growing confidence as the atmosphere of the time lightened. Even under the protectorate of Oliver Cromwell, himself a great lover of music, Sir William Davenant produced the first English opera, *The Siege of Rhodes*, as a private entertainment in his own Rutland House in 1656. In somewhat elusive circumstances two or three 'nursery playhouses' were also established; one was in Hatton Garden, where it was also known as the New Playhouse. But it may have moved. Another was established in Finsbury Fields. This was 'a booth or playhouse' where the company of John Perin 'acted several plays' for nine weeks. The playhouse itself survived until 1682. These playhouses pose a puzzle. Who managed them? Who acted in them? What was their likely future? They are historical anomalies that cannot be resolved without piling doubt upon conjecture.

It has been generally accepted that the Restoration and the Stuart revival opened the doors of the theatres to the clamorous public. General George Monck, after his successful march into London and the restoration of the old Parliament, issued an order prohibiting all stage plays. That order seems to have had no effect after the return of Charles II. Two patents were issued for the foundation of two new acting companies; Davenant managed the Duke of York's Men at a new theatre in Lincoln's Inn Fields, while

Sir Thomas Killigrew led the newly established King's Men, which began in Clare Market before moving to the new Theatre Royal in Drury Lane. All was 'new'. Three other companies emerged under the royal dispensation, at the Cockpit, the Red Bull and Beeston's Salisbury Court. These were well-known venues, and it is possible that they had always been there while hiding their theatrical lights under a bushel or two.

The king gave ten of Shakespeare's plays to the Duke's Men, including *Hamlet*, *Macbeth* and *King Lear*; their leading actor was Thomas Betterton, a man of middle height but strong voice and with a natural air of authority. In all, he played some one hundred and twenty roles. After the death of Davenant he became leader of the Duke's Men, while Killigrew and the King's Men no doubt scrambled for the twenty-seven or so plays of Shakespeare that had not been granted to their rivals; but they felt obliged to commission new or recent works in order to entice the audiences. But the presence of two companies under royal auspices was expensive and sometimes redundant. Killigrew preferred the older and more experienced players – despite, or perhaps because of, his preference for more recent drama – while Davenant looked for fresher recruits.

Killigrew's choices included Michael Mohun and Charles Hart. They were two of the leading players, and the diarist Samuel Pepys reported that Mohun himself was considered 'the best actor in the world'. He ranged widely from old to new and from comedy to tragedy; he played Face in *The Alchemist* and Truewit in *Epicoene*, and performed as Iago and Hannibal. Among his closest colleagues in the King's Company were William Wintershall and Theophilus Bird. Bird had been one of Beeston's Boys, but on joining the King's Men he adopted a series of masculine roles including dukes, lords and second lords. The aristocracy, at least on stage, had returned. Wintershall was also able to run the gamut of familiar roles, and was described as a 'most judicious actor, and the best instructor of others'. The older players seem to have felt it their duty to train up the young after the recent period of silence.

John Lacy, also of the King's Company, was praised by Pepys for his role as an Irish footman 'beyond imagination', and 'so well performed that it would set off anything'. The celebrated diarist also described Edward Kynaston as 'the loveliest lady I saw in my life', which may give some indication of Kynaston's most significant roles. But he could move from woman to man and act accordingly, and he was well known for his Henry IV.

Davenant was more enterprising in taking on younger actors who had not been instructed in the old tradition. He picked, among others, Thomas Betterton and James Nokes. Many of them had once been part of the children's companies, where they were expected to dress and act in female parts. Nokes, who was known as 'Nursery Nokes' for his eloquence in that hard profession, remained a comic with Davenant's company even after it had merged with its rival. According to the *Oxford English Dictionary*, the word 'nokes' became a synonym for fool, dullard or ninny. He was able to provoke 'general laughter' by his 'silent eloquence'; he simply had to look, expressively, and not speak. John Dryden wrote a play specifically for his strengths, *Sir Martin Mar-all* (1667), which Charles II attended on eight separate occasions. The actor-manager (and later Poet Laureate) Colley Cibber describes Nokes as 'an Actor of a quite different Genius from any I have ever read, heard of, or seen, since or before his Time', marked by 'a plain and palpable Simplicity of Nature, which was so utterly his own, that he was often as unaccountably diverting in his common Speech, as on the Stage'. He was perhaps the greatest comedian of his age.

But the ruling assumption of the children's companies, that they would dress and act in female parts, was about to change. The arrival of the king heralded a new dispensation that for the first time allowed women on to the stage. In the autumn of 1660 the first female performers acted before an audience, and two years later a royal edict decreed that all female parts should be taken by women rather than boys. It was, in a literal sense, a revolution.

Davenant, under the aegis of the Duke of York's Company, introduced Mrs Jennings, Mrs Norris, Mrs Davenport, Mrs Saunderson, Mrs Davies, Mrs Long, Mrs Gibbs and Mrs Holden; he had the confidence and support of the king in building the new theatre in Lincoln Inn's Field, where a large forestage made it available for Restoration spectaculars. He also introduced, following the example of the French, moveable and changing scenery, which greatly assisted the flow of the narrative. Killigrew in turn constructed a new theatre, the Theatre Royal, between Bridge Street and Drury Lane. He also added seven female actors in Mrs Corey, Mrs Eastland, Mrs Hughes, Mrs Knepp, Mrs Marshall, Mrs Uphill and Mrs Weaver.

The previous lives of these actresses remain obscure. Their livelihoods were not considered either proper or suitable. The women who performed in the masques of the era were prominent ladies of the Court, and stepped out beyond even the shadow of scandal. But it was quite another matter with Mrs Davies, Mrs Corey and all the other professional actresses, who were considered in the popular imagination as little better than women of the street. They did in fact spring from different occupations, as can be discerned from later examples. Some were once dancers, or coffee-house waitresses, flower girls or street singers. Some came from a theatrical family or had married actors and needed extra income, while others had worked in milliners' shops. It is reported that some of the female players lodged with Killigrew or Davenant, and no doubt they were coached and rehearsed by the managers as well as the other actors. The 'nurseries' were still in operation, and provided a rudimentary training. Yet it is certain that some of these women had more than a spark of ambition or talent, as well as an irresistible determination to play before an audience.

The first English actress on the stage was Margaret Hughes, of Killigrew's company, who took the part of Desdemona on 8 December 1660. It is worth noting the date if only to emphasize the immediate and ineluctable flow of actresses who at one point almost took over the stage. They even played 'breeches parts' and were substituted for the men. By the middle of 1661, in fact, women had become an indispensable aspect of the London theatrical scene. Two of the earliest were Elizabeth Barry and Anne Bracegirdle. They arrived at an appropriate time, as the vogue for heroic drama was gradually superseded by what was known as 'pathetic' or 'affective' drama; by the 1680s a fashion for 'she-tragedies' began to cultivate the public taste for the innocent suffering of the virtuous woman.

But the sexual element could not be ignored, especially when a number of female performers led less than virtuous lives. Tragedies increasingly began to include rape in the plot, while Restoration comedy was ribald and salacious in a different manner. The air of arousal or prurience was excited by the general belief (especially among the male members of the audience) that female players were little more than whores or courtesans in their private lives. In the late 1670s and 1680s there also arrived a vogue for plays concerning calculating or rapacious mistresses, the most eminent of these actors being Elizabeth Currer. Her parts were in the comic vein, which allowed her a certain latitude in her boldness and deceit. Part of the fashion for these players was the common knowledge that the Court and its attendants kept mistresses and courtesans one after another in an endless cycle of concupiscence.

Charlotte Butler was one among the players of dubious reputation, in life as well as on the stage, and a contemporary satire notes: 'But if she's hungry, faith I must be blunt/ Sh'l for a Dish of Cutlets shew her Cunt.' There were many verses, epigrams, profiles and pamphlets of a similar kind, and it often took a great deal of courage or wit to confront and conquer a salacious or sarcastic audience.

One of those who did so was Nell Gwyn, the quondam orange-seller who became the mistress of the king. It was said that she began life as a serving maid in a brothel before being promoted to fruit-seller in the theatre, where her familiar cry was 'Oranges! Will you have any oranges!' She was well known to the actors, and her good looks were combined with a merry laugh so vivacious that her face puckered up and her eyes became almost invisible; she had a sharp wit, too, and as a result of her employment as orange-girl was quick at banter with her male customers.

Thomas Killigrew, the manager of the King's Men, saw her potential, and before long she was given the female lead, Lady Wealthy, in a low comedy. Her vitality and vivacity swept her triumphantly on to the stage, and she was soon given the major roles in comedies high or low. She was reputed to be lewd, but she was always cheerful; Pepys visited one of the 'tiring-rooms' for dressing, to which men were still admitted, and found her in company with another actress: 'But Lord! To see how they were both painted would make a man mad, and did make me loathe them; and what base company of men comes among them, and how lewdly they talk!'

Gwyn may have been debauched, but she was also the epitome of gaiety. Such a combination of good humour and good living turned her into the most renowned of Restoration actresses. She invented with Charles Hart a comic turn known as 'the gay couple'; they are fundamentally drawn to each other, but they hold back in the belief that marriage will confine them. They must be assured of a generous love, when 'we will be both as mad as we please'. They are witty and lively, and engage in playful repartee. Gwyn and Hart carried on their joint career in Dryden's *Secret Love* (1667), and for the next two seasons they were rarely off the stage. In this part Gwyn was supreme, despite the fact that she was illiterate and had to learn the lines by rote. She had once been Hart's mistress, although in later years they quarrelled and parted. Her most famous lover was the king himself. She did not live long enough fully to enjoy her good fortune, however, and died of apoplexy at the age of thirty-eight, or thirty-nine, or perhaps even forty. Dates were sensitive material in the theatre.

Hart was one of the best and most versatile of the King's Men, and excelled in dignified tragic roles as well as lively comedy. A contemporary stage prompter, John Downes, wrote in his historical review of the stage, *Roscius Anglicanus* (1708) that 'if he Acted in any one of these but once in a Fortnight, the House was fill'd as at a New Play, especially [in the part of] Alexander, he Acting that with such Grandeur and Agreeable Majesty, That one of the Court was pleas'd to Honour him with this Commendation; That Hart might Teach any King on Earth how to Comport himself.'

The Duke's Men introduced their own gay couple, but their equivalent of Gwyn, Moll Davis, had begun an affair with the king in 1667 and became unavailable for public spectacle. Gwyn followed suit a year later. In Gwyn's absence the King's Men settled on Elizabeth Boutell, who was no match for her predecessor; she had a 'Childish Look' and her voice was 'weak, tho' very mellow'. She managed a few more comic parts, including Margery Pinchwife in William Wycherley's *The Country Wife* (1675), but then found her proper medium in pathos and tragedy, where she was paired with Rebecca Marshall in heightened conflict between two women of opposing temperaments: purity against corruption, shy modesty against strong-minded bravura. Boutell was the sweeter of the two.

The Duke's Men in turn took up Jane Long for Davis's part in their comedies, but she did not display the right measure of vigour and vivacity. The company had more success with its tragedy queens, Mary Betterton and Mary Lee. The former, the wife of Thomas Betterton, was, according to Downes, 'so great a

Mistress of Nature' that she could 'throw out those quick and care-less Strokes of Terror from the Disorder of a guilty Mind . . . with a Facility in her Manner that render'd them at once tremendous and delightful'.

Lee began as a sweet-faced juvenile, but her natural capacity was for violent and martial parts. She fought a duel, killed a king and killed herself on at least two separate occasions. In a parody of her more violent tirades, the writer Thomas D'Urfey gives her a stirring oration: 'Blood is my province; therefore with you all I am resolv'd to fight.' Her father laments over her corpse, in one sanguineous episode, that she was 'one of us; For tho she were a Virgin, she was martial'. It is an indication, perhaps, of the blood and thunder that were characteristic of Restoration heroics and Restoration tragedy. The sudden reversals of political life, and the bloodshed that accompanied them, seemed to have fostered a taste for theatrical sensationalism among the London public.

The most popular actress of her generation, Elizabeth Barry, was taken up and trained by the Earl of Rochester with the guar-antee that she would be the finest actress of her generation. So, at least, runs the popular legend. He kept his promise, and by 1676 she was at the height of her profession as comedienne and tragic heroine who played threatened virgins, witty wives, adulterous wives, shameless courtesans and all the variations between. She also became known as 'the queen of tragedy'. Her private life was not stainless, and the audience once erupted into laughter on her line as Cordelia in Nahum Tate's version of *King Lear*: 'Arm'd in my Virgin Innocence, I'll fly.' But her acting superseded all scandal, and a contemporary critic, John Dennis, noted that 'no Stage in *Europe* can boast of any thing that comes near to her Performance . . . That incomparable Actress changing like Nature which she represents, from Passion to Passion, from Extream to Extream, with piercing Force, and with easie Grace, changes the Hearts of all who see her with irresistible Pleas.' As did many players, she also changed companies when it became convenient to do so, beginning with the Duke of York's, moving to the United Company and finishing with Betterton's new troupe. She played at least 142 parts, and even revived the fashion for the 'gay couple'. She was pathetic, erotic, comic, tragic, majestic and malicious, and sometimes all at once.

Seven

The changing audience

This affords the opportunity to consider more fully the great male favourite of the Restoration, Thomas Betterton, who played opposite Elizabeth Barry as rival as well as colleague. Betterton was from the beginning a sensation. He was in the phrase of the time a 'juvenile Roscius', and was, according to Samuel Pepys, 'the best actor in the world'. The key characteristics of his acting were restraint, simplicity and gravity. There was no violence of movement, or extravagance of gesture (he rarely lifted his arms); his voice was low and serious, dexterous rather than melodious; he restrained his passions and forced the audience to focus on the slightest alteration of his gestures or speech. Facial expression was also a key part of his acting repertoire. The focus of a Betterton performance was on the clear presentation of the play's words and action.

Betterton played Hamlet at the age of twenty-five, and appeared as Macbeth and Othello at the Haymarket at the age of seventy-two. It has been assumed that he adopted a ponderous or mannered style, and it is possible that he used a musical chant for certain passages. He possessed a voice 'more manly than sweet'; he was of middle height and inclined to corpulence, which increased as he grew older, but, according to Colley Cibber, 'from the harmony of the whole' there emerged 'a commanding mien of majesty'. Betterton knew well enough that there were many ways of provoking the spectators to cheers and loud applause, 'but to keep them hushed and quiet, was an applause which only truth and merits could arrive at'. It was the stillness of total observation at which he aimed.

One of Betterton's most eminent parts was that of Hamlet, which, according to John Downes, gained him 'esteem and reputation superlative to all other plays'. When he saw his father's ghost, for example, it was noted that he 'turned as pale as a neck-cloth' – a physiognomic feat in itself – 'when every article of his body seemed to be affected with a tremor inexpressible' and his stuttering response reduced the audience to silence until it was broken 'in a thunder of universal applause'. As the *Tatler* put it, 'the perfection of an actor is only to become what he is doing.' As a result, Pepys said that he dominated, rather than leavened, a production; the diarist also noted two slight defects. Betterton sometimes mislaid his lines and sometimes 'corpsed' or laughed at a mistake by actor or stagehand. But the English player, Anthony Aston, remarked on a more interesting characteristic when he noted that 'Betterton from the Time he was dress'd to the End of the Play, kept his Mind in the same Temperament and Adaptness.' Betterton aimed to 'transform' himself into the person he represented and to lose all consciousness of being on stage, so he remained 'in character' throughout, an unusual attribute at that time. It was also a remarkable feat in a period when the spectators could be restless and querulous. *Blackwood's Magazine* observed in 1861 that 'the magnetic influence of tone and expression seemed to mesmerise an audience.' It was, and is, a gift that few actors possess. That is why Betterton was considered to be inimitable.

For his last performance, as Melantius in Beaumont and Fletcher's *The Maid's Tragedy*, it is reported that 'the curiosity of the public was so much excited that many spectators got into the playhouse by nine o'clock in the morning and carried with them the provisions for the day.' The actor, Barton Booth, remarked that 'divinity hung round that man'. This was the age of the actor. There was no director, no producer, only perhaps a prompter. Betterton was, in one sense, the last of his kind; his formal delivery and mannered action were going out of fashion with the arrival of David Garrick and his imitators.

With the passing of the Betterton school, the apostolic line of Shakespearean actors also came to an end. The vacuum was filled by a plethora of acting manuals, which described the gestures and tones of voice an actor ought to employ in order to convey particular emotions and to create certain effects. These handbooks became the bibles of aspiring players, and were blamed for promoting the new 'artificial' style that prevailed on the English stage from the 1720s. By 1735 the dramatist Aaron Hill was complaining that 'players are shockingly unnatural' and that audiences 'receive little benefit from being told that every passion has its peculiar and appropriate look, and every look its particular gesture'. Many actors of the new school would halt the action of the play, advance to the front of the stage and declaim their lines to the audience in either a sing-song or bombastic voice, all the while accompanying them with a series of outlandish set gestures. Their bodies were as mechanical as their speech; they 'strutted' and 'ranted'. They had little interest in creating, or conveying, 'individualized' characters, instead acting 'types' and regarding the play primarily as an opportunity to demonstrate their acting prowess. They had little interest in the action, the plot, the nuances of the lines, or in interacting with other performers on stage. The focus was on their showy 'stage business'. But many of the players, according to one chronicler, ascribed 'the coarseness of their own performances to the corrupted taste of the age'.

It is salutary to consider in this context the often forgotten role of the audience. The drama is not a mass but a liturgy, and its magic is incomplete without a congregation. There was in the Restoration a new kind of audience that had been through a time of trial and had no wish to see misery enacted; hence the swift demise of Dryden's tragedies and the popularity of Nahum Tate's softened version of *King Lear*. Bawdiness, licence and optimism became the master-themes. And, with the return of the merry monarch and his laughter-loving lords after so long and dreary an absence, the habits of the aristocracy became associated with the humours of the coffee house and, more importantly, the tavern.

In this revived drama, the audience was above all a circle of friends. The cast, more often than not, would be dressed quite as opulently as the members of the audience. The lead actor would have been a master of ceremonies as much as a participant. We may imagine a swivelling motion in the gait as he swung out, at certain periods, from fellow actors to address the audience. Even when he spoke to the audience he was not entering their reality, but summoning them into his. That restive audience would have been part of his world. It was there by invitation, indeed by command.

Colley Cibber first appeared on stage in 1690, at the age of nineteen; he was not an immediate sensation but, like other players, he was skilful enough to take advantage of his weaknesses, which included a thin, piping voice, a fallible memory and a wholly unheroic figure. He was also an accomplished mimic and learned the key to general laughter. He had his wig brought to him on the stage in a sedan chair. He had a habit of amusing the audience by bending over to the prompter and asking 'What happens next?', even when he himself had written the play. His acting was a considerable success, largely because he claimed as his own the fashionable and pernickety figures whose names gave away their appeal. He was Sir Novelty Fashion in 1696, Lord Foppington in 1697, Sir Courtly Nice in 1703 and Sir Fopling Flutter in 1706. He played these parts to the life, since he was known to be 'something of a coxcomb'.

In tragedy Cibber was not so successful. He played Othello to general laughter, and Charles Macklin, who played his Iago,

Eight

Fickle fashion

The combined costs of the two new troupes, the Duke's Company and the King's Company, were prohibitive; bad management compounded the problem, as well as an unwelcome return of the plague in the summer of 1665 that closed the doors of the theatres for eighteen months. This was a severe blow to the finances of both companies and a calamity to players and management alike. The players were no longer, in Pepys's words, 'proud and rich'. Disaster followed catastrophe when in January 1672 the Theatre Royal burned to the ground. The King's Company migrated to the playhouse in Lincoln's Inn Fields, the theatre that had been vacated eleven weeks earlier by the Duke of York's Company, and at once began an appeal for funds to establish a new Theatre Royal to be erected on the same site as its predecessor. This may have been the impetus, beside the burden of double payments, for the two managers, Thomas Killigrew and William Davenant, to combine in a union of their patents. Thus in 1682 the Duke of York's Company and the King's Company became the United Company.

The theatre was now the vogue, especially for the more affluent. There were companies in Bath, Plymouth, Exeter, Norwich, Bristol and assorted country towns. Prices had risen, so that pennies had become shillings. The temperature had also climbed higher; theatrical riots were now almost commonplace, with the audience storming the stage or wrecking the interior for real or imagined grievances. The smallest tumult might arise from the recent fashion of throwing rotten fruit at the players. Prizefighters and troops were enlisted to assist opposing factions.

Davenant sold his shares to a lawyer, Christopher Rich, who promptly took over the management of the United Company. All was not well. Betterton became alienated from the new management and, gathering around him as many actors as he could, established his own company, which, naturally enough, became known as Betterton's Company. He began well, with a production of William Congreve's *Love for Love* in 1695, but the new venture was not an overwhelming success. The theatrical revival of the late 1690s, however, prompted the arrival of three female players, Susannah Mountfort, Anne Bracegirdle and Elizabeth Barry, all of whom were welcomed for their inventiveness and vivacity. Their dominance in the United Company, and then in Betterton's Company, emphasizes the unprecedented extent to which female actors had taken over the stage.

Mountfort was well known for her aptitude at playing the role of a grotesque, low-born as well as ugly. In her more conventional roles she became a lady of wit and delicacy, but she could change her manner and appearance completely. In Thomas D'Urfey's *The Bath* she became 'almost another Animal', ugly, dowdy, dirty, with a 'broad laughing Voice, a poking Head, round Shoulders, an unconceiving Eye'. This technique of malapert transformation was followed by other female players who wished to do no more than entertain.

Bracegirdle took a different road to fame, portraying virtuous heroines and serious-minded heiresses, yet seriousness on the Restoration stage did not preclude sensuality. Cibber noted that

her Youth and lively Aspect threw out such a Glow of Health and Chearfulness, that on the Stage few Spectators that were not past it could behold her without Desire. It was even a Fashion among the Gay and Young to have a Taste or Tendre for Mrs Bracegirdle . . . In all the chief Parts she acted, the Desirable was so predominant, that no Judge could be cold enough to consider from what other particular Excellence she became delightful.

Actresses were expected to have sex appeal, and to charm audiences through their movements, gestures and expressions; this obliged them, or afforded them the licence, to be more 'natural' than men. It was noted as remarkable, however, that in *Love for Love* Bracegirdle was not 'guilty of the affectation to insert witticisms' of her own devising. That may therefore have been one of her familiar ploys to engage the attention and affection of the spectators.

Bracegirdle assumed the chaste part, in comedy or melodrama. She and Barry excelled, also, in pathetic tragedy, and such was their distinction that they played similar parts for twenty years. It must be one of the longest double acts in dramatic history. Barry herself became celebrated in both comic and tragic roles, although it is clear that she veered towards the latter. Betterton himself said that she could bring 'success to plays that would disgust the most patient reader', while John Dennis described her as 'that incomparable Actress changing like Nature which she represents, from Passion to Passion, from Extream to Extream, with piercing Force and with easy Grace'.

Anne or 'Nance' Oldfield was living with her mother at the Mitre Tavern in St James's, where she was 'discovered' by the playwright George Farquhar, reading a play out loud behind the bar. Her distinct voice and turn of phrase convinced him on the spot that 'the Girl was cut out for the Stage.' Like other females of the period, she made the leap from barmaid to actress. After a polite hesitation before springing on to the stage, she admitted that 'I longed to be at it, and only wanted a little decent entreaties [*sic*]'. It was not, however, an easy ride. Oldfield was taken into the rebuilt Theatre Royal at Drury Lane, where she remained mute and inglorious for approximately a year before taking on a leading role in a trifle, John Vanbrugh's prose version of John Fletcher's *The Pilgrim*, where she enjoyed her first public success. Slowly she ascended the ladder of theatrical life; she became adept at prologues and epilogues (the staple of the actor's public repertoire), but she also played leading roles in several plays by Richard Steele, Cibber and others. Her most famous creation, perhaps, was that of Lady Betty Modish in Cibber's *The Careless Husband* (1704). Her success brought her enmity with Bracegirdle, who walked out of the theatre in disgust when Oldfield was given the first 'benefit night'; this was the night when the proceeds were given to the actor in question, and it seems she received £500 for her efforts. Oldfield carried on working, despite ill health and eventual cancer, and died in 1730 before being carried off for burial to Westminster Abbey.

Fashions changed, however, and in 1728 John Gay's *The Beggar's Opera* captured public attention as a conflation of musical, melodrama and burlesque. The songs were splendid, and the dialogue crisp. But the object of all eyes was the actor who played the central role of Polly Peachum, Lavinia Fenton, whose carriage on the way home was surrounded by admirers. There always seems to have been one female player who was the cynosure of London, and Fenton fitted the bill admirably. Her portrait was taken and sold all over the city; books about her life were written; ballads and songs were composed in celebration of her; and her image was engraved on playing cards, teapots and fans so that, according to Gay himself, 'her popularity outstripped that of the play itself.' The ideas of 'star' and 'celebrity' did not emerge until the nineteenth century, but these terms accurately describe her contemporary status. Fenton's natural and untrained voice, together with the evident sincerity of her acting, led to her being described as wholly English for her lack of formal constraint and her absence of artifice. Of course, she retired and became a duchess, and subsequent portraits signified her new social status as well as her femininity.

Catherine or 'Kitty' Clive also specialized in burlesque and comic opera. She was discovered, according to report, singing as she washed steps near the theatrical venue of the Old Bell Tavern in Fleet Street. Stranger debuts have been recorded. She was recommended to Cibber, who, sensing her potential, hired her for the Theatre Royal in Drury Lane, of which he had become manager. She played more than two hundred parts in that theatre, but specialized at the rougher end in viragoes, hoydens, whores, maidservants, dowdies, faded beauties and less than innocent country girls. She was not altogether at ease with the high life. 'I choose my company as I do my fruit,' she said, 'therefore I am not for damaged quality.' In common with other players who are obliged to understate their talents, she was particularly open to sympathetic company. Samuel Johnson remarked that 'Clive, sir, is a good thing to sit by, she always understands what you say.' But her temper was as sharp as her wit, and she engaged in several theatrical feuds. Horace Walpole, one of her greatest friends, noted that 'applause had turned Garrick's head, and yet he was never content even with that prodigality: he hated Mrs Clive till she quitted the stage, and then cried her up to the skies.'

Clive's feud with her contemporary Margaret or 'Peg' Woffington was well known to anyone who picked up a newssheet, and a chronicler noted that 'No two women of high rank ever hated one another more unreservedly than these great dames of the theatre.' The rivalry or enmity between players was a familiar part of the theatrical scenery. Wigs were torn off and costumes filched or cosmetics stolen; there were also a hundred little tricks to distract the audience's attention from a rival. Claques in the audience were inclined to support one actress rather than another, which might result in hisses, boos and shouts as well as the occasional rotten apple or overripe orange. There were fainting fits, screaming fits, hysterical fits and fits for their own sake.

Woffington, however, was for a while the best known of the eighteenth-century actresses. She was most famous for playing elegant society women in comedies, since her voice was not regarded as dignified enough for tragedy. It was said that she had 'great sensibility' and that 'she has, more than most players, given a loose to nature in expressing it'. In other words, she let it rip.

Some aspects of Woffington's performances, however, may have diminished the effect of 'naturalism'. She sometimes interacted with the audience by gazing at individual spectators and directing certain lines their way. The introduction of her personality and private life on to the stage may also have detracted from the effectiveness of her performances by revealing her acting as an 'act'. Similarly, she was notorious for her louche lifestyle, and sometimes exploited her reputation on stage; she took on raffish roles, and played them with audacity. She was a celebrity actor, so people wanted to see Peggy, and to see Peggy act, as much as they went to see her in a particular part.

The 'breeches part' was one of the most favoured among those who wished to display their shape or expedite their movements, and Woffington was no exception. In her early days it was noted that 'she never displayed herself to more advantage than in characters where she assumed the other sex.' Her male costume had one fortunate result, when she was elected president of the nominally all-male Beef-Steak Club. When she played Sir Harry Wildair in Charles Johnson's *The Country Lasses* (1715), no male actor later wanted the part in rivalry with her. She was the subject of various anecdotes, ribald or otherwise. After one breeches part she declared that 'in my conscience, I believe half the men in the House take me for one of their own sex!', to which an acerbic female colleague replied, 'it may be so, but in my conscience, the other half can convince them to the contrary.' Woffington gave as well as took. When Catherine Clive declined to have tea with her, she explained that she had a reputation to lose. 'Madam,' Woffington replied, 'so should I too if I had your face.' Like many illustrious players, she was known by the definite article, 'the Woffington', as if she were a natural phenomenon.

Frances Abington began at a young age at the King's Theatre in Haymarket, after previously earning a living as a tavern reciter, a prostitute, a flower-seller and a milliner's servant – some of the more plausible introductions to the theatrical world. Under the less than benign guidance of Theophilus Cibber, the actor-manager and son of Colley, she was whisked away from the Haymarket and settled in Dublin, a city that, with its thriving theatrical culture, was a convenient destination for actors temporarily out of work. She enjoyed success there in a number of parts, but became the taste or toast of the town in a play of 1759 entitled *High Life below Stairs*, by James Townley. In that part she wore a distinctive cap, and within days, according to one theatrical chronicler, 'there was not a milliner's window, great or small, but was ornamented with it, and in large letters ABINGTON appeared to attract the passers-by.'

That was the value of the popular female actor, who could influence and change fashion with the smallest item. Abington was not universally admired. Garrick remarked that 'she is below the thought of any honest man or woman; she is as silly as she is false and treacherous,' and described her 'cold counteracting discourse'. But she also had admirers, such as the biographer James Boaden, who pronounced upon her 'very peculiar and hitherto unapproached talent' and her deportment 'beyond even the conception of modern fine ladies'. The general observation was not favourable, however. One contemporary wrote that 'she had been on the stage for thirty years; she was one-and-twenty when she came, and one-and-twenty when she went.' She seemed to have aged gracefully, in other words, but perhaps not without the aid of artifice. It was noticed that none of the theatrical profession attended her funeral.

Sophia Baddeley was more admired for her looks and her voice than her acting. When an actress in *King Lear* was indisposed, Baddeley took her place at Drury Lane. She was unacquainted with the play, even in its bowdlerized version, and when Edgar appeared as mad Poor Tom she uttered a scream and fell down unconscious on the stage. It was not the best introduction to her public. She migrated from lover to lover before dying at the age of forty-one.

Dorothea Jordan, or Mrs Jordan as she was more generally known, had a more fortunate fate and drew crowded houses throughout her career. Leigh Hunt described her as 'the first actress of the day', and according to the *Morning Herald*, 'her face, if not beautiful, is said by some to be pretty . . . her voice, if not peculiarly sweet, is not harsh; if not strong, is clear.' That might pass muster as a favourable verdict, but it is contradicted by more earnest admirers who celebrated her 'spirit of fun' and her 'most melodious voice', which, according to a contemporary actress, 'is harmony itself . . . she has the most *distinct* delivery of any actor or actress I ever heard.' Jordan was strikingly 'animated', especially when she performed comic roles; like other comic actresses, she was believed to lack the 'dignity' for tragic parts, but that did not prohibit her from playing, among others, Ophelia, Imogen and Emilia.

Jordan was believed to be entirely unschooled, a not uncommon fate among female players, who lacked the long inheritance or tradition of male acting. 'Mrs Jordan's excellences', wrote Hazlitt,

were all natural to her. It was not as an actress, but as herself, that she charmed everyone. Nature had formed in her most prodigal humour; and when nature is in the humour to make a woman all that is delightful, she does it most effectually . . . Mrs Jordan, the child of nature, whose voice was a cordial to the heart, because it came from it, rich, full, like the luscious juice of the rich grape.

The *Morning Post* agreed with this favourable assessment. 'Nature', its critic wrote, 'has endowed her with talents sufficient to combat and excel her competitors in the same walk. Her person and manner are adapted for representing the peculiarities of youthful innocence and frivolity; and her tones of voice are audible and melodious.' Jordan played her parts as though they were 'real' people, in 'real' situations, however we define that term in its eighteenth-century sense; she gave her audience the illusion that this was the manner in which the characters would behave in the world. Paradoxically, she often achieved these effects by 'playing' herself.

As a comic player Jordan aroused more laughter than other actors, and Charles Lamb noted that 'her laughter is the happiest and most natural on the stage'; it was 'the laughter of the feelings' that complemented her 'bewitching voice'. As soon as she stepped on to the stage her spirits seemed to rise, and she was able to elevate her audience with her gaiety.

A contemporary noted that 'when the whole stream comes out, nothing can be fuller of heart and soul.' Jordan, when introduced to the actor-manager of the York circuit, Tate Wilkinson, was asked whether she specialized in tragedy, comedy or opera. To this she replied, 'All.' Although astonished, he took her at her word and hired her as one of his travelling company. It was a hard baptism, made harder by a pregnancy and an increasing dislike of the conditions of her employment. Jordan found refuge on the stage of the Theatre Royal, Drury Lane, in an adaptation of David Garrick's *The Country Girl* in 1785 and, with this introduction to London, she found success. She became an integral part of the Drury Lane season, where she excelled in a variety of roles, including Rosalind.

But she was perhaps not in life the 'fair princess' of Orlando's imagination. She fought successfully for a large pay rise and was not above using the newspapers to advance her cause. A genius in acting is often a genius in publicity.

It was perhaps inevitable that Jordan should become bored with conventional amours, and instead she took up with the Duke of Clarence. It would have been rude not to. Her audiences were not indifferent to her dalliance; the ladies hissed through their fans, and their manservants were less polite. But she pulled through with the determination of a seasoned actor. Her private life was in any case dramatic; there were more babies and more miscarriages. It is in some ways an old and familiar story, when a pretty and accomplished young lady plunges into the deep end of London. Jordan no longer had innocent youth as an excuse, however; she was thirty by the time she met the duke, embarking on a relationship that endured twenty years.

But that made no difference. She wrote to the duke in 1811 that 'the Theatre last night was greatly crowded and from the applause and admiration one would think that I had but started on the profession.' She had one of the great skills of the gifted actor in transforming herself on the stage. It is now something of a cliché to note that an actor, even of the highest quality, can be morose, taciturn or oddly ordinary and thus a great disappointment to his or her admirers, but once the paint is on the face and the cue is called, the actor becomes a different being. Strength, suppleness, memory and vigour all return. That, at least, is the theory.

The success of *The Beggar's Opera* had already stimulated less conventional forms of theatre, including other ballad-operas and musical revues. It was evidence that the London public rejected bawdy dramas but was still willing and even eager to be entertained. Oliver Goldsmith and Richard Brinsley Sheridan can perhaps be associated with some new-minted actors. The great successor of Betterton was Barton Booth. Betterton saw his potential and took him from the theatre in Lincoln's Inn Fields to the new Queen's Theatre in Haymarket. There Booth proved his worth, in part by imitating the manner of Betterton himself. It is possible that Booth accentuated some of Betterton's formal mannerisms, but he had the advantage of a distinct and melodious voice so that the merest whisper could be heard from the back of the theatre. Unlike some of his contemporaries, he trained himself 'never to speak out of tune, or a proper key'. There was no more chanting, and no more bellowing, even though there were still actors who were unable 'to distinguish noise from passion, and ranting from sensibility'. His face acted with him, so that his voice and countenance presented a unity. It was said that the blind could see him in his voice, and the deaf hear him in his countenance. He struck picturesque attitudes from the statuary and painting he admired, and preserved them in stillness, at which the more sensitive members of the audience might applaud. This was in fact a perhaps unconscious inheritance from the medieval miracle plays. It might be worth noting, in passing, that players on stage characteristically wore white gloves.

By dint of hard work, constant playing and managerial skill, Booth took the leading role at Drury Lane before entering its management. He remained with that theatre for the last twenty years of his life. He was Cato, King Lear, Timon of Athens and many other of the more disciplined and serious roles that suited the temper of the time. One critic noted that he had the gift 'of discovering the passions where they lay hid in some celebrated parts by the injudicious Practice of other Actors'. Criticism sometimes fell his way, however, and he received a message from one of the boxes when he was playing Othello, to enquire 'whether he was playing to please himself or his audience'. After Booth's death in 1733, the tradition of Betterton finally faded from public notice.

Following the deaths of Betterton and Booth, a player made his way forward who was, according to one notice, 'almost a great

actor'. James Quin was reputed to have substantial comic potential. He was judged to have followed some of Booth's precepts
while adding a sprinkling of Falstaff to them. He began as a novice,
or 'faggot', on the English stage, but advanced soon enough. In
tragedy he excelled in secondary parts, since Lear and Hamlet
were unfortunately beyond his range. That was not an uncommon
disadvantage among early eighteenth-century actors. A critic in
the *Gentleman's Magazine* noted that Quin was always perfect in
his lines, but the lines were not enough. It was said of him that
'the calm, divine stoic Cato, the jealous furious lover Othello,
the debauched drunken Sir John Brute speak in the same tone; a
hoarse monotony goes through them all.' Tate Wilkinson observed
of Quin's tragic manner that it was 'strutting, pompous, languid,
tiresome and wanted spirit'.

Quin was credited with a 'natural dignity', but dignity can
go too far; he all but ignored the other players, and remained
inattentive until his own cue came on. This was, and is still, one
of the vices of certain actors. Yet Quin had virtues of his own. He
radiated dignity and impersonated majesty, often with a sublime
indifference which amplified the effects; he was also possessed
of an elegant voice, comparing favourably with the ranting and
wailing which other players deemed appropriate to their high
heroics. Quin was not helped in later life by his bulk and double
chin. The Duchess of Queensbury once asked him, perhaps indeli-
cately, 'Pray, Mr Quin, do you ever make love?', to which he
replied, 'No, Madam, I always buy it ready made.'

Tate Wilkinson also had a more general complaint, about the
theatrical costumes of the period, 'which had done many years'
service at Lincoln Inn's Fields, having graced the original wearers'.
The ladies were in large hoops, and wore heavy velvet petticoats
that were burdensome on the stage. Woffington herself had only
one 'tragedy suit'. Wilkinson also complained about the beaux,
the nobles and the ladies who considered it a point of honour to

congregate on the stage so that a renowned actor spent 'several minutes before he could pass through the numbers that wedged and hemmed him in, he was so cruelly encompassed around'. The stage, not for the first or last time, copied the condition of London.

One player succeeded another, but in the absence of superlative personalities among performers, only anecdotes and vignettes survive. A few became more eminent. Charles Macklin earned his fame as Shylock, a part he studied by lingering in the Jewish quarter of London; he turned the character into a complex human being who was by turns serious, witty, shrewd and wicked. His performance inspired intense and varied emotions in his audience. His natural or at least naturalistic performance, on its first presentation at the Theatre Royal, Drury Lane, was so powerful that George II could not sleep afterwards. Such was the acclaim that the part of Shylock was never again played as a buffoon or caricature. Macklin did not adopt the 'ranting' or 'sing-song' style then in vogue, but continued with his 'natural manner'. He became famous for 'breaking the tones of utterance'; he sometimes mouthed 'half-form'd sounds' mid-phrase; he always modulated his voice and altered his expression, according to his lines. In consequence, the lines came alive and the shifting moods of his character were conveyed. 'Imagine', one contemporary noted, 'a rather stout man with a coarse yellow face and a nose generously fashioned in all three dimensions, a long double chin, and a mouth so carved by nature that the knife appears to have slit him right up to the ears.'

Macklin also worked as a dramatic teacher who told his students to unlearn everything they had been told. He instructed them to research their parts thoroughly, to pay attention to details of costume and follow the specifics of a scene or a line. He taught three types of pause – the moderate, the longer and the grand – and the occasions on which each should be used. This suggests the meticulousness and variety of his own acting. Macklin was also revolutionary in his insistence on regular rehearsing. Under the orthodox system, famous actors knew countless parts by heart, and rarely – or barely – rehearsed with the other actors before a production. After all, *they* were the stars of the show, with their 'points' and 'aria'-like set pieces; the production was their vehicle. Yet Macklin made all the performers rehearse together regularly; the main characters interacted with the lesser parts and as a result the production appeared integrated, the play coherent. He detested what he called 'the hoity-toity tone of the tragedy of that day'. One aspiring student tried to recite in front of him, to be met with 'Bow, wow, wow, wow.'

Charlotte Charke, the daughter of Colley Cibber, earned her living as a strolling actress, fiddle-player, gardener, grocer, alehouse-keeper, *valet de chambre*, sausage-seller and puppet show-woman. She spent much of her time in male dress, until she was arrested as a 'rogue and vagabond'. But she slipped her bonds and finished her days in the purlieus of Clerkenwell with a monkey, a cat, a dog and a magpie for company. An essayist described her as a person of considerable talent, but entirely under the government of the most irrational impulses. She died on 6 April 1760, a little early for Charles Dickens, who loved the company of players and considered this the most intelligent of professions. He could have immortalized her.

Hannah Pritchard, in contrast, concentrated on her acting. Samuel Johnson said that 'her playing was quite mechanical. It is wonderful how little mind she had. She no more thought of the play out of which her part was taken than a shoemaker thinks of the skin out of which the piece of leather is cut.' This is an example of his words running away with his wit, since he added that on stage she 'seemed to be inspired by gentility and understanding'. This is one of the deeper mysteries of acting. But Pritchard had the merit of playing opposite Garrick on several occasions, so that she became almost his 'partner' until the end of her career; perhaps as a result of her association with him, she acquired fame and popular success even though she did not cultivate them as much as her contemporaries. It is plausible that she was overshadowed by Garrick himself, since they appeared so often together on the same stage. Some due recognition of her merit is to be found in the fact that a monument to her memory was placed in Poet's Corner, Westminster Abbey, near her more illustrious colleague.

Pritchard is an example of the gradual disassociation of the female actor from the prostitute. In the seventeenth century the identification had been a familiar one, but the growing popularity of female actors together with their strong connection with the aristocracy, even in some instance with the royal family, would break that unfortunate link. One fact of lineage may be of some interest. Sixteen eminent female actors were the daughters of provincial theatre managers; twenty-six of them were the daughters of actors of either sex.

Nine

Damme, Tom, it'll do!

The annals of acting take us ineluctably to the two greatest players of the eighteenth century, David Garrick and Sarah Siddons. Garrick was generally considered to be the greatest of all English actors, although there were other eminent players who contested that claim. Perhaps some still do. Others were ambivalent. 'Damn him!' Kitty Clive exclaimed. 'He could act a gridiron!' In truth, he could act almost anything, and took great pleasure in doing so. At a private gathering he performed the dagger scene from *Macbeth* to cries of praise, and at the next moment played a pastry-cook's boy who drops his pies and bursts into tears.

Garrick's countenance was infinitely malleable, and, as Denis Diderot reports of another of his party pieces, his expression changed in a matter of seconds 'from wild delight to temperate pleasure, from this to tranquillity, from tranquillity to surprise, from surprise to blank astonishment, from that to sorrow, from sorrow to the air of one overwhelmed, from that to fright, from fright to horror'. He felt obliged to act both on and off the stage. He was once describing to James Boaden the sculpture of Henry VII at Strawberry Hill, the very image of an avaricious and care-worn tyrant. 'Stop,' he said, 'I think I can give you the expression.' Boaden noticed that it was 'singular, and not to be forgotten'. When Boaden later visited the house, 'I immediately recognised the head.'

Garrick was born in Hereford in February 1717, at a time when the theatre was the god of public idolatry. His real life began in 1737, when he and Samuel Johnson, a friend and erstwhile teacher, walked together to London. He was supposed to become a wine-merchant, but another vocation lured him on. He joined the theatrical company of Henry Giffard, then based at Goodman's Fields Theatre. The theatre itself was in a delicate position as a result of the Licensing Act, just recently passed, but need knows no law.

By 1741 Garrick was playing Richard III, and, according to reports, a string of coaches was to be seen travelling from Westminster to the Fields. From where had this young man come? How had his skill been overlooked? In the following year he played King Lear, when it was known to be the undoing of more experienced actors. That was enough to seal his reputation. There is a story behind this success. Some effects were taken from the life. Garrick had an acquaintance in Leman Street, Whitechapel, who accidentally dropped his two-year-old girl out of an upper window. She died instantly, and such was the father's grief that he was driven insane. Garrick often came to visit and observe him, and that, he said, was how he learned to act Lear's madness. He knew that it worked. In the middle of an impassioned scene from that play, when the audience was like Niobe all tears, he turned to a fellow actor and whispered, 'Damme, Tom, it'll do!'

Garrick could make others feel while himself remaining quite detached. One critic declared that he had never seen the actor laugh or cry. His laughter on stage 'was well put on, but it was not a natural laugh'. Arthur Murphy, one of his contemporaneous biographers, told the poet Samuel Rogers that '*off* the stage he was a mean, sneaking little fellow. But *on* the stage – Oh my great God!' Garrick's ordinary speech was not that of a trained player, but rather 'vague, repetitive and ejaculatory'. Here we have the paradox of a great actor, magnificent and spellbinding on the boards but ordinary and unimpressive in life, majestic in the theatre but jealous and petulant in the ordinary transactions of the world. It has often been said of great performers that they can never quite live up to their personae. It is so common a predicament as to have become predictable, and many of them knew it themselves. It may be one of the penalties of genius.

Garrick was taken up by Charles Fleetwood, and in the spring of 1742 moved from Goodman's Fields to the Theatre Royal, Drury Lane, where he remained for five years. He played each part with attention to minute details of manner, countenance and voice. In *Macbeth* he hissed to an actor the line, 'There's blood on thy face!' He said it so naturally that the actor, starting back, quite forgot his reply. 'Is there, by God!' he exclaimed instead.

Garrick's style was volatile and various, and more than one critic noticed how he transformed or transcended the melodramatic and declamatory styles of acting with a manner 'young and light and alive in every muscle and in every feature' as he came 'bounding on the stage' to stir the audience and challenge the players. One contemporary journal reported that 'he was not less happy in his mien and gait, in which he is neither strutting nor mincing. When three or four are on the stage with him, he is attentive to whatever is spoke,' without 'unnecessary spitting, or suffering his eyes to wander through the whole circle of spectators'. We have here an intimation of the habits of bad actors.

Nature took the place of artificiality, as the Victorian actor-manager Henry Irving put it, and originality supplanted conventionality. Garrick was small, at approximately 1.6 metres (5 ft 4 in.), but he was elastic. His idiom was conversational, complete with pauses and even silences. It must have seemed to the spectators that the real thing stood before them. He took on more than ninety roles and, in the process, sharpened and refined his style so that he seemed almost to become a force of nature. A young boy was seen rolling on the ground in ecstasy when Garrick imitated a turkey-cock 'in a seeming flutter of feathered rage and pride'. He had the habit, according to the dramatist George Colman, of 'flashing the lightning of his eye' as a serpent might mesmerize a bird. Clearly it mesmerized the public, too, who flocked to his performances in such numbers that many of them could not get into the theatre. Two minor faults were noted, however. In tragedy he sometimes stammered and hesitated for no good reason, but this may have been the famous 'Garrick pause'. In comedy he might introduce a risqué joke to please the audience.

Such was Garrick's success that in 1747 he bought a half share in the patent of the Theatre Royal, Drury Lane. Now he possessed his own kingdom. He enlarged his Shakespearean repertoire, spending two months rehearsing Benedick, and at the same time spurred the plays and players into more rapid action; although some of his contemporary comedies were not successful, the first season yielded a profit. In the second season both Covent Garden and Drury Lane advertised *Romeo and Juliet*. It became known as 'the battle of the Romeos', and is evidence of the heights the rivalry of the playhouses could reach. In a city where drama ruled, the upper echelons of society talked of little else. It was as good as a war, even if the combatants wore powdered wigs. When *Othello* was played for one day only, the House of Commons suspended its session. The theatrical rivalry continued on a less exalted level when both theatres hired wire-dancers in direct competition with each other.

But Garrick's own genius had not been forgotten among the various fracas. In a mediocre historical tragedy of 1754 entitled *Virginia*, he summoned all his energy to condemn the villain in a low and melancholy voice, 'Thou traitor!' It is surprising what two words can do, and the whole audience was reported to respond 'with a thunder of applause'. It is proof, too, that Garrick was keen to observe the minutiae of his performance. When he saw the Ghost in *Hamlet* he scared himself more than the audience.

In Henry Fielding's *Tom Jones* (1749), Partridge exclaims, 'if that little man there upon the stage is not frightened, I never saw any man frightened in my life.' His curse at the end of the first act of *Lear* 'caused a kind of momentary petrifaction through the house, which he soon dissolved as universally into tears'. Garrick himself was known to observe that some of his greatest strokes of acting came unplanned and unexpected.

There were, of course, those who criticized the idol of the day. Some felt that Garrick overacted as much as his immediate predecessors; it was just that his overacting took a different form, and was ostensibly in the service of a more convincing 'naturalism'. Theophilus Cibber spoke of Garrick's 'over-fondness for extravagant Attitudes, frequently affected Starts, convulsive Twitchings, Jerkings of the Body, Sprawling of the Fingers, slapping the Breast and Pockets'. Was he being too natural, or too artificial? It is a question impossible to answer in a world of mirrors and mimicry. For Cibber, Garrick was being too 'natural' or overzealous in his desire to imitate, or present, nature, but to others the same manner might seem to be artificial. Garrick also introduced oil lamps instead of candles to light the auditorium, and used the lanterns to illuminate the stage. The audience might have chosen to believe that they were looking at daylight.

By the 1750s taste had revolved again, with the return of spectacle, pantomime and opera, but the introduction of French dancers to the London stage was a step too far. The hisses were louder than an ocean, the dancers hid in corners, and the experiment was not tried again. But in general the theatres of this period were more decorous than their predecessors. John Galt, in *The Lives of the Players* (1831), noted that 'a vulgar person scarcely ever frequented the pit, and very few women . . . In that part of the house the audience was composed of prosperous young merchants, barristers and students of the Inns of Court. Riots rarely disturbed the tranquillity of the pit.'

Nevertheless, Garrick himself was afraid of failure. One contemporary wrote that 'anxiety for his fame was the manager's reigning foible, on the slightest attack he was *tremblingly alive all o'er.*' Another observer noted that 'Vanity was his Prominent Feature and a Troublesome and Watchfull Jealousy the constant Visible Guard of his Reputation.' He was always looking in mirrors. Horace Walpole said, 'I do not mention the things written in his praise, because he writes most of them himself.' Garrick's faults were said to derive from 'the fire and hastiness' of his character. No one could equal him, or rival him; otherwise, hell flowed over. But his contemporaries did not necessarily flatter him. He once asked his old friend Samuel Johnson to respect his feelings; 'Sir,' Johnson replied, 'Punch has no feelings.' The painter William Hogarth told him that 'you are in your element when begrimed with dirt, or up to the elbows in blood.'

Garrick's criticism of his contemporaries, however, was often just. 'The name of players makes me sick,' he wrote. As for the strolling players who roamed over the kingdom, they 'are a hundred years behind . . . they still keep to their Strutting, bouncing and mouthing, that with Whiskers on, they put me in mind of the late Czar of Russia who was both an Ideot & a Madman.' As always, he noticed the detail. He once wagered a German author that they could not ride through a town as if they were drunk. They almost got away with it, but Garrick noted that 'your legs weren't drunk.'

When Garrick struck upon the notion of a 'Shakespeare Jubilee' in the autumn of 1769, he of course had the complete management of the proceedings. It was, however, something of a disaster. Heavy rain stopped play, and the streets of Stratford-upon-Avon were deluged with water. He did his best to enliven proceedings, but his greatest achievement was to signal the beginning of what became known as 'Bardolatry'. Perhaps that was enough. He appeared on stage for the last time in June 1776, as

Don Felix in Susanna Centlivre's *The Wonder*, but he did not enjoy his retirement; he was always restless and busy. George III noticed that 'he was a great fidget.' Garrick's doctor said he looked older than he was, 'for his Face has had double the business of another Man's'. But he had more than double the genius.

As a study in contrast, Sarah Siddons was known for her coolness, and maintained a distance from her contemporaries. To say that she was majestic would be an understatement. 'She was a grand artiste,' one theatrical historian recalled, 'but a very disagreeable woman.' She came from the theatrical family of the Kembles, but was born at the Shoulder of Mutton inn at Brecon, Mid Wales, in 1755. She was recruited into the theatrical profession at an early age. It is said that as Sarah Kemble she began as a strolling player but was trained in singing and elocution by her mother; she seems also to have attended a number of day schools during her travels. She is first mentioned in a playbill of 1767, and was also known to have taken the part of Ariel. One of her fellow players was William Siddons, with whom she contracted a relationship, whereupon she was sent by her family into service as a lady's maid in Warwickshire. It was not a promising beginning, but her parents eventually withdrew their opposition to the match and she married Siddons in 1773. The following year the newly married couple joined a theatrical company in Cheltenham, where her charm and gracefulness provoked admiration among the more discriminating members of the audience.

Garrick was alerted to her potential and travelled to Cheltenham to see her. He snapped her up for five pounds a week, but she was too inexperienced to fulfil her potential, so she left what must have seemed a favourable situation and toured the better provincial theatres. In York, according to Tate Wilkinson, 'all lifted up their eyes with astonishment that such a voice, such judgement, and such acting' should go unnoticed. She moved on to the prestigious theatre in Bath, where she remained for three years and where her beauty, as well as her 'picturesque and striking' manner, won her many admirers. She had her own way of achieving this. When she once heard of the unexpected death of a close friend, for example, she put her hand to her brow and fell backwards into a chair. Even as she did so, she told herself that she could use the effect at that evening's performance.

All the other famous eighteenth-century actresses possessed 'sex appeal'; Sarah Siddons had none. She was not 'coquettish' on stage, but 'sublime' and 'maternal'. While other actresses culti-vated (or were forced to foster) a dubious celebrity, Siddons had a respectable off-stage image as a loving mother and faithful wife; this dovetailed with, and reinforced, her 'chaste' and 'spiritual' performances. She invariably chose roles that would enhance her fame as a 'good' woman, and sometimes performed while pregnant, her unborn child becoming a sort of prop, or signifier, of the mater-nal side of her character. Siddons also invested the 'bad' women she played with 'delicate' and 'maternal femininity'. That was her appeal. Her genius, however, lay in her intense concentration on character. James Boaden, prompter and theatrical chronicler, wrote that 'I never felt the least indication that she had a private existence, or could be anything but the assumed character.' She always kept the door of her dressing room open, so that she could hear everything on the stage; she said that by these means 'the spirit of the whole drama took possession of my mind.' Then, as soon as the play was over, she dropped her characterization.

In the summer of 1782 Siddons was invited back to Drury Lane to play the heroine in a minor tragedy, *Isabella* by Thomas Southerne, which was for her a moment of triumph. She had over-come her critics, and on the night itself she enjoyed a 'scene of reiterated shouts and plaudits'. Boaden wrote that 'so natural are her graduations and transitions, so classical and correct her speech and deportment, and so intensely interesting her voice, form and features, that there is no conveying an idea of the pleasure she communicates by words. She must be seen to be known.' Hazlitt noted in her 'those reaches of the soul, in which it looks down on its sufferings, in which it rises superior to nature and fortune, and gathers strength and grandeur from its despair . . . She seemed formed for scenes of torture and agony.' And she was seen by more and more; she became what was known as 'the rage of the town'. The daughter of a Welsh innkeeper had the ambition and endurance of one who sensed her own genius. Social success followed her new-found fame, and her drawing room in Gower Street was much favoured. George III cried at her acting, and the queen invited her to Court. It was reported that 'her door saw more carriages daily before it than any other.'

In her second season at Drury Lane Siddons ventured into Shakespeare with *Measure for Measure*. But her favoured mode was tragedy. With all her intensity and gracefulness, she could not manage comedy. In tragedy her innate dignity, her sometimes statuesque poses and her expressive countenance did the work for her. François-Auguste-René Chateaubriand noted that 'an extreme sensibility united to a profound melancholy characterized her look, and her smile had something in it scarce earthly.' Some called her ironically the 'queen of tragedy' or 'the queen of tears', but in all her social relations she was restrained and composed; like her dramatic utterance, according to her biographer, her voice was 'measured and deliberate'. A draper sold her some material and was struck dumb by the tone in which she said, 'But will it wash?' She could also draw on depths of suppressed passion. Watching her in the famous sleepwalking scene from *Macbeth*, Lord Byron had a convulsive fit and several women fainted. James Sheridan Knowles stated that 'well, sir, I smelt the blood! I swear I smelt the blood!' This the mesmeric power of the actor at full blast.

Actors themselves are far more aware of the audience, and individual members of the audience, than they are generally willing to admit. They will notice if someone leaves, or whispers to someone else. One unnamed actor confessed that the sight of someone sleeping in the stalls dried up his tears in a pathetic scene. A female player noticed a 'peculiarly stolid and stony woman of fashion', and was determined to affect her or perish in the attempt. It was quite common for actors to count the members of the audience, as they acted, and to reckon up the proceeds.

Siddons sat for Sir Joshua Reynolds as 'The Tragic Muse'. And that is what she had become. She played Lady Macbeth thirteen times, but found it difficult to extract the requisite earnings from the 'purse manager' of Drury Lane, Richard Brinsley Sheridan, who – despite his reputation as a comic dramatist – was as close as an oyster. She made her money by embarking on provincial tours, where she was greeted as a wandering Sibyl. She was drawn, painted and sketched in a hundred different attitudes, and her image was in every print-shop. But her picturesque attitudes were closer to Melpomene, the goddess of tragedy, than to Siddons herself. She had already lost two daughters, and her husband, overshadowed by her fame, was becoming more and more estranged. But the story of the goddess with a troubled past only increased the adulation that surrounded her. Her whisper could chill an audience into silence. The phenomenon of 'Siddons fever', the electric charge that ran through the audience, caused fainting fits, hysteria and physical paroxysm of an alarming nature, and became a commonplace.

And Siddons kept on working. She had a compulsion to act. She returned for the season of 1802 to Drury Lane, where she took the part of Hermione, who poses as a marble statue before stepping down as the long-lost heroine. It could be said that she acted the statue better than the woman, because of her extraordinary poise. Her final season, in 1811–12, was marked by her assuming fifty-seven performances in fourteen different characters; she was fifty-six and naturally showing signs of wear.

Siddons's farewell performance was that of Lady Macbeth, who had almost become her shadow; the spectators were enthralled and would not let the play continue after the sleepwalking scene. The audience were not simply spectators, but active participants in the drama; darkening the front of the stage and using a lighted background conveyed a marked illusion of reality. Every expression was scrutinized, every movement watched, every syllable apprehended. Hazlitt noted that 'power was seated on her brow, passion emanated from her breast as from a shrine. She was Tragedy personified . . . To have seen Mrs Siddons, was an event in every one's life.'

On 31 May 1831, aged seventy-five, Siddons fell ill with acute erysipelas, a bacterial skin condition, before falling into a coma a week later. She died in her house at 27 Upper Baker Street the next morning. She was buried in St Mary's churchyard in Paddington, where a crowd of five thousand sent her to the rest that she had never known in life.

Ten

Wonders and ranters

After the death of Garrick and Siddons, the stage may have seemed bare. But the theatrical world abhors a vacuum, even if it fills the vacancy with peculiarities. A case in point can be made of William Henry West Betty, known as 'Master Betty' or the 'young Roscius'. His father took him, at the age of eleven, to see Siddons on stage in Belfast, whereupon he declared that 'I shall certainly die if I may not be a player.' He must already have possessed advanced histrionic tendencies, since, on watching him, the manager of the Belfast Theatre observed that 'I never indulged in the hope of seeing another Garrick, but I have seen an infant Garrick in Betty.' He was taken up at once and, still only eleven, played a Turkish sultan in a play by Voltaire to great applause, before going on at the same age to Young Norval in John Home's *Douglas*. His fame quickly spread south to Dublin, where he performed a variety of roles and is said to have learned the part of Hamlet in three hours. The Irish authorities extended the curfew for an hour to accommodate his performance. News of his extraordinary precocity was soon heard in Europe: 'This is a clever boy,' one lady remarked, 'and had I never seen boys act, I might have thought him extraordinary.'

Of course Betty had to visit London as part of his progress, and guards were called to control the crowds who clustered around the Covent Garden theatre where he was performing. One report notes that 'Shrieks and screams of choking, trampled people were terrible. Fights for places grew; constables were beaten back, the boxes were invaded. The heat was so fearful that men all but lifeless were lifted and dragged through the boxes into the lobbies which had windows.' Betty made his fortune more quickly than he had expected, since the theatres raised their prices whenever he appeared, but, with great good sense, he abandoned the stage at the age of eighteen and entered Christ's College, Cambridge. He tried to resuscitate his career a few years later, but was not a success. After a failed attempt at suicide he settled into the comfortable surroundings of Dulwich with his savings to support him.

It is difficult to explain the extraordinary success of an eleven-year-old boy. It was said that Betty was guided by divine inspiration, but it might have been a case of mass hysteria, a condition to which we are now accustomed. He was pretty, he was bold and he was word-perfect, and he must also have possessed a genuine ability or talent to excite the audience. He would have passed muster in the sixteenth century as one of the boy actors of Blackfriars. He happened to be born at a fortunate time, when fashion and frivolity reigned.

But the key to Betty's achievement was his passion for acting; he had loved what he did ever since seeing Siddons. One critic remarked that 'he had amazing docility, and great aptitude at catching what he was taught; he could convey passions which he had never felt, nor seen in operation but upon the stage; grace, energy, fire, vehemence were his own; the understanding was of a mature brain. He seemed, however, to think all he said.'

Betty had his detractors, in particular other actors who wished to prick the 'baby bubble'. Dorothea Jordan remarked, 'Oh for the days of King Herod!' One theatrical manager called the whole affair 'a Humbug'. A Polish dwarf, Józef Boruwłaski, compared him to the previous fashion in Paris for a rabbit who beat upon a drum. Siddons's brother John Philip Kemble, asked if he would act with Betty, replied that he had never seen him *play*, while Siddons herself refused to have anything to do with the infant phenomenon; he was beneath her dignity.

Sturdier ground is reached with Spranger Barry and John Philip Kemble, even if they have not survived in public memory. Despite his peculiar Christian name, Barry has not avoided oblivion, even though at the time he was considered by many to rival Garrick himself. A nineteenth-century critic wrote that Garrick 'did not have the physical attributes of Barry. Certainly he was nowhere with Barry in *Othello*, and came up to him only in the banishment scene of *Romeo*.' Barry was born in Ireland in 1717 and, after two seasons in Dublin, took the road in the 1740s to Drury Lane, where he soon distinguished himself with his voice no less than his bearing. The name Spranger suited him; he might spring from a castle keep, or stride across a stage, with the same vigour. He was tall and handsome, with a voice to match, and he had all the Irish bonhomie in the world. Who could resist the charm that he distributed in bucketfuls? He was magnificent as Othello (a part that Garrick never played after his encounter with Barry), less so as Macbeth, but back to peak performance in a sequence of lovers' parts. He was not as convincing in violent parts as he was in tender roles, since he made a speciality of 'elegant distress'. Perhaps he knew his weaknesses.

Despite his dignity and commanding presence in public, Barry used to ask experienced stagehands during rehearsals to give him their opinion on his performance. He had the ability to stir his audience with modulations of the voice or changes of behaviour, a habit that was known as 'clap-trapping'. His was essentially what one critic has called 'a pantomimic representation of the passions' rather than an 'ability to represent the so-called "real" life of the naturalistic theatre'. It was not necessary to be real, but rather to seem real; he did not wish to convey individualistic responses, as did others, but typical ones.

When Garrick took up the management of Drury Lane in 1747, he and Barry were in a sense forced together. They played opposite each other, or played the same role on alternate nights, and the question that animated London society consisted in the relative merits of their personalities and performances. Romeo was a case in point. Hannah Pritchard, the actor, found Garrick 'so ardent and impassioned . . . I should have expected he would have come up to me in the balcony; but had I been Juliet to Barry's Romeo – so tender, so eloquent, and so seductive was he, I should certainly have gone down to him.' In the autumn of 1750, when Barry had migrated to Covent Garden, they both played Romeo for twelve nights until even the enthusiastic admirers of either man grew tired of the contest. It seems that Barry took the prize largely because he looked like a lover. He was not adept, however, at plumbing the depths of feeling, being better at the 'showy' side of the business. It is significant that his greatest roles, Othello and Romeo, rarely *think*. The two actors also played King Lear. A critic noted that Barry was 'every inch a king and Garrick every inch King Lear'. Leigh Hunt remarked that 'Barry was one of the old artificial school who made his way more by person than by genius.'

Barry seemed to shuffle between London and Dublin as circumstances permitted until he was finally reunited with Drury Lane in 1767. But there were always problems with Garrick, perhaps from extravagant living on the part of Barry and jealousy on that of Garrick. Performances were cancelled and, as a result, finances straitened. Barry eventually left Drury Lane, and in 1774 he went back to Covent Garden. He was now too old to play the romantic lead, and took less significant parts. He died three years later, but Garrick refused to provide an epitaph for his tomb. For once he was at a loss for words. That may have been appropriate. A contemporary noted that 'the best and worst of Barry's character is that he had none.'

It is only just to mention Siddons's younger brother, Charles Kemble. He was dismissed by some as second-rate compared to his older siblings, but according to the contemporary actress Helena (or Helen) Faucit he 'had an ease and distinction which set him apart, even from actors conventionally graceful and spirited', and possessed 'that freshness which arises when an actor seems to speak from the impulse of the moment, and when his utterances were apparently as fresh to himself as to the listener'. This is a valuable and important gift that is often noticed only in its absence. But Kemble was also considered to be one of the originators of the 'heroic school'; with hand on hip, it was known as the 'teapot style'. He made steady if unspectacular progress, even if he was in the perpetual shadow of his two more gifted siblings, and even if he sometimes traded on his surname. He died at his home in Savile Row in November 1854.

He is perhaps the best introduction to his older and more successful brother. John Philip Kemble was born in Lancashire in 1757, and when he was fourteen his mother insisted that he should enjoy or endure a thoroughly Catholic education at Douai College in northern France. But he was not destined for the priesthood, and partly with the help of his sister, now Sarah Siddons, he became a strolling player with all the travail that belonged to that profession. His first secure base was Liverpool, where he remained for three years, often accompanying Sarah on the stage; he had a repertory of 158 parts, some comic and some tragic, but he may still have felt overshadowed by his sibling (and also, perhaps, by the reputation of Garrick). He could be difficult and easily insulted, and was as a result excessively self-important.

Kemble joined the company of the Theatre Royal at Drury Lane in 1783, and under the lax management of Sheridan he was given the choice of various Shakespearean roles. He managed to hold himself together in the parts of Hamlet, Shylock and Richard III, but it was noticed that he lacked fire or vigour and was more concerned with his precise elocution. 'To be critically exact', wrote James Boaden, 'was the great ambition of his life.' But that was in itself exceptional. He thought through every detail of his performances, and so mastered them that he could rivet the audience with his expressions, his gestures, and the enunciation of a certain word.

Kemble also looked good in a toga and made a flourish with Joseph Addison's *Cato* in the second season at the Theatre Royal. Hazlitt remarked that he paraded 'a studied piece of classical costume – a conscious exhibition of elegantly disposed drapery, that was all: yet, as a mere display of personal and artificial grace, it was inimitable'. It was customary at the close of the play for all the characters to stand immobile on the stage, 'frozen in an attitude', as the theatre echoed with the applause of the audience. They became statues in front of a painted cloth. The pose seemed to suit him.

Kemble's sister was often close at hand. He and Sarah played Othello and Desdemona, as well as the Macbeths. There must have been something in the blood of the Kembles. Both of them adopted a statuesque and picturesque style that they borrowed from the portraitist. They had the same firmness and control, the same dignity of behaviour, the same iron will and the same sternness of temper. Both knew how to practise restraint. Kemble was described as having a 'classical dignity', and Hazlitt remarked that 'he is the only one of the moderns, who both in figure and action approaches the beauty and grandeur of the antique.' Sir Walter Scott described Kemble as 'tall and stately, his person on a scale suited for the stage . . . with a countenance like the finest models of the antique, and motions and manners corresponding to the splendid cast of his form and features'. In turn critics spoke of Sarah Siddons's 'grand deportment'.

Kemble had other props, too, in the form of alcohol and opium. But he did not succumb to these potions, and in 1788 he agreed to take over the management of Drury Lane. This only accelerated his ambition and, in particular, he triumphed as Coriolanus, Macbeth and King Lear. Scott reported that during the death scene of Coriolanus 'we have repeatedly heard screams from the female part of the audience.' In the less tremulous world of caricature, Kemble is depicted as a 'theatrical ranter' who declaims directly to the audience, with a distorted expression on his face, his arms whirling around him like the sails of a windmill. He was also charged with showing minimal interest in any particular play and in the actors around him. He compensated for what he lacked in speed, range, flexibility and 'naturalness' with his wonderful elocution, and with his painstaking penetration of the character he played. That is why he preferred to personate characters with one overpowering characteristic or passion into which he could dig more deeply. Hazlitt observed, 'we think the distinguishing excellence of his acting may be summed up in one word – *intensity*; in the seizing upon some one feeling or idea, in insisting upon it, in never letting it go.'

In consequence, the audience's attention was taken away from the play and the other players, and Kemble's acting dominated the production, so that he was a lone star. Deliberate and deliberately artificial, he poured scorn on the idea that he 'became' the parts he played, famously remarking that 'if Garrick really believes himself to be [Richard III] he ought to be hung every time he plays it.' As a result, Kemble was successful in a limited range of roles; as Coriolanus and Macbeth he was superb, as Lear and Hamlet he was wooden. He was described as 'an icicle on the bust of tragedy'. Like most other actors, he lacked Garrick's versatility. Nevertheless, as manager he improved both sets and scenery so that one memoirist described him as 'the parent of the modern improvements of the stage'. That did not necessarily make him more popular; the employees called him 'Black Jack'.

Theatres were in any case often places of misfortune. This was the period when, according to *The Theatrical Speaker* of 1807, 'the English stage has lost much of its former splendour; and . . . its eventual decay approaches rapidly . . . the actors dress with less taste on the London stage than in other countries.' The anonymous author also mentions an actress over forty, who could only have been Dorothea Jordan, playing the part of a girl of sixteen; elsewhere she would have been hooted off the stage. He mentions that English actors speak in a very loud voice, as if they were declaiming their lines. That is why 'the English do not usually succeed in expressing soft and inward emotions.'

In the autumn of 1808 the Theatre Royal succumbed to the perennial peril and was burned to the ground. Insurance, and quick finance, allowed the new theatre to open a year later, with Kemble and his sister in their fireproof roles of the Macbeths. But on this occasion they were not enough. The costs of the new theatre had been large and Kemble took the opportunity of generally raising prices and erecting new boxes in order to generate additional income. There followed the most notorious and damaging of all theatrical wars, which became known as the 'Old Price Riots'. They lasted for sixty-seven nights, and the new theatre was reduced to a wreck. There were some characteristics of the eighteenth-century theatre that may have provoked riot, among them perhaps the close proximity – but careful gradation – of the various classes so that it could be seen as a microcosm of London. The city was in any case the haven of crowds, fights and riots, which migrated quite naturally into the playhouses. In December 1809 Kemble surrendered to the violence and signed a peace treaty with what was now a disgruntled mob.

He went back to work with a sequence of familiar roles, interrupted in part by the retirement of Siddons at the end of the 1811–12 season. He made provincial appearances in Liverpool, Edinburgh, Dublin, Bath, York and Bristol. Each town had its own reputation in the theatrical community. York was universally considered to be 'the stepping stone to London', while the inhabitants of Bristol were known as the 'Bristol hogs' because they paid no attention to London celebrity. Retirement may have been much on Kemble's mind, and some noticed that in the 1814 season he had lost some of his energy; there may have been only a remote connection with any valedictory mood. It so happened that twelve days later Edmund Kean made his debut. Kemble finally retired, with the role of Coriolanus, on 23 June 1817. He died of a stroke some six years later.

It is worth considering those who never reached the level of fame or notoriety that their more celebrated contemporaries achieved. It was calculated that approximately six thousand people were known to claim the title of actor, male or female, but according to *The Road to the Stage* (1815), 'the number of persons claiming those honours are perhaps nearly seven times that number.' What was the life for those whose light has failed? William Hazlitt, a year or two later, described them 'with sinking hearts – engaged, dismissed again, tampered with, tantalised, trifled with, pelted, hooted, scorned, unpitied . . . And all this, without any fault in themselves, any misconduct, any change, but in the taste and humour of the audience.' One biographer recognized that 'the actors lived in a ragged half-world, desperately pretending not to see the real while hopelessly failing to create the illusory.' The life of an actor, then and now, could be one of anxiety and neglect.

THERE IS THE FAMOUS oil painting by James Northcote of Kean when young, playing Brutus, his hair swept back, looking forward intensely and with an expression of vivid alarm; his dark eyes are enlarged and the brows raised; his mouth is slightly open, as if he were about to speak; and his neck is bare, with an open collar. It is one of those portraits that, once seen, is never forgotten. A contemporary wrote of Kean's 'entire mastery over his audience in all striking, sudden, impassioned passages', leaving refinement and details to other actors. Leigh Hunt remarked that he had 'an instinctive natural reason' for everything he did, and commented that Kemble was statuesque while Kean was vibrant; that Kemble delivered his lines in a formal, 'sing-song' way, whereas Kean brought in the pauses and hesitations of natural speech. Neither was particularly realistic, in any current sense, but at the time it was believed that Kean had made a decided thrust towards nature.

Kemble saw Kean as Richard III and observed that 'our styles of acting are so totally different, that you must not expect me to *like* that of Mr Kean; but one thing I must say in his favour – he is at all times terribly in *earnest*.' Samuel Taylor Coleridge declared that 'to see him act, is like reading Shakespeare by flashes of lightning.' To some Kean was most memorable, and most himself, in passages of vivid animosity, what a contemporary described as 'striking, sudden, impassioned passages'. As a result he has been associated with the contemporary Romantic movement, in which sensibility and sentimentality were the twin engines of passion. But in his playing there was no question of random impulsiveness. Kean told Garrick's widow that

> these people don't understand their business; they give me credit where I don't deserve it and pass over passages where I have bestowed the utmost care and attention. Because my style is easy and natural they think I don't study, and talk about 'the sudden impulse of genius'. There is no such thing as impulsive acting; all is premeditated and studied beforehand.

Nevertheless the fully fledged Romantic actor, taking his or her cue from Kean, was intent on communicating what were known as 'the passions'; he or she wished to convey feelings so that they could be internalized by the audience, and the subjective experience shared.

There is perhaps one large distinction between the styles. Kean was the master of inner feeling, where Kemble was the master of the external sign. Fanny Kemble, the actor's niece, went to the heart of the matter when she noted that Kean possessed 'no taste, perhaps, and no industry, but let his deficiencies be what they may, he has the one atoning faculty that compensates for everything else, that seizes, rivets, electrifies all who see and hear him, and stirs down to their very springs the passionate elements of our nature. Genius alone can do this.' It is perhaps worth noting in this context that the first melodrama, Matthew Lewis's *The Castle Spectre*, was staged at Drury Lane in 1797. The gothic, the mysterious and the sensational were coming slowly to a climax. They just needed the right players.

Kean was born – by general consensus, in 1789 – into a family that can be called, in the phrase of the time, 'shabby' rather than 'genteel'; his mother divided her time between prostitution and acting, a familiar combination for those who had to make their own way unaided in the world. Neither father nor mother took much interest in the boy, and he was farmed out to the midwife at his birth. He was a weakly child who was obliged to wear irons on his legs until the age of seven. But this did not prevent him from becoming an excellent fencer and, after much practice and perseverance, a dancer. According to one nineteenth-century biographer, he was 'a born Bohemian, and would leave his home sometimes for weeks together, to wander about the country with acrobats and tramps'. He was called by one performer 'Alexander the Little'. 'Yes,' he replied, '*but with a great soul.*'

The boy Kean was put to work as an infant entertainer in drinking clubs and cider cellars, and progressed to acrobatics at Bartholomew Fair. He soon became adept at pantomime and was said particularly to excel in 'the pantomime of tragedy'. He would have been a master of silent film. There is an extant playbill of a 'Master Kean' in 1796, playing a minor part in *The Merry Wives of*

Windsor. It seems a little too young, even for an infant phenomenon, and there may have been a different Master Kean. But he
did come to rely on his good looks and physical agility. It could
be the story of a hundred London children.

Kean was of modest height, at 1.7 metres (5 ft 7 in.), but his dark
eyes and somewhat striking features found him work with a company in Sheerness. He subsequently undertook several theatrical
circuits, and in 1802 he gave a short recital at Covent Garden. He
once said that Sarah Siddons caught sight of him and, patting him
on the head, observed, 'you have played very well, sir, very well.
It's a pity, but there's too little of you to do anything.' That, at
least, was his story. He found employment as a casual actor, but
seems sometimes to have been reduced to begging. Here, perhaps,
were the seeds of his self-hatred and occasional malevolence. He
seemed to mock and discourage any assistance; he allowed his
inner wounds to fester and took to the comforts of drink to dull
the pain. He was the enemy of society, and that innate bitterness
fuelled his acting.

Kean's first proper engagement, perhaps prompted by his success as Harlequin in one extravaganza and his unusual appearance
as a dark-eyed dancer, was with the company in Sheerness managed at the time by Samuel Jerrold; he moved on to Gloucester and
Stroud before returning to Jerrold. But he wandered on. He was
seen in Exeter in 1812 and 1813, and performed later in Guernsey.
The tracks of a strolling or at least mobile player are hard to follow.
He joined the 'Gloucester circuit' and married an actress eight
years his senior, with whom he had two sons. Her dowry was
poverty; more wandering and more heavy drinking were followed
by further misery and self-reproach. 'He used to mope for hours,'
his wife said, 'with his hands in his pockets, thinking intensely on
his characters.' While at Dorchester he was observed closely by
the acting manager of Drury Lane, Samuel Arnold. Arnold must
have had a good eye, since Kean's first major performance was as

Shylock at the Drury Lane theatre on 26 January 1814. 'My God!' he exclaimed. 'If I should succeed I shall go mad!'

Kean's blazing personality and vigorous feeling made him quite unlike anyone else, and he tapped into his reserves of bitterness and misanthropy in his portrait of the Jew. Hazlitt recalled later, 'we wish we had never seen Mr Kean. He has destroyed the Kemble religion and it is the religion in which we were brought up.' Gone was the solemn majesty and the sudden pause for applause. The first night had not been particularly well attended, but the second was filled to capacity. Jane Austen wrote to her sister, Cassandra, that 'places are secured at Drury Lane for Saturday, but so great is the rage for seeing Kean that only a third and fourth row could be got.'

Hazlitt had already obtained a seat, as a dramatic critic, and commented that 'the character never stands still. There is no vacant pause in the action; the eye is never silent.' He added else-where, 'For voice, eye, action, and expression, no actor has come out for many years at all equal to him.' The word of the time was 'electric'. George Henry Lewes wrote that it was impossible to watch Kean 'without being strangely shaken by the terror and the pathos, and the passion of a stormy spirit uttering itself in tones of irresistible power'. But Kean was not all storm and lightning; before each performance he carefully measured the number of steps he should take to find the required spot. One actor sought his advice:

'When I place my hand on your head to curse,' Kean said, 'mind you keep your eyes fixed on mine.'

'Is that all, sir?'

'Yes – do whatever you like after that. It will all be the same to me.'

Kean played to packed audiences, and chose only those parts that suited his rebarbative temper. He played Richard III and Iago as often as he did Othello. 'Was not Iago perfection,' Byron wrote to his fellow poet Thomas Moore, 'particularly the last look? I was close to him (in the orchestra) and never saw an English countenance half so expressive.' Kean preferred to see human life *in extremis*. He sat up all night in an adjacent room to watch the hanging in 1820 of the Cato Street conspirators, and said to an acquaintance that 'I mean to die like Thistlewood tonight; I'll imitate every muscle of that man's countenance.' The more he seemed to suffer, the greater his inner contentment. In this, we may discern a thread; in the twentieth century Charles Laughton also found ease in affliction.

Hazlitt was Kean's most significant critic, however, because he divined the essence of the change this actor brought to the theatre. Hazlitt noted 'the hesitation, the bewildered look, the coming to himself' that Kean brought to Macbeth, as well as 'the rapidity of his transition from one tone and feeling to another' in Shylock. The actor was also able to give 'effect to the conflict of passions arising out of the contrasts of situations'. His voice was taken for granted, resembling 'a hackney-coachman at one o'clock in the morning'. He had once been Harlequin, as previously noted, and *The Examiner* reported that 'he is the best actor we ever saw in what may be called *the pantomime of tragedy*; his acting is *inimitable* where there is *no speaking*.'

Kean was not so adept at comedy, except, perhaps, as an imp of the perverse. Lewes observed that 'he had no playfulness that was not as the playfulness of a panther, showing her claws every moment.' By his fourth season, in 1816, he was performing the solitary wildness of Timon of Athens. And, as always, the pit – which in those days represented the best of theatrical audiences, combining art, letters, law and other distinguished professions – rose to him.

Kean himself was coming close to megalomaniac madness. He wrote to one aspiring dramatist that no one should write a tragedy for Drury Lane without making its entire centre around the character he himself would perform. All his death scenes were magnified beyond the bounds of any text. He paraded a lion through the streets and established a 'Wolves' Club' devoted to debauchery and self-destruction. By his thirties he was losing his fire or, rather, quenching it in increasing volumes of alcohol. He was not helped by the unexpected appearance of William Charles Macready as the newly favoured taste of the town. But Kean received a large salary that helped to inflate the income of other principal actors; where they were once happy to receive twenty pounds a week, they now demanded twenty pounds or more a night.

In 1820 Kean took ship for the United States, where he seems to have been soothed with all the signs of his success, but on his return he discovered that the manager of Drury Lane had also taken on Macready. More insidious problems followed, when a cache of letters he had written to his latest lover, Mrs Charlotte Cox, resulted in his arrest for 'criminal conversation' with a married woman. The subsequent trial, which he lost, was the sensation of the day, and from that time forward his appearances on the stage were at the mercy of the London public, which was not always kind. In 1825 he left again for the United States and Canada, where the presence of an eminent actor, now as famous a Romantic as Byron, kept the audiences contented.

But his health had gone, more than likely hastened by the mercury treatment for syphilis. Kean acted off and on, but his vivacity and charisma had left him. A contemporary reported that when waiting for his cue he was 'a hapless, speechless fainting mass bent up in a chair'. When the call came, according to one biographer, 'he looks about as if in a dream, drags himself painfully to his feet, totters towards the stage, and by an extraordinary conscription of his forces, walks strongly on, plays his scene with a simulation of energetic brilliance, and collapses again.' If he forgot his lines he could 'vamp' – that is, make up his own. It is a description that could be applied to many actors, past and present. Kean died from disease, drink and drugs at the age of forty-six; but was refused his proposed burial beside Garrick.

As a postscript, the career of his son is instructive. As the off-spring of a famous father, Charles Kean gained much interest, but his abilities were always in the shadow; he relied not on his father's bolt of lightning, but rather on a meticulous and scholarly re-enactment of his part. As a director he kept a dinner bell by his side during rehearsals and, when a problem arose, he would ring it ferociously until everyone stopped. Two-hour rehearsals were considered sufficient for any play, but in his case they often continued all day.

Charles Kean fought a running battle with Macready, who became the most famous and popular player of the early decades of the nineteenth century, and as a result Macready, despite his success, resented the younger actor's skill and eventual reputation. Macready's friends generally wrote for the critical journals, and under the actor's influence Charles Kean was conventionally criticized and scorned. But his skill kept on breaking through. In the autumn of 1837 he joined the Theatre Royal, Drury Lane, and effectively restored that theatre's fortune. In the process he began entirely to revise the interpretation of Shakespeare in a natural-istic fashion. 'We can't now be bound by old rules,' he said, 'and keep troubling ourselves about what John Kemble didn't like or Macready wouldn't do.' He was praised for quieter and less exub-erant parts, restraining the excitement of Romanticism for a more sober naturalism that did indeed become the style of later years; the vogue for domestic drama is one example. Kean was so real, and so natural, by the standards of the time, that he did not seem to act at all. In his way, he was a true pioneer. He died in London on 22 January 1868, at the age of 57.

Certain comic performers can act as an interval before the arrival of the nineteenth century. Charles Kean's fame was rivalled by that of Charles Mathews, a specialist in what he called 'monopolylogues', which, as the word suggests, consisted of one actor playing all the parts of a short play and doing so by means of stock phrases, comic asides, mannerisms and the mimicry of dialects. He specialized in the garrulous female, the urchin, and the foreigner with a funny accent, with so many rapid changes of voice and manner that he seemed to observe the urban world without disclosing any personality of his own. His real skill, in fact, lay in his dexterity and responsiveness; he could 'represent seven or eight different, and very varied, characters in an evening'.

Mathews was born in the Strand in 1776, and his youth was spent in his father's bookshop, generally with a play in his hand. He was finding his repertoire. He was not at first successful. 'Sir,' Tate Wilkinson told him, 'you are too tall for low comedy. I never saw anything so thin to be *alive*.' Mathews spent two years in Dublin, imitating the idiosyncrasies of famous actors, and was applauded by a responsive audience. He had not only acquired a repertoire; he had found his vocation. He was equally at home with inanimate objects and could spend a full ten minutes in trying to sit upon a chair.

Boaden described Mathews as a 'comic world in one', but Byron put it more ingeniously: 'He seems to have continuous chords in his mind that vibrate to those in the minds of others, as he gives not only the looks, tones and manners of the persons he personifies, but their very train of thinking.' Critics recognized and commented on Mathews's 'possessed' or 'demonic' qualities. He could sit at dinner, and be universally mistaken for a completely different person. If there had then been the term 'psychic' (not coined until 1870), it could undoubtedly have been applied to what seemed like his extrasensory gifts. It is true that the greatest actors have also been the greatest mimics. Mathews was known to be restless and irritable, and, according to Henry Barton Baker in *Our Old Actors* (1879), there were times when it was 'necessary to put away his razors, lest he should commit suicide'.

After Dublin, Mathews was engaged in the usual business of moving to a theatre where employment was offered. After three years in Swansea and three years in York, where he learned the art of ventriloquy, he eventually reached London, where he spent two years at the Haymarket. He was hailed as the comic genius of the day. He then mastered Drury Lane and in 1808 migrated to the Lyceum with a series of comic mishaps entitled *The Mail Coach Adventure*, before removing himself to Covent Garden. He was by now the premier comic of London, and in 1828 he became half-owner of the Lyceum. But his proprietorship did not last for very long; on a sea voyage back from a tour of the United States he contracted a lung disease, and in 1835 he died at Plymouth.

The second significant comic was of a different species. Joseph Grimaldi was not really a comic at all, but a harlequin. It is to his immortal credit that he invented the Clown as an English institution and his name, Joey, was his calling card. But he was an artist, not a farceur or jokester. He was also an avid and expert collector of butterflies. 'I never saw any one to equal him,' Charles Dibdin, the singer and songwriter, said. 'There was such *mind* in everything he did.' Throughout his life, from 1778 to 1837, Grimaldi was the emperor of foolery for the box, pit and gallery of Drury Lane and Covent Garden. Two of his most popular songs were 'Hot Codlins' and 'Tippity Witchet', and it was he who coined the great pantomimic phrase 'Here we are again!' He would enquire of his audience, 'Shall I?', to which the raucous answer was 'Yes!' His most popular pantomime was *Harlequin and Mother Goose*, and Mother Goose herself has survived into the present century. Dressed in a blanket, large tin plates for buttons and a hat fashioned out of a pie dish, and carrying a bunch of carrots as a bouquet, he would arrive on stage in a large wicker basket with four single Gloucester cheeses as wheels.

Grimaldi had a white face, red triangles on his cheeks and a comic wig; his dress was a coloured shirt, flowery tunic and baggy trousers. His voice was an amalgam of 'laugh, scream and speech'. More colourfully, it was described as like 'the utterance of a boy laughing, talking, and eating custard all at once'. He was unmistakable. Other characters gradually joined him, most notably the Dame, the Principal Boy and Pantaloon. Hey presto! It was the pantomime without which, until recently, no self-respecting theatre could survive. As *The Atlas* of 1 February 1829 put it, '"Have you seen the new pantomime?" is as familiar as "Have you seen the new tragedy?"'

Grimaldi's industry and popularity were his undoing, like those of the music-hall performers who followed in his wake. There were occasions when he had to play three 'heavy parts' in three different theatres on the same night. He had to perform the most laborious jumps, leaps and revolutions without ceasing for forty years, and by then he was almost fifty. His weakened body could no longer take the strain. His farewell speech was greeted with 'a shout enough to rend the roof; he stood up, his knees tottering, and every feature of his face convulsed.' Among his last words were 'it is four years since I jumped my last jump – filched my last oyster – boiled my last sausage . . . I used to have a fowl in one pocket and sauce for it in the other. Eight and forty years have passed over my head and I am sinking fast . . . Farewell! Farewell!' It was a night of tears as he stood trembling on the stage to which he had devoted his life. He died at the end of May 1837.

Joseph Shepherd Munden was born in Leather Lane in the spring of 1758; little is known of his early life except that he joined or accompanied several sets of strolling players before being taken up by Canterbury, and then Covent Garden in 1790, as what was known as a 'low comedian'. His speciality was faces; he could put on a different one at a moment's notice and, according to one essayist, 'was not so much a comedian as a company'. A fellow comic described him as a 'great actor' who 'followed his art *con amore*'. He once drank a bottle of lamp oil by mistake, and pulled such a face that the response of the audience was hysterical laughter. When asked why he kept on drinking it, he replied that 'there was such a glorious roar at the first face I made on swallowing it I hadn't the heart to spoil the scene.'

Charles Lamb wrote that 'a tub of butter, contemplated by him, amounts to a Platonic idea. He understands a leg of mutton in its quiddity.' By this he may have meant that Munden treated inanimate objects with the same reverence as the animated. Munden had one piece of advice that he passed on to a fellow comedian: 'Always fix your eye on some one man in the pit, sing at him, till he laughs, and then you have 'im – the rest are sure to follow.' Of his face it was said that 'Munden has none that you can properly pin down and call *his*.' Whether playing Sir Francis Gripe, Caustic, Old Rapid or Nipperkin, he studied the part with as much intense and careful attention as if he were playing Shakespeare. Indeed he did play Malvolio, Launce and other distinguished parts. But he could not be called a learned man. He once confessed, 'I never read any book but a play, no play but one in which I myself acted, and no portion of that play but my own scenes.' On hearing this, Lamb replied, 'I knew Munden well, and I *believe* him.' He died in 1832, and was remembered as a caricaturist, a grimacer, a buffoon, but principally as a great comedian.

Munden was succeeded by John Liston, who turned drollery into a form of art by identifying with the audience rather than with the play. He stood outside the drama, and in fact he stood outside himself to watch the ludicrousness and incongruity of it all. Hazlitt wrote, 'no one is *stultified*; no one is *mystified* like him – no one is so deep in absurdity, no one so full of vacancy, no one chuckles so over his own conceit, or is so dismayed at finding his mistake.' Comics sometimes seem to come in types, and here we might find the seeds of Tommy Cooper. In his last years Liston would stand at the window of his house in Hyde Park Corner and time the regularity of the omnibuses; if one happened to be late, 'he would be in great distress.'

The comic who inherited Liston's popularity was J. B. Buckstone, who joined the Adelphi in 1827 and soon became known for 'a union of shrewdness and drollery'. He was also a prolific writer of plays and farces, with which he continued when he joined the Haymarket six years later. A contemporary critic judged that 'Mr Buckstone has much waggishness, but Mr Buckstone has no refinement. A double-entendre lurks in each eye, his smirk is the hint of an unclean presence . . . He has the true low comedy air in his walk and gesture, his face looks dry and red with long roasting before footlights. He is the son of mirth and vulgarity.' It can be supposed that this description, written in 1862, suggests a certain unease and even distaste for Buckstone's lubricious and facetious comedy. Ellen Terry's later comment may be added. 'It is a curious paradox', she wrote, 'that the play for which everyone has a good word is often the play which no one is going to see, while that which is apparently disliked and run down is crowded every night.'

Eleven

Lights! Action!

When we go from Edmund Kean to William Charles Macready, the most prominent Shakespearean actor of his day, we enter another age. In approximate terms we travel from the Georgian period to the Victorian period, with all the manifest changes that journey implies. It could also be said that we associate Kean with Byron, and Macready with Dickens.

Macready was in some ways acutely theatrical, with an expressive face, powerful voice and sonorous manner; like many of his Victorian contemporaries he was diligent and purposeful, hard-working and indefatigable. The biographer and critic John Forster commented that he had never seen 'such a grasp of thought, never such a sustained exhibition of single, profound and enduring passion'. It is significant that the critics always devoted their attention to the leading figure of the drama, and that the notion of 'ensemble' acting had never occurred to them as being important.

Another contemporary wrote of Macready that 'he was a thorough artist, very conscientious, very much in earnest.' Earnestness was the key to the mid-nineteenth century, and it marked out his dramatic style. Although he took on the great and familiar roles, he seems to have been more effective in those that expressed passion rather than nobility; he was a master of pathos, remorse and the more bravura aspects of melodrama. He was very intelligent, if inclined to be short-tempered; he was also a 'gentleman' who suffered terribly from the suspicion that his was not a gentlemanly profession – 'over-sensitive to the imaginary disrespect in which his profession is held', as George Henry Lewes put it, 'and throughout his career hating the stage, while devoting himself to the art'. He was, in other words, a thoroughly complicated and sometimes difficult actor.

Macready was born off the Euston Road in early March 1793, and had an orthodox childhood and schooling. A friend at Rugby noted, however, his 'wonderful talent for acting and speaking', which 'may be turned to good account in the Church or at the Bar'. The fact that Macready had played truant to see the child actor Master Betty, however, suggests that the compass had moved in a different direction. His father was manager of a Birmingham company and, when the boy was withdrawn from school because of debt, he sheltered under his father's patronage. This misfortune may, according to one biographer, account for the 'morbid sensitiveness on the subject of his social status that tortured him in after-years'. He joined his father's company, where his first appearance as Romeo was successful enough to lead him on to seventy different roles, including two parts opposite Sarah Siddons. 'You are in the right way,' she told him, 'but remember what I say: study, study and do not marry till you are thirty.' Siddons was always good at giving, if not taking, advice, and he followed her counsel.

The London managers, alerted to his skill, sought Macready out, and he joined Covent Garden in 1816. Leigh Hunt described him as 'one of the plainest and awkwardly made men that ever trod the stage'. Nervousness and self-consciousness may have combined to create that impression. He was pacing about the green room when he stopped a theatrical employee. 'Can you tell me, sir,' he asked him, 'about what time they generally begin to hiss tragedies at this house?' The sight of his name on the playbills thoroughly unnerved him, and throughout his life he crossed the road to avoid the experience. On his opening night at Covent Garden, in September 1816, he experienced the nervous tension that was always to beset him, with shortness of breath, palpitating heart, blurred vision and fear of forgetfulness. But these were all obstacles he was able to surmount.

Macready's roles were uneven, but he acquired his reputation with Richard iii, Hamlet, and a play by James Sheridan Knowles entitled *Virginius* (1820), one of those pseudo-classical compositions that passed for high art. It remained one of his favourites since it suited his sonorous voice and, despite Hunt's remark, his grand bearing on stage. In fact, Hunt himself observed that in Richard iii 'we expected to find declamation, and we found thought giving a soul to words.' The enterprising actor also perfected what became known as 'the Macready pause'.

Macready's most suitable role, however, was that of Macbeth. John Westland Marston, a critic and dramatic poet, observed 'his artistic power of translating his emotions into strikingly appropriate – often absolutely symbolic – forms of expression'. It is a tradition, and a technique, that survives. Another method was more obvious. Before the third act of the *Merchant of Venice* Macready would work himself into a towering rage by cursing under his breath and violently shaking a ladder fixed to the wall.

After a European holiday, Macready moved himself from Covent Garden to Drury Lane, where predictably he opened with *Virginius*; there followed a series of what might be called bread-and-butter parts. He continued a long quarrel with the manager, Alfred Bunn, who took him through fifteen classical parts including Antony; Macready had already acquired a veto over any melo-dramatic roles that he believed to be beneath his dignity, and this may have been one cause of disagreement. But he did participate in contemporary drama, adopting fifty new roles in plays recently written. In that endeavour he helped to alter the nature of stage tragedy from the heroic and the ideal to the domestic and the individual. *The Spectator* wrote that 'naturalism (an ugly but useful word) is at the basis of all Mr Macready's impersonations. To seize on an impersonation, to make it perfectly comprehensible to every capacity, to familiarise the creations of the dramatist to the spectator, rather than to hold them in a state of august elevation, seems to be his constant aim.'

Macready took over the management of Covent Garden, with the opening production of *The Winter's Tale* in the autumn of 1837. At the beginning of the following year he restaged *King Lear*, followed by *Coriolanus*. For the latter part much preparation was needed; according to Ellen Terry, no actor worthy of his hire can play it properly 'until he has been doing it for fifty nights'. That was the advantage of ensemble playing and the long run. Macready's second season was much like the first, conservative, orthodox and popular, in which he fostered new plays by Byron, Sheridan Knowles and others. It was his last season in that theatre. He returned to acting at the Haymarket in 1840 but, with the encouragement of Dickens and others, took over the management of Drury Lane in a thespian version of musical chairs.

Macready remained in charge for two seasons, from 1841 to 1843, during which time Shakespeare emerged as the most applauded among what was otherwise essentially a congeries of minor dramatists. He made very little from the enterprise, and tried to replenish his wallet with a number of short engagements and 'farewell nights'. An article in *Blackwood's Magazine* blamed the actors for the shortcomings of the London theatre; their refusal to join stock companies for long engagements, their demand for high salaries and short runs, and their domineering attitude towards the dramatists had provoked the crisis. The author added that 'it is no longer the play, but the actors, that the public are called to see.'

Macready's final visit to the United States, in 1849, was not a success. On his return to England his last, his very last, appearance was as Macbeth at Drury Lane in 1851. He then retired from the stage. He had throughout his career dominated the English theatre both with his presence, which to many was overbearing, and with his disciplined rehearsals, which for many were exacting and oppressive. He was not sympathetic to the problems of other actors, a fact that may have been part of his general dislike for his profession. Everything had to be perfectly prepared and rehearsed, and the slightest mistake elicited such searing rebukes that some actors refused to work with him.

Yet Macready did help to change the terms of tragedy from the heroic to the domestic, and from the ideal to the real. His firm and conventional manner, especially after the disciplined rowdiness of Edmund Kean, helped to raise the status of the actor in the public imagination, just as he helped to elevate legitimate drama from the 'clap-trap' and cheap spectacle that had become more and more evident. Robert Browning found Macready 'one of the most admirable and, indeed, fascinating, characters I have ever known; somewhat too sensitive for his own happiness, and much too impulsive for invariable consistency with his nobler moods'. 'It was not the loss of money that made him resign,' according to one scholar, 'but wounded vanity.' The reason is clear enough. Macready was no longer fashionable. The later nineteenth-century stage became open to unfamiliar and unexpected performers from Ellen Terry to Henry Irving. They were not a completely new breed – far from it – but they settled more comfortably within the new dispensation of steam, machinery and Queen Victoria.

This was also the era of amateur theatricals, when two or three affluent households would stage scenes or plays for the benefit of friends or neighbours. It was perhaps the most histrionic era in English history, in which the actors were as interested in social as in theatrical advancement. A few examples will suffice; Miss Fenton became Duchess of Bolton, Miss Farren became Countess of Derby, Miss Brunton became Countess of Craven, Miss O'Neill became Lady Beecher, Miss Stephens became Countess of Essex, Miss Foote became Countess of Harrington, Mrs Nisbit became Lady Boothby. And so on.

The theatre itself was the principal staple of entertainment, but in the mid-Victorian era that included Gothic melodrama, corrupted Shakespeare, opera, operetta, sentimental comedy, domestic farce, romantic drama, burletta and every conceivable form of pantomimic extravagance. The 'stock system', by which a group of actors would congregate around a principal and produce five or six plays a week, was in full flower; it was characterized by extravagance and passion rather than the development of plot or the exploration of character. That would come later, with 'long runs' and ensemble acting.

The audiences changed only slowly. The passage of the Reform Bill in 1832 expedited the progress and self-confidence of the middle class, who were the most likely candidates for the better seats. But in certain quarters, and in certain theatres, the populace was unmoved. A German observer noted 'an unheard roughness and coarseness . . . the noise and mischief so incessant that it is difficult to understand how such distinguished artists can perform at all with so brutal, so indifferent and ignorant an audi-ence'. The middle class had not entirely supplanted the traditional playgoers. It is a salutary reminder of the conditions in which Kean or Garrick, for example, had been obliged to work.

Lesser actors were still treated with contempt, and were gener-ally considered to be members of a trade rather than a profession. 'Almost every young person', Lewes wrote, 'imagines he could act, if he tried.' A different response came from the young Charles Dickens, who himself took up acting for brief periods. He recalled 'the poetry, the lights, the music, the company, the stupendous changes of glittering and brilliant scenery'. He was more than a little stage-struck, but he conveys the allure the theatre held for many Londoners in the nineteenth century. There was in fact a theatrical 'boom'; three playhouses opened in the 1820s, but no fewer than fourteen were established in the 1830s. After the duopoly of Drury Lane and Covent Garden was abolished by parliamentary edict in 1843 (with the Haymarket still considered 'low'), there was a further resurgence of London drama. Ten theatres were in operation for the winter season of 1807, but thirty-four had emerged by the 1870s. The number of actors increased in proportion. It has been surmised that the total of 1,357 actors in 1841 had risen by almost three times twenty years later, and doubled again by 1891. The theatres themselves had not improved greatly. Gas lighting, instead of candlelight, was introduced at the Olympia in 1818, but by the 1830s it was still relatively uncommon; candles, which stayed alight for the entire performance, and oil lamps were still standard. This was the ambiance in which the Victorian actors worked.

One of the earliest, raised and cultivated in the nineteenth century, was Samuel Phelps; he was born in Plymouth in 1804, and spent his formative acting years on the provincial circuits. It was a hard apprenticeship, lasting in effect from 1826 to his performance as Shylock at the Haymarket in 1837, but he gained favourable attention for his rigorous characterization and his command of an audience. There must have been many who believed that his talents were wasted, and he seemed destined to be compared unfavourably with the players of the previous generation, such as Kean, Kemble and Macready.

The early nineteenth century was not necessarily bursting with great actors, but any available talent was snatched up. After the success of Shylock, Macready wrested Phelps from the grip of Benjamin West at the Haymarket, and installed him at Covent Garden. This was the way of the London world. Phelps joined Macready no doubt in response to vague promises of glory, and began to play a number of Shakespearean roles, including Hamlet, Othello and Richard III. But Macready sensed a rival. When

Phelps triumphed in *Othello*, Macready decided to confine him to secondary roles. He could not bear any hint of comparison.

Phelps ended his servitude in 1844, when he was hired as manager of the Sadler's Wells theatre; it was not quite the centre of the English theatre, but it sufficed for Phelps's plans to present 'the real drama of England'. He opened that year with *Macbeth*, in which he played the lead to great acclaim. Six of Shakespeare's dramas followed. One of his actors commented that Phelps 'had something of the irritability of Macready, and was not slow to give stupid, or, still more, careless people the rough side of his tongue; but his heart was so evidently in his work . . . never sacrificing other scenes to his own, or other actors to himself.' He helped to reverse the fashion for the individual 'star', who was often the actor-manager, in favour of the 'ensemble' system, in which all played a part. This, after Kean and Macready, was a welcome change.

Phelps also received much praise for his reworking of Shakespeare. Of Falstaff it was noted that he 'lays stress not on *Falstaff's* sensuality, but on the lively intellect that stands for soul as well as mind in his gross body . . . [Falstaff] is not vulgarised in Mr Phelps's reading.' He managed fifteen seasons at Sadler's Wells and can be said to have been successful in them all. That theatre's reputation spread so widely that according to Marston in *Our Recent Actors* (1888), 'it became a sort of pilgrim's shrine to the literary men of London, to the younger members of the Inns of Court, and to those denizens of the West in whom poetic taste still lingered.' It also became the resort of 'our working classes in a happy crowd, as orderly and reverent as if they were at church'. They had come to see Shakespeare, but they had also come to watch Phelps, who, according to Henry Morley's *Journal of a London Playgoer* (1866), had 'of late years been the personator of about thirty of the characters of Shakespeare. Great men or small, heroes or cowards, sages or simpletons, sensual or spiritual men, he has taken all as characters that Shakespeare painted, studied them minutely, and embodied each in what he thinks to be a true Shakespearean form.' He acted in an unaffected and restrained manner; by his example, Morley continued, the other actors learned 'how to subdue excesses of expression that by giving undue force to one part would destroy the balance of the whole'.

Sadler's Wells also rivalled the provincial companies in its willingness to train young or inexperienced actors in the ways of the stage. It resembled the provincial stock companies, too, in performing a different play each night. This was in itself a memorable achievement, worlds apart from the chicanery and greed of most actor-managers of the time. Certainly it was the best possible complement of Phelps's acting. One theatrical historian recorded: 'He was at his very best in the keen analysis of human weakness – in happy and credulous vanity, in the dry raillery that satirizes human failings and inconsistencies, in the crabbed regrets and fretting apprehensions of age, and in the obsequiousness which sees through and despises those whom it flatters.' It was said of Phelps's method that 'not a speech, not a sentiment, not a line, but shows an immense amount of study; and the meaning is brought out by all the resources of the histrionic art – the emphasis, the pause, the intonation in all of its varieties of modulation and falsetto.' Two words would become susceptible of change, 'histrionic' and 'falsetto', which indeed were eventually considered to be mannered and rhetorical.

So Phelps lived long enough to hear his acting style ridiculed and his mannerisms disparaged. No actor has ever emerged unscathed from the scythe of time and fashion. Poetic drama had been abandoned, for example, and such traditions as the necessity of the players standing during a tragic scene were ignored. How much of this was affected by the changes of audience, as well as those of social convention, cannot properly be gauged.

The strain of sole management had worn Phelps down, but he continued his acting career at Drury Lane for another seven years. His wife and two sons died in the interim, but acting is a fever that, for some players, no amount of misfortune can alleviate. He died in 1878, having seen through much of the century whose theatrical tradition he refined and developed. Of all the great actor-managers, he is the one still most overlooked, having fallen into the shadowland between Macready and Irving. But it can perhaps be remembered that, at a speech in the Mansion House in 1876, he passionately advocated a national theatre to carry on the Shakespearean tradition.

One of Phelps's near contemporaries, Alfred Wigan, began life as a 'wandering minstrel', but by the age of twenty, in 1834, he was appearing at the Lyceum and then at the Queen's Theatre in Tottenham Street; in what capacity he played is not entirely clear, although he seems to have specialized in music and singing. He moved from small part to small part, from a play by Dickens to the role of Tom Tug in Dibdin's *The Waterman*. His most illustrious role was opposite Madame Vestris at Covent Garden. He remained there for five years before moving in shuttlecock fashion from the Strand to the Lyceum, from Drury Lane to the Haymarket, from the Olympic to the Princess's and on to the Adelphi. Clearly he was in demand, but the *Dictionary of National Biography* describes him as 'actor, rope-dancer and performer on stilts'. Perhaps he practised all three at once. Wigan was also reputed to be a scholar of the French language, and he did not waste the opportunity of becoming a stage Frenchman for the London public. He was characterized, however, for 'refinement, delicate perception and truth to nature, combined with deep though quiet feeling'; *The Times* describes how in *The Corsican Brothers* 'everything like commonplace exaggeration is shunned, and the language is made to approximate as much as possible to that of real life.' He worked in watercolours rather than in oils. It was said in a critical survey that 'the character of Mr Wigan's acting was almost unique in his time.'

We might place Wigan beside Frederick Robson, who was at his best in the burlesque of such diverse characters as Shylock and Medea. Of the latter part it was said that 'the foundation of the acting was essentially tragic,' and that the exaggeration of style comprised the burlesque. With some actors it would have been difficult to distinguish exaggeration from deliberate comedy. Of Robson's Shylock, *The Times* reported that it belonged to the 'histrionic phenomena of the day'.

Robson began his professional life in a small theatre in Whitstable as 'second utility', although no one now knows what that meant; possibly it refers to a part that is small but vital, the sort of role known in opera as 'fifth business'. But it was only the beginning of a career that *The Times* considered to be that of 'the greatest actor on the English stage since the days of Edmund Kean'. Robson's style was that of burlesque but, as Morley put it, 'his merit – and it amounted to genius – lay in his rare power of combining tragic passion and real hints of the terrible with ludicrous burlesque.' It was reported that 'Robson made the listener feel because he felt himself.' Marston remarked that 'nothing could be more microscopic than his observation of characteristics.' That is perhaps the highest accolade for a comedian.

Robson engaged in seasonal tours, by which winding road he arrived in London and, specifically, at the Olympic Theatre, where in 1853 his song 'Villikins and His Dinah' was one of the most popular of the age. When he played in Henry Mayhew's *The Nervous Minstrel* at the same theatre, a critic wrote that 'so vivid a picture of an outcast street musician, ragged, miry, miserable, his limbs racked and distorted with rheumatism, his voice hoarse and broken with constant exposure to rough weather, had not been seen before on the stage.' And yet 'what a roar of merriment greeted the appearance of the woebegone little figure of Robson . . . where with an intensely comic look of abject misery, he silently surveyed the already convulsed audience.' He combined the terrible with the droll, so that audiences were never sure whether to laugh or cry.

Robson possessed an extremely nervous personality, and would moan in the wings, 'I daren't go on, I daren't go on.' A dash of liquor and a hefty push would resolve his doubts. He was very small, at 1.5 metres (5 ft), with a very large head but small feet and hands. He had a passion for flowers, which soothed him. It was an arduous life, however, and he died at the age of forty-three in August 1864.

Twelve

Females in front

Some female actors in this period could take over the stage in managerial as well as theatrical terms. One such was Lucia Elizabeth Mathews, known universally as Madame Vestris, who emerged into the world by way of Dean Street, Soho, in 1797. At the age of sixteen she married a dancing master, Armand Vestris, and began her career as a mezzo-soprano. But in a city where opera singers were idolized, she did not quite meet the required standard. She took to the stage, and in 1820 to breeches parts at Drury Lane, where she was admired for the next ten years. Male costume suited her.

In 1830 Madame Vestris leased the Olympic Theatre on the understanding that she would present musical entertainments, or at least entertainments with music, in which she often played a not inconsiderable role. This she did with brio, and she refurbished the theatre at the same time; performances finished at eleven, which allowed the affluent middle class to make their way home. 'It was, I fancy,' Westland Marston wrote in *Our Recent Actors*, 'her practice of taking the house into her confidence, combined with her coquetry and personal attractions, that rendered Vestris so bewitching to the public.'

Vestris had a change of heart in every sense. In 1835 she hired Charles Mathews, the son of the famous comedian with the same name, and three years later she married him, her first husband

146

having died some years before. They made an engaging couple, or duet, in the light comedy that they introduced to the Lyceum, of which they purchased the management. Mathews himself wrote later that 'the lighter phase of comedy, representing the more natural and less laboured school of modern life, and holding the mirror up to nature without regard to the conventionalities of the theatre, was the aim I had in view.' Madame Vestris fully shared his enthusiasm, but their hopes for similar success in the United States were not always fulfilled.

On their return to London, however, they leased Covent Garden, where they commissioned contemporary comedies as well as Shakespearean revivals that avoided all the historical paraphernalia that had previously weighed down the dramas. Madame Vestris was attuned to lightness, extravagance and gaiety. One theatrical historian recalled that 'her highest effort . . . was in portraying of a tremulous and giddy joy, a rapture bordering on frenzy.' Her greatest success was in Dion Boucicault's *London Assurance*, materially helped by her concern for detail and her taste for lavish interiors. It was said that 'when not on the stage she was constantly in her private box, watching the performance, noticing the slightest imperfection.'

There followed, however, a period in which lightness and gaiety were noticeably absent. It was a time of vicious internecine warfare between managers and theatres, of deceit and double-crossing that could rival any pirate drama. It concluded in debt, disaster and unremitting work simply to maintain the standards that Madame Vestris expected. In 1847 she and her husband once more leased the Lyceum, among the repertoire of which were French imports in which they again performed as a light-hearted comic couple. One of their collaborators was James Robinson Planché, who, despite his surname, was born in Piccadilly; he shared the keen interest of Madame Vestris in classical burlesque, and in the space of the Lyceum he embroidered his burlesques into extravaganzas close to operatic models. Vestris herself complemented the effect with luxurious interiors of carpets, furniture and ceiling cloths. She was one of the pioneers of the 'box set'. It was successful dramatically but disastrous financially. People were dressed and brought in to fill the theatre; they were known as 'Humphs' after the actor who first employed the trick, Humph Barnett. Mathews was imprisoned for debt, and was released five days before his wife died of cancer on 8 August 1856. As an actress Madame Vestris was renowned for her glamour; as a manager she was unrivalled for her efficiency and probity.

In the latter decades of the nineteenth century, when the middle-class family became the paradigm of domestic life, there emerged a social drama in which representative middle-class characters, fortunately blessed by wit and elegance that might otherwise have been in short supply, became engaged in domestic complications and moral dilemmas of a generally discreet or reticent kind. It was known as cup-and-saucer drama. The masters of this art were Oscar Wilde, Arthur Wing Pinero and perhaps George Bernard Shaw, while its early practitioners included Squire Bancroft and Lady Bancroft, who played opposite each other in a series of modern comedies.

Squire Bancroft admitted that 'often as I went to the play, dearly as I loved the theatre, until I tried to become an actor I had never known one.' So he ventured on to the provincial stage, playing 346 parts in four years and in the process encountering a new generation of actors who would flourish in the 1860s and beyond. One of these, Marie Wilton, he married; together they became the Bancrofts, who played society comedy with a carefully selected and loyal cast. Bancroft said of one such play, *Caste* by Thomas William Robertson, that 'the characters looked and talked so like beings of everyday life that they were mistaken for such, and the audience had a curiosity to know how they were getting on after the fall of the curtain.' This may be considered the triumph of naturalism. The Bancrofts also fully developed the style of the box set, so it seemed to the audience that they were looking into a real drawing room with its sofas, chairs and table. The dialogue did not necessarily rise above that level.

In 1865, the year after they met, the Bancrofts took over the Prince of Wales's Theatre in Tottenham Court Road, where they opened appropriately with Thomas William Robertson's *Society*. It was the year in which John Stuart Mill was elected to Parliament with a demand for women's suffrage, but this made it no easier for female actors. There were no schools or academies, and their only assistance came from mutual friends in the profession or from letters of recommendation. Even if they were accepted for minor parts they were forced to lead a precarious and often impoverished existence. Their hope was to join a touring company where employment, at least, was assured. And they were still only paid half the amount given to the men. Theatrical conditions were also less than ideal. Clement Scott, in *The Drama of Yesterday and Today* (1899), wrote that 'there was an interval of stage squalor and untidiness, a careless slipshod method of dressing the stage.'

This was all to change. As Scott put it, 'The Bancrofts came at the right time to reform that vulgarity altogether.' The pair eventually moved on to the Haymarket, where they lavished all the expense that comfortable audiences required. The pit was abolished and the raucous days of the Old Price riots were over. When Mrs Bancroft made her entrance she reported that there was 'a roar of affectionate welcome, hearty and prolonged'. The Victorian middle class had at last taken over. Henry James surveyed the new Haymarket and wrote that the theatre had become 'the perfection of a place of entertainment. Brilliantly luxuriant, softly cushioned, and perfectly aired . . . and the stage set all around in an immense gilded frame, like that of some magnificent picture. Within this frame the stage, with everything that is upon it, glows with a radiance that seems the very atmosphere of comedy.'

The old order was passing away, with the demise or retirement of Macready, the Keans and the original Kembles. But the 'new school' of domestic realism, coming into prominence, was not altogether a success. There was no Shaw or Ibsen among the playwrights, and at this late date it is difficult to distinguish their different styles.

A 'natural' style, however, was eventually employed by Fanny Kemble, who remained on the stage without scenery or props. She stood in front of her audience and for an hour recited passages from Shakespeare. It was not a novel approach – her father and aunt had done it before her – but it acquired the atmosphere of the theatre without the paraphernalia she hated. She had begun in more conventional circumstances as an integral member of the Kemble family. Her parents were both accomplished actors; Sarah Siddons was her aunt, and John Philip Kemble her uncle. Her blood might as well have been stage blood. In 1829, in the face of familial bankruptcy, she took the stage as Juliet. The *Monthly Magazine* remarked that 'the illusion she was Shakespeare's own Juliet came so speedily upon us as to suspend the power of specific criticism . . . In boldness and dignity she unquestionably approaches more nearly to Mrs Siddons.' There may have come a time when she grew tired of being compared to her aunt. But in the beginning she was grateful. It was the first role she had ever played and, even so, she was a great success. How much of this was owing to her lineage, and how much to her individual talent, is impossible to gauge.

Kemble filled Covent Garden for the rest of the season, and she attempted in the new fashion to convey the 'mental state' of the character. But how could she do this in a culture of spectacle and sensation? It was one of the reasons for her distaste for the acting profession. She was not conventionally attractive, being short and dark-eyed, and possessed an unusually deep voice that she described as a baritone. But her real problem lay in the fact that she had been thrown head first on to the stage without any training in elocution or deportment, let alone in acting. She may have felt that her family would see her through, and as a result she relied on the twin forces of instinct and inspiration as the alternatives to technique and training. On one occasion she shrieked at a violent scene and then ran off the stage, still screaming, hastening down the stairs into the street until she was brought to her senses.

Kemble was a quick learner, however, and mastered a different play every month. When the London theatres were closed after the season, she toured the provincial theatres. But for some reason, despite her heritage, she believed the theatre was somehow beneath her. She confessed, 'I do not think it is the acting itself that is so disagreeable to me, but the public personal exhibition, the violence done . . . to womanly dignity and decorum in thus becoming the gaze of every eye and theme of every tongue.' Most of the critics disagreed. In the 'Noctes Ambrosianae' of *Blackwood's Magazine*, one critic wrote that 'her attitudes . . . her appearance, her apparition [are] beautiful . . . they are also classical – that is to say, the spirit of Art breathes in and over the spirit of Nature . . . [she] is a girl of genius.' Just as hostile journalists could plumb subterranean depths of vitriol, so the more benevolent could reach effortlessly for hyperboles of praise.

In the early 1830s the economic troubles of the London theatre, always in a perilous state, sent Kemble and her father to the United States for a tour of two years. There she married, and to her great relief abandoned her acting career. But her relief was short-lived; she discovered that her husband was a slave-owner, and eventually decided to put some distance between them. In 1847, having left her husband, she gave her first solo readings of Shakespeare in a tour of the country. It inaugurated a career that she pursued to great acclaim for the next fifteen years.

By the time she returned to London in 1877, Kemble had created a repertoire of twenty-four plays with particular attention to 'the beauty of the plays as poetical compositions'. Everyone left satisfied at this demonstration of what was known as 'rational entertainment'. It has been recorded of this period that 'education, refinement, and general knowledge, have rendered all classes more exacting'; as a result, 'modern audiences are less enthusiastic in the outward and visible tokens of their delight' and less given to applause, cheers, hisses or even riot. But Fanny Kemble had left all that theatrical mayhem with relief. She had earned enough to live comfortably in both England and America, dying in London in 1893.

Helena Faucit survived Kemble by only five years, but she accumulated enough experience and expertise to turn herself into the greatest actress of her generation. Faucit came, like so many actors, from a theatrical family, in which her uncle 'taught me the value of the different metres in blank verse and rhyme . . . he made me understand the value of words, nay, of every letter of every word, for the purposes of declamation.' She made her first appearance on the stage at Richmond in 1833, at the age of nineteen, when inevitably she played Juliet.

But Faucit was disappointed by her performance because 'I had not the true artistic power to lose myself in the being of her character.' This was an art that she tried all her life to master. She studied her characters with intense sympathy and careful imitation; she shared their emotions, as far as she could, and exhibited their shifts of mood and motive as if she were living them. 'If she has not the art to conceal art,' one critic said, 'the art she does not conceal is true, is founded on quick and refined perception of the poetry she is interpreting.' Such praise became familiar.

Faucit bided her time at the small theatre in Richmond, and in Brighton, but after two years she was called to London to fill the gap left by Fanny Kemble on her travels. In 1836 she made her debut at Covent Garden, playing Julia in James Sheridan Knowles's *The Hunchback*, and she aroused so much enthusiasm that she was given a three-year contract as leading lady. A reviewer of that play noticed her 'rare merit' of responding to other actors' words 'as if hearing them for the first time'. This is a more difficult gift than is generally imagined. But her spontaneity was part of a larger attempt to depict the psychological truth of the character, whom for the duration of the play she imagined to be real.

Faucit came under the tutelage of Macready when he became manager of the theatre shortly afterwards, and in the next season she acted with him, and also with Charles Kemble. She nourished a real though unconsummated devotion to Macready, so that when he moved on to the Haymarket, she moved with him. She also accompanied him when he subsequently joined Drury Lane. In this period she took on nine separate Shakespearean roles and many more new parts. Macready described her as 'beyond all compare the best English actress'.

When Macready sailed to the United States, Faucit started on a provincial tour of her own country, where she earned more plaudits than ever. She played Pauline in Edward Bulwer-Lytton's *The Lady of Lyons*, and Lady Macbeth in Edinburgh; the *Glasgow Stage* described her as 'Glasgow's favourite actress', and she created a frenzy in Cork and Limerick. When she played Antigone in Dublin, it seemed to the audience that the past itself had been resurrected. She combined the statuesque with a living radiance, the classical form with felt emotion. She was so successful in Paris that Macready, after his return from the United States, refused to act with her.

On her arrival or, rather, renaissance in London, Faucit played Lady Macbeth at Drury Lane, where once more she caused a sensation. The *Morning Post* remarked that 'there has been rarely, if ever, a more truthful or more impassioned performance.' She practised a technique known as 'dilation', by rising on her toes, lifting up her head, extending her arms and expanding her voice. This strategy could stop the show with calls and cries or what were known as 'enraptured bursts of applause'. Her work and her travels never ceased, but any account of them would be a recital of critical applause and popular success, gifts and dinners and laudatory addresses. It is perhaps remarkable, however, that in her early fifties Faucit was still playing the parts she had first taken on as a juvenile lead. 'People saw in her not only a great actress,' her biographer wrote, 'they felt themselves in the presence of one who was in herself the ideal woman of whom poets have written.'

In 1851 Faucit married Theodore Martin, whom she had first met eight years before, and the couple settled in Wales and London, interrupted by her occasional forays into theatrical territory. She died in 1898 and was buried in Brompton Cemetery. She was without doubt the most versatile and accomplished actor of the period. She may not have had the face of Sarah Siddons, but she possessed 'the whole beauty arising from powerful and changing expression', with a voice whose 'deep intonations and flexible richness' captivated an audience. She was described as 'psychological', or 'intellectual', or 'poetically natural', which means only that there were no appropriate words to describe her unique apprehension of character and style. The dramatic critic Joseph Knight perhaps put it more simply when he called Faucit 'the greatest interpreter of the poetic drama that living memory can recall'. She had emerged at a time when drama had frequently degenerated into burlesque or song and dance. In her wish to elevate it, she took up the standard of her sex. Her predecessors in the nineteenth century had wanted to become respectable; she simply wished to be professional.

Thirteen

Studies in contrast

'For an actor who can't walk, can't talk and has no face to speak of,' Henry Irving once told Ellen Terry, 'I've done pretty well.' This most puzzling of actors, born in 1838, came to the stage at a moment of theatrical transition. As a result, he became an enigma. Some called him naturalistic, and others romantic; some called him melodramatic, and others realistic. Some thought him artificial, while others considered him genuine. Some criticized his voice and others praised it. He was for some the last representative of the old school, and for others the beginning of a new. He was considered a great stage manager, but the sole object of attention was himself. He was a selfish and self-absorbed man, but he thoroughly understood his public. He was an obsessive who from morning to night thought only of the theatre, yet he behaved like the most restrained of Englishmen.

Irving knew his own contradictions. People said he was 'always Irving', but no one knew what that really meant. He took pains to create his part on stage, but not necessarily to interpret it; he always retained control over his emotion. 'In his assumed character,' the artist Walford Graham Robertson said, 'he was anxious to give expression to everything; as himself he was careful to tell nothing.'

Irving's real name was John Henry Brodribb, and at the age of eighteen, feeling that it sounded too middle-class for a young man with aspirations, he changed it. He was born in Somerset and for the first eleven years he lived with his aunt and uncle in Cornwall. Despite his slow climb to eminence, he never entirely lost his rural habits. Terry was amazed that, before he picked her up on stage, he would spit on his hands. At the age of eleven he returned to his parents in London, where he trod the familiar path from schoolboy to clerk, but – like most great actors – he had immortal longings, and, having seen Samuel Phelps as Hamlet, he acquired the edge of steel to cut down the obstacles in his way.

One member of Phelps's company introduced the young Irving (as he now called himself) to the actor, who offered him a minor role. But, understanding that it would be catastrophic to fail on his first appearance in London, Irving preferred to test himself on the provincial stage. He joined the Lyceum Theatre in Sunderland and spent the next fifteen years learning his trade or, rather, his profession in a succession of small theatres; it is recorded that he played more than seven hundred parts in this period, during which he became a confident 'heavy' despite his very thin legs and odd nervous mannerisms. His voice was a mystery, elucidated by Henry James as 'the strange tissue of arbitrary pronunciations which floats in the thankless medium of Mr Irving's harsh, monotonous voice.'

Irving was not sturdy, nor was he particularly graceful. He was tall and thin, with a long face. One friend recalled 'his walk, somewhat resembling that of a fretful man trying to get very quickly over a ploughed field'; the critic William Archer believed that his locomotion 'was not a result of volition, but an involuntary spasm'. Some believed he had a wooden leg, but no one knew which of the two it was. He was often troubled and uncertain but covered his insecurity with the force of mid-Victorian energy and bravado.

The artist Mortimer Menpes sensed the presence of some inner conviction. '[Irving] radiated some subtle force,' he said, 'before which all men became modest and even reverential.' His legs may have been weak but his eyes were piercing and his hands long and graceful; he took care that they should always be seen as if they were engaged in some form of the mesmerism that was then fashionable. That is why he made himself the object of all eyes. It was often noticed that there was a strong feminine streak in Irving's style, but that is by no means unusual, and may be inevitable in a great actor who must learn the dimensions of being fully human. Other critics offered a different interpretation. 'He danced, he did not merely walk,' Edward Gordon Craig wrote, 'he sang, he by no means merely spoke. He was essentially artificial in distinction to being merely natural.'

But Irving's strongest gift was the power of will. One critic noted that 'his artistic life was one long struggle towards perfection, fault after fault he conquered, one by one he laid by his mannerisms, line by line he modelled the beautiful, sensitive face that he had evolved from his original immobile and rather ordinary features.' He was to be seen with 'a huge silk hat, monkish features, iron-grey hair'. He had an overcoat with a fur collar, which became the characteristic dress of an impresario, and a broad-brimmed 'wide-awake' hat like that of a Quaker. He had created himself as a sculptor might fashion a statue. He escaped from himself or, rather, he hid from himself. When he played Hamlet 'he was one of those who . . . will pace rooms like wild animals, will gaze into looking-glasses until they are frightened at the expression of their own eyes, will talk aloud.' It is not necessary to believe that Irving was just such a man, only that he could drag him up from the depths.

If Irving was indeed a neurasthenic hero, it may have in part stemmed from guilt. He was raised a strict Methodist, for whom the theatre is the devil's plaything. It was often said that he possessed a 'magnetic personality', whatever that means, but it is also a fact that he never stirred his audience to wild enthusiasm. He did not necessarily inspire. Seeing him was like reading Shakespeare by the roseate hue of an oil lamp.

In the summer of 1870 Irving was the principal character in a new play, James Albery's *Two Roses*, which ran for almost three hundred nights at the Lyceum. But this was only the prelude to what was to become his most enduring success in the same theatre, Leopold David Lewis's *The Bells*. But it came at a cost. Returning home with his wife after the successful first night, he turned to her: 'Well, my dear, we shall soon have our own carriage and pair.' She was not impressed. 'Are you going to go on making a fool of yourself like this all your life?' Irving stopped the carriage and stepped out. He never spoke to his wife again. It was as if she had ripped out his heart.

But no force on Earth could tear Irving away from his vocation. His *Hamlet* ran for two hundred nights. After the death of the manager of the Lyceum, he eventually took his place and remained there for twenty-three years, during which period he became, in the slang of the day, a 'theatrical legend'. Everyone knew Henry Irving. 'Here', a critic wrote, 'was the Hamlet who *thinks aloud*; here was the scholar, and so little of the actor.' His reign was unrivalled in nineteenth-century theatre, and everyone imitated him, respectfully or maliciously. He presented generally uncut and uncensored Shakespeare as well as the melodramas that were the fashion of the time. He also became an expert in scenic illusion and, for the first time, darkened the auditorium so that the play became a glowing picture. Shaw said, however, that if you looked closely at him you would find he has no face.

Irving insisted that everything be, in the phrase of the day, 'rotten perfect'. When asked about his best part, his response was Hamlet. 'Oh no, sir,' his companion replied, 'Macbeth. You sweat twice as much in that.' He never economized on theatrical effects, and worked with artists such as Lawrence Alma-Tadema and Edward Burne-Jones, as well as with musicians such as Arthur Sullivan. He garnered the fruits of mid-Victorian culture and, in the process, fashioned the theatre into the supreme public art. But it was not an easy journey. Irving said, in memory of Edmund Kean, that 'the road to success lies through many a thorny course, across many a dreary stretch of desert land, over many an obstacle, from which the fainting heart is often tempted to turn back.'

Irving began working with Ellen Terry in a production of *Hamlet* in 1878. Their first encounters were not promising; he found her frivolous, while she found him dull and awkward and described him as 'conceited and almost savagely proud of the isolation in which he lived'. She noticed, too, that his technical accomplishments were not comparable to her own. But theatrical differences do not last for ever. She joined Irving's company at the Lyceum that year, and they made a perfect theatrical couple, who played together for twenty-five years. They revived their great successes and rejuvenated Shakespeare's more difficult plays. They even mixed some 'blood and thunder' drama into the brew. There were rumours of a romance offstage, but nothing was known for certain. Perhaps they both had too much to lose in their ascent.

Irving reached the summit in social terms when in 1895 he was the first actor to be offered, and to accept, a knighthood from Lord Rosebery. But misfortune often succeeds success. Melodrama, to which he had devoted much time and energy, was losing its appeal for the public. Nevertheless, Irving turned his back on the new acting and the new drama of ideas in order to continue in his strong vein of Shakespeare and melodrama. He surmounted criticism by his consistent regard for character, and for his understanding of minute detail in gesture, voice and movement. One critic described his acting as 'evidently the result of much thought and psychological study'. That would never become old-fashioned. Shaw, however, was one of his fiercest critics. He wrote that 'the history of the Lyceum, with its twenty years' steady cultivation of the actor as a personal force, and its utter neglect of the drama, is the history of the English stage during that period.' It was a direct hit against Irving.

But private misfortunes also assailed Irving. He became seriously unwell with emphysema, and a fire in the scene storage of the Lyceum destroyed the sets for forty-four plays. He died in October 1905 and was buried in Westminster Abbey with all the signs of national mourning for a Cornish boy who had risen unaided to the pinnacle of his profession. But that profession had already suffered a sea change. James Anderson, a contemporary actor, noted as early as 1860 that 'the change that has taken place in things theatrical in the past few years is something wonderful . . . all is now hurry-scurry, bustle and haste; melodrama and burlesque have taken the place of tragedy and comedy; poetry and romance are voted slow; and the actors speak with such rapidity of utterance as to give one the idea that they are rushing to catch an express train.'

This was perhaps the setting for Ellen Terry, who, like so many of her professional colleagues, came from a theatrical family and was introduced to the stage at a very young age. At nine she played Puck, and Mamillius in *The Winter's Tale*. Soon afterwards she was at the Royalty, and at the Theatres Royal of Bristol and Bath, before returning to London at the Haymarket. Her journey may have been expedited by her position in what would become known as 'the Terry family'. London could in fact be said to be governed by a number of theatrical dynasties for whom the green rooms were a second home.

Terry enjoyed a wholly professional education in every sense. She married into the artistic hierarchy with an artist, George Frederic Watts, but then began a liaison with an architect, Edward William Godwin. Only the best would do.

At the age of twenty-seven Terry returned to the stage in the conventional roles of Shakespearean heroines, but the following year she joined with the Bancrofts at the Prince of Wales's Theatre in Tottenham Court Road. There she experienced an epiphany. She was playing Portia in *The Merchant of Venice* when she realized that the response of the audience was radiant beyond any of her experiences. She was possessed by 'the feeling of a conqueror ... "What can this be?" I thought. "*This is different.*"' *Fraser's Magazine* wrote that 'as she moved through the changing scene, every new incident seemed to touch some new feeling; and each change of feeling expressed itself by voice, countenance or gesture in a manner so lively and natural that it was felt at once to be both true in itself and in harmony with the rest.' She was praised for her 'natural' style of acting, combined with a gaiety that seems to have been a familial trait.

Herbert Beerbohm Tree said of this production that it marked 'the Renaissance of theatrical art in England'. In her *Memoirs*, Terry associated the powerful effect of the production with the burgeoning aesthetic movement, which had changed the appearance of the stage for ever 'with a more gorgeous and complete little spectacle [that] had never before been seen on the English stage'. But it also changed her. She had discovered herself, and for the next twenty years she was the classical heroine nonpareil. It was at this point that she joined Irving's company at the Lyceum, to remain for more than twenty years. Irving said that her pathos was 'nature helped by genius'. *Iolanthe* was produced for her, together with *Romeo and Juliet*, *Much Ado about Nothing* and *Twelfth Night*.

Terry learned by experience, by trial and failure, to find the wit and self-confidence of a strong woman, however nervous she might appear off the stage. She wrote once that 'my real tears on the stage astonished some people ... but they have often been a hindrance to me. I have had to work to restrain them.' She helped to fashion the 'new woman', even though she insisted on the significance of love and devotion in marriage. Bram Stoker, Irving's personal assistant, wrote that 'Ellen Terry's art is wonderfully true. She has not only the instinct of truth, but the ability to reproduce it in the different perspective of the stage.' She herself argued that the women of Shakespeare's time inspired his heroines. 'Wonderful women!' she wrote. 'Have you ever thought how much we all and women especially, owe to Shakespeare for his vindication of woman in these fearless high-spirited, resolute and intelligent heroines!'

Some notes on Terry's copy of *Romeo and Juliet* provide an indication of her approach:

Get the words into your remembrance first of all. Then, (as you have to convey the meaning of the words to *some* who have ears, but don't hear, and eyes, but don't see) put the words into the simplest vernacular. Then exercise your judgement about their sound . . . so many different ways of speaking words! Beware of sound and fury signifying nothing. Voice unaccompanied by imagination, dreadful . . . Imagination and intelligence absolutely necessary to realize and portray high and low imaginings. Voice, yes, but not mere voice production. You must have a sensitive ear, and a sensitive judgement of the effect on your audience. But all the time you must be trying to please *yourself* . . . Get yourself in *tune*. Then you can let fly your imagination, and the words will seem to be supplied by yourself. Shakespeare supplied by oneself! Oh! Realism? Yes, if we mean by that real feeling, real sympathy. But people seem to mean by it only the realism of low-down things . . . To act, you must make the thing written your own. You must steal the words, steal the thought, and *convey* the stolen treasure to others with great art.

It is as good an introduction to acting as any.

It is often clear that the newspaper critics of the nineteenth century will treat each actor's version of Lady Macbeth differently, to the extent that no comparison can be made between them. The public might attend *The Merchant of Venice* or *King Lear* several times because on each occasion it was, for them, an entirely different play. Throughout that century 'pictorialism' was the theme, and the long, tender lines of the picturesque scenario were as important as any of the lines spoken on the stage. The scenic artist would often imitate paintings of the period in which the play was set, as Irving managed with Paolo Veronese in *The Merchant of Venice*. In the same spirit the scene-painters took on added significance, and at the beginning of the century landscape artists, such as Clarkson Stanfield and David Roberts, were intimately connected with the production. Irving at the Lyceum and Bancroft at the Haymarket turned their respective stages into kinetic works of art. It was said of Terry herself that 'somehow or other Miss Terry always is a perfect version of the picturesque . . . no lady on the modern stage is so much of a picture in herself, or falls so readily into the composition of the larger picture formed by the combination of a drama.'

In 1903 Terry took over the management of the Imperial Theatre, where she specialized in the work of Shaw and Ibsen. She was one of a number of female actors who assumed management in this period, and it can be celebrated as the most successful era of the female actor-manager. By 1912 there were four female performers who were successfully organizing London theatres. Perhaps the most notable of them was Lilian Baylis at the Royal Victoria Music Hall, which became known as the Old Vic. This was also the period when the female player came to the fore. In theatrical terms the mid- to late nineteenth century was the age of the woman.

Terry's association with artists encouraged her interest in visual symbolism and the decoration of sets. More significantly, she took an intense interest in costume, to the extent that the clothing she wore demanded a certain type of character and thus a different type of acting. Henry James said that she resembled a pre-Raphaelite drawing; that produced one recognizable style. In 1906, to mark her fiftieth year on the stage, the crowds cheered and danced in the streets adjoining Drury Lane.

Terry's heroines under Irving's management might threaten to become a crowd with, among others, Ophelia, Portia, Desdemona, Juliet, Viola, Cordelia, Imogen and Lady Macbeth. She sailed on imperturbably. Dublin's *University Magazine* suggested that 'All the deeper human emotions are closed to her. She cannot command, she cannot defy, she cannot even despair.' Perhaps it is true that at the centre of many great actors there lies a vacancy. But, by the alchemy of popular acclaim, she became a feminist icon before the concept of feminism was introduced.

Terry carried on acting even as she took over the management of the Imperial. She recited, she lectured and she experimented with the Talking Machine Company with extracts from Shakespeare. She could not resist the allure of the new medium of the cinematograph; from 1916 she appeared in a number of silent films even as she continued a conventional career on the stage that was not concluded until 1920. She died of a cerebral haemorrhage in 1928, at the age of eighty-one.

There could be no greater contrast with the actress who followed Terry in public recognition. Mrs Patrick Campbell, baptised Beatrice Stella Tanner, was born in Kensington in 1865. She started in amateur dramatics but began her professional career in Liverpool, having made an ill-advised marriage, and moved on to melodrama at the Adelphi in London, where she was judged to be a success. The 'break' for which actors secretly long was given her in 1893, when she was offered the lead role in Arthur Wing Pinero's *The Second Mrs Tanqueray*, a sombre play about a 'woman with a past'. One contemporary noted that she was 'tall and slight and dark, not pretty but attractive, the type of face that excites curiosity: and she has nervous, characteristic hands. There is a tinge of commonness about her, though, which helps the part to a certain extent.' The *Daily Chronicle* was more adulatory, recording that 'she showed a genius which gives her from this time forth an enviable place on the English stage'.

But Campbell did more than that; she divested women of the false conventions that restricted them. Her success encouraged the emergence of other risqué heroines who denied the Victorian standards and certitudes that still dominated the productions of the West End and were treated by actor-managers as holy writ. The first shot had been fired by Henrik Ibsen, whose plays were damned or celebrated, discussed and performed, as if they were at the centre of all theatrical endeavours. He was acclaimed as a genius by some, and denounced as a cesspool by others. Female actors such as Elizabeth Robins and Florence Farr devoted their careers to his plays, while many others rejected them utterly. Henry James was one of the admirers. He wrote of *The Master Builder* that Ibsen's 'independence, his perversity, his intensity, his vividness, the hard compulsion of his strangely inscrutable art, are present in that full measure, together with that quality which comes almost uppermost when it is a question of seeing him on the stage, his peculiar blessedness to actors'. The conventions and clichés were thrown away; the melodrama was gone and the 'costume drama' had vanished. In their place rose plays of contemporary life and modern preoccupations. For the actors it was an unexpected and, to begin with, unknown challenge.

The success of *The Second Mrs Tanqueray* launched Campbell on a career that lasted for most of her life. She became identified with women who seek desperately for physical or artistic freedom, only to fail in miserable circumstances. She followed this triumph, in which she was compared to Sarah Bernhardt and Eleonora Duse, with another 'problem play' by Pinero, *The Notorious Mrs Ebbsmith*, on the dilemma of the 'new woman'. William Archer wrote that 'here we have character working itself out entirely from within.' One theatrical historian wrote of the play that 'the actress took us to wonderland, and she kept us there until she had done with us.' It was succeeded by *Fedora* in the Haymarket. Campbell had some instinct for what would work in this period, with a new audience and a new theatre. She did not follow the conventional mannerisms of the traditional roles, and Archer was moved to write that 'if Mrs Campbell's Juliet passes muster as a good, not to say great, performance, there is an end of [conventional] Shakespearian acting.' 'Mrs Pat', as she was generally known, understood this perfectly.

But Campbell's instinct vied with her temper, and she could be sarcastic, dilatory and unprofessional. One critic wrote that she 'took her art and her own great gifts too lightly. She would lose interest in a part and play with it instead of playing it.' For some managers the experience was agonizing. The actor George Alexander stated bluntly, 'go on for another play with Mrs Campbell I will *not*. I'd rather die.' She played hysterical women on and off the stage, but her feeling for the falling or fallen woman could electrify the audience. In the summer of 1895 she began a partnership with the actor-manager Johnston Forbes-Robertson that lasted for five years; it was more than a professional relationship, but their affair and their theatrical duet were both sundered by a number of failures on the stage. It was said that they perfectly complemented each other – his 'skill without temperament' and her 'temperament without skill'.

Campbell embarked once more on her own, managing a small theatre, the Royalty, while embarking on a number of American tours to replenish her ever-diminishing treasury. She married again only a few days before her success as Eliza Doolittle in Shaw's *Pygmalion*. Her friendship with Shaw was in fact the most important of her life; it was perhaps on his advice that in the 1920s she played in several of Ibsen's dramas that were still considered radical or at least unconventional. But they argued all the time, with the balance between actor and playwright constantly shifting until the time came when Shaw became the most famous dramatist of his time.

Campbell realized that her style would soon become only a reminiscence, and in 1922 she wrote that 'the "school" today is lighter – the personalities have somehow adapted themselves to a more girlish, or what is termed a "flapper" style.' A few years later she wrote that the characters of the modern drama were 'pretty puppets who did not get the chance to voice the great independence, courage and humour of our time'. She preferred dignity and repose, but that did not stop her from playing the flower girl, Eliza, in *Pygmalion* once more, at the age of fifty-five. She died in 1940, twenty years later.

Opinions varied concerning Campbell's acting, and some declared it to be fabulous while others disdained it as artificial. One actress, Kate Terry Gielgud, noted that 'passion, the deep tragedy of the classic stage, she cannot touch; she is too fin-de-siecle, too much the morbid, introspective modern woman.' She had been so in touch with the pulse of her age that she had now become old-fashioned. Few, if any, actors can escape that fate.

Janet Achurch, born the year before Campbell, was also often associated with the fashion for Ibsen. She claimed to derive from a long line of actors, and in fact her maternal grandparents managed the Theatre Royal in Manchester, so it seemed only natural that she would entrust herself to the stage. She made her first appearance in a farce at the Olympic in 1883, and after the required tour of the provinces she took the leading role in Wilkie Collins's *The New Magdalen*, for which Shaw acclaimed her in the *Saturday Review* as 'the only tragic actress of genius we now possess'. She had joined the Olympic for one season only before moving between London and the provinces as opportunity offered. Then, at the age of twenty-five, she took over the management of the Novelty Theatre. Her first major production was the English premiere of Ibsen's *A Doll's House*, in 1889, in which she took on the role of Nora. It materially advanced Ibsen's reputation, as well as her own, and was considered by many to be the theatrical debut of the decade.

After her marriage to the actor Charles Charrington, Achurch began a two-year tour of Australia, which was extended to New Zealand, India and Egypt. Whether this advanced her London career is doubtful. She suffered a miscarriage and from that period became addicted to morphine. On her return to England she joined the Avenue Theatre, and played once more in *A Doll's House*. After some less significant dramas she took the leading role in Ibsen's *Little Eyolf*. One of her consistent admirers, George Bernard Shaw, recorded that 'she played with all her old originality and success, and with more than her old authority over her audience . . . For the first time one clearly saw the superfluity of power and the vehemence of intelligence which make her often so reckless as to the beauty of her methods of expression.' She returned the compliment by playing, in the following year, the leading role in Shaw's *Candida*; this was followed by his *Captain Brassbound's Conversion*. In a letter on this production, Shaw congratulated her: 'Lady Cicely is the first sign you have given of reaching the wise age of comedy and being able to play the fiddle as well as the trombones and drums.' She played two or three more roles, but her addiction to morphine eventually overcame her and she died of poisoning at the age of fifty-two in 1916. She was one of the now unacknowledged pioneers of a new drama.

On the stage Achurch never lost her self-control. She wrote, 'I have often cried bitterly while rehearsing a part, and yet been dry-eyed on the first performance.' In common with other actors, she relied on observation, and confessed that 'everything that comes, or ever has come, into my own life, or under my observation, I find myself utilising; and in scenes of real personal suffering I have had an under-consciousness of taking mental notes all the time.' Few actors would admit to this, even though many experience it.

Fourteen

Management and melodrama

The male actors of the latter years of the nineteenth century seem somehow diminished by their female counterparts. Perhaps that is because some of them accepted the useless appendage 'Sir', an absurd trinket that did nothing but diminish their achievement and place them firmly in a traditional mode. Some of them also became associated with Oscar Wilde's comedies, which required only modest allowances of wit, agility and elegant diction. You could not be a great actor in the world of Wilde, if we except one or two outrageous female parts. But that is another story.

Herbert Beerbohm Tree, whose real name was Herbert Draper Beerbohm, was born in London in 1853. He spent his early years in his father's business, but at the age of twenty-six the call of the stage became irresistible. His principal roles were foreign princes or foreign eccentrics. His first real successes came as a vicar in Charles Hawtrey's *The Private Secretary* and a spy in Hugh Conway's *Called Back*, diverse roles that seemed to prove his versatility; these were followed by a number of not terribly distinguished plays by writers who have now been forgotten.

Tree must have possessed great self-confidence, however, when in 1887 he took over the management of the Comedy Theatre in Panton Street. He moved on a few months later to the Haymarket, where he divested himself of traditional Victorian dust and velvet. He was eager to associate himself with 'new drama', including that of Wilde, Maurice Maeterlinck and Ibsen; he even instituted a tradition of contemporary theatre on Monday nights, in marked contrast to most of his competitors, who put their trust in the tried and tested and trivial. He could even compete with Henry Irving with a series of Shakespearean revivals. Tree's style as manager was decidedly odd, however, largely because his sense of the absurd was stronger than his feeling for realism. He said once to an actor, 'I want you to suggest – well you know, don't you? – a cross between a whitebait and a marmoset.' He read over the account books with bafflement, as if they were composed in Sanskrit.

Tree was successful enough to take over a new theatre in 1897, Her Majesty's, of which he was manager for twenty years. In this long period he mingled plays classical and modern, foreign and domestic, comic and melodramatic, tragic and farcical. Among the sixty plays were Shaw's *Pygmalion* and sixteen of Shakespeare's dramas, the spectacular sets and expansive scenery of which turned Her Majesty's into the quintessential Edwardian theatre. It had become the era of visual realism in which built-up sets, pivoting scenes, sliding scenes, platforms, lighting effects and painted sets minimized the contribution of the actual players.

As an actor, Tree was most attracted to 'character' parts, in which certain dominant traits guided his speech and movement. Perhaps it helped that his voice came from his throat rather than his mouth, and that his gestures were often curious or bizarre. A critic wrote that 'a character actor is one who does not excel chiefly in certain recurrent situations, but in building up before our eyes a definite human being. Beerbohm Tree possessed the power of conceiving character in a very high degree.' He was a most accomplished Fagin, Shylock and Svengali, but he could also become Ulysses, Richard II and Macbeth.

Tree disliked the name 'character actor', however. 'The cant of "character acting"', he said, 'has wearied me to death. Every part is a character, and therefore every actor is a character actor.' He went on to state that he played one style of character to please the public, and another to please himself. But, as a critic pointed out, 'there is one character that he is very fond of playing – and that is himself.' There were others who described him as a romantic actor in the sense that 'he believed in inspiration. He was to the last an improviser, trusting to the emotion of the moment.' Character actor or romantic actor? Perhaps he was both. One critic wrote that 'he was always better in representing weakness rather than strength, passivity than resolution.' He did seem to prefer characters who had a strain of the artist in them. But he was also an actor who could change his appearance, and with make-up he was unrecognizable. His eyes and hands, like those of few actors, could coax the audience into willing belief. He turned down Barrie's *Peter Pan*, in which he would have been an illustrious Captain Hook. When asked why he had rejected it, he replied, 'God knows, and I have promised to tell no one else.'

Henry Chance Newton, the theatre critic, recalled how a budding starlet once insisted that she be given equal billing with the great man. She wanted: 'Sir Herbert Beerbohm Tree *and* Miss (So and So)'. Genially puzzled, Tree responded with, 'Yes, my dear child, but why "and"? Why not "but"?' We must charitably assume that he had not prepared that remark in advance. In any case, the example shows a man whose true gift always lay in comedy, and whose tragedy was to consider himself a tragedian.

Present-day actors are earnestly encouraged to think of themselves as reacting rather than acting. This was not Tree's method. Indeed, his sublime self-preoccupation is as charming now as it must have been vexing then. Shaw recalled an instance when the play required Mrs Patrick Campbell to throw a pair of slippers at Tree. She proved to be an excellent shot and Tree, blithely unaware that this was in the script, collapsed in tears. 'It seemed to him', Hesketh Pearson wrote, 'that Mrs Campbell, suddenly giving way to an impulse of diabolical wrath and hatred, had committed an unprovoked and brutal assault on him . . . The worst of it was that as it was quite evident that he would be just as surprised and wounded every time, Mrs Campbell took care that the slippers should never hit him again, and the incident was consequently one of the least convincing in the performance.'

Tree died in the summer of 1917, but not before he had performed one other service for the English theatre. In 1904 he established the Royal Academy of Dramatic Art (RADA), which was housed above what had become His Majesty's Theatre. Two years later the voice teacher Elsie Fogerty established the Central School of Speech and Drama; the education of the actor, hitherto reserved for managers and other actors, could begin. Before the establishment of these two institutions there had been no comprehensive scheme for the training of players. During the Renaissance the apprentice learned from his master, and in the Restoration the players were taught informally by the older actors or the playwright. There were two conservatoires, LAMDA (the London Academy of Music and Dramatic Art) and the Guildhall, but in the Victorian period they trained only musicians.

The emergence of provincial repertory theatres, where a settled company present a number of specified plays, hastened the process of training. The Gaiety Theatre in Manchester was founded by Annie Horniman, and there she prepared actors for both small and large roles. The Birmingham Rep, established in 1913, also vied with the drama schools as a forcing ground for players. Between 1900 and 1914 there were as many as 250 touring companies on the road, although William Archer denounced them for their 'hopeless vulgarity and blatant imbecility . . . A glance at the hoardings in any provincial town is enough to make one feel suicidal.' But RADA and the Central School were quite different; they first established the context in which, according to one actor, Mrs Kendal, 'there is at last a recognised social position for the professional player.'

Johnston Forbes-Robertson, another actor-manager and eventually another 'Sir', was born in the City of London at the beginning of 1853. It was believed by his family that he was destined to be a painter, and he spent three years at the Royal Academy, but then, for reasons that may have been obscure even to him, he climbed on to the stage. It was not a profession he particularly savoured. 'Rarely,' he wrote, 'very rarely have I enjoyed myself in acting.' But he needed the means to support his family, and one sister and two brothers joined him in the profession. He had what might be called an Edwardian face, all angles and pallor, that made him irresistible to the more conventional managers of the time. This was combined with a resonant voice, which, according to Clement Scott, 'reminds one of the moan and wail of the cello'. The voice was the thing. It was said that he spoke blank verse as if it were conventional speech.

In the spring of 1874 Forbes-Robertson was hired by W. G. Wills for his play *Mary Queen of Scots*, and soon afterwards he began a short tour with Ellen Terry. From that time forward he was never short of engagements both in England and in America. When he played Orlando in *As You Like It*, a critic noted that 'Forbes-Robertson's embodiment, a little grave and severe and somewhat too intellectual, was, nevertheless, instinct with the right feeling . . . His air of high breeding and his perfect taste commended him to cordial sympathy.' This hits the true Edwardian note. But to many, that was not as Shakespeare intended. It had come too close to contemporary domestic drama, with little majesty and no thunder. Yet Forbes-Robertson brought something else in their place: incessant vocal training, arduous self-discipline, restraint and perfect pitch.

In common with many Edwardian actors, Forbes-Robertson ascended into management – as Irving's replacement at the Lyceum in 1895 – but his first season was not a resounding success. His leading lady was Campbell, whose temper and tantrums were well known. He offered her Ophelia, but she refused; it had to be Juliet or no one. And so it was. It may have been she who pushed Forbes-Robertson into management in the first place. He confessed that 'I would have gladly remained an actor pure and simple . . . On the other hand, several actors younger than I had taken up management very much earlier in their careers and there was nothing for it but to take a theatre if I was to maintain my place.' The pair muddled through until a final parting in 1899, and the following year he married the woman who became his new leading lady in every sense. She was the daughter of a sea captain and her stage name was Gertrude Elliott. She was soon Ophelia to his Hamlet.

Forbes-Robertson remained successful, and in 1907 Shaw remarked that 'I wrote *Caesar and Cleopatra* for Forbes-Robertson, because he is the classic actor of our day, and had a right to require such a service from me.' Of him, Shaw wrote, 'He does not utter a half-line; then stop to act; then go on with another half-line . . . He plays as Shakespeare should be played, on the line and to the line, with the utterance and acting simultaneous, inseparable and in fact identical.' Shaw had already seen him as Hamlet, and recognized that 'he can present a dramatic hero as a man whose passions are those which have produced the philosophy, the poetry, the art and the statecraft of the world.' The critic James Agate echoed the praise: 'Forbes-Robertson was a gracious and noble actor, and in his private life a gracious and noble gentleman.'

Happily, it was not all a matter of grace and nobility. Those ethereal virtues were offset by a saving sense of humour, not to mention quick-wittedness. On one occasion, an actress playing opposite Forbes-Robertson found that her necklace had broken in the middle of the scene. More and more jewels began dropping on to the stage, and Forbes-Robertson had to rescue as many of them as he could, all the while staying in character. He succeeded, but 'I could not stow the things into my pockets without exposing the mishap to the audience . . . She at that moment gave a deep sigh which caused a momentary hiatus between her bodice and her chest.' At that, eyes averted, he stuffed the jewels down her cleavage, to a whispered, 'Thank you!'

Forbes-Robertson had by indirection or instinct changed the temperature of the stage. As *The Athenaeum* put it, 'gradually, but surely, that natural and realistic style of acting in tragedy is overpowering the conventional and declamatory.' The *Quarterly Journal of Speech* records that 'the realists were having hard enough time preserving any sense of decorum in the melodramatic and farcical aspects they had forced themselves into . . . Their voices were becoming shrill, their linen and their laces disarrayed. They entered the drawing rooms of [Arthur Wing] Pinero and [Henry Arthur] Jones with polite sighs of relief and took up their duties as mouthpieces of the dramatist with eagerness . . . Domesticated animals like well-regulated homes.' The dramatist had taken over from the actor and, for many, the 'golden age' of the theatre had come to an end. Forbes-Robertson's last London season occurred in 1913 – which was described by one contemporary critic as the 'swan-song of the Old Drama' – and he subsequently went into comfortable retirement until his death in 1937. At his height, however, he was the quintessential Edwardian actor who formed the link between Victorian and modern.

George Alexander Gibb Samson was born in Reading in the summer of 1858 and seemed destined for a life of trade, but at the age of twenty-one he loosened the shackles and also dropped his two last names. He joined a repertory company in Nottingham, and that eventually led him to the Standard in Shoreditch; Henry Irving spotted him there and brought him to the Lyceum, where he played a variety of roles. But then, at the relatively early age of thirty-two, Alexander leased the Avenue Theatre. Some mediocre dramas followed in what was essentially a mediocre theatre, but his fortunes changed later in the year when he leased the St James's Theatre; he remained there for the rest of his career.

As Irving and Tree had already demonstrated, this was the age of the actor-manager. The reasons for the rise of this figure seem mysterious at first, but any smoke soon dissolves. Some actors had attained sufficient eminence and wealth, for example, to be able to run their own show. The conditions of late Victorian England were ripe, the stars in every sense set fair. As gas gave way to electricity, as stage sets became more and more naturalistic and therefore elaborate, as swelling hordes of backstage assistants were required for a play to be mounted, so the actor-manager began to assume a central role – including, it should be noted, that of 'director'. He was well placed for such a position, being attuned both to the needs of actors and to the logistics of production. But this role was so far informal, and indeed it had yet to be given a name.

Alexander was good at his work, hiring the best actors and paying appropriate salaries. He was precise, punctual and even-tempered, and he ran the theatre like a Swiss clock. He did not introduce many foreign plays, but relied on the comfortable dramas of high, and almost high, life. In these he often played the leading role with his debonaire manner and suave demeanour. Wilde once complained that Alexander did not act on the stage; he behaved. He was as elegant and fashionable as his plays, and men would study his clothes before ordering their own.

Alexander's two great playwrights were Oscar Wilde and Arthur Wing Pinero. Now only Wilde survives, but Alexander had the acumen to present *Lady Windermere's Fan* in 1892 and Pinero's *The Second Mrs Tanqueray* the following year. The omens could not have been more favourable, and were strengthened by the first production of *The Importance of Being Earnest* in 1895. Wilde's four great comedies were in fact all produced at the St James's Theatre under the aegis of George Alexander.

A glance at the cast lists reveals that there was no stock company and no 'old favourites' for any of Wilde's work; the players for each comedy were different, scotching the belief that there was a standard 'Wilde style'. If such a thing existed, it lay only in the alchemy between dramatist and manager. There can be no suggestion that the cast was not at the top of their profession; Lord Windermere in *Lady Windermere's Fan* was played by Alexander himself, and the following year Lord Illingworth in *A Woman of No Importance* was taken by Tree. Lady Bracknell in *The Importance of Being Earnest* was played by the sensation of the moment, Rose Leclercq. According to Irene Vanbrugh, who played her daughter Gwendolen, Leclercq's walk, her voice, her manner and even her 'long bottle of eau-de-Cologne' were exact in every detail.

The first nights were dramas in themselves. Hesketh Pearson wrote that Alexander 'catered to the tastes and foibles of that Society' like a restaurant manager. So, in a typical St James's play, the humorous characters were 'charmingly playful', the serious characters 'pleasantly sentimental', and the plot had to 'savour of scandal without being in any way truthfully objectionable. Adultery was invariably touched on and inevitably touched up . . . theft was made thrilling and murder romantic.' Stylistic consistency was one of Alexander's priorities, testified to perhaps by the long ripples of laughter and applause throughout the play. He insisted on consistency, and, again according to Vanbrugh, 'everything was well thought out and executed with the utmost dignity, which did so much to raise the theatrical profession.' Of course, it was the dignity that provided the humour.

The leading man was the epitome of 'modern masherdom', which may be defined as languid elegance with just a hint of eroticism, but he played his role with gravity. No one should know that the players shared the joke with the audience. For the first night of *The Importance of Being Earnest*, on 14 February 1895, the ladies all wore sprays of lilies to decorate their puffed sleeves while the gentlemen wore buttonholes of the same bloom. The streets outside the theatre cascaded in applause when Wilde and his wife stepped out of their carriage. Wilde's conviction and imprisonment put an end to what would otherwise have been a fruitful collaboration, however, and the play was dropped until a revival in 1909.

But Alexander's reputation was not diminished, and he continued to produce costume dramas, melodramas and musical dramas. One of his great successes came in 1896 with *The Prisoner of Zenda*. But the days of incipient glory could not endure indefinitely. In March 1918 he died of consumption and diabetes; with the promotion of Oscar Wilde, however, it cannot be said that his career was in any sense a failure.

A rival for public attention lay in Charles Wyndham, who managed the Criterion from 1874 to 1899 and who specialized in comedy of a more sophisticated nature. 'The modest villa', as one critic put it, 'is changed into a luxurious "boudoir" with all the wealth of colour that Messrs Liberty can introduce.' In 1899 he moved to the theatre that was renamed Wyndham's and, with the collaboration of the dramatist Henry Arthur Jones, provided a sequence of 'Society comedies'. Their principal actor was Irene Vanbrugh, who, with her older sister, Violet, came to dominate the late Victorian stage. They were the scions of an ecclesiastical family, but they both trained at a stage school in Margate. John Gielgud wrote that 'the Vanbrugh sisters were remarkably alike in appearance. Tall and imposing, beautifully spoken, they moved with grace . . . They were elegantly but never ostentatiously dressed, entering and leaving the stage with unerring authority . . . Violet never struck me as a natural comedienne, as Irene was.'

By the turn of the century the theatre was coated in sugar and spice and all things nice, which included sentimental melodramas, domestic comedies, adventures and romances. Ideas or 'problem plays' of any kind were avoided and, as for Ibsen or Shaw, they were not worth the bus ticket. Shakespeare, however, was still welcome. Between 1900 and 1914 there were 150 Shakespearean revivals. They were, according to *The Stage*, 'Shakespeare of the picture frame, with lopped texts, performances large, slow and declamatory, and representational colour-plate sets'. Fortunately, there was no shortage of theatres. Between 1900 and 1924 twelve new establishments were opened in the West End of London. The gallery cost a shilling or a 'bob' while, way past the pit and the dress circle, the stalls were 10/6.

The most famous of the Edwardian players was Gerald du Maurier, who was taken in hand by Mrs Patrick Campbell, scrubbed and polished until he became an acceptable actor. His first success was at the Duke of York's Theatre in 1902 with J. M. Barrie's *The Admirable Crichton*, in which he played Ernest Woolley; he then took on the double role of Captain Hook and Mr Darling in *Peter Pan*, before reaching his summit in 1906 with his leading role as a gentleman crook in E. W. Hornung's *Raffles*, which became the progenitor of the 'crook-dramas'. The parts in which du Maurier was most accomplished, however, were not to his taste. 'I have never had a happy day in the theatre,' he once confessed, and a contemporary, Cedric Hardwicke, recalled that du Maurier 'despised the playwrights who supplied him with such dross which with his alchemist's touch he persistently made to look like gold'. It was said that he always played the same part, but that, more often than not, was the fault of the writer. He was admired by younger players, such as Gielgud and Ralph Richardson, because of his nonchalant elegance and his ability to make everything look easy. He made it quite natural, for example, to light a cigarette on stage.

Du Maurier was rivalled only by Madge Kendal, or Mrs Kendal as she preferred to be known, who was already called 'the Matron of the English Drama' because of her emphasis on 'respectability' both on and off the stage. She had gained a reputation as a representative of the new school of 'naturalism', and was for a time hailed as the sensation of the day. But, like most self-proclaimed new schools, it was too little and too late. The English theatre had lost its way, from which it proceeded directly into burlesque and melodrama. It was said of Kendal that 'she looked like a plum pudding and acted like a machine.'

Kendal in turn was rivalled, albeit in a friendly spirit, by Athene Seyler, who was born in London in 1889 and, having been coached for a while by her next-door neighbour, Henry Irving, won a scholarship to RADA. She first appeared on stage in 1909, but soon won applause and more importantly an enthusiastic audience by playing eccentric old ladies with more than a hint of theatricality; she was Mrs Frail, Mrs Candour, Mrs Malaprop and Lady Bracknell. There was no shortage of demand for dotty or determined old ladies, and she became an outstanding female actor in comic parts. She had a theory about it: 'I never acted what is described as "all out". One should hold one's part *in*.' In some respects she preferred the old theatrical style. 'The old actormanagers', she wrote, 'never gave you a complete script, just the pages on which you had something to say. Nowadays directors try to tell you even how to move your hands. In the old days the author would say "Miss Seyler, the first scene is yours. How would you like it arranged?"' The increasingly intrusive director was thus already on the rise. James Agate praised Seyler's ability to keep and hold contact with an audience, 'the most understanding game of shuttlecock and battledore ever played between an actress and her adoring public'. She was also an accomplished writer on theatrical matters. In *The Craft of Comedy* (1943) she made a series of significant distinctions: 'I should say that a woman ought to *dance* as she moves in a seventeenth century play, to *sail* in an eighteenth century one, to *swim* in a nineteenth century dress . . . and to *stride* in the twentieth century.' After an equally successful career in film, Seyler died in 1990 at the age of 101. She had maintained the English comic tradition, equalled only by Edith Evans, who put her own twist on eccentric matrons.

At the turn of the century one of the prominent figures of the English theatre was Frank Benson. He was born in 1858 and at the age of twenty-two he managed and played the major role of Clytemnestra in a college production of Aeschylus's *Agamemnon*. In the circumstances it was only a limited success, but, more importantly, it sharpened his taste for all matters theatrical. He grazed around the edges of the stage until his first engagement in 1882 as Paris in *Romeo and Juliet*, with Henry Irving and Ellen Terry in the principal roles, and with the bravura of youth he took over a touring company, which was renamed the F. R. Benson Company. A wandering troupe has its difficulties, including in Benson's case a disastrous fire, but he managed to build up a large enough wardrobe for any conceivable drama. Actors came and went, but a solid core of performers remained loyal; they became known as 'Old Bensonians'. As is not unusual, this loyalty was offered to a man who, for all his generosity, could be a martinet. On one occasion he rehearsed *Macbeth* for seven hours without allowing his actors a meal. He had just come to the moment when Macbeth cries out, 'They have tied me to a stake,' when another actor felt obliged to exclaim, 'I wish to God they would tie me to one!' Abashed, Benson at once called a halt.

In 1886 Benson was asked to direct a Shakespearean festival at Stratford-upon-Avon, and the association continued. Over the next thirty years he produced all but two of Shakespeare's plays. But his eyes were always on London. From 1899 to 1916 he managed Shakespearean seasons at a number of West End theatres, including the Globe and the Theatre Royal, as well as some 'outer theatres' in Hammersmith, Wimbledon and elsewhere. They were not always a success, at least in comparison with the lavish productions of Herbert Beerbohm Tree, but no one could dispute Benson's energy and enthusiasm.

Nor did he lack the eccentricity so often apparent in the English actor. Benson's passion for the theatre, for example, was matched by an obsessive love of cricket. The actor-manager Seymour Hicks recalled that Benson's contracts for other actors were worded,

Fifteen

The new styles

The most notable theatre in England at this period was the New Court at Sloane Square (as the Royal Court was then known). It was under the joint management of J. E. Vedrenne and Harley Granville-Barker, who presented thirty-two plays of which eleven were by George Bernard Shaw. Among the Shavian offerings were *Major Barbara*, *Man and Superman* and *Captain Brassbound's Conversion*. The two managers can be said to represent the 'Theatre of Ideas' in all its uncommercial glory. They created an informal ensemble for that purpose, with Shaw himself taking part in staging his dramas. Over three seasons they presented Shaw's plays, together with work by John Galsworthy and Henrik Ibsen. The Court became the centre of high drama, and helped to foster the concept of the 'new drama', which was notable for its absence from the West End. It was an experiment, and an innovation, in every sense. It was certainly the single most important venue in Shaw's long career.

Granville-Barker asked that the actors should speak quickly, as in Shakespeare's time, with due regard for the music and pace of the verse. He detested elaborate sets as both distracting and ana-chronistic, and he also differed from other directors and actors in the intimacy and detail of his approach. He was a true actor's direc-tor. He was an interpreter of the text, not an actor-manager more concerned with the look of the thing or the box-office receipts, or with his own importance.

Shaw in turn required that his actors should play 'their parts with a relish' and 'without the least fear of over-acting and extravagance'; they were part of the gush of words that W. H. Auden described as Shaw's 'wonderful displays of conspicuous waste'. Shaw wanted all their stops 'to be pulled out'. It was part of the passionate excitement that his ideas were meant to convey; the characters were intended to embody those passions, so that all the alarm bells of intellect could sound at once.

The challenge was to detach the actors from their Edwardian mannerisms. Shaw detested the 'cup-and-saucer' style of genteel dialogue and asked Granville-Barker for 'the drunken, stagey, brass-bowelled barnstormers' of the old style. What the Kembles or Sarah Siddons could achieve was now considered to be outdated. Instead there were points to be made, declamations to be delivered and rhetoric exploited, even if this was quite beyond the range of most contemporary players. One critic wrote that 'early Shaw struck people with its torrential loquacity, overtaking the playgoer's bewildered mind because all that he had to say was charged with thought and new ideas, whimsical perversions, the formlessness of the plays and the characters alternating between the fantastic and the real.'

In 1914 Shaw consolidated his reputation with *Pygmalion*, assisted by an extravagant performance by Mrs Patrick Campbell who, back from touring the United States and blazing in the part that Shaw had written for her, played Eliza Doolittle with a strenuous Cockney accent. As a true actor, despite some initial reservations, she did not allow the disparity between her age and that of her character to pose any problems. She had an imposing voice, but she was good at contrasting tones from light to heavy, and she had a fine comic sense that often seemed to be directed at herself. As a result, she outperformed the rest of the cast with no real effort.

Shaw himself was rivalled by J. M. Barrie and Arthur Wing Pinero, with occasional intrusions from Henry Arthur Jones. Jones and Pinero were in fact the most popular of the Edwardian dramatists, principally because they could fashion a story that did not linger or sag. 'Whatever may be the loftiness of your ideas and opinions,' Jones said in an interview, 'until you have smelted them into a story, you will have no play that will hold a general audience.' Their plays may not have been of outstanding quality, but they served their purpose. The theatrical world immediately before the First World War was designed to divert attention from the horrors elsewhere.

Granville-Barker, one of the principal players at the New Court as well as its manager, emerged on to the stage of the Comedy Theatre at the age of fifteen, began writing plays in 1894 at seventeen and became a theatre manager ten years later. It was rumoured that he was Shaw's son, a fact that, given his proficiency, can at least be entertained. John Gielgud described him as 'a sort of young genius [who] wore sandals and ate nuts'. Amid these various pastimes he even found time to write plays, among them *The Voysey Inheritance*.

Yet Granville-Barker's principal concern was to elevate the national drama, with the New Court for his stage and the Ibsenite enthusiast William Archer as his colleague. He moved on to the Savoy, where he had a predictable mixture of failure and success; a national theatre was still in sight, but the war destroyed the pleasing mirage. His subsequent work was infrequent and inconclusive, and he died in Paris in 1946.

It is also worth recording that Anton Chekhov's *The Seagull* was first performed in translation at the Scottish Repertory Theatre in Glasgow; the year was 1909, long before the playwright had acquired an international reputation. Something else was stirring, however, and *Variety* of that same year wrote of the new 'electric theatres'. Their hour was come at last.

The first films were entertaining diversions to display the strange process itself, with rushing trains and speeding cars hurtling forwards as if they were about to break through the screen. The actors of the Edwardian theatre were not used to film, and no one really knew how to act before a camera. It was an unnatural and unnerving experience. Some actors responded by over-compensating, with arms flung out and eyes searching upwards as if for inspiration; others relied on familiar comic routines in which, for want of an audience to sustain them, they tended to overact. There were some, however, who tried to ignore the camera altogether, and although at the time they might have been considered to be under-playing, they now seem the most convincing. This was a virgin form, for which no tradition existed. Consequently, naturalism was not necessarily the aim; it was often quite the opposite.

If the style of the early cinema is 'theatrical', that is simply because these are filmed versions of stage productions. One of these novel houses, showing 'moving landscapes and seascapes', was the Old Vic in Waterloo Road, managed by Lilian Baylis. The first films were born out of the demands of a smaller and more intimate audience, but the voice and gesture of the players were attuned to a wide stage and a large auditorium. It is essentially a style in which body and voice are pushed beyond their normal range, which included the enlargement of stock gestures and exaggerated reactions. It was a style, too, that demanded ensemble acting. Negligent actors might be lost, but in fact there were few negligent actors on film. Even in the most trivial adventure they all seem to know what they are doing.

Only a fragment remains of Herbert Beerbohm Tree in the death scene of *King John*, prepared in 1899, the first Shakespearean play ever filmed. It is no more than one or two minutes long, but it creates an undeniable impression of writhing pain. In 1901 a different style of cinematic acting is employed in *Sporting Colliers and a Bobby*, which, although it seems to employ actors, conveys a less theatrical impression. It concerns a group of amateur gamblers who are betrayed to a passing policeman. There follow the usual chase and mayhem but, unlike the American 'Keystone Cops' productions of a decade later, they seem not to be orchestrated or carefully directed. The players themselves may have been told not to act, which suggests an alternative approach to the new medium. For the multiple faces of the actor, however, it is only necessary to watch *Mr Moon* of the same year, a 'test' for the music-hall artist Percy Honri, with pouting lips, raised eyebrows, winks and tears. A *Daring Daylight Robbery* (1903) makes use of passers-by who are not extras, and of trains, cars and horse-drawn vehicles, in a story of a foiled burglary. It has been suggested that most of the cast were working-class men who had been persuaded to perform, in which case this is the first example of working-class cinema.

Johnston Forbes-Robertson, in the first filmed version of *Hamlet*, in 1913, is taken from the stage and thrust into a world where the artificial and the formal combine. When Horatio sees the ghost on the battlements, he puts one hand to his breast and flings the other backwards; it is the familiar sign from the acting manuals and had remained the same for at least two centuries. It also displays the extent to which the Edwardian theatre still comprised the art of gesture. Arms are raised in greeting or farewell, spread wide in horror or amazement, and hands are clasped in prayer or supplication, or raised to ward off an angry gaze or word. But this is not an exercise in extravagance; these are all minimal gestures within a deliberate and definite range. They convey a somewhat eerie effect as of synchronized swimming, flowing from one statuesque pose to the next. There is much ceremonial in the scenes at court, but a glance at the face of Forbes-Robertson, careworn and haggard from thought, might be considered to introduce an element of naturalism. Even though the expressions are real, they are suitably heightened.

In the play scene, we see Hamlet at his most persuasive and disturbing. His body seems twenty years younger. He bounces about, bowing and curvetting, and beaming a maniacally happy smile on those around him. This relatively elderly actor – Forbes-Robertson was then sixty – seems positively boyish. Then, as the story comes to its crux, as the king grows visibly uncomfortable, Forbes-Robertson's body becomes slow and taut; he crawls towards the king, his eyes as bright as a flaring candle.

Another vignette from the following year, of Tree playing Svengali in Paul M. Potter's *Trilby*, is a masterclass in Edwardian acting. It is clear that the two principal means of conveying emotion were the hands and the eyes. The eyes in fact dominate the performance, moving from mad eagerness to soft wheedling, from triumph to astonishment. But the hands are also the key. Each actor employs them with great care and attention, pointing, gesticulating and soothing; for Tree each gesture conveys total command. There is no tremor or ambiguity in the movements, and none of the gaucherie of those modern actors who seem never to know what they should do with them. Even the fingers are placed in a lexicon of gestures. On stage Tree would have known how to reach the dress circle, by commanding it or perhaps by mesmerizing it. Yet on the screen he relied on movement. Moreover, he seems to have been an actor who understood the role of synergy on the stage; he plays in close collaboration with the other actors, feeding them as well as feeding off them. And then, as he leaves, he performs the most distinctive music-hall gesture of 'cocking a snook' at the others. Solemnity was not necessary in Edwardian melodrama. But we gain at least some inkling of his commanding presence on the contemporary stage.

The effect is that of a stage where the face is essentially a mask. This is a truism. But the first film actors miss the audience and are working in a vacuum. That may account for the extravagance and the heavy reliance on stock or standard gestures. The director would know no better and would in fact encourage the players to do what they knew best. As a result they strain for effects, and strive for excesses of expression and gesture that they can only really accomplish in front of a live audience. There are moments when the performers seem ill at ease or unprepared. We are now used to the convention of film acting that 'less is more', but at that time more was more, and that is why the actors from the music hall, rather than the theatre, took readily to the camera.

A player in a different mould, Ivor Novello, was first more celebrated as a film actor, but he acquired his technique from the drama. He was deeply theatrical, with every gesture poised, every movement considered and every expression eloquent. The eyes in particular command the camera in the same fashion that stage actors demand the attention of the audience. But the cinema had already influenced a change in the performer's style. 'Modern English acting', the journalist Ivor Brown wrote in the *Saturday Review*:

provides usually an adequate and sometimes a brilliant medium for the modern English play. It is life-size. It is deft and slick . . . Like the drama itself it goes about its business quietly. Within its limited range it has a well-groomed competence . . . He who goes in search of a new Bernhardt must provide them with a new kind of play or else a very old one.

We may or may not consider Sybil Thorndike to be another Sarah Bernhardt, but she became the epitome of a certain Edwardian style. She was born in Gainsborough, Lincolnshire, in 1882 and enjoyed a stage career at a very young age, with its beginning in amateur dramatics and her mother's decision to start a company for musical comedies. 'Of course I can act,' she said, 'I've acted since I was four.' That may have been a slight exaggeration, but it reveals at least her early inclination. On the urging of her brother, Thorndike joined the Central School of Speech and Drama, then under the guidance of Elsie Fogarty at the Royal Albert Hall in London. At the age of twenty-one she joined the Ben Greet Players, close to the Strand, and in 1904 she made her stage debut in Greet's production of *The Merry Wives of Windsor*. In 1908 she migrated to Manchester, where she worked with the vigorous and innovative Annie Horniman's Repertory Theatre. She was introduced to the 'new drama', and was in turn noticed by George Bernard Shaw when she played the understudy for the title role in his *Candida*.

In 1914 Thorndike was enrolled at the Old Vic under the watchful eye of Baylis. In wartime her post was not well paid, but it was work. She soon made a favourable impression in a number of roles, as the theatre instituted a succession of classic and Shakespearean productions. Shaw remarked that the Old Vic 'seems to be at the centre of the dramatic movement nowadays'. The effect of the First World War was to create a dearth of male actors, and Thorndike was thrilled to have the chance to change sex on the stage. 'When you're an actor,' she noted, 'you cease to be male or female, you're a person.'

She also proved herself to excel in tragic roles. But even the greatest tragic actors are sometimes at a loss. The role of Lady Macbeth baffled Thorndike until help came from an unexpected quarter. She could not find, as she put it, 'the heart of that foulness', but Baylis put her right in the sternest tones. 'Don't be so nonsensical!' she told Thorndike. 'You love your husband, don't you?' Thorndike found herself forced to consider what she would be capable of doing for her husband's sake, or for her children's. The 'heart of that foulness' became in a moment the heart of a wife, and Thorndike could enter it. So it was a hard-nosed producer more interested in opera than in drama – Baylis never, to Thorndike's knowledge, watched a play through to the end – who had to make the cogent point to the sensitive, empathetic artist.

Thorndike stayed at the Old Vic until 1918, after which she took part in several productions in a variety of theatres. Her next major success came with the title role in Shaw's *Saint Joan*, a part that he had written for her in particular. After its London premiere in 1924 it was a resounding and public success, easily the most considerable production of the year. Thorndike herself became, in critical jargon, a 'household name' and remained so for the rest of her life. She was deemed to be England's greatest tragedy actor, while other equally important but less tragic roles were consigned to Edith Evans.

That the mistress of tragedy should herself be irrepressibly jolly and unpretentious is a paradox only when we forget that an actor's business is to become 'the other'. Ralph Richardson, recognizing with some dread that Thorndike was the first great star he had acted with,

wondered if I dared pay court and wish her well. I went to the door of her dressing-room, but I was afraid to knock in case she was communing with herself before that big part. Then I heard a buzz of talk inside, and tapped. 'Come in, Ralph dear,' Sybil said. 'Won't you have a bun?' She was feeding half-a-dozen schoolgirls with buns a few moments before the performance.

Thorndike was, like other stage actors, intrigued by the possibilities of film. She found the necessary techniques to be successful and remarked that 'it's like tiny miniature painting compared to scene painting . . . The film is a taking away of everything but essential movements and far, far tidier and cleaner-cut than the stage.' The stage nevertheless shines through her performances, and there are occasions and gestures that come directly from her theatrical training. Her acting is restrained, and is largely controlled or dominated by her eyes. In *Dawn* (1928), a study of the nurse Edith Cavell, her stoicism becomes a form of serenity. A sideways dart of the eyes dismisses a nervous maid; when the maid turns back, flustered, a taut stare cut off by the eyelids sends her back again. Her eyes, too, both display and seem to master her fear. She raises an authoritative finger to command silence, and when she points to a door or hiding place she uses swift, efficient movements in ways not usually employed on film sets. The tilt of her head and an upturned palm signify that she can do no more for a suppliant. She can be wary and authoritative at the same time, with only a raised eyebrow and pursed lips. This was not something to be devised by a film director.

Thorndike stands upright with a stance that demonstrates how much in command of herself she remains, and this self-control is retained to the end of the film, with a dry-eyed mastery that was certainly not customary among film actors. When in *Dawn* she begins to contemplate her own fate, and that of her fellow workers, her face betrays no indication of pathos or misery in the old style; she is simply thinking things through to the end, and this rare blend of economy and sincerity is all the more convincing for it.

Thorndike also had little tricks of her own. When another actress held the stage, Sybil might wink at the audience, a habit that Evans considered unprofessional. In one play in which they worked together, while Evans made an impassioned speech Thorndike held the audience's attention by slowly crossing and uncrossing her eyes. 'If you have no audience,' she said, 'then act to the kitchen poker.' Gielgud remembered her last appearance at the Old Vic. Thorndike was by this time in a wheelchair, and it hindered her not at all. 'Lively, passionate, argumentative,' he recalled, 'always travelling, acting, learning a new language or a new poem, a magnificent wife and mother, she was surely one of the rarest women of our time.'

'Oh Lewis,' Thorndike cried once to her husband, Lewis Casson, 'if only we could be the first actors to play on the moon.'

This tells us much: the heart of the tragic actor does not necessarily weep or brood, rather it yearns.

No Edwardian actor could be more different from Thorndike than Tod Slaughter, who has generally been identified with bloodstained melodramas; he managed the Elephant and Castle theatre, where such productions were the principal attraction, from 1924 until its closure in 1927. Yet it was at the New Theatre in St Martin's Lane that he first played Sweeney Todd in 1931. It was a great success, largely because of the presence of Slaughter, whose face is at first a mask of rubicund welcome and innocent geniality; he rubs his hands at the sight of a prospective victim in the manner of a 'ham' villain, writhing and wheedling before his wealthy customers. After his cinematic success in the role, five years later, he became known as 'Mr Murder' and fitted Sweeney Todd as Bela Lugosi fitted Dracula. Slaughter was an actor of the old school, brought up on the popular stage, and he retained the theatrical characteristics of the wide eyes, the beckoning finger, the savage grin and, most powerfully, the mad laughter. His slang phrase, of double meaning for a barber, was 'I'll polish you off.' It can be surmised that those who had been trained on the stage exercised a larger presence on screen than did those who were deprived of the experience.

Sixteen

Short and quick

The English theatre of the 1920s was not connected with the experimentalism of its Continental neighbours. With the exception of Harley Granville-Barker, it played the old favourites or the new replicas in the conventional way, with revues, melodramas and musical comedies leading the parade. The First World War only intensified the appetite for melodrama, bringing a flood of cheap patriotic plays with such unsurprising titles as *The War Baby*, *Brave Women Who Wait*, *The Enemy in Our Midst* and *Are We Disheartened?* Overt propaganda and obvious stereotypes were mingled with flimsy or practically non-existent plots. It was not the theatre's finest hour. These crude fabrications were soon accompanied or replaced by comedies and intimate revues that stayed on the right side of bawdiness. *A Little Bit of Fluff* (1915) ran for 1,241 performances at the Criterion, for example, but it was outscored if not outclassed by the great success of the decade. *Chu Chin Chow*, a musical comedy based on the exploits of Ali Baba, opened at Her Majesty's Theatre on 3 August 1916 and ran for five years. It was a sign of the times.

Other plays followed the clipped and tight-lipped exploration of repressed feeling. The master of this was Noël Coward, whose first play, *The Vortex*, opened in 1924, followed by *Hay Fever* the following year. His laconic delivery and elegant manner were copied by other actors. But there was still no shortage of farce and melodrama. *Rookery Nook* by Ben Travers opened at the Aldwych in 1923 and lasted for ten years.

An actor of some eminence from this period, Felix Aylmer, was born in 1889; after being introduced at Oxford to the dramatic society there, he set himself to the task of acting. He appeared in *Romeo and Juliet* at the age of twenty-two before appearing in two Shakespearean productions under the scrutiny of Granville-Barker. The war brought an unfortunate hiatus to his career, as it did for so many actors, but he hurried back uninjured to his fiancée in Birmingham and for a while strode across the stage in that city. But that was not enough.

Aylmer made the journey to 'the Smoke', as the capital was then called, and appeared in many West End plays, where his severe – not to say solemn – manner marked him out for lawyers, judges, diplomats and solicitors. It was said that judges themselves imitated his demeanour. Aylmer was unusual in one respect. He rarely made space for Shakespeare, and did not have much time for the dramatist. He said that

> Shakespeare has done so much harm to actors. He has been responsible for so much work that is artificial and unreal that in my time he has seemed a machine for manufacturing ham actors who do not understand the psychological contents of the parts and the poetry. Everyone has to do Shakespeare if they want to make a reputation but it seems to me that they seldom do their best work in his plays.

Melodrama and intense romance faded in the theatre of the 1920s. Where once the actors had ruled, at the end of the nineteenth century, they had been beguiled by the cinema and lost some of their authority in the world of the stage. Perhaps the cinema had also abbreviated the longer monologues and dialogue that had depended on a certain pattern of rhythmic speaking, and were substituted by the clipped or laconic expression of the later decade. This was the age of terse conversation and succinct remarks: 'brief, short, quick, snap' were the catchwords. It was a time, as one critic put it, of 'sharp, brittle intolerance' and fast-paced if uneasy gaiety. In the lower quarters of the West End, thrillers and sentimental comedies, as well as musical revues and farces, drew in the crowds. Plays migrated from one theatre to another as public taste and affection for various performers altered, while in the provinces repertory theatres wilted in the glare of the moving pictures.

Despite – or perhaps because of – these changes of mood, it is probable that the female actors of the 1920s were superior to the male. Constance Collier was born into a theatrical family in 1878, and made her debut at the age of six at the Theatre Royal in Hull. For three weeks she played small roles as a 'Gaiety Girl', one of the chorus girls at the New Gaiety Theatre at the end of the Strand. She was remarkably tall and had some difficulty in finding suitably elongated parts, but in 1901 Herbert Beerbohm Tree invited her to be the leading lady in *Antony and Cleopatra* at Her Majesty's; this was an occasion when her height was a positive advantage. In common with many actors of her generation, she had a vigorous personality not untouched by self-parody.

Gladys Cooper was born in Lewisham in 1888, and after a voice audition she was recruited at the age of seventeen for what was known as a 'musical dream play'. *Bluebell in Fairyland* was principally for children, but no doubt some members of the audience took pleasure in the antics of a nubile actor who would for a while become a photographer's model. Her first permanent employment was with George Edwardes's company at the New Gaiety, where she took on singing and dancing parts. This was the destination of many pretty young females, but it was not the fate she had envisioned for herself. She wanted to be a serious actor in the mould of Thorndike.

In 1916 Cooper began acting at the Playhouse on Northumberland Avenue, where she starred in a comedy entitled *Please Help Emily*. She herself did not need much help, but she allowed herself to be coached in comedy by Charles Hawtrey. In fact she made such an impression that the proprietor offered her the role of joint manager in 1917. She continued to act, and took part in the direction of several successful plays, including work by Shaw and Pinero. She began to work with W. Somerset Maugham as well, who said, 'it's interesting to consider how Gladys Cooper has succeeded in turning herself from an indifferent actress into an extremely accomplished one.' She had also become a 'pin-up', whose photographs adorned the barracks and the trenches. In a similar search for diversity she starred in a few early films, among them *The Sorrows of Satan* (1917). In the same period she formed a close friendship with Ivor Novello, a circumstance that merely stoked the publicity around her, but his sexuality prohibited any closer union. A similar situation pertained with Gerald du Maurier, whom she had met four years earlier, except that in his case the impediment was a happy marriage.

By the late 1930s Cooper's youthful enthusiasm for the stage had all but evaporated, and she chose to emigrate to the United States to follow a cinematic career, in the course of which she completed thirty films. On her return to England she settled in Henley-on-Thames, where she died in 1971. Henry Sherek, the theatre manager, recalled that 'she was a great lady of the theatre. Whenever she made an exit she always gave the impression that she never in her life had to open a door for herself.' That is a kind of compliment. Her son-in-law, the actor Robert Morley, said that 'she could be very sharp at times. She was not good at feeling sorry for people, perhaps because she never felt sorry for herself.' Dirk Bogarde's recollection can be added as a postscript: 'She had all the charm of an electric carving knife; she was precise, hard, efficient, very cool, very beautiful, and I was terrified of her.'

Cooper's name has, for various reasons, not faded. When one of her two younger sisters decided to mount the stage, she fled on hearing what she thought were a multitude of sibilant hisses. In fact, the members of the audience were whispering to one another, 'It's Gladys Cooper's sister!' She is an example of the evident truth that female actors were often unlucky in their husbands; more often than not they married beaux who were either feckless adventurers or inconsequential aristocrats. The female actors themselves, with few exceptions, were remarkably witty and articulate or, if not witty, at least lucid and confident.

Lena Ashwell was born in 1872 and began training as an opera singer, but she was persuaded by Ellen Terry to change her profession to that of actress, at which she was singularly successful. By 1892 she was touring with George Alexander in *Lady Windermere's Fan*, and she continued her work in the West End and in the provinces. Shaw spoke of 'the divinely gifted Lena Ashwell', although he did have an especial fondness for female players of this decade. By 1900 she was one of the leading actors of the day, and was celebrated on a visit to the United States as 'the great emotional English actress'. She became known for taking on 'modern' parts in leading roles, and as a result became less than enamoured of the conventional dramatic diet.

Of the musical theatre, which ruled the West End, Ashwell said, 'I believe that the drama is undergoing a period of active transition . . . I think the people have been literally choked with musical comedies. They are all the same, you know. I believe the London season opened with no less than seven of them. I think the fad for that kind of entertainment is soon going to be a thing of the past.' She took over the management of the Savoy, but her confident prediction of change never materialized.

From the Savoy Ashwell went to the newly named Kingsway Theatre in Great Queen Street, where she tried to advance modern drama. In *The Stage* in 1929 she described the difference between the styles old and new:

> Where before in Shakespeare's plays there had been the rhythm of the spoken word to explain the motives and the feelings, and to build up the power of the scene, the Transition Drama of the newer school had a hidden swirl of unspoken emotion, which had to be communicated to the audience by no other means than the actor's concentrated power of thought and feeling.

It was written of her that 'when the woman theatrical manager was practically unheard of she made a brilliant success of an enterprise that gave the public a series of plays in which the woman's point of view was never left out; and so she won another outpost for the advancing woman's army.' Ashwell was in every sense a pioneer; she campaigned for a national theatre, and during the First World War she organized companies of players to entertain the troops, a philanthropy shared by many of her fellow actors. After the war she set up touring companies, and a training academy for aspiring players. She died in London in 1957.

Some female performers shone brightly for a short period before lapsing into semi-obscurity. Dorothea Baird, for example, created the title role in Tree's *Trilby*; she played the part barefoot and smoking a cigarette, two breaches of protocol that would once have banished her from the stage. She also created the role of Mrs Darling in *Peter Pan*.

On the acting style of these performers there is little information; the reviews are trite and generally adulatory without affording much reason for being so. Several qualities emerge, but more often than not these must be teased out from the silences. To be 'sweet' was to be pretty and well behaved. If a female actor is praised for her 'passion' or 'conviction', it can be assumed that she had a commanding presence on the stage, perhaps with a tincture of acid in her relationships with other actors. The Canadian actor Raymond Massey wrote that 'all through the twenties the theatre in England was undergoing an important change; stylized, mannered plays were giving way to realistic drama and comedies, and actors had to make some adjustments to their acting style.'

The distinctive aspect of the late Edwardian period was still the prominence of the music-hall artiste. At least half of the most prominent female actors began their theatrical life in that setting. It is salutary to note that critics wrote of actors 'impersonating' a role. It was the preferred term, although it would be unthinkable to employ it now. It seemed to assume that acting was, ultimately, play-acting. Of course in one sense it is, but it was also of a piece with contemporary critics' obsession with hairstyles, sets and costumes. Everything of consequence lay on the outside. It was Athene Seyler who remarked that diction and elocution had declined as the stage sets grew more grandiose.

Two other female performers still stand out. Irene Vanbrugh, whose real name was Irene Barnes, was born in Exeter in 1872. The success of her older sister Violet on the stage prompted Irene to embark on the same career. In 1888, while training at the Theatre Royal, on the recommendation of Lewis Carroll she played the White Queen and the Jack of Hearts in a revival of *Alice in Wonderland* at the Globe, off the Strand. She followed her sister in joining J. L. Toole's company, where she played a number of substantial roles before moving from the Haymarket to the St James's, and then from the Royalty to the Court theatre. Her sensitive intelligence, her quickness and her command of mood seem to have captivated her audiences. But she had reservations about her skill. 'Who and what', she wrote, 'is the person who spends most of his or her life impersonating other people, impersonating them strongly enough not only to convince themselves but to convince thousands of others . . . What then is the reality, how far has this constant recreation of yourself obliterated the original? . . . a sort of double life must be led.' Her question has never been satisfactorily resolved. In any event, her first successes were repeated in Pinero's *His House in Order*, performed in 1906, and from that time forward she was continuously successful almost until her death in 1949.

We may add to this litany of Edwardian actors Vesta Tilley, if only to emphasize the popularity and dominance of female performers in the music hall. She was born Matilda Alice Victoria Powles in 1864 and began her professional career as a touring player at the age of five; she was known as 'the Great Little Tilly' and had her first London season in 1874, two years after she had begun cross-dressing on the stage. It was an exhausting dramatic life, with three or four 'turns' in different music halls on the same evening. The music hall itself was gradually becoming more respectable, with the old bawdiness replaced by what was called 'variety'; there was also a certain frisson in seeing an attractive girl pulling out all the stops as a male. One critic, Maurice Wilson Disher, wrote that 'instead of merging her own personality into that of the character, she brought her wits to bear on him critically – we had to see them ourselves, not as we could see them in real life, but as they were when viewed through a clever woman's eyes.' It is as good a description of acting as any. Tilley's popularity was enormous, and by the 1890s she was the highest-paid performer in the country. She was a splendid principal boy in pantomime, and took command of American vaudeville. Her last tour was in 1919, finishing in 1920 at the Coliseum, where her final song received a forty-minute standing ovation. The 'idol of London' died in that city in 1952.

Last, but also first, must be Edith Evans. She was born in 1888 in Pimlico, London, and at the age of fifteen she was apprenticed to a milliner. Her first professional engagement, at the age of twenty-two, was with the Streatham Shakespeare Players as Viola in *Twelfth Night*. Two years later fate, in the shape of William Poel, took her in hand. Poel is now almost forgotten, but in his lifetime he was acclaimed as an actor and producer who changed English taste by insisting that Elizabethan plays should be played in Elizabethan conditions. He abolished the ornate scenery created by Irving and Tree, and required that the plays be performed uncut. He became associated with the Shakespeare Reading Society, with which he remained until 1897, with the simple lesson that Shakespearean verse should be spoken faithfully but lightly and musically. He insisted on authentic costumes and established the Elizabethan Stage Society to propound his principles. He also had an eye for genuine theatrical talent, hence the rise of Edith Evans.

Evans's first Shakespearean performance under his auspices was in 1912 as Cressida, at the King's Hall in Covent Garden and then at Stratford. Her professional career, which lasted sixty-six years, really began in 1914, when she acted in four plays, including Gertrude in *Hamlet* at the Little Theatre in the Adelphi and the Royalty; but it rose ever higher in the early 1920s with Lady Utterwood in Shaw's *Heartbreak House* and then Cleopatra in Dryden's *All for Love*. James Agate asserted that her Cleopatra 'was the most finished piece of acting on the London stage today'. She climbed even further in 1924 with Mrs Millamant in William Congreve's *The Way of the World*. Arnold Bennett wrote in his diary that 'Edith Evans gave the finest comedy performance I have ever seen on the stage.' There is an explanation. 'When I come on to the stage as Millamant,' she said, 'I assume without question that I am the most beautiful woman in town, and on the assumption of that consciousness I base all my behaviour.' She would gaze into the mirror at her lopsided, almost hatchet, face and murmur, 'I am beautiful, I am beautiful,' over and over again, until with the last incantation she swept on to the stage, charm at the ready.

Like most actors, Evans was utterly dedicated to her profession, and played over 150 leading roles. The critic Kenneth Tynan noted that 'she has an enviable facial mobility with one unique attribute:

the gift of suggesting vulgar-hearted disdain.' She came to regret the fact that her most famous part was that of Lady Bracknell, in which there is indeed a hint of vulgarity. It was her swooping voice that was memorable, but in any case her voice was such a flexible medium that despite herself it became her trademark. Michael Redgrave wrote that few realized that her performance was largely the magic of verbal control: 'We talk of her personality, her magnetism, her wonderful assumption of beauty, all of which she has in abundance. They are so compelling that the audience does not analyse the result.'

It was Evans's voice that held the key, her voice together with her eyes. As Lady Bracknell she offers us a fruitcake of a voice: high-octane, rich and flutey, full of every note, rattle and caw. But it is in her eyes that we see the great actress. Each pupil carries a flea circus within it, dancing in puckish delight, as if her eyes are telling another story, full of wicked gossip, while her throat and lips play Lady Bracknell. When she waited in the green room she sat very quietly with only her hands moving across her lap; she was allowing the character to take over, and friends noticed that at such moments she became a stranger to them. They fell silent. One contemporary, watching her ready to perform, remarked that, 'I always feel that she's saying, "don't get too close to me; don't touch me."' In preparing for her part she was tentative and hesitating, adding a tone here and a gesture there. Out of all this the character was born. It was sometimes assumed that Evans was word perfect in advance, but in fact she did not consult the script until the time of rehearsal. She gave the impression of aloofness, and had no sympathy for those who interfered with her work. One of her secretaries recorded that 'as far as her own work was concerned Edith was completely ruthless, anyone and everything that might injure it was out.' 'If one accepts that Edith is only interested in Edith,' Sybil Thorndike once said, 'one can be quite fond of her.'

Although we need not suppose that the malice in this was more than mischievous, some rivalry undoubtedly simmered between the comic and the tragic queens. Sheridan Morley wrote that while 'Dame Edith cascaded from a great height . . . Dame Sybil contented herself with playing Schumann on the stage [in N. C. Hunter's *Waters of the Moon*] and, when the grandchildren weren't in front, capturing the few good scenes she did have almost by stealth.' Legend has it that when the play had been running successfully for a year, the manager announced to Evans that she would be receiving an entirely new wardrobe from Balmain. 'Good,' said Edith, 'but you'd better do something for Sybil too, what about a new cardigan?' And if Evans could be an egotistical, which is to say a professional, actress, she was notable for another characteristic. The director William Gaskill recalled how 'waves and waves of warmth came from her.'

Hers had been a long career. Evans started work in the silent cinema in 1915, but gave her last screen performance, singing and dancing, in 1976 as the dowager queen in *The Slipper and the Rose*. In the autumn of that year she died at her home in Kent. John Gielgud wrote, 'supreme mistress of high comedy and farce, a brilliant and versatile character actress rich in power and emotional conviction, the name of Edith Evans must surely rank with the greatest of her sisters in the history of our theatre'.

Seventeen

A quartet

In the 1920s the male actors had been eclipsed by their female counterparts, but all that was about to change. There was in any case one interloper who passed effortlessly from the 1920s into the 1930s and beyond. This was Charles Laughton. He was to all appearances a plump Yorkshireman with a cracked and fricative voice. But within this Caliban was a Proteus able to outplay all his contemporaries. He was born in Scarborough in 1899 but contracted a glandular condition that enlarged his size; his family directed him towards hotel management, which was partially interrupted by his being gassed during army service in the First World War, but hotels were in any case not to his taste.

In 1925 Laughton enrolled as a student at RADA, where two years later he was awarded a gold medal. He was immediately taken up for his odd but striking appearance, as well as his natural gift for the stage. George Bernard Shaw watched him as the male lead in *Pygmalion* and went backstage to tell him that 'you were perfectly dreadful as Higgins. But I predict a brilliant career for you within the year.' He had seen the light within the actor. And so it proved.

Laughton began with Russian plays, under the guidance of a Russian director, but was soon chosen for the roles his demeanour seemed to demand; that is, he specialized in oleaginous villains, neurotic malcontents and other somewhat sinister characters. He lowered the temperature with Hercule Poirot in Michael Morton's *Alibi* and Samuel Pickwick in a Dickensian adaptation, but then went on to play a gangster in Edgar Wallace's *On the Spot* and a murderer in C. S. Forester's *Payment Deferred*.

It was inevitable that Hollywood would summon Laughton, and there among other roles he played his first Nero and his only Dr Moreau, together with four other films, including *Devil and the Deep* and *The Old Dark House* (both 1932). In *Devil and the Deep* he uses that unmistakable languorous voice in which he hammers a trochee on each two-syllabled word and follows it with a lingering cadence, as in 'womaa-aa-aan' and 'LETTaa-aas'. There is nothing more gripping than his final scene, when he emits an eldritch howl – inhuman and for that reason utterly convincing – and a hysterical laugh before drowning in a sinking submarine. This is not madness; it is something peculiar, almost unnameable and close to cockeyed genius.

In 1932 Laughton performed in six Hollywood films. It could no longer be assumed that an English actor would appear only in British films. It should also be noted that the 1930s were a very lean time for adaptations of Shakespeare, which had been the lifeblood of native players. The fashion for the filmed stage performance had in any case waned, replaced by a taste for cinema as cinema. Basil Rathbone, for example, was well known for playing that most English of characters, Sherlock Holmes. But the paramount English player on the screen was still Charles Laughton.

Fame and success, however, would spring from closer to home. On his return to England in 1933 Laughton embarked on a series of biographical films, including *The Private Life of Henry VIII* (1933), *The Barretts of Wimpole Street* (1934) and *Mutiny on the Bounty* (1935). They would make him the most significant film actor (if not the most accomplished actor) of his generation. Henry VIII was for Laughton the part that required perfect pitch. We see aspects of his style that were already familiar – the bumbler, the boy, the ogre, the jealous husband – together with a schoolboy's preening smirk and a slight bounce in his walk; like many bulky people, he was surprisingly light on his feet. While he waits for Anne Boleyn's execution he taps the windowpane, a tap that manages to be both gloating and impatient. A capacity to convey sudden and complete shifts of feeling, with no artificiality, was Laughton's forte. He could display contempt, resentment and even menace followed by almost comic glee and a laugh of innocent joy. It would not be facile to claim that he deployed the same skill on stage. Sometimes he accompanied an authoritative voice with an ever-deepening pout. He had singular expressions that other actors could not imitate. He could also make a gargoyle of his face, sometimes followed by his familiar full-chested laugh, which always began with a double-barrelled report. There was also the moue of the mouth, with raised eyebrows and half-sulky posture. He managed to convey so much, and transform himself so completely, largely through meticulous preparation. Only by that attention to detail could he achieve such astounding spontaneity and such precision in performance.

In 1933 Laughton also joined the Old Vic, where his work on the stage was as much admired as that on celluloid. With the exception of Chekhov, his roles were out of Shakespeare, including the title roles in *Henry VIII* and *Macbeth*, Angelo in *Measure for Measure* and Prospero in *The Tempest*. 'He doesn't tell you what to think or feel,' one critic wrote, 'he brings you face to face with the thing itself.' Of his *Measure for Measure* one theatrical historian wrote that 'he did little justice to the verse, but the performance was a shuddering glance at a cankered mind.' This naked exposure may have been one of the legacies of film-acting. His compulsion spilled over on all sides. In every one of Laughton's performances there is a transformation, not just a trajectory. He said of 'method acting' that it gives a photograph where 'real acting gives an oil painting'. Laughton offered something more direct and powerful.

Uniquely, perhaps, he invites you to *share* his character's feelings. 'You don't direct Laughton in a picture,' Hitchcock remarked, 'you referee it.' His covert homosexuality might have altered his life, but it also lent eccentricity and tension to his acting. He died in Hollywood in 1962.

Within six years, from 1902 to 1908, were born Donald Wolfit, Ralph Richardson, John Gielgud, Laurence Olivier and Michael Redgrave; to level the field somewhat, we must include Peggy Ashcroft. Here were some of the greatest actors of the century, clustered as if in a cabinet of curiously bright lights. The principal dramatists could not be fully associated with these new and diverse actors. Shaw was still writing, and writing, and writing, but he could no longer share in the shock of the new; J. M. Barrie and Arthur Wing Pinero, although of lesser genius, suffered a similar fate and were contemplating the final curtain of their stage success.

New dramatists did emerge in the 1920s and 1930s. Noël Coward, J. B. Priestley, James Bridie and W. Somerset Maugham did not quite match the standard of the emerging actors, but, as prolific as they were popular, they kept the players in work. By the end of the 1930s Coward had composed more than twenty plays as well as two revues and two operettas, while Priestley finished nineteen plays and Bridie twenty. The alternative was the verse drama for an English audience pioneered by T.S. Eliot, whose *Sweeney Agonistes* and *The Rock* were followed later in that decade by *Murder in the Cathedral* and *The Family Reunion*.

The coming actors were not, however, interested in contemporary blank verse, perhaps Wolfit least of all. He was an actor in the old style, beetle-browed, gruff and stubborn. He was born in 1902 near Newark in Nottinghamshire, and from an early age was determined to become an actor. While teaching in Eastbourne in 1920 he came upon Charles Doran's touring Shakespearean company, where his extravagance and energy at the age of eighteen were considered outstanding. Four years later he made the pilgrimage to London and took a number of small parts under the guidance of Matheson Lang, a stage and film actor from Canada who had arrived in England eleven years before and now managed the New Theatre. In 1927 Wolfit joined the Sheffield Repertory Company, but then returned to London.

Wolfit settled on the familiar wandering life of touring and repertory, interrupted only by marriage and a daughter, before he found a path to possible success through Lilian Baylis at the Old Vic. But the path was wayward. He was not popular with the other players because of his remoteness and self-concern. Other actors share similar characteristics, but Wolfit compounded the error by conceiving an envious dislike for the leading man, John Gielgud, perhaps because Gielgud *was* the leading man. Yet Wolfit had immense presence on the stage, with a characteristic fierce and dark gaze that never left him. He had total control of his voice, and had the signal ability to convey and to project an inner life.

Although he was not wanted for a subsequent season at the Old Vic, Wolfit found work easily enough in London or on tour. From 1931 to 1936 he travelled from theatre to theatre, until he joined the company at the Shakespeare Memorial Theatre in Stratford. It was a short season, but he managed to play eight parts, including Hamlet, Orsino and Cassius. Other roles were relatively minor, a circumstance that dismayed him, but his Hamlet was judged to be a notable success. The critic Audrey Williamson was impressed by his 'electric drive and force of suffering . . . there was thought behind every gesture and line, and again and again one was struck by the subtlety of detail.'

Wolfit returned to Stratford for the 1937 season and, as a result of his success, he set up a touring company of which he was naturally manager and leading actor, a role he maintained for the next twenty-six years. Hermione Gingold once remarked, 'Olivier is a tour de force and Wolfit is forced to tour.' He was deeply hurt by criticism of any kind and formed a carapace of pomposity, grandiosity and brutality tempered by genuine modesty and humility. He gave the impression of embarking on a hard and harsh journey, and having never been thanked for his pains.

But Wolfit's stage presence was itself harsh and unyielding, leaning more towards the melodramatics of Irving and Macready than any contemporary. The style was so passionate and unruly that in certain circles he became synonymous with 'ham'. But in truth his career was as diverse as it was energetic, encompassing Shylock, Touchstone, Macbeth, Richard III, Othello, Falstaff and many others. His Lear of 1943 was considered to be outstanding. James Agate commented that 'Mr Wolfit had and was all the things we demand, and created the impression Lear calls for . . . his performance on Wednesday was the greatest piece of Shakespearian acting I have seen since I was privileged to write for the *Sunday Times*.' Kenneth Tynan wrote that Wolfit 'has dynamism, energy, bulk and stature, and he joins these together with a sheer relish for resonant words . . . he moves very slowly and predatorily, with immense finesse, and rises to his climaxes in clear and cogent steps.' At the end of each performance Wolfit enacted a little drama of his own by clutching the curtain as if for dear life.

In 1951 the director Tyrone Guthrie invited Wolfit to join the Old Vic with Lear, Timon of Athens and Tamburlaine, and in the last-named role he came into his own. One critic compared him to a giant bear, which in some moods he resembled, while another noted that 'he projects an adolescent relish in animal cruelty, and rises in the second half to a kind of madness which is turned in on itself in a lust for destruction.' That is perhaps the abiding image of Wolfit, who could never seem to be at ease anywhere, and who could not settle down with other actors whom he considered much less eminent than himself.

It was Wolfit who had to be the star, and if he was not, he sulked and generally misbehaved. He was '*the actor*' with a dark, wide-brimmed hat and cloak. Guthrie complained of his anger and occasional brutality to the rest of the cast, with the result that Wolfit left the Old Vic. He formed a new company, but it was generally supposed that he surrounded himself with second-rate players so that he might shine all the brighter. When he was criticized for cutting a passage from *Twelfth Night*, he replied that 'I can't learn it and, if I can't learn it, Shakespeare didn't write it.' He carried on working and touring as if his life depended on them. He always believed that he had never received his due, in fame or acclaim, and remained a disappointed man. He died in London in 1968.

Ralph Richardson was born in the same year as Wolfit, but two actors could not be more different. Richardson's upbringing and education were erratic, but in common with many actors he had a Catholic childhood. He was an altar boy at a Roman Catholic church in Brighton, along which ritual path he was accompanied by Laurence Olivier, Michael Gambon and John Philip Kemble. There is clearly a connection between the experience of ceremony and the love of acting. He graduated from school to an office, but he was rescued by £500 that his grandmother left him in her will. Bolstered by the bequest, he joined a group of semi-professional players managed by Doran, but after his marriage in 1924, he and his new wife joined the Birmingham Repertory Company, with which he first ventured into London with a small part in Sophocles' *Oedipus at Colonus*.

The next four years were spent in minor West End roles, of which Richardson commented that 'those years of grind formed the first thread of nervous tissue connecting what I had in my mind and what I was doing with my body.' In 1930 he was enlisted at the Old Vic, where he met Olivier and Gielgud. 'Unlike me,' Gielgud said, 'he is intensely interested in machinery and in all the intimate details of science and engineering . . . He is inclined to despise the petty accessories of theatrical life.' Richardson's first season at the Old Vic was dominated by Shakespeare, from Caliban to

Toby Belch, and his playing was so widely admired that he was persuaded to continue with a second season at the head of the company. The producer Harcourt Williams described his Richard II as 'a tall, willowy figure in black velvet, surmounted by a fair head, the pale agonised face set beneath a glittering crown'. Richardson had had enough of Shakespeare, however, and his second season was his last. He began to work on the plays of contemporaries or near contemporaries, such as Shaw and Maugham. In 1934, for example, he played at the Duchess Theatre in Priestley's *Eden End*, in what turned out to be a fruitful collaboration.

Richardson migrated to Broadway the following year to play Mercutio in *Romeo and Juliet*, but he hated the experience, and the theatregoers of New York were bemused by an ordinary-looking man who did not set out to dazzle as his contemporaries did. In 1936 he returned to London and a crime adventure, Barré Lyndon's *The Amazing Dr Clitterhouse*, at the Haymarket. But he was back on the stage of the Old Vic two years later in the role of Bottom, and then Othello to Olivier's Iago. Richardson did not approve of Olivier's homosexual interpretation of the part, however, and that may in fact have affected his performance. James Agate commented that 'the truth is that Nature, which has showered upon this actor the kindly gifts of the comedian, has unkindly refused him any tragic facilities whatever . . . He cannot blaze.' But he knew how to burn brightly, and was praised for his work in 1939 on Priestley's *Johnson over Jordan* at the New Theatre, which was inevitably overshadowed by the imminent war. During the hostilities he became lieutenant-commander of the naval reserve, a post in which he was not a particular success. But he was largely preoccupied by the long illness of his wife, who suffered for thirteen years from encephalitis lethargica and died in 1942.

By 1944 Richardson had been released to rejoin the Old Vic as its manager, together with Olivier, and in the same year he married for a second time. For four seasons he worked with Olivier, Thorndike and Margaret Leighton, and created a memorable Falstaff, who, in Tynan's words, 'was not a sweaty fat man, but a dry and dignified one. As the great belly moved, step following step with great finesse lest it over-topple, the arms flapped fussily at the sides as if to paddle the body's bulk along. It was deliciously and subtly funny, not riotously so: from his height of pomp Falstaff was chuckling at himself: it was not we alone, laughing at him.'

Paul Scofield, who acted with Richardson in Graham Greene's *The Complaisant Lover* in 1959, said of him that 'I found the gradual hostility, which grew in him throughout the play, almost frightening. Something very hard – an iron in his soul – something dangerously combative, very masculine . . . just sometimes more alarming.' Perhaps the remote and absorbed persona Richardson sometimes adopted was a way of controlling his less attractive qualities. Of his role in *Peer Gynt*, he wrote, 'I don't remember . . . it's a funny thing about acting. I have nothing to say about it at all which is a bit odd because one does take such immense trouble to try and find the character, to create the character, that it is rather as if the memory vanishes.' The effect is similar to those people who cannot remember the events of a traumatic past. He was as a result unceremonious about his skill. 'Acting', he said, 'is merely the art of keeping a large number of people from coughing.'

Richardson's manner, on stage as well as screen, seems understated and even unfelt, but he is in fact performing in a deliberately lower key than those around him, who may have preferred the Grand Guignol manner. Richardson, however, could subdue himself to the material he worked in; in front of an audience he conveyed an irresistible charisma, but he knew how to suppress it when needed. However instinctive in his approach to acting, he would often puncture an otherwise fluent performance with knowing or clownish asides. His register of facial expression is remarkable, with an arched eyebrow, a commanding glance or a look of horror, all admirably conveyed with an inner conviction that precludes theatrics. It is all very subtle, but unmistakable.

It could be said that Richardson was at his most persuasive when his character was in some way faulty. He had the habit of keeping his inner reality in reserve so that, when he was required to release it, it came out with all the greater conviction. He could combine grievance with menace together with weary resignation. He did not need to act it out. It was one of his characteristics that he could blend the most incongruous feelings. He could shift his manner in a moment, and convey complex emotions with a glance. Only someone of keen observational skill – or very deep self-awareness – would know, for example, that an expression of rage is often the truest sign of absolute terror.

In 1975 Richardson joined the National Theatre, beginning with Ibsen's *John Gabriel Borkman*. Gielgud commented, 'I shall never forget the noise he made when Borkman died. As if a bird had flown out of his heart.' Richardson had an indeterminate quality in his acting, as if he were not sure whether his emotions were true or untrue. He illuminated the maxim that absence is presence. He was like the dreamer who dreams and forgets. He himself wrote that 'acting is to some extent a controlled dream. In one part of your consciousness it really and truly is happening . . . The rest of it is technique.' In John Osborne's *West of Suez*, one critic noted the 'false innocence' of Richardson's character, Wyatt Gillman, which brings with it 'a hint of a whimper, calculated self-reproach, a touch of unction'. But he noted later 'a touch of steel' somewhere within it.

Peter Hall, who directed Richardson in *The Cherry Orchard* for the 1978 season, noted his preparation for the part of Firs. It evokes a very English way of 'getting into character'. The means are quite different from those used by the 'Method' school of actors, but the intent and the result are identical. Hall wrote:

I shall never forget Ralph walking through the last bit of Firs; not acting it but commentating on it to himself and to us:

'Now I come through the door in my slippers. Good heavens, there's nobody here. Good Lord, they've all gone. So I go off to the window and look out. Can't see anything. So I go over to the sofa feeling very tired now, sit down, drop my stick, too tired to take it up. So I lie back, want to put my legs up, but can't, I'm too tired. Then I die.'

This is the manner in which Richardson felt his way into his role, gently and without fuss. A fellow actor commented that 'when you're acting with him there's no eye contact. He never looks at you and he never touches people on stage.' He was most powerful when portraying characters who are curiously empty and who are terrified of that emptiness. A *New Yorker* profile in 1977 described him as 'very odd and absent-minded and solitary, and absurd, and noble, and desolate. When he spoke he sounded at once defiant and merciful.' Here, then, are six characters in search of a personality.

Although Hall, among others, considered him the greatest of the great four, Richardson himself was always diffident about his abilities. He sometimes referred to himself as a 'second-class' actor in comparison with his famous contemporaries, in the belief that he lacked substance. Perhaps that is why he never exerted a hold upon the public like that of Gielgud or Olivier. 'We don't know exactly who we are, do we?' he once said. 'We're a mystery to ourselves, and to other people.' But that can be seen as an advantage, and may account for the secret springs of his acting. He observed of Charlie Chaplin that 'the audience didn't realise how odd he was because he was so near to reality in his madness.' Richardson could have been talking about himself, although it should be noted that he took care to release only so much of himself as he could bear. In interview, he was adept at playing the part of the bewildered, but knowing, eccentric, always steering matters away from anything too intimate. Charles Laughton was to make a professional virtue out of his inner wounds; Richardson made one out of concealing them. He died in October 1983, at the age of eighty. He was the supremely human actor, at once magical and mundane.

The third of the famous quartet, John Gielgud, was born in the spring of 1904 in South Kensington. He was part of a famous theatrical family, and his great-aunt was Ellen Terry. He was not a natural scholar, and became a day boy at Westminster school; at the age of seventeen he persuaded his parents to fund his drama lessons on the understanding that, if he was not a success at twenty-five, he would give up the whole business. In this first year he enlisted in a private drama school under the control of Constance Benson, the wife of the actor-manager Sir Frank Benson, who was well known for his Shakespearean revivals. Constance commented that the young man 'walked like a cat with rickets', which may have had something to do with incipient bow legs. He took part in several amateur productions, and was hired by the Old Vic in non-speaking roles, which, given his eloquence, may have been a mistake.

In 1922 Gielgud's cousin Phyllis Neilson-Terry offered him a part in her company with *The Wheel*, a trite melodrama, and he gladly abandoned his early mute and inglorious career for a period of study at RADA. The actor and director Nigel Playfair, a friend of the family, saw potential in Gielgud, and for his London debut put him in Josef and Karel Čapek's *The Insect Play*, where he was cast, perhaps appropriately, as a poet-butterfly. 'I am surprised', he said, 'that the audience didn't throw things at me.' He went on to play Charley in *Charley's Aunt*, itself already a venerable institution, then joined the Oxford Playhouse, where work was more readily available. This was 'rep' as he had never known it, with a new play every Monday, seven performances a week, and rehearsals for six days. He played for several months in 1924 and 1925 in a variety of dramas, but it was his experience as Trofimov in Chekhov's *The Cherry Orchard* that convinced him that, after all, he might become a successful actor: 'It acted as a kind of protection from my usual self-consciousness . . . Instead I must try to create a character utterly different from myself.' When he looked in the mirror, complete with sparse wig, small beard and steel glasses, he said to himself, 'I know how this man would speak and move and behave.'

In May 1925 Gielgud repeated the role at the Lyric, Hammersmith, and his beguiling voice led him ineluctably to BBC Radio, for which he worked off and on for seventy years. He possessed one of the most recognizable voices in England. At once liquid and airy, relaxed and yearning, it might be the voice of a prophet foreseeing both darkness and the hope to follow. He seemed to cosset and cherish every word, however banal, and this could make him the despair of radio producers; he could not simply repeat the words, but had to give them wonder and wings. Such loving attention to vowel and consonant could not but attract parody, but the parodies were as warm as they were respectful.

By 1929 Gielgud had returned to the Old Vic, from which the envious Wolfit had disappeared, and soon formed a relationship with a new recruit by the name of Ralph Richardson. There was frost at first. 'He was a kind of brilliant butterfly,' Richardson recalled, 'while I was a very gloomy sort of boy. I found his clothes extravagant. I found his conversation flippant. He was the New Young Man of his time and I didn't like him.' Wounds were healed when Gielgud gave Richardson some pertinent hints about Caliban, and it was not long before they recognized the flame in each other. Gielgud glided through the repertoire with *Romeo and Juliet*, *The Merchant of Venice* and *Richard II*; the unhappy king was always one of his favourite parts, and a fellow actor commented that 'the infinite variations of his beautifully modulated vice hypnotised both audience and actors.' The mesmerism was complete. He once remarked of playing Shakespeare that, since nobody understands what you are saying, you can make up the lines if you forget them.

Tynan, in *He that Plays the King*, wrote that 'Gielgud is an actor who refuses to compromise with his audience . . . They must accept him on his own intellectual level or not at all. This aloofness and rigid dignity of his represent his only unique quality.' After other plays at the Old Vic, Gielgud enjoyed his first commercial success in 1931 with Priestley's *The Good Companions*, which ran for 331 nights; he participated in the filmed version two years later. He was not an admirer of the cinema, however, which 'appals my soul but appeals to my pocket'. He finished two films in 1941, including the part of Benjamin Disraeli, but otherwise he ducked the opportunity whenever it presented itself, while Olivier and Richardson backed into the arc lights. He did not really return to the cinema until the 1950s.

In 1932 Gielgud was willing to direct *Romeo and Juliet* for the Oxford University Dramatic Society, and more than willing to work with Peggy Ashcroft as Juliet and Edith Evans as the Nurse. In one of his many notorious slips of the tongue, he described them as 'two leading ladies, the like of whom I hope I shall never meet again'. He meant that they were indispensable, not disposable. In 1935 he staged *Romeo and Juliet* once more, with Ashcroft and Olivier. In this production Olivier and Gielgud swapped roles, from Romeo to Mercutio, each week. All seemed set for a triumph, but Olivier took matters in hand. One cast member recalled that 'Larry was out to dominate the play by the sheer force of his presence, and to ride roughshod over the rest of us as we went about things in our rather restrained Gielgudian fashion.' Olivier also took exception to the critics who noted Gielgud's effortless superiority in the speaking of verse. Olivier, who was not accustomed to being compared unfavourably with anyone, never really forgave Gielgud for a fault that was hardly of his making.

Gielgud was knighted in 1953, providentially before he was arrested for soliciting. He feared that his career would crash and burn after that unfortunate incident, but, if anything, it increased his popularity. The strain on him was so great, however, that he suffered a nervous breakdown. For the next two years he absented himself from the stage and concentrated on directing. In 1955 he ventured in front of an audience with *King Lear*, which was not a success, and *Much Ado About Nothing*, which was. Shakespeare was in effect his safety rope. He once said that 'I was haunted all through my childhood by the shade of Henry Irving.' This meant that he feared the slight flavour of being old-fashioned.

Throughout the 1960s Gielgud divided his time between directing and film work, with one or two forays into acting that were not altogether successful, with the single exception of the part of the headmaster in Alan Bennett's *Forty Years On*. The role suited him perfectly, and one critic commented that it represented, 'from the great mandarin of the theatre, a delicious comic creation'. His next great performance was in David Storey's *Home* in 1970, with Richardson, a duet that has been described as 'two of the greatest performances of two careers that have been among the glories of the English-speaking theatre'. In this Gielgud is sardonic and meticulous, holding himself intact in opposition to Richardson's more distracted and confused character, until both are invaded by grief. Only slowly does the audience realize that they are locked in a mental institution; they are Lear's 'poor bare, forked animals' transposed to a different and more suppressed key.

In a profile of the period, Gielgud declared that acting is 'half shame, half glory. Shame, at exhibiting yourself; glory, when you can forget yourself.' He believed that there were two stages in an actor's career: the first concerned with self-revelation, and the second with detachment and self-presentation. He could say to himself that 'I know my powers. I have tested them thoroughly. And I am fairly sure that some of them are unique and theatrically valid quite apart from the roles I play.'

In 1974 Gielgud resumed acting with the part of a depressed and introspective Shakespeare in Edward Bond's *Bingo* at the Royal Court. He went on to play another partnership with Richardson in Harold Pinter's *No Man's Land* at the Old Vic, which was an extraordinary success with Gielgud as a garrulous and slightly menacing stray; it ran for three years through the West End, Broadway and the National Theatre. This was in turn followed by Julian Mitchell's *Half-Life* at the National. One critic reflected that Gielgud was 'a past master at portraying suffering: here he displays, with great art, the numbed stupefaction of one who has seen too much in others.' He then went back to film and television, in which, after innumerable performances, he had become most famous and recognizable. For many of a younger generation, this was all they knew of him. Lacking any theatrical vanity, he was not dismayed by this sea change in a long career. 'They pay me very well for two or three days' work a month,' he said, 'so why not? It's nice at my age to travel all over the world at other people's expense.' The film critics shared his enthusiasm. Pauline Kael observed of his role in *Arthur*, for example, that 'John Gielgud can steal a scene simply by wearing a hat.' He used the persona he created on stage to make his way in front of the camera. In his final film appearance, in Samuel Beckett's *Catastrophe* of 2000, he did not speak. True silence then finally descended, and he died later that year.

The fourth member of this renaissance of English acting, Laurence Olivier, was born in Dorking, Surrey, on 22 May 1907. He once said, 'I believe that I was born to be an actor.' Certainly the circumstances were right; his father was a priest of High Anglican persuasion and the young Olivier was brought up in a world of ritual and ceremony. At ten he appeared in his choir school's production of *Julius Caesar*, and Ellen Terry noted in her diary that 'the small boy who took the part of Brutus is already a great actor.' His father sensed it, too, and in 1924 he agreed that his son might join the Central School of Speech and Drama. Two years later Olivier was invited into the Birmingham Repertory Theatre, for which he played a variety of roles. It was more useful than any university, and from the beginning he was driven by an insensate appetite for the stage; in 1929 he appeared in seven plays. He once confessed that 'I have never been conscious of any need other than to show off.' He expedited this by playing in Noël Coward's *Private Lives* in 1931, but when it moved to Broadway he decamped to Hollywood in the company of his new wife, the actor Jill Esmond. The film industry was not as exciting or productive as he had anticipated, but he threw one last dice in playing opposite Greta Garbo. He was fired after a few days, however, on the supposition that he was scared to death by the leading lady.

Safely ensconced in London, Olivier resumed a theatrical career already embellished by his good looks and his athleticism. His versatility was once more pre-eminent. In one West End play he jumped 2.5 metres (8 ft) over a balcony, amazing the audience and his fellow actors. Compared to his animation and drive, other actors seemed more casual, their roles more lightly executed. They were always somehow quieter or more dispassionate.

But Olivier had not yet fulfilled any of his ambitions. He was not a star, but he had reached the foothills as a virile romantic actor. In 1934 Gielgud offered him the part of Bothwell in Gordon Daviot's *Queen of Scots* at the New Theatre; Gielgud, as director, had seen Olivier's potential at once. He then proposed that Olivier should alternate with him the roles of Mercutio and Romeo, as we have seen, with Peggy Ashcroft as Juliet. Gielgud had the words, and Olivier the action. Olivier himself once said, 'I've always thought that we were reverses of the same coin: the top half John, all spirituality, all abstract things, and myself as all earth, blood, humanity if you like, the baser parts of that humanity without the beauty.' In a memoir he insisted that 'you must have the strength, the will and determination of an ox.' He once said of a fellow actor, 'he's a good actor, very good, but he's too nice . . . he lacks the killer instinct.' There was another side to that argument; it meant that Olivier himself knew that he possessed just such an instinct.

His blood and guts landed him two major film parts, and Tyrone Guthrie invited him to join the Old Vic. At last Olivier was a classical actor. He played the leading role in *Hamlet*, of which James Agate wrote that 'Mr Olivier does not speak poetry badly. He does not speak it at all.' Instead he complimented him on his 'pulsating vitality and excitement'. Hamlet led to Toby Belch, and Belch led to Henry v. Macbeth and Othello followed, consummated at the end of 1938 by his most accomplished part as Coriolanus. One critic celebrated it as 'a pillar of fire on a plinth of marble'. He summed it up by hurling himself in a somersault down some stairs and coming to a halt just at the edge of the stage.

Then Olivier vanished from the stage for six years. This was in part the consequence of the Second World War and his role in propaganda films, and in part the influence of Hollywood. He seems to have made the transition from stage to screen with very little difficulty. Tynan confided to his diary, however, that Olivier was 'an essentially cold actor'. He had a point. Tenderness did not come easily to him, but when he found it, it is as persuasive as any other quality he displayed. In a cinematic version of *As You Like It*, however, he does not seem to be a natural paramour, for all his charm. Required by the script to be in love, he shows something more like mooning self-pity. The sense is of some vague, Wertherian, unreal anguish; it has a self-caressing quality. And then there is Agate's point of his speaking verse. It is in some respects very curious. He hammers on the metre without releasing the rhythm; the verse is painstaking without necessarily being accurate. His fundamental weakness may be that he was too aware of his good qualities.

Allowance may be made for his relative youth, but Shakespeare's roles, however young, require weight and depth and delicacy; these are not qualities that Olivier always demonstrated.

He was not always good at responding to other actors. That was betrayed by his eyes. When he registered shock, for example, he was sometimes content with a grimace. In fact he found shock a very difficult emotion, or sensation, to present. He also had problems conveying vulnerability; something in him needed to show off, to discard the revelation of truth in favour of the flourish. When called upon to love, Olivier's heroes and anti-heroes gave the impression of loving only themselves, the eyes downcast and the voice elaborately soft. He appeared suspicious of emotional spontaneity.

There is a sense in which Olivier was always on his guard; in certain roles, and at certain moments, he found the baring of the soul almost embarrassing. In other scenes he has a way of trusting to his native charm where there is more work to be done. Yet he never had difficulty in finding and presenting anger. He often presented moods of irritability, a state with which he seems to have been more comfortable. Like Coriolanus (1937) and Heathcliff (1939), parts that he played admirably on stage and on screen, he forged himself. That is not, however, how he remembered it. In an interview he confessed that the director of *Wuthering Heights*, William Wyler, 'was a marvellous sneerer, debunker; and he brought me down. I knew nothing of film acting or that I had to learn its technique; it took a long time and several unhandsome degrees of the torture of his sarcasm before I realized it.' In one scene Olivier was obliged to endure sixty 'takes' to find any emotional reality for the camera. It is often salutary to remember how innately and instinctively theatrical he was. He may have known Richardson's maxim that 'films are where you sell what you've learned on the stage.' Yet there is always that indefinable and unlearnable quality known as charisma.

Olivier returned to England in 1941 and joined the Fleet Air Arm; like Richardson, he was not a successful pilot, and he was persuaded that he would aid morale better with lines than with bombs. So he set to work on *Henry V* as both leading man and director; it was a triumph of propaganda in 1944 but, more importantly, it was a feat of film-making. At the beginning he is playing not Henry but a Tudor actor playing Henry. Thus he opens his arms to the audience and bows to them. His verse-speaking is now more attuned to his character; his voice has the familiar timbre, but he has rendered it more majestic. It is harsh and hard for the most part, which makes the dips into tenderness or reflection all the more striking. Actors confronting a particularly cerebral piece of Shakespeare are usually encouraged simply to follow the thought and forget about 'acting'. This is what Olivier seems to be doing here.

In the same year, when he was filming at Denham Studios, Olivier was persuaded by Richardson to join him and John Burrell in managing a newly formed Old Vic, which might be the nucleus of a national theatre. They started the process by inaugurating a continuous repertory and by selling inexpensive tickets from one shilling and sixpence to four shillings and sixpence. With a company that included Margaret Leighton and Alec Guinness, it might be considered cheap at the price. There was even talk of an 'expansion scheme' in 1946, but it was suffocated by theatrical politics; the only tangible and beneficial result was the foundation of the Young Vic.

The third play of that 1944 season was also one of Olivier's greatest, *Richard III*, the study of an uneasy king whose outward benignity and inner turbulence bore some relation to the actor's own temperament. The clipped delivery, the eyelid-batting asides and the lurching of moods elicit from the audience not so much applause as recognition and illicit consent. Olivier was never more plausible as a seducer than when he played the long-nosed, hunchbacked cripple. Over the next three years he performed a range of parts, from Oedipus to Mr Puff, which exemplified what was now being called his theatrical genius. 'The Old Vic season', one critic wrote, could be set as a 'starting date for the modern English theatre'. Olivier's only weakness lay in tragedy. He was not a great Lear, and one critic remarked, 'I have the conviction that Olivier is a comedian by instinct and a tragedian by art.' There may be another aspect. Cedric Hardwicke once said that 'anyone who has been an actor any length of time does not know whether he has any true emotions or not.'

A subsequent ten-month tour of Australia and New Zealand was not altogether a success. Olivier's marriage to Vivien Leigh, who toured with him in a number of roles, was unravelling. He suffered cartilage injury that required extensive morphine. And he was informed in a letter from the chairman of the Old Vic that the services of the triumvirate were no longer required; Olivier, Richardson and Burrell were out. Olivier returned for a last season in 1949, but his need for success and recognition on the stage seems to have been eclipsed by his acquisition of film 'stardom'. He spent much time and attention, also, on caring for Leigh, who was suffering from manic depression. They eventually divorced in 1960, and soon afterwards he married Joan Plowright.

In 1955 Olivier enlisted in the Shakespeare Memorial Theatre at Stratford-upon-Avon, where he played in succession Malvolio, Macbeth and Titus Andronicus, and in the last two of which he rescued his reputation as a tragic actor. Comic pathos and tragedy were aligned when in 1957 he took on the leading role in Osborne's *The Entertainer* at the Royal Court. This role of the fading comic suited him well. Osborne said, 'I suspect that Olivier has a feeling sometimes that he is a deeply hollow man.' William Gaskill, artistic director at the Royal Court, commented, too, that 'that kind of heartless clown's mask is very much part of Larry Olivier.' Olivier's success with Osborne's play may have helped him to embrace the 'new theatre', and in 1960 he played Berenger in Eugène Ionesco's *Rhinoceros*. This was succeeded by Jean Anouilh's *Becket*. He was moving from character to character without much sense of progress. It might be thought that this did not matter any more, given his achievement and reputation, but a flying arrow needs a target. Gaskill also noted that the 'sense of a man driving himself forward was reflected in his verse-speaking, in the way that he carried lines through to the end, and the famous upward inflection'.

Olivier had indeed found a direction, in the neighbourhood of Chichester. He was offered the management of the new Chichester Festival Theatre, with the opening season set for 1962. The third play was immediately the most successful; *Uncle Vanya* included Michael Redgrave, Plowright and Olivier himself. It was fortuitous that in the same period a national theatre was planned and seriously proposed; Olivier was offered the post of founder and director, which he accepted with alacrity.

It was a position for which he had always wished, and he could use Chichester as a focus to bring together an accomplished company. Olivier recruited two directors from the Royal Court, John Dexter and Gaskill, and asked Kenneth Tynan to become his literary manager. Gielgud and Richardson were not considered, and one of the first recruits, Redgrave, did not last for long. Instead Olivier relied on new players to invigorate the enterprise, among them Maggie Smith, Derek Jacobi, Colin Blakely and Anthony Hopkins. The early productions were sometimes inventive, with Peter O'Toole playing Hamlet for a brief period without much success. Geraldine McEwan once said of Olivier as director that 'if you got into a hole, you had to get out of it yourself.' Franco Zeffirelli summed it up as 'steel discipline, and [being] merciless with himself and with others – no excuses, no weakness'. Olivier liked to address his colleagues as 'baby'. During rehearsals he would insist, 'Give me more, more, more.'

For four years the National was a resounding success, com-
mercially as well as artistically. Tom Pate, the theatre manager,
recalled that Olivier

> was very interested in the returns – particularly if he was
> appearing in that night's show. He would go on stage for
> his first scene, have a squint around the auditorium, and
> a few minutes later the internal phone would go, and it
> would be Sir Laurence asking for the night's figures. The
> thing was, somehow he would find it difficult to come out
> of character during the show – so in *A Long Day's Journey
> into the Night*, say, he'd ring with his American accent,
> and the next night I'd have Shylock on the end of the line
> asking why there were six empty seats in Row O.

Olivier said that an actor must work on three levels at once, 'line,
thought and audience'. *Othello* itself demonstrated his mastery.
One critic, recognizing his 'spine-tingling performance', noted that
'Olivier constantly shows there is a heart-felt passion aching to
penetrate the actorish façade.'

After four years of success, however, things began to fall apart.
Olivier contracted prostate cancer, while Dexter and Gaskill
left. There was also a public controversy about Rolf Hochhuth's
Soldiers, in which Olivier overruled Tynan's championship of the
play. Olivier received a life peerage in 1960, the year he played
Shylock once more. Was he a living theatrical force or a member
of the establishment? It was hard to tell. As early as 1971 plans
had been made to replace him with Peter Hall, and the following
year he was officially notified of the decision. For him it seemed
to be a betrayal, but he managed to delay his departure until
November 1973.

Olivier spent most of the next fifteen years making money for
his new wife and family. He made commercials, and appeared on

film and television. One of his most animated performances was his work with Michael Caine in the screen version of *Sleuth* in 1972. Caine recalled that 'once you start acting with him you'd better watch out, because he is completely and utterly merciless . . . there's this tornado of acting comes straight at you.' Olivier put it in another context when he confessed to Caine that 'I'm not like you. You can act as yourself; I can never act as myself.' That is why Gielgud called Olivier 'a great impersonator'. Only when he was transformed into another person could he perform. He worked as he steadily weakened, and continued until three years before his death of renal failure in 1989. He had been a film star, an acclaimed actor, a director, a producer and an impresario. So great was his devotion to the theatre that, if he had not harboured immortal longings, he might have been a dresser, a prompter and a stage carpenter as well. He has joined the company of Garrick, Kean and Irving.

Eighteen

Female persuasion

The testosterone of male achievement has perhaps reached the brim, and it is time to push it to one side. Edith Margaret Emily Ashcroft, known as Peggy, was born at the end of December 1907 in Croydon, Surrey. Her mother was an enthusiastic amateur actor, and her father achieved the rank of major before being killed in the Second World War. At school she was inspired by her elocution teacher and, at the age of sixteen, decided to attach herself to the stage. She enrolled at the Central School of Speech Training, of which Laurence Olivier was also a member, but she seems to have been more influenced by reading Konstantin Stanislavski in 1924 and by watching a season of Russian plays two years later at a repertory theatre in Barnes, southwest London. Her ambition was to become part of a company, however, and in 1926 she was taken on by the Birmingham Repertory Theatre. She was always determined, with a hint of obduracy, about her future.

Ashcroft's salient qualities were already apparent, although perhaps 'salient' is the wrong word; her talents did not leap out at the audience but, rather, drew it in. As a result, the adulation she deserved was slow to come. Delicacy, a refusal to play to the gallery if it meant sacrificing the truth, and an economy and grace of movement were her characteristics, together with simplicity, and a supreme sensitivity to words. A bedizened excess was not part of Ashcroft's repertoire. Here was the thing itself. Her only equivalent, tellingly, was Eleonora Duse, who once remarked that, away from the stage, 'I do not exist.' Herself no beauty, Ashcroft was free to be as beautiful or as ugly as the role demanded.

Her first significant role was as Desdemona, playing opposite Paul Robeson at the Savoy in 1930. John Gielgud recalled that 'when Peggy came on in the Senate scene, it was as if all the lights of the theatre had suddenly gone up.' Two years later he directed her in an Oxford production of *Romeo and Juliet*, and then between 1932 and 1933 she took on ten leading roles at the Old Vic. There was hardly time thoroughly to explore each role, but it was noticed that she had an impassioned naturalness to see her way through.

Ashcroft was in many senses adrift. In 1940 the privations of war postponed any plans she might have conceived for the stage. Nothing could deter her for long, however, and her stamina was no more in doubt than her talent. During the Blitz, a 'buzz bomb' caught her coming out of rehearsal and blew her straight into a barber's shop. She landed, as her biographer tells us, 'in the unresisting arms of a fat man who had only asked for a shave'. She was injured by shards of glass in her knee, but was able to rejoin the company shortly afterwards. In a production of 1949 she played Beatrice to Gielgud's Benedick in *Much Ado About Nothing*, and according to one critic, 'they set off each other's best points, call[ed] out in each other the highest art.'

The 1950s gave Ashcroft the opportunity to blossom. Going from Enid Bagnold's *The Chalk Garden* at the Haymarket to Bertolt Brecht's *The Good Woman of Setzuan* at the Royal Court, she demonstrated to one reviewer through her role in the former her native 'sincerity and candour'. In 1952 she played in Terence Rattigan's *The Deep Blue Sea*, where she managed 'playing of such truth and tenderness . . . not harrowing, finally, because so courageous and yet infinitely more pathetic for its unhysterical decency'.

In 1956 Ashcroft supported the notion of a Shakespeare Memorial Theatre that would provide premises for classical and contemporary plays both in London and Stratford, under the guidance of Peter Hall. In its first season, in 1960, she played Kate in *The Taming of the Shrew*, Paulina in *The Winter's Tale* and the leading role in John Webster's *The Duchess of Malfi*. It was after these successes that Ashcroft committed herself to *The Wars of the Roses*, a conflation of Shakespeare in which she played Margaret of Anjou. For some, it was her greatest achievement. Harold Pinter described it as 'pretty staggering . . . it is her combination of ferocity and tenderness that is singular.' Hall remarked on 'the extraordinary immediacy and passionate naivety she's carried into old age . . . it makes me think that there is a particular Englishness which is to do with extreme passion and extreme sexuality, contrasted with a wide-eyed English quality.'

Ashcroft's firmness and determination had sculpted her career, and it was this inner strength that projected both sense and sensibility. Her biographer, Michael Billington, sensed 'an aura of solitude' about her that she may have inherited from childhood, but she derived her strength from what he called her 'emotional attack, imaginative sympathy, and tonal accuracy'. She was more than a match for her male contemporaries. She died in London in the summer of 1991 after a stroke.

In some ways Ashcroft was the inspiration for, and representative of, the female actors of the period. One of the most remarkable, and recognizable, was Margaret Rutherford. She was born in Balham, south London, in the spring of 1892. After the early suicide of her mother and the confinement of her psychotic father, who had killed his own father, she was haunted by the possibility of inherited mental illness; perhaps her frequent role as a 'dotty old maid' was a way of dispelling her fears through comedy. She continued her schooling and joined the Royal Academy of Music to train as a music teacher. She could not fulfil her aspiration to act, however, until her aunt left her a small legacy. In 1925 she joined the Old Vic, where she played small roles in Shakespearean productions, but she was not hired for the next season and returned to teaching.

Two years later, however, Rutherford was engaged as an understudy at the Lyric in Hammersmith, before becoming involved in weekly repertory in a number of towns. While she was in Oxford her unusual personality captured the attention of Tyrone Guthrie, who put her in two plays at Her Majesty's. Her first great success, under the direction of John Gielgud, came in 1938 as a comical aunt in M. J. Farrell and John Perry's *Spring Meeting* at the Ambassadors Theatre. It was the first of many such roles but, as Gielgud put it, she was 'in herself a deeply serious person' whose splendid comic persona was touched by sadness. It is often thus.

Rutherford's next memorable role came the following year as Miss Prism in Oscar Wilde's *The Importance of Being Earnest*, with Edith Evans as Lady Bracknell, a role that Rutherford took over when the production migrated to Broadway. She seemed invincible, but suffered a nervous breakdown in 1941 while playing Madame Arcati in Noël Coward's *Blithe Spirit*, in the belief that she was mocking spiritualism. It seems likely that she suffered from bipolar disorder. But this did not prevent her from playing a domineering or absent-minded old woman, even though there were occasions when she disliked becoming a figure of fun or the object of fatuous remarks. She generally seemed unaware of the comic ambiance that she created, and made little effort to be funny in herself, relying on her face and its expressions to do the work. She was variously described as a 'spaniel-jowled actress', 'a splendidly padded windmill' and a gargoyle from Notre Dame. She was perpetually distracted, her jowls quivering in disbelief or surprise, often forgetful and sometimes strident. Kenneth Tynan's backhanded compliment was that she could act simply with her chin.

Rutherford's facial characteristics were made for the camera, and she made many films in which her personality scarcely changes; she tends to be indomitable and strong-willed, implacable and energetic, qualities that are emphasized by her surprisingly decisive moments and her sprightly delivery. On the screen she repeated her most memorable stage performances, while gaining a new audience as Agatha Christie's Miss Marple. She married in 1945; she and her husband remained a devoted couple for the rest of their lives, and in 1972 she pre-deceased him by only one year.

Gertrude Lawrence experienced a far less destructive childhood. She was born in the summer of 1898; her Danish father was a music-hall singer, and her mother a part-time actor. They were divorced while she was very young, but she moved from one to the other in an atmosphere imbued with stage business. She joined the training school of Italia Conti, and with her influence she appeared in four plays. Noël Coward met Lawrence as a fifteen-year-old performer. 'Her face was far from pretty,' he recalled, 'but tremendously alive.' From the age of sixteen she lived at the Theatrical Girls' Club in Soho, from which base she was engaged in various musical tours. She began a new career as a cabaret singer, albeit briefly, which took her on to the music-hall stage. A fellow chorus girl, Rose, told her that 'you're not exactly pretty, and you're too thin for everybody's taste, but you've got *class*. You need to be seen by the West End toffs.' And so she was.

Lawrence's first success came with Coward's *London Calling!*, which he wrote specifically for her when she was twenty-five. In the following year she became part of *Charlot's Revue* of 1924, which moved on to 1925 and 1926, crossing the Atlantic. She now pursued her career in New York, where the critic Alexander Woollcott described her as 'the personification of style and sophistication', which was high praise in that city. There she starred in the Gershwins' *Oh, Kay!* and *Pygmalion*, enchanting her audiences with what Coward called her 'witty quick-silver delivery of lines; the romantic quality, tender and alluring; the swift, brittle rages'. The critics did not necessarily agree, but, as Ronald

Bryden observed in a perceptive passage, 'the actors that critics write about best are those whose effects bear analysis; who offer a vividly thought-out impression, a lucid communicable approach to the whole role. The notation for Gertie's kind of acting does not yet exist. In the cerebral sense she was scarcely an actress at all.'

Coward had in a sense become her mentor. In 1931 they played together in *Private Lives*, with Laurence Olivier, and in 1936 they again acted jointly in *Tonight at 8.30*. In 1941 Lawrence took the leading role in a musical, *Lady in the Dark*, for which she was celebrated as 'the greatest feminine performer of the American theatre'. Orson Welles sent her a telegram after the premiere, 'YOU ARE EVERYTHING THE THEATRE LIVES BY'. The show's Broadway run and subsequent tour lasted three years, and she stayed with it until its final performance. During the Second World War she returned to London, and became well known for her visits to the troops. London itself was a severe disappointment since, as was painfully apparent, it had changed much since her last stay twelve years before. In her imagination she was still in the 1930s, but that air of ebullience and gaiety had gone. That may in part have been a reflection of the fact that she no longer had the charisma or the popularity of the past. Her last and most successful stage production was *The King and I*, by Richard Rodgers and Oscar Hammerstein, which opened on Broadway in the spring of 1951. She was not the success she had anticipated. Her voice, never very strong, had gone. In the course of one performance she suffered a fainting fit and was later diagnosed as suffering from liver and abdominal cancer. She died in New York on 6 September 1952, and was buried in a Massachusetts cemetery.

WE CAN CONCLUDE with the two Hermiones. The first, Hermione Gingold, was born in 1897 in Maida Vale, northwest London, and made her professional debut at the age of eleven in a children's delight, Walford Graham Robertson's *Pinkie and the Fairies*. She was promoted to *The Merry Wives of Windsor* and, after a spell at stage school, was cast in Clifford Mills and John Ramsey's *Where the Rainbow Ends* in December 1911. Among the cast was a young Noël Coward. In her teenage years she was in demand for her quick wit and eccentric demeanour. Adult life was more difficult, when lack of work was compounded by nodules on her vocal cords, which made her sound, according to the critic J. C. Trewin, like 'powdered glass in deep syrup'. 'One morning it was Mozart,' she said, 'and the next "Old Man River".' This was an example of her raucous humour, for which she became famous.

In fact this drop in pitch helped her career, and Gingold found her métier in the fashionable revues of the 1930s. One of her writers, Alan Melville, described her portraying 'grotesque and usually unfortunate ladies of dubious age and, occasionally, morals'. After the Second World War she went back to revue, but lost some of her bite. She continued to make films, work on the radio and appear on television shows. A review of one of her later plays described her as 'blatant as ever, deafeningly loud, strutting like a parody of every tragedy queen, male or female, since time began, she was in splendid relishing form, her lips drawn over her fangs and her voice swooping campingly through a whole two octaves of sneers.' That epitomizes her quintessential performance. She went on to play in Stephen Sondheim's *A Little Night Music*, both on Broadway and in the West End, and to narrate the revue *Side by Side by Sondheim*. She died from heart disease and pneumonia in 1987.

The second Hermione, Hermione Baddeley, was born in Shropshire in 1906. Her film career, which began in the 1920s, encompassed a number of entertaining comedies, such as *Passport to Pimlico* (1949), *The Belles of St Trinian's* (1954) and *Mary Poppins* (1964). She played the bold and brassy types indispensable in English comedy, but sealed her reputation as Ida in *Brighton Rock* (1948). On stage she was often paired with Noël Coward in

the 1940s and 1950s. She packed a powerful punch; a performance lasting two minutes and nineteen seconds in the film *Room
at the Top* (1958) won her an Oscar nomination for Best Supporting
Actress in 1959. She was also nominated four years later for a Tony
Award for Best Performance as a Leading Actress for her part
in Tennessee Williams's play *The Milk Train Doesn't Stop Here
Anymore*. Baddeley married twice and had a brief relationship
with the actor Laurence Harvey, but the difference in age proved
too vast to pull together. She died at the age of seventy-nine and
was buried in Amesbury, Wiltshire. Will there ever be room for
a third Hermione?

Nineteen

The enigmas

There have always been renowned theatrical families, the talent or genius of which is passed from generation to generation. Michael Redgrave, the only child of two actors, was the benefactor or even founder of one such family. He was born in actors' lodgings in Bristol in 1908, but embarked on a conventional education at Clifton College in that city and at Magdalene College, Cambridge; in both these places he enjoyed the amateur theatre. He then became a teacher of modern languages at Cranleigh School in Surrey, where he also enlisted in the semi-professional Guildford Company close by. He had all the makings of an actor; he was strikingly handsome, muscular and, at a height of 1.9 metres (6 ft 3 in.), difficult to miss. He left teaching at Cranleigh and gave an audition to Lilian Baylis, who offered him a modest contract. Instead, however, he opted for the Liverpool Playhouse, where he played a variety of parts from 1934 to 1936, in the course of which he married an aspiring actor, Rachel Kempson; they worked together frequently.

In 1936 Tyrone Guthrie invited husband and wife for a season at the Old Vic, where Redgrave played Orlando against Edith Evans's Rosalind (she was then forty-eight but, as was said, 'game') and then Laertes against Laurence Olivier's Hamlet. Redgrave then migrated to the Embassy Theatre and the St Martin's Theatre for two minor comedies. The Redgraves had three children in the late 1930s and early 1940s, Vanessa, Corin and Lynn, all of whom joined the acting profession. It would seem that theatrical blood may be inherited, as well as what Redgrave described as 'the divine gift' of acting, which for him consisted of spontaneity and the unforced expression of inward feeling.

Redgrave had in fact already made an impression, and John Gielgud offered him a variety of roles in 1937 and 1938 at the Queen's Theatre, from Tuzenbach in *Three Sisters* to Sir Andrew Aguecheek in *Twelfth Night*. He was a difficult actor to describe, in part because of the chameleon tendency he brought with him from his private life. One review of his performance in *Three Sisters* noted that 'his very bones seemed to shape themselves differently, and his physical habits to adapt themselves to the mental habits he took on with his character.' It could be that he had no real, central character at all. His children confessed that he could sometimes seem cold, distant and inaccessible; it was a quality, or absence of quality, that others mentioned. Tynan wrote that 'this actor always startles me by behaving as if he were suffering from persecution mania; he is at least apart from and at most actively hostile to his audience.'

Following the period at the Queen's Theatre, Redgrave was cast in the first production of T. S. Eliot's *The Family Reunion* in 1939. He used to quote Stanislavski, who wrote that every actor must 'love the art in himself, and not himself in the art'. In 1940 Redgrave was cast as the highwayman, Macheath, in *The Beggar's Opera* for a tour from Glyndebourne. The following year he was called up for service in the Royal Navy, but after seventeen months he was discharged for medical reasons; he had a crooked arm.

In 1942 Redgrave returned immediately to the stage and acted in a number of plays for a variety of companies, from Norman Armstrong's *Lifeline*, set on an oil tanker, to *The Duke in Darkness*, set in sixteenth-century France. He did not achieve the success for which he must have hoped for his Macbeth at the Aldwych in 1947, and that was followed unfortunately by the title role in August Strindberg's *The Father* at the Embassy, which was also disappointing. Redgrave decided that it had been 'another half-successful assault on a great part'.

As did so many of his contemporaries, Redgrave took part in several English films, but perhaps his most celebrated cinematic role came in 1951 with *The Browning Version*. His character was that of a dry teacher of classics at a public school who had lost the idealism and enthusiasm of his early career, and such is the subtlety of his interpretation that it is possible to see both aspects of his character simultaneously. Redgrave has the gift of exploring depression and disappointment, which may be seen as his distinctive quality. The quiet intensity of his performance is remarkable, and it was described as 'mesmerising' and 'hypnotic' by its first critics. It may seem to belong to the age of 'method' acting, but the method is entirely and uniquely his own.

The next season found Redgrave at the Shakespeare Memorial Theatre, where he took on the parts of Prospero, Richard II, Shylock, King Lear and Antony. When he also played Hamlet, a critic remarked on his 'absolute mastery of the vocal line . . . It is an exemplary performance as a piece of verse-speaking, without tricks, mannerisms, or affectations, but immensely various, always absolutely true, always perfectly in tune.' He found playing such complex and isolated characters, however, a unique strain. Unlike actors of the Noël Coward school, he could never quite dissociate himself from the parts he adopted. As he once observed, 'in simulating hysteria you're bound to experience it.'

In 1955 Redgrave was directed by Harold Clurman at the Apollo in Jean Giraudoux's *Tiger at the Gates*; of his performance Clurman said that 'Michael Redgrave is so intelligent that he destroys all by himself the silly notion that actors are or ought to be stupid.' It may even be that his sharp intelligence deterred any pleasure he took in acting. Tynan repeated the accolade, however, by writing that 'this is a monumental piece of acting, immensely moving, intelligent in action, and in repose never less than a demi-god.'

At the opening of the National Theatre in the autumn of 1963, Redgrave played Claudius to Peter O'Toole's Hamlet. By the 1960s he had developed Parkinson's disease, but he continued to work by touring Shakespeare; he also travelled overseas, taking in four continents and one hundred and twenty-six theatres. His last stage play was Simon Gray's *Close of Play* at the National in 1979. He was by then confined to a wheelchair, and he died in a nursing home six years later, in March 1985. He cannot be said to have had a happy or contented life; his bisexuality was pronounced and his promiscuity well known. These faults, if such they were, caused him embarrassment, guilt and sometimes grief, but they also lent his acting a singular distinction.

Alec Guinness was born in Paddington, London, at the beginning of April 1914. It was once believed that he was a member of the famous and respectable Guinness family, but his origins are in fact obscure. When he was five, his mother married a lieutenant in the Royal Army Service Corps, Daniel Stiven, but when he was fourteen he was told that his real name was Guinness. The truth is unknown. It is likely that he was illegitimate, and this may account for his ambiguous relationship with the world, slipping in and out of roles. He had a conventional education at a minor public school in Eastbourne, then became a copywriter at an advertising agency in Lincoln's Inn Fields.

But Guinness was close to the West End and frequented the Old Vic for sixpence; his first real exposure to the theatre had come in Bournemouth in 1930, when he saw Sybil Thorndike and Lewis Casson in Ibsen's *Ghosts*. In an act of unusual courage he telephoned John Gielgud, whom he had never met, and asked for advice on a possible theatrical career. Gielgud, perhaps nonplussed, recommended an acting coach. He suggested that

Guinness apply for a place at RADA, but in fact he ended up at the Fay Compton School of Drama, where in 1934 he performed in two mediocre plays.

Perhaps his acting coach may in part be blamed. Martita Hunt was an actress with pretensions to Continental elegance. Gielgud had assumed that Guinness belonged to the wealthy family of that name, and so, it transpired, did Hunt. Guinness recalled how her eyes dimmed perceptibly when she saw his poor clothes and shoes. 'I need a drink,' she said. As Guinness attempted the opening speech from *Henry V*, she 'buried her face in her hands . . . while the smoke from her cigarette drifted through her hair'. He was then dismissed: she was 'expecting someone important'.

For a man later known for his modesty and circumspect behaviour, the young Guinness was remarkably brave, not to say audacious. He tracked down Gielgud at Wyndham's, and during the interval reminded him of their previous short conversation. Gielgud promised him some part in a new production. Later the same year Guinness went to a matinee of *Richard II* at the Old Vic, in which Gielgud played the main part, and hovered in the actor's vicinity until he was recognized. Gielgud promptly invited him to play Osric in a forthcoming production of *Hamlet*, an offer that he had no difficulty in accepting. He had already told a friend, 'I feel I have the seeds of genius in me,' and Osric was at least an early bud. It is perhaps the archetypically theatrical role, comically overblown, and thus very unlike Guinness himself. But the actor always had a weakness for a part that could pluck him from his familiar territory.

In 1935 Guinness appeared in André Obey's *Noah* as well as *Romeo and Juliet*, and the following year he played in Anton Chekhov's *The Seagull* and joined the Old Vic. Over the next three years before the Second World War he took part in thirteen productions, primarily directed by Tyrone Guthrie and Gielgud himself. Guthrie liked improvisation and the inspiration of the moment, which it seemed that the young actor might supply.

Guinness seemed at his best when playing supporting parts, hiding in plain sight, but real success came when he played Hamlet in a modern dress production at the Old Vic in 1938. Modern dress suited him; it bolstered his anonymity. The war intervened, and he joined the Royal Navy in 1941, suffering no obvious damage as a result.

After the war Guinness went straight back to the stage, where at the Old Vic, then ensconced in the New Theatre, he was cast in a plethora of roles that seemed to emphasize his malleability; he was the Fool in *King Lear*, Comte de Guiche in Edmond Rostand's *Cyrano de Bergerac*, Abel Drugger in Ben Jonson's *The Alchemist*, the Dauphin in George Bernard Shaw's *Saint Joan* and Khlestakov in Nikolay Gogol's *The Government Inspector*. Of this last part the critic Harold Hobson wrote that 'he is as delicate as a butterfly . . . this pale and fragile actor, whose gaiety seems always haunted by sadness.' Some critics compared him to Stan Laurel.

But these parts were in a sense the prelude to Guinness's first substantial achievement in the sphere of film, in which he cast his spell over five of what are now known collectively as the 'Ealing comedies', and confirmed the greatness he had sensed in himself as a young man, as well as that single-minded ambition and courage that characterized his early years. Simon Callow noted perceptively that Guinness worked 'by becoming a sort of ontological magician. He was able to release himself into character, or rather, perhaps, he was able to allow himself to be seduced by, to be taken over by, another self.' In that way he was able to control and direct the insecurity he had experienced as a child. Tynan noted of his eyes that, although 'superficially guileless, they are in truth sly and wary and, rather than meet your gaze, they will wander contemplatively from side to side . . . The whole presence of the man is guarded and evasive. Slippery sums him up.' Another profile of him noted also that 'the eyes are guileless, but they are also sly, and his manner communicates intimacy as if from a great distance.'

That is why he was still something of an enigma, almost anonymous or self-effacing among the colourful characters who surrounded him on the screen. It had been observed that, according to his biographer Piers Paul Read, Guinness 'had a reserved and brittle personality, and could quickly take offence'. Olivier could be particularly unpleasant to him, as numerous contemporaries have testified. After seeing Guinness in a 'run-through' of *Twelfth Night*, he murmured to him, 'Fascinating, old dear. I never realised before that Malvolio could be played as a bore.' The slight stayed with Guinness throughout his performance.

After leaving the Old Vic in 1948, Guinness appeared later on the stage in *Hamlet*, Eliot's *The Cocktail Party* and Georges Feydeau's *Hotel Paradiso*, among others. But his most accommodating medium was still film. In 1950 he gave an excellent imitation of Benjamin Disraeli in *The Mudlark*, although there were scenes in which he was too suave or formal. He gave the impression, whether from instinct or from deliberation, that Disraeli had no interior life and that he was an actor playing the game of life. Guinness always was attracted to characters who relished play-acting. He was one of the actors who depended on the possibilities of expression directed by true if disguised feeling. His faint smile is otherworldly and glacial, but his eyes are alert and piercing.

We may assume the lure of the cinema lay in the large sums of money it brought, which would have seemed impossibly grandiose in earlier years. An egregious example was the original *Star Wars* trilogy (1977–83). In an interview in 1999 Guinness confessed, 'I just couldn't go on speaking those bloody awful banal lines. I'd had enough of the mumbo jumbo.' He took on two or three plays, including Alan Bennett's *The Old Country* in 1977 at the Queen's Theatre, which was regarded by the *Sunday Times* as 'one of his finest performances; both erect and crumbling, he conveys a sense of tenacious indecision and dignified self-disgust.' His last stage appearance, in Lee Blessing's *A Walk in the Woods*, was performed at the Comedy Theatre in 1989; it was his seventy-eighth part.

In 1956 Guinness was received into the Roman church, and became a devout Catholic. There were rumours of his bisexuality, but that comes with the territory; all great actors accommodate both masculine and feminine characteristics. He died of cancer in the summer of 2000, having equalled the achievements of his quondam mentor, John Gielgud, and, as one of the most versatile of film actors, he is to be compared only with Olivier, Scofield and Redgrave.

Paul Scofield always preferred the theatre to the screen. He was born in Birmingham in January 1922, but within a few weeks the family settled at Hurstpierpoint, Middlesex, where his father became headmaster of the local school. At the age of twelve Scofield moved to Varndean School in Brighton, where a play by Shakespeare was an annual event. It is perhaps not surprising that an introduction to Shakespeare should provide an impetus or inspiration for so many actors, and Scofield followed his youthful ambitions by joining the Croydon Repertory Theatre at the age of seventeen. When it closed down, he migrated to the London Mask Theatre School and played walk-on parts in three separate plays. His only lines were 'Yes, sir.' In 1941 some of the Mask students fled the bombs of London and migrated to Bideford in north Devon, where they established a small repertory company. His robust presence and somewhat strangulated if gravelly voice had already provoked both attention and applause.

In the autumn of 1944 Scofield accepted an offer from the Birmingham Repertory Theatre, known as the 'Old Rep', where he found what he called 'a certain amount of technical balance as an actor'. He played roles in *The Winter's Tale*, Oliver Goldsmith's *She Stoops to Conquer*, Shaw's *Man and Superman* and other plays, three of which were directed by Peter Brook. Brook recalled, 'I looked into a face that unaccountably in a young man was streaked and mottled like an old rock, and I was instantly aware that something very deep lay hidden behind his ageless appearance.' From the 'Old Rep' Scofield was accepted at the Shakespeare Memorial Theatre in Stratford, where, with Brook as director once more, he achieved great success with *Love's Labour's Lost*. He played the lead in *Pericles* in 1947 and *Hamlet* in 1948. Kenneth Tynan wrote, 'I know now that there is in England a young actor who is bond-slave to greatness.' It was the usual rodomontade, but there was an element of truth in it. Scofield seemed to prefer characters who are in some way magnificently flawed or faulty. His biographer Garry O'Connor noted that 'Paul's great roles are the losers and self-destroyers, the victims of passion or envy.'

In the 1950s Scofield acted in a variety of plays in diverse theatres, from *Richard II* at the Lyric to *Hamlet* at the Phoenix. His demeanour was characteristically subdued and undemonstrative, his expression calm and ironic in a way that captures both modesty and strength. The smile sometimes freezes on his face or turns into a frown, while his voice conveys both courage and vulnerability. This is the performance of an actor who loves words and relishes their sound; he does not raise the volume or tone very much, but relies instead on more subtle changes in emphasis and inflection. These qualities are also evident in his role at the Globe in Robert Bolt's *A Man for All Seasons* of 1960, in which he played Thomas More convincingly as a mild-mannered servant of the king who did not until the end manifest his iron belief and determination. His delivery is more formal and more serious, in accordance with the circumstances, but there is an oboe-like intonation that conveys his strength of will. Helen Mirren recorded that 'he aspired to the soul rather than the character. He has no sense of personal ambition.' He did not care to be photographed because, as he told Cecil Beaton, 'he did not know, in front of the camera, which role he was playing.'

An actor of Scofield's merit could not escape the cinema completely, and he made a brilliant success, for example, of the filmed version of *A Man for All Seasons* in 1966. He continued to work through the 1970s and 1980s, choosing only roles that best suited him, and quite remote from the blandishments of directors. Simon Callow described him as a 'late flowering of that astonishing generation which included Olivier, Gielgud, Ashcroft, Evans, Redgrave and Richardson'. Scofield always managed to convey the irresistible force of inner feeling; if the outer life is an act of conjuring, a skill that, once mastered, will never fail, the inner life is summoned up by a kind of spell, contingent for its success on the aid of unpredictable forces. The same was true of Sybil Thorndike and Charles Laughton. Scofield's performance as Macbeth, which began at Stratford and ended at the Aldwych, shows once more his mastery of gesture and expression. As he speaks he pauses frequently, lingers over single words, covers his eyes, puts his finger and thumb together and lifts them to his face. He always has time; his acting is unhurried, he is unconcerned by pauses because he knows they can be eloquent. His voice has an imponderable resonance which passes from actor to audience. It compels us to enter the drama and not simply to observe it. When a character's expression can change with a word or glance, and can do so with conviction, we have an actor who is fully engaged in the feelings of that character. Scofield died of leukaemia on 19 March 2008.

We should note that Scofield's radical interpretations of character might never have reached us without the genius of Peter Brook, apostle of magic. It has become a commonplace to mention that the stage director is yesterday's child. But, like the actor himself, the director is a blend of many, older functions. In the early medieval period, the actors in the *Visitatio* would have been led by a choir master. For the civic Mysteries, a pageant master took charge. Perhaps the playwright 'directed' in the Elizabethan period, although we have no evidence for this. Certainly he would not have played any instructional role; the actors knew their business too well for that. In later years some actor-managers fulfilled what might be termed a directorial function. Henry Irving was intimately involved in all aspects of production and Harley Granville-Barker was never afraid to train his actors when he saw fit.

It was during the Second World War, however, that the origins of the modern theatre director are to be found. We know that the conflict was of some advantage to female actors – so many men were away at the front – but it also ensured that the producer, still known by that name, was suddenly forced to take on far more responsibilities than before. With many seasoned actors in the forces, it was necessary to train the untutored; with so many new logistical problems to solve, he had to take charge of the minutiae of production. More by accident than by design, and little by little, the producer – an organizer, fundraiser and *metteur en scène* – became the director. Someone who told the actor where to move became someone who not infrequently demonstrated how to act.

It is true that even early direction could often have a pedagogic element: Richard Burton was trained in verse-speaking by Gielgud, for example. But the role of teacher was never central, and it was still understood that the actor should know the rudiments of the art. The producer's role was to ensure that a visually attractive tableau should be established and maintained, and that the actors knew their lines, were aware of their props, could remember their moves and, above all, pick up their cues: unintended pauses make for a sluggish performance. Naturally, they were not to bump into the furniture.

Until the 1950s, and even into the 1960s, 'producer' was still the expression preferred. Then, and partly under the influence of cinema, the term 'director' appeared. Almost immediately it began to colonize the virgin plains of theatre. The word had associations foreign to English theatre; it connoted, even when it did not mean, a grand and universal creator, a Hitchcock or Murnau. Peter Hall, on the other hand, summed up his role with gentle good sense. 'Theatre work is essentially collaborative,' he remarked, 'although it requires a chairman or a leader – it may be the leading actor or the director or the writer. It finally requires an editor and inspirer.' He also observed that if actors are not given a director, 'they will tend to evolve one,' and uncovenanted authority can be far more dangerous and arbitrary than authority agreed upon.

With the rise of the director came a new development in theatre criticism. When an actor performed well, credit for this was increasingly given to the director. It became commonplace to read that such and such a director 'coaxed' a fine performance from such and such an actor. This term, or one like it, is to be found almost every week in the review sections of newspapers, magazines and blogs. It is only just to mention, however, that directors do occasionally need to 'coax' a performance out of an actor. Some actors are much more passive than others and will blossom under a firm directorial hand where others might feel stifled.

However, the Continental notion of the *auteur* or the director as creator has now taken root. It is often believed that the director is responsible for the artistic vision. He or she may not always, indeed may not often, displace the playwright, but the actor's role is significantly more passive than it was in the early modern period; the knight is now a pawn. Whether this has helped to create remarkable drama is another question. The modern director can be a teacher, a master of ceremonies, a drill sergeant, a mage or a prophet. The idea of director as demiurge, however, was taken for granted in the United States and on the Continent decades before it was so much as entertained in England. Thus, in most senses that matter, 'the director' is a foreign import, one of many that have enriched English theatre.

The director can now be displaced by an actor. Alec McCowen was born in Tunbridge Wells on 26 May 1925, and went to the

Skinners' School in that town before being accepted to RADA in 1941. He lasted there for only one term before being told that he was wasting his time. But that did not deter him. He remained in repertory theatres for the next few years in Macclesfield, York and Birmingham, while also touring India and Burma in 1945. His London debut came as Maxim in Chekhov's *Ivanov* at the Arts Theatre in the spring of 1950, and he then tried his luck in New York; he was rewarded only with small parts towards the end of 1951. He returned to London, where he played a number of roles at the Arts Theatre and again in repertory, slowly climbing to recognition before in 1959 joining the Old Vic, where for two seasons he concentrated primarily on Shakespeare with a dose of Wilde shaken in. He seemed to be a steady and unobtrusive actor on a gradual rise, partly unregarded, which seemed to represent his somewhat diffident personality, but at the Old Vic he was given much larger and more challenging parts. He played the title role in *Richard II*, Mercutio in Franco Zeffirelli's *Romeo and Juliet*, Oberon in *A Midsummer Night's Dream* and Malvolio in *Twelfth Night*. He seemed to absorb rather than reflect his characters, if the distinction can be made. He was a sponge rather than a polished gem.

In 1962 McCowen moved to the Royal Shakespeare Company, shuttling between Stratford and the Aldwych as Antipholus in *The Comedy of Errors* and the Fool to Paul Scofield's Lear. He then took on the difficult role of Father Riccardo Fontana in Hochhuth's *The Representative* in December 1963. It was not the last time he would play a cleric. In the spring of 1968, for example, he played Father Rolfe in *Hadrian VII* at the Mermaid, for which performance he won the *Standard*'s Best Actor award. It was a great success, a fact that prolonged its run at the theatre to accommodate the ever-growing audiences. One critic wrote that 'I cannot recall an occasion on which this splendidly underestimated actor has been better used.' The play then travelled to Broadway, where it enjoyed a similar popularity. McCowen had at last risen to the top of his profession.

Arguably his greatest achievement, however, was his one-man dramatization of St Mark's Gospel at the Riverside Studios in January 1978, which one critic characterized as 'the familiar story with all the precision, irony, intelligence and faintly controlled anger that characterise all his work'. McCowen himself wrote that the gospel 'is amazingly suited to the theatre. It is amazingly theatrical.' It moved on to the Mermaid and then to the Comedy before being transferred to Broadway. Back at the Mermaid in 1982, he took on the part of Adolf Hitler in Christopher Hampton's adaptation of George Steiner's *The Portage to San Cristobal of A.H.* Michael Billington of *The Guardian* described it as 'one of the greatest pieces of acting I have ever seen: a shuffling, grizzled, hunched, baggy figure, yet suggesting the monomaniac power of the Nuremburg Rallies, inhabiting the frail vessel of this old man's body'. Two years later, again at the Mermaid, McCowen ventured upon another one-man show in a portrait of Rudyard Kipling. This also transferred to Broadway. In November 1987 he enjoyed a vivid change of character at the National Theatre as Vladimir in Samuel Beckett's *Waiting for Godot*. He remained active and busy through the late 1980s and 1990s in work ranging from Eliot to Beckett, Shaw to Shakespeare. He died, aged 91, on 6 February 2017.

Twenty

Female stars

The female actors born in the 1930s or on its margins were some of the most skilful and entertaining of the century, and should be seen beside Edith Evans, Sybil Thorndike and Peggy Ashcroft. Joan Plowright was born in Lincolnshire in October 1929, and formally trained at the Bristol Old Vic Theatre School; she first appeared in repertory at the Grand Theatre, Croydon, in 1948 before becoming a member of the Bristol Old Vic Company. She then became affiliated with the West of England Repertory Company, and moved from theatre to theatre in the familiar fashion.

In 1956 Plowright caught the eye of the theatre manager George Devine, who hired her for the English Stage Company at the Royal Court, where she appeared in plays by George Bernard Shaw and Eugène Ionesco and played the leading role in William Wycherley's *The Country Wife*. Of the last, one critic reported that 'Joan Plowright jumps to the forefront of our young actresses with her lively performance in the title role; she is all cunning and mischief. A richly endearing flirt.' Like Evans, she was blessed in having an extraordinarily distinctive voice. At once commanding, flute-like and tremulous, it was the voice of a schoolmistress perpetually shocked at the naughtiness of her charges.

When *The Entertainer* moved from the Royal Court to the Palace Plowright took over Dorothy Tutin's role as Jean Rice, the daughter of Laurence Olivier's Archie. This was the occasion of her meeting the actor with whom she began a romance that would culminate in their marriage. She continued working both in London and in New York as her reputation steadily grew, not necessarily unassisted by her marriage in 1961. In 1958 she returned to the Royal Court, but this did not prevent her from working elsewhere. In 1960 she played opposite Olivier in Ionesco's *Rhinoceros*, then flew to New York with him and took the role of Josephine in Shelagh Delaney's *A Taste of Honey*; it was during this visit that they were married. A range of plays and roles followed during the 1960s and 1970s, culminating in Chekhov's *The Cherry Orchard* at the Haymarket and William Congreve's *The Way of the World* at Chichester. Encroaching blindness put an end to her career in 2014, but at the time of writing Plowright still lives in the Sussex house where she and Olivier spent the last period of their married life.

Dorothy Tutin was born in London the year after Plowright, and in what had already become a familiar pattern she had the rudiments of a conventional education before being accepted at RADA. In 1950 she joined the Bristol Old Vic, where she played a number of Shakespearean roles; then, in 1952 and 1953, she migrated to the Phoenix and enjoyed great success with Graham Greene's *The Living Room*, of which Kenneth Tynan wrote that 'Miss Tutin's performance is masterly; the very nakedness of acting.' In the spring of 1954 she starred at the New Theatre as Sally Bowles in John Van Druten's *I Am a Camera*, of which the theatre critic Caryl Brahms noted that 'she somehow contrives to combine the satiric with the entirely credible'; she also remarked on Tutin's voice, a 'kind of curdled cooing that could only come from a turtle-dove with laryngitis'. Tutin moved on to the Royal Court and then the Shakespeare Memorial Theatre, in which she played a whole gallery of Shakespearean females. There was never any criticism in the stalls or the dress circle at the familiar and perhaps over-familiar parts. They were to be expected, and even considered obligatory for the development of the classical female actor. The years of Rosalind and Viola, Portia and Ophelia were mingled with Chekhov and Shaw, Wilde and Rattigan and a score of then popular playwrights. Her last plays, in the 1980s, were more unusual and adventurous, with Harold Pinter's *A Kind of Alaska* and Neil Simon's *Brighton Beach Memoirs* among them. In her last years she contracted leukaemia, from which she died on 6 August 2001.

Claire Bloom was born in London in February 1931 and, inspired by the sight of Norma Shearer in the 1936 film adaptation of *Romeo and Juliet*, studied acting at the Guildhall School and then at the Central School. Her family had spent the early war years in the United States, but in 1946 she made her first appearances in a number of plays at the Oxford Repertory Theatre. At the age of seventeen she was invited to join the Memorial Theatre at Stratford under the aegis of Robert Helpmann, where among other productions in 1948 she played Ophelia to Paul Scofield's Hamlet. Kenneth Tynan described her as 'the best Juliet I've ever seen'. She had a formal perfection of feature that rendered her angelic in her youth and aristocratic in maturity. Her subsequent stage career was filled with success, beginning with Christopher Fry's *The Lady's Not for Burning* in 1949, opposite a young Richard Burton, and then in Peter Brook's production of Fry's *Ring Round the Moon* at the Globe, in which she played a ballerina. The critic in *Plays and Players* noted that 'she seems to feel with intensity the part she plays and she allows one that always unforgettable leisure of forgetting that she is acting.'

It may have been Bloom's performance in *Ring Round the Moon* that caught Charlie Chaplin's imagination, because at the age of twenty she was cast alongside him in *Limelight*, a film in which she plays a young ballerina whom Chaplin saves from suicide. In the garish light of Chaplin's theatrical style she conducted her role lightly and gracefully; as a portrait of a young female actor, her image went around the world and boosted her career enormously. At the time she said, 'I couldn't just be a film star. I'm much too ambitious for that.' In 1952 she moved to the Old Vic, where she played among other roles Jessica, Ophelia, Helena and Juliet; in all her parts she was praised by the critics. Of her Juliet, Tynan wrote that 'she gave a sweet new agony to the supreme love-drama in the language. The silly lamb became a real, scarred woman.' In a production of Jean Giraudoux's *Duel of Angels* in 1958, one critic noticed that 'she seems to be maturing as an actress, having acquired that indefinable something which invests her performance with a new poise and authority.'

In January 1959 Bloom travelled to New York and played opposite Rod Steiger. Subsequently she married him and for the next nine years became his travelling companion as he wandered the world in search of films; she followed his example and found stage and film work wherever she could. Her reintroduction to her public came in 1971 when she played Nora in Ibsen's *A Doll's House* as well as Hedda Gabler at the Playhouse in New York. In 1973 she brought *A Doll's House* to London at the Criterion, in a production that manifested what one critic called 'a perform-ance of high theatrical intelligence'. This was surpassed in 1974 by her portrayal of Blanche du Bois in Tennessee Williams's *A Streetcar Named Desire*. It was an extraordinary performance, and Williams himself stated, 'I declare myself absolutely wild about Claire Bloom.' She herself had said that 'I've never been in the mainstream. I've always had to do things for myself. So I'll go on doing it.' She still lives in London.

Margaret Natalie Smith, otherwise known as Maggie Smith, was born in Ilford, east London, at the end of 1934, but was brought up in Oxford, where she trained at the Oxford Playhouse School. 'One went to school,' she said, 'one wanted to act, one started to act and one's still acting.' She made her first stage appearance in 1952 as Viola in *Twelfth Night* under the aegis of the Oxford

University Dramatic Society. Her early steps were those of a budding comic, and she travelled to New York in 1956 in order to appear in a revue, *New Faces of '56*, at the Ethel Barrymore Theatre. Returning to England, she appeared opposite Kenneth Williams at the Lyric, Hammersmith, in another revue, *Share My Lettuce*, which was successful enough to transfer to the Comedy Theatre.

In November 1958 Smith took on her first 'straight' role, as Vere Dane in *The Stepmother*. The play was not deemed to be a success, but she was not in the least daunted, and she joined the Old Vic company for the 1959–60 season, during which she took part in William Congreve, Shakespeare and J. M. Barrie. She was still being described as a 'comedienne', and it did seem that she preferred laughter to tears in the parts she had been given. She had a natural gift for comedy that has never dimmed.

In 1963 Smith joined the Old Vic at the National Theatre. She received predominantly favourable reviews, even if their terms were somewhat ambiguous: 'As to sensuality an iceberg might seem hot in comparison . . . the mournful little voice, so perfect in comedy, is sometimes a problem in tragedy . . . she was sweetly serious, besides sporting a most wringable neck.' The last review came from her role as Desdemona opposite Olivier; in this part she was gentle and tender, using an entirely different register from the one to which she was accustomed. She could sometimes be described as ingenuous, but this part demonstrated how broad and deep her bounds could be set. In the following year she played in Ibsen's *The Master Builder* and Coward's *Hay Fever*. There was now no doubt of her range. At the same time she began working in films, culminating with the title role in *The Prime of Miss Jean Brodie* in 1969, for which part she could have been created. Films were also now part of her acting life, although she expressed reservations about the medium. She once said, 'I think films are totally baffling. It's desperately hard . . . I would choose the stage if I had to.' Fortunately for her, she was not obliged to make that choice.

Back at the National Theatre, Smith played Chekhov, Ibsen and Coward, and followed them with *Peter Pan* and a play in 1974 entitled *Snap*, in which the critic Alan Brien described her as 'forever enmeshed and tangled in her clothes and in her ideas, blinded by her hat, struck dumb in mid-sentence, falling over her own ankles, colliding with her own syntax'. It is better imagined, or watched, than described. She toured the United States and then settled for four years in Stratford, Ontario, where at the Stratford Shakespeare Festival she embarked on a number of roles that seemed to gather her as much acclaim as she had enjoyed in London.

Smith returned to the capital in 1981, and the *Evening Standard* welcomed her back with another award for her performance in *Virginia* at the Haymarket. A critic noted that 'Smith suggests a mind shimmering with intelligence – a mind so perceptive she is often cattily funny and so sensitive she finds the world insupportable.' In 1987 she played Lettice in Peter Shaffer's *Lettice and Lovage* at the Globe in Shaftesbury Avenue; in the part she becomes a gorgeously theatrical tour guide who, when she is fired, adopts her familiar nasal twang and becomes very much a pantomime dame, thumping her consonants and twisting her vowels with a camp, aggrieved petulance that only she can muster.

In 1997 Smith was Claire in Edward Albee's *A Delicate Balance* at the Haymarket, in which she provided most of the comedy; her voice was raucous and jarring, her carriage that of an aristocrat. The costume designer Anthony Powell added another note when he remarked that 'she is more scared of being touched and hurt than anyone I know.' There is no reason to believe that Smith will cease to be so prolific and so skilful. There is no part that she cannot make her own, and at her heightened, bedecked best she is the country's finest comic actress.

The year 1934 was an enchanted one. Not only was Maggie Smith born, but the same year also greeted the arrival of Eileen Atkins and Judi Dench. Eileen Atkins was born on 16 June in the

Salvation Army Mothers' Hospital of Lower Clapton, a district of east London. Her mother, Annie Ellen, was a barmaid and her father a gas meter-reader. She was not born under a dancing star. She might be considered, however, as part of that generation of working-class actors who first emerged in the 1950s, were it not for the fact that she neither celebrated nor identified herself with her background in the same manner as, for example, Albert Finney or Richard Burton. Nevertheless, a gypsy fortune-teller told her mother that the little girl would become a great dancer. Unfortunately she divined the wrong profession, but Annie Ellen swallowed the story whole and enlisted her daughter in dancing lessons. Eileen did not care for them but attended for the next twelve years. From the age of seven to fifteen she toured the working men's clubs as 'Baby Eileen', no doubt all-singing and all-dancing, but she also performed at the Stage Door Canteen in Piccadilly for American servicemen. By the age of twelve, just after the war, she had begun working in pantomime in local London theatres, such as the Kilburn Empire and the Clapham Grand.

When it was pointed out to her mother that Atkins had a 'Cockney accent', it was agreed that a friend of the family might pay for her early education at the independent Parkside Preparatory School in Church Lane, Tottenham, north London. From there she was accepted into the Latymer School in nearby Edmonton, an independent grammar school where the remains of her native accent were erased. This was not merely common practice, but was expected (although, as we shall see, some actors resisted such emasculation – as they saw it). At Latymer Atkins also took part in 'drama demonstrations', which accelerated her propensity for performance. She stayed at the school until she was sixteen, at which point she applied or was told to apply for a RADA scholarship. She was not accepted, however, and instead attended the Guildhall School of Music and Drama in the City of London, a more than acceptable substitute.

Atkins graduated in 1953, and first appeared on a London stage that year, as Jaquenetta in *Love's Labour's Lost* at the Open Air Theatre in Regent's Park. She was also a member of various repertory companies before performing in a number of London venues, from the Saville to the Vaudeville, from the Royal Court to the Aldwych, from the Haymarket to the Cottesloe. The variety of her roles, from Medea to St Joan, is testimony to her diversity as well as her ability. In the 1980s and 1990s she took on fifteen different roles in thirteen London theatres. Further comment on Atkins's strength and durability might seem superfluous. She also played the title role in *Honour* by Joanna Murray-Smith at the Cottesloe, in 2003, for which part she won her second Olivier Award for Best Actress. The critic Benedict Nightingale wrote of this performance, 'Eileen Atkins may be our finest actress: a glint in the eyes, a sly and subtle sense of danger, a feeling that she has looked into the abyss of others and herself.'

But the role from which Atkins has forged her own particular star is that of Virginia Woolf. She first played the celebrated writer on stage in 1989 at the Hampstead Theatre, in Patrick Garland's adaptation of *A Room of One's Own*, for which she won the Drama Desk Award for Outstanding One-Person Show. In the same year she toured England and elsewhere with this dramatized version of Woolf's lectures, in which she played a woman quite in control of her feelings, powerful though they certainly were. She was entirely convincing. Everything was in place: the unemphatic superiority, the carriage, the grace, the gravitas and, above all else, the cold and glittering seam of irony running through her voice. It was in the best sense theatrical, bigger than realism but true to reality, everything full of urgent but gracious intent. Her abiding quality as an actor, however, is her sincerity, exemplified by that earnestness which informs even her comedy. In 1992 she again played the role of that troubled novelist in *Vita and Virginia*, written by herself, at the Ambassadors Theatre. *The Guardian*'s critic wrote that 'even though I prefer plays to epistolary exchanges, acting of this calibre keeps one engrossed and illuminates the waywardness of passion.' Atkins's most recent work was to have been Amy Herzog's *4000 Miles* at the Old Vic, but the COVID-19 pandemic, which has blighted so many prospects, intervened. That pandemic has been the single most crucial event in the lives of all stage actors, emphasizing the precariousness and anxiety of their careers. Ever since the days when plague closed the doors of the Fortune and the Globe, acting has been a difficult and hazardous profession.

Judi Dench was born in York in 1934 and attended a Quaker school, Mount School, in that city. She attended art college but soon discovered that this was not her real vocation; John Gielgud and Ralph Richardson had both made the same wrong decision and had grown equally disenchanted. Persuaded in part by her brother, Dench joined the Central School of Speech and Drama, then ensconced in the Albert Hall, where she won the Gold Medal as Outstanding Student. She once wrote that at drama school 'you cannot learn to act, but you can learn technique – how to breathe properly, how to relax and how to project your voice.' The most significant lesson she learned, in fact, was that of 'projection'.

Dench's first entrance on the professional stage was as Ophelia in *Hamlet* at the Royal Court Theatre in Liverpool, a production that made its way to the Old Vic in London. She remained with that company, which she considered to be 'invaluable training', playing the smaller parts at first before performing, among other roles, that of Maria in *Twelfth Night*, Katharine in *Henry V* and Juliet in *Romeo and Juliet*. One of the company, Alec McCowen, remarked of her last performance at the Old Vic, in *A Midsummer Night's Dream*, that 'her speed is phenomenal, and she can make you gasp at the quickness of her speech, which is always crystal clear. She doesn't hang about.' It was also said of her that 'the release of feeling, a sort of glorious shiver with an instantly recognisable crack in her voice', is characteristic of her performances.

The same observer, the critic Michael Coveney, noted that 'Judi Dench is known to be a cosy, comfy creature with good manners, good breeding and a pronounced liability to burst into giggles and gales of laughter.'

Dench joined the Royal Shakespeare Company in 1961 at the age of twenty-seven, where she first performed as Anya in Chekhov's *The Cherry Orchard* and Isabella in *Measure for Measure*. After two years she moved on to the Nottingham Playhouse, where she made a decided hit with Lady Macbeth, in which role she toured from January 1963 to April 1964. In 1968, after performing a multiplicity of roles, she was offered by Hal Prince the part of Sally Bowles in *Cabaret*. This seemed to her an unusual decision, because she believed that she croaked rather than sang, but despite her misgivings it was a great success and managed a long run at the Palace Theatre. A contemporary wrote that she was the only actor playing Sally Bowles who could intimate that she would never actually come to anything; this is what the text makes clear, and Dench gave a funny and touching performance as someone marked for oblivion.

When the curtain finally fell on the musical, Dench returned to the Royal Shakespeare Company, working for nearly twenty years in Stratford and in London. She was now, in that most overworked of all descriptions, 'a star', yet still appeared in ensemble productions like Shaw's *Too True to Be Good* in 1975–6. 'The important thing', she said of returning to the RSC, 'is getting to be part of a family, being with the others . . . It's a family feeling where you can let your defences down.' This says as much about her disposition as it does about her career. In 1976 she was with Donald Sinden in *Much Ado About Nothing* before tackling Lady Macbeth opposite Ian McKellen. 'If this is not great acting,' the critic of *The Guardian* noted, 'I don't know what is.' Another critic remarked of the same production that 'the test of great acting is not impersonation but revelation.'

As Lady Macbeth, Dench followed every twist and turn of the text with absolute precision. You are never left wondering what she said or thought, never overwhelmed by a cascade of beautiful sound. She gives us not evil, although she has every opportunity to do so, but rather the pain of conscience in unsuccessful revolt. When Macbeth leads her offstage, having promised to enact yet further atrocities, her plump, tear-stained face, a picture of hopelessness and incomprehension, manages the inconceivable: it elicits our sympathy for Shakespeare's most vilified villainess. It is a mesmerizing performance.

Dench was with the National Theatre Company in 1982 and 1983 in Wilde's *The Importance of Being Earnest*, where she quite changed the received playing of Lady Bracknell as exemplified by Edith Evans. In the 'handbag moment', for example, Dame Edith gave her famous roller-coaster inflection, while Dench first removed her lorgnette and peered, her face nobly incredulous. Only then, with delicate disbelief, did she ask, 'A *hand*bag?' In 1987 she was once more with the National Theatre to play the female lead in *Antony and Cleopatra*, with Anthony Hopkins as Antony. This was her favourite Shakespearean role; she is small but here she seemed titanic. She skipped and stamped and twirled, at once light and muscular, and had complete command of the stage even when playing opposite Hopkins.

Other plays followed, since Dench seemed constitutionally incapable of resting. In 1989 she was Gertrude in Hamlet, followed by leading roles in *The Cherry Orchard*, Sean O'Casey's *The Plough and the Stars*, and *Coriolanus*. Her speaking of verse is always exquisite; it is sometimes loose, but always perfectly pronounced. She elevates discourse to a humane and comprehensible level. The director Richard Eyre has said that her gift is 'innate' and, although she has demurred, he was quite right. You cannot *learn* to hear. But the text itself was always her master and mentor. Like other actors, Dench has a quality rather than a 'style'; hers is freshness, with a bracing truthfulness or candour combined with spontaneity. She is endlessly adaptable; the chameleon changes its colour, but it remains a chameleon.

Geraldine McEwan, originally McKeown, was born on 9 May 1932 in Old Windsor, Berkshire. She won a scholarship to a local private school, Windsor County Girls' School, but she also took private lessons in elocution. This would at least be useful in her earliest dramatic roles. 'The plays we did at school', she once said, 'always loomed large in my life. I was the one who recited poems on Speech Day.' In a later interview she recalled that 'I was very shy, very private,' but, after reading a speech by Lady Macbeth at a public concert, 'I realised it was going to be a way in which I could manage the world. I could protect myself by losing myself in other people.'

At the age of fourteen, while McEwan was still at school, she was taken on by the Theatre Royal in Windsor, and played walk-on parts essentially to fill the stage; her first appearance was an attendant of Hippolyta in *A Midsummer Night's Dream*. But the theatre was now her goal, and after leaving school she began to pursue a theatrical career. Her earliest assignment was as assistant stage manager at the Theatre Royal itself, but at the same time she was allowed to take on larger roles than before. In 1951 she played an Irish girl in a comedy, John Dighton's *Who Goes There?*, which moved on to the Vaudeville in the West End with McEwan in tow. This was the time when her surname was simplified.

One critic reported that McEwan 'could probably have continued in the commercial theatre trading on the idiosyncratic voice and personality', but in truth she had transformed herself into a striking and resourceful heroine. Often her sense of irony and her fastidiousness are subtly intermingled. She could be plaintive and quizzical at the same moment, too, and in her more ferocious moods she possessed a feline quality with claws to match, which was irresistible; her voice could be fluted or sharp according to circumstance, and at times of stress it seemed in need of a lozenge. Sometimes it could be unctuous and drawling; sometimes a mew, and sometimes a purr. But it was always captivating.

Wisely McEwan took up Olivier's invitation in 1965 to join the National Theatre Company, and she appeared in eleven plays over the next five years. In the summer of that year she played opposite Albert Finney in John Arden's *Armstrong's Last Goodnight* before travelling with the Company to Moscow and Berlin. On her return to England she performed in Georges Feydeau's *A Flea in Her Ear*, followed by her first collaboration with Olivier in the 1967 production of Strindberg's *The Dance of Death*. Of the latter, Martin Esslin wrote that 'she has the sense of the grotesque, the timing and the comic invention needed for the part, and at the same time succeeds triumphantly in evoking sympathy for the sufferings of this insufferable woman.'

It is always useful to study McEwan's face in such a part. There is the collusive, cheeky, simpering smile she offers her cousin, and the horror in her gaze, despite all her venom, when she thinks her husband has died. Her face is weary, worn down by a love that, although real, has turned septic. Sometimes, for all her ferocity and self-absorption, she shows a smile that is warm, associated with looks of true hurt and of grief that she cannot help or hide. These moments, of humanity or of deep despair, appear quite suddenly and are just as suddenly suppressed.

During this period with the National McEwan also performed in Congreve, Coward, Webster and Brecht, thus consolidating her reputation as an actor of great versatility and subtlety. In 1971, still with the National, she was Alkamena in Jean Giraudoux's *Amphitryon 38*, of which one reviewer noted that her 'voice and comic stylisation . . . are both used here to make of the vamp-like wife a funny, sensual and appealing character'. She went on to Peter Nichols's *Chez Nous* with Albert Finney and Denholm Elliott, where she was noted for her impression of 'catty fastidiousness'.

In 1978 she played the title part in Coward's Feydeau adaptation *Look after Lulu!*, where, according to one notice, 'she proves herself the mistress of double meaning and sexual innuendo, lowering her voice to the limits of suggestiveness.'

One of McEwan's outstanding roles, however, was that of Mrs Malaprop in Sheridan's *The Rivals* in 1983. Michael Billington of *The Guardian* remarked, 'It is easy to play the word-mangling Mrs Malaprop as a comic buffoon. But the whole point of McEwan's performance was that she took language with fastidious seriousness, fractionally pausing before each misplaced epithet as if ransacking her private lexicography. As I said at the time, it was like watching a demolition expert trying to construct a cathedral.' For this role she was voted Best Actress by the *Evening Standard*. She won the same award in 1995 for her role as Lady Wishfort in Congreve's *The Way of the World*, where, according to one critic, she 'comes on looking like an ostrich which has mysteriously been crammed into a tambourine lined with fresh flowers'. Sometimes it seemed that she was born to play dotty or over-dressed dowagers.

Most great actors tend to cast off the mannerisms of their youth. McEwan chose to keep hers, filling them out with the authority and ease of age. Her natural rhythm was light and bird-like, but, as we can see in *The Dance of Death*, she could by sheer effort assume weight and stateliness. Her face was naturally ageless; she never quite looked young, since her features were too jarring and busy, and she never seemed old. She remained, as she began, a queen of pixies. She died at the end of January 2015, after suffering a stroke.

Vanessa Redgrave was born in Blackheath, London, on 30 January 1937, the daughter of Michael Redgrave and Rachel Kempson. As a result of the air raids over London during the Second World War, her family moved to Herefordshire, where she attended the Alice Ottley School in Worcester; the Redgraves returned to London in 1943 and she attended the Queen's Gate

School in South Kensington, where she played Shaw's St Joan, before 'coming out' as a debutante in the orthodox fashion. But in 1954 she began studies at the Central School of Speech and Drama, which offered a much more suitable preparation for her adult life; her biographer Dan Callahan writes that 'fellow students remembered her as awkward, disorganised and rebellious.' She made her first appearance on stage at the Frinton Summer Theatre three years later, in a play by William Douglas-Home aptly titled *The Reluctant Debutante*, before moving on to the Arts Theatre in Cambridge and then to the Royal Court, where she played Sarah Undershaft in Shaw's *Major Barbara*.

Redgrave joined the Shakespeare Memorial Theatre for the 1959 season, but her parts in *A Midsummer Night's Dream* and *Coriolanus* did not provoke much interest. Since she was working with Charles Laughton, Laurence Olivier and Edith Evans, that was perhaps not surprising. In March 1960 she went on to the Comedy Theatre for Joan Henry's play *Look on Tempests*, and in August she was at the Queen's Theatre to work with her father in Robert Bolt's *The Tiger and the Horse*. At the request of Peter Hall she returned to Stratford in July 1961 to play Rosalind in *As You Like It* for the Royal Shakespeare Company; the *Financial Times* reported that her pursuit of clarity, meaning and passion represented a wholly new approach to Shakespeare. Gielgud was more descriptive when he remarked, 'this Redgrave girl is very charming and talented, though dreadfully tall.' This success was followed by Katharina in *The Taming of the Shrew* and Imogen in *Cymbeline*.

Redgrave played Nina in Chekhov's *The Seagull* at the Queen's Theatre in 1964, and in 1966 she played the leading role in Jay Presson Allen's adaptation of *The Prime of Miss Jean Brodie* at Wyndham's, for which performance she won the *Evening Standard*'s award for Best Actress. She was uncomfortable with the role of a semi-fascist schoolmistress, however, and stated that she 'split right open – my greatest fear was that I would actually go mad on stage.' It may have been this experience that sent her spinning into film and television, where she remained for three years.

In the spring of 1972 Redgrave was Viola in *Twelfth Night*, in which a critic recognized her 'phenomenal gift of allowing us instant access to her thought', which is the mark of an exceptional actor. At the Globe in August 1973 she was Cleopatra, directed by her ex-husband Tony Richardson, culminating in what was described as 'an enraptured dignity in death and desolation'. She changed direction completely in November of that year with the leading role of Gilda in Coward's *Design for Living*.

In 1984, having again concentrated on film and television work, Redgrave returned to the theatre with Ibsen and Tennessee Williams. A fellow actor, Imogen Stubbs, commented that 'she has greatness – charisma, daring, insanity. It is not even technically controlled . . . But Vanessa has that element of catharsis.' In 1992 Redgrave starred with Paul Scofield at the Haymarket in Shaw's *Heartbreak House*. Another period of film-making followed, about which she is illuminating. In her autobiography she remarks that 'film acting is a process that demands the utmost understanding of the fact that any moment in life will contain more in it than any single person in it is conscious of, and the actor or actress has to accept and use this all the time.' In 1996 she reappeared on stage with Scofield in Ibsen's *John Gabriel Borkman*. 'She has a slightly odd voice,' the director Tony Palmer had said of her earlier. 'It is not a beautiful voice by any stretch of the imagination. But she has an instinct for poetry and getting the rhythm perfect.' She was also the mistress of her voice. As a suffragette in *The Bostonians* (1984) it is an uncertain chirrup, but as Agatha Christie in *Agatha* (1979) it is cool and sweet.

In January 2006 Redgrave received the Ibsen Centennial Award for her 'outstanding work in interpreting many of Henrik Ibsen's works over the last decades'. 'I give myself to my roles as to a lover,' she said in an interview with *Time* magazine, 'and so

I save myself for my work, to lose myself in a role. It's the only way.' In her autobiography she remarks that 'every actor knows such moments, when it seems that someone else has taken possession of him. It is the union of the conscious with the unconscious. The problem is that everyone knows it when it happens, but artists spend most of their lives trying to understand *how* it happens.' It is worth remarking that her father used similar terms, when he wrote of 'the god descending'.

To speak of Redgrave's style of acting would be misleading. That suggests something like the nobility of Olivier or the sophistication of Coward. Like Edith Evans and Maggie Smith, she seemed to hear a tune that no one else could quite catch. Her eyes are always alive, and always alight. There is endless activity beneath her performances, sometimes quick and sometimes slow. Two of her salient characteristics are feyness and danger; her presence can sometimes be consolatory, but never cosy. We see innate erudition in her performances; she seems to know more than the playwright, more than the director, and more even than the character she plays.

Helen Mirren was born in 1945 in Hammersmith, west London, with the full name of Helen Lydia Mironoff, the surname bequeathed to her by her Russian father, who changed the family name to Mirren when she was six years old. The newly minted Mirrens moved to Leigh-on-Sea in Essex, and she attended schools in Westcliff and Southend before pursuing her real interests at the New College of Speech and Drama in north London. She became interested in the theatre after seeing a summer show at the end of the pier, according to her memoir, *In the Frame* (2007), and by a production of *Hamlet* by the Southend Shakespeare Society. A school contemporary recalled that 'Helen always knew she could act and wanted to go into the theatre. She had a ruthless streak even then. She was going for it and nothing deterred her.' 'I wanted,' she wrote, 'and was destined for, the theatre.' At the age of eighteen she auditioned for the National Youth Theatre, and was accepted. Two years later she was playing Cleopatra at the Old Vic, which effectively 'launched my career'.

Mirren had made a definite impression, and was invited to join the Royal Shakespeare Company. There she first appeared in *The Revenger's Tragedy*, directed by Trevor Nunn, followed by four Shakespearean plays as well as *Enemies* by Maxim Gorky in 1971 at the Aldwych and Strindberg's *Miss Julie* at the Other Place in the same year. The director Ken Russell saw her in that play and remarked that 'she has a quality of self-possession that is irresistible . . . that marvellous blend of instinct and cunning and compassion and vulnerability . . . She invests her characters with a hint of steel that reads as pride or strength.'

It would be more accurate to speak of an 'approach' rather than a style. Mirren's acting at the beginning of her career bears little resemblance to what she later became, and in this perhaps lies her secret. She, more than most actors, adapted her mode to her age and, perhaps, to public perception. The impression she first made was as something of a sex symbol, with her large mouth and distinctly odalisque figure. In the late 1960s, as for example in the filmed version of Hall's *A Midsummer Night's Dream*, she manifested a unique blend of sensuality and innocence.

In 1972 and 1973 she was attached to Peter Brook's recently formed International Centre for Theatre Research, and with this group of actors she toured North Africa and the United States. But she went back to the RSC in 1974, playing Lady Macbeth opposite Nicol Williamson at Stratford and in the following year at the Aldwych. She believed that 'I had really begun my life as a professional actress.' During this period she wrote a letter to *The Guardian*, criticizing her own company for over-expenditure as 'unnecessary and destructive to the art of the theatre', with the art of acting obscured in an 'abyss of costume and technicalities'.

In September 1975 Mirren appeared as Maggie in David Hare's *Teeth 'n' Smiles* at the Royal Court, before moving on to the Lyric, Hammersmith, for *The Seagull* and a new farce by Ben Travers, in which she was described as 'stirringly voluptuous'. She was back at the RSC by 1977, moving between Stratford and the Aldwych, playing Queen Margaret in the three parts of *Henry VI*; in 1979, she was Isabella in *Measure for Measure* at the Riverside Studios, directed by Peter Gill. She possesses a vivid but natural direct-ness that allows her to cut to the heart of her characters. When her performances came across as callow, that was because they were meant to be callow. Such callowness was accompanied by a half-embarrassed sensuality, by a girlishness and, above all, by what can only be called luminosity.

In 1981 Mirren returned to the Royal Court for Brian Friel's *The Faith Healer*; later that year she was remarkable in the title role of Webster's *The Duchess of Malfi*, of which one critic wrote that 'Miss Mirren never leaves it in doubt that even in her absences, this ardent, beautiful woman is the most important character of the story.' When she went on to play Moll Cutpurse in Thomas Dekker and Thomas Middleton's *The Roaring Girl*, she was described as having 'swaggered through the action with radi-ant singularity of purpose'. She acted in 1989 with Bob Peck in Arthur Miller's *Two Way Mirror*, of which Miller said: 'what is so good about English actors is that they are not afraid of the open expression of large emotions.' That is not always the case, but it may justly be said of Mirren's clarity and naturalness of feeling. In 1994 she performed in Ivan Turgenev's *A Month in the Country*, which in the following year was transferred to New York for her Broadway debut.

In 1998 Mirren again played Cleopatra at the National Theatre. In that performance, however, she was not considered to be at her best. Perhaps she had visited the role too often. It is not uncommon for even the finest actors to allow familiarity to numb a performance. She went on to the Donmar Warehouse to play Lady Torrance in Tennessee Williams's *Orpheus Descending*, where one critic remarked on her ability to convey 'resilient toughness'. One of her biographers remarked that 'the eyes are eagle-like, predatory and perceptive.'

Mirren returned to the National in 2003 for Eugene O'Neill's *Mourning Becomes Electra*, and then in 2009 for the title role in Jean Racine's *Phèdre*. Her particular kind of directness or plainness, close to severity, was evident in her performance as Elizabeth II in Peter Morgan's *The Audience* at the Gielgud in 2013; it is a character she had already played on film, in *The Queen* (2006), with the same unaffected and perceptive candour. A typical quality of Mirren's late work is restraint or, rather, self-suppression; it is what one might call 'the pressure-cooker effect', which is common in many great actors. It tends to produce a performance of depth and conviction. Her characteristic qualities, then, are authority without authoritarianism, combined with tenderness.

Twenty-one

The impossible players

When Vanessa Redgrave was a girl of fourteen she spent the summer holiday with her family in Stratford, and they passed every evening at the Memorial Theatre, where for a time Richard Burton played Prince Hal. She wrote later that

he was the only actor I have ever seen whose voice and eyes literally compelled the audience to listen and observe his every move . . . when he turned his deep steady gaze upon the audience his eyes seemed to search you out . . . His raw, resonant Welsh voice, sorrowful and sometimes harsh, his physical stillness, and that steady piercing gaze, were unique.

Burton was born Richard Walter Jenkins on 10 November 1925 at Pont-rhyd-y-fen in the Afan valley of South Wales, the twelfth of thirteen children. His father was a miner, and his mother a barmaid. She died when he was two years old, and for a while he was brought up by his older sister and her husband. He seems to have been an anxious and unhappy child until he came under the influence of a teacher at secondary school in Port Talbot, Philip Burton. The young Jenkins became his ward and changed his name to Burton by deed poll.

Burton's father could never summon up the slightest interest in his son's chosen profession. In any case, watching films or going to the theatre would have clashed with vital visits to the public house. In later years, Burton looked his father up at the local pub and introduced himself as his son. 'Which one?' was the nonchalant question in Welsh. 'Number twelve,' replied his son, equally unperturbed. He expected no more. There are perhaps few sharper spurs to artistic ambition than an absent father.

Burton's legal guardian seemed to sense his dramatic abilities and arranged for him to hold an audition in front of Emlyn Williams in Cardiff. This led to his first play, Williams's *The Druid's Rest*, which opened at the Royal Court, Liverpool, in November 1943 and transferred in the following year to St Martin's in London. The critic of the *New Statesman* wrote that 'in a wretched part, Richard Burton showed exceptional ability.' Burton later claimed that that short sentence determined his future. At the close of the production he was called up for the RAF and spent six months on a special wartime course at Exeter College, Oxford, where his tutor, Nevill Coghill, was an enthusiastic director of plays. He placed Burton as Angelo in an Oxford University Dramatic Society production of *Measure for Measure*, and subsequently called him a 'genius'. Burton's contemporary Robert Hardy recalled that 'there were moments when he totally commanded the audience by this stillness. And the voice which would sing like a violin or with a bass that could shake the floor.'

When he left the RAF in 1947, Burton returned to the stage under the auspices of H. M. Tennent Ltd in *Castle Anna*, from a novel by Elizabeth Bowen, at the Lyric, Hammersmith. Almost immediately he was signed up for a film written by Williams, *The Last Days of Dolwyn* (1949), and in this production he met his future wife Sybil Williams, with whom he had two daughters. In 1949 Burton returned to the stage in Christopher Fry's *The Lady's Not for Burning*, directed by John Gielgud, which moved to New York in 1950. Gielgud said of him that 'he was marvellous at rehearsals. There was the true theatrical instinct. You only had to indicate – scarcely even that. He would get it and never changed it.'

In 1951 Burton was in Stratford once more to take part in a Shakespearean history cycle at the Shakespeare Memorial Theatre, in which he played Prince Hal. This was the performance that Redgrave had seen, and her observations were confirmed by Kenneth Tynan, who wrote that 'Burton is a still, brimming pool, running disturbingly deep; at twenty-five he commands repose and can make silence garrulous'; this was followed by Henry v and the role of Ferdinand in *The Tempest*, a part he loathed – as do most actors. Two years later he joined the Old Vic, where he began by playing Hamlet.

In this production Burton worked against his instincts, as do, at some point, most great actors. He was celebrated for his presence and the power of his address, but for this performance he moved lightly and uncertainly. He would rub his hands and seem almost to totter. In his craggy landscape of a face, the eyes darted in fear and perplexity. At the most seemingly inopportune moments, he would laugh. The laugh was genial, not mocking, as when Ophelia spoke of the 'rich gifts' he had given her once. At the notorious injunction to 'Get thee to a nunnery,' he lowered his voice almost to a murmur. The arms seemed frail, the gestures small and almost etiolated. Then, suddenly, as he roared in anguish at his former love, his arms whipped out, his legs spread out to leap. We often speak of how some actor 'roars' the line, but Burton's roar is a true roar, like a lion seeing his rival. But when, on seeing the ghost in the first act, he addressed the 'angels and ministers', his voice had become angelic.

We should remember that by both men's accounts Gielgud needed to 'direct' Burton very little, since the younger man would usually anticipate Gielgud's suggestions. When Hamlet gives Polonius the piece of paper, it is with a sudden dart of the arm. His posture, generally so cramped and hunched, serves as the perfect foil for these sudden 'unleashings'.

'Alas, poor Yorick', he says, genially, and we may note how often Burton can be conversational and easy. He was, *pace* his reputation, very much at home in that mode. He said that Hamlet could be played fifty ways, and he was prepared to demonstrate this. His version at the Old Vic was that of an unsettled and unsettling figure, a spreader of fear, sardonic, vulnerable only to himself; he was a lord of the *danse macabre*. It was an imperfect performance, but then formal perfection was never to be the chief concern of this defiantly rebellious actor. He observed in conversation with Kenneth Tynan that 'I wouldn't want to be that kind of actor, who goes on stage and every night perfectly gives the same cadence to the same speech . . . I would prefer to be free, so that I'm invited to be bad some nights, if I happen to be bad that night.'

After his Hamlet was released upon a receptive world, Burton took on King John, Coriolanus, Sir Toby Belch and Caliban; in December 1955 he was Henry v, for which he won the *Evening Standard*'s Best Actor award and was welcomed as 'the natural successor to Olivier'. In 1956 he alternated between Othello and Iago. After his tenure at the Old Vic came to an end, he migrated to Switzerland as a tax exile and appeared only once more on the English stage, as Doctor Faustus in a production to benefit the Oxford University Dramatic Society in 1966. It was not particularly well received, and, if the filmed version is any indicator, it is possible to understand that lack of success. His last speech, however, showed him at his best. What more fitting part for a tortured soul than that of a soul in torment?

Burton made a few appearances on Broadway, but his principal focus was now on film, so at this point we must leave him – perhaps lamenting the loss to the English theatre, where he had made such a strong first impression. In a world of flamboyance and bravura, as well as delicacy, he had retained a powerful sense of origin as a working-class boy and as a result became an example to later actors. Having the voice of Zeus and the eyes of Hades, he needed to *do* very little. Supremely poetic, his acting was nonethe-less too earthy to be called lyrical and too intense to be described as worldly. And this was his gift. Ordinary passion was often beyond him – he could seem strained, self-pitying and theatrical – although he remains the laureate of intensity. But when a spirit or mood was needed that transcended the ordinary or even the human, he came into his own. He was, as are many of his countrymen, a mystic, and his atheism was no bar to that. He once said that 'God put me on earth to raise sheer hell.' He died suddenly of a brain haemorrhage on 5 August 1984.

One actor was particularly associated with Burton, an actor who was in some senses his soulmate and in others his opposite. Burton once said of him that while for most actors acting is chiefly a matter of craft, occasionally an actor arises whose originality amounts to wizardry. Peter O'Toole was born in Leeds in August 1932 and began life in the working-class area of Hunslet. 'When you're pressure-cooked into a Catholic slum upbringing,' he once said, 'you don't forget it very easily.' His father, originally from Ireland, was a bookmaker of uncertain fortune. O'Toole attended St Joseph's, a school outside Leeds administered by nuns and Jesuit priests. He became an altar boy and, like Olivier and other actors, came to adore the theatricality and ritual involved in that activ-ity. 'I loved every second of it,' he said. 'The mass was my first performance.'

At the age of eight O'Toole was evacuated from Leeds as a result of the war, and taken in by a family from the Midlands for a year or so before returning to Leeds and St Joseph's. He left school at the age of fifteen, and began wrapping parcels in a warehouse before being taken on at the *Yorkshire Evening News* as a 'copy boy' and general factotum. At eighteen he was called up for national service in the navy, but after the obligatory two years he returned to the *Evening News*. Quite by chance he was offered a role in Turgenev's *Fathers and Sons* by a local drama group, and was smitten with the idea of becoming an actor. With a friend he hitchhiked to London and braved the portals of RADA. It was fortunate that the academy was then holding auditions for the next year of students, and O'Toole was offered a scholarship in a class that included Albert Finney, Alan Bates, Richard Briers and Frank Finlay.

After RADA O'Toole joined the Bristol Old Vic Company at the Theatre Royal in the autumn of 1955. He began with small roles, in Thornton Wilder's *The Matchmaker* and Chekhov's *Uncle Vanya*. He remained with the company for four years, and in 1956 he was still playing minor roles in works by Jonson, Shaw, Sheridan and others. By the following year, however, he was being given larger parts, including Alfred Doolittle in Shaw's *Pygmalion* and, more importantly, Jimmy Porter in John Osborne's *Look Back in Anger*. It was a part he entered with relish.

Patrick Stewart, a student at the Bristol theatre, commented that 'O'Toole has been my benchmark for stage charisma ever since – just the intensity of his presence.' When in 1958 O'Toole played John Tanner in Shaw's *Man and Superman*, a contemporary recalled that 'you couldn't take your eyes off him on the stage. Real stars all have a slightly dangerous quality about them, and Peter had an unpredictability that bordered on menace.' This was succeeded by his Hamlet in April of that year. In January 1959 he played Private Bamforth in Willis Hall's *The Long and the Short and the Tall*; of his performance, Tynan wrote, 'I sensed a technical authority that may, given discipline and purpose, presage greatness.'

O'Toole joined the Shakespeare Memorial Theatre at Stratford for the 1960 season, and there, perhaps surprisingly, under Peter Hall's direction he was cast as Shylock. Bernard Levin called his performance a 'radiant masterpiece', and the critic for *The Tribune* affirmed that it 'will stand as a great chapter in theatre history'. O'Toole also played Petruchio opposite Peggy Ashcroft in *The*

Taming of the Shrew, and Thersites in *Troilus and Cressida*. But he had only just begun to fulfil his early promise. A fellow actor, Ian Holm, recalled that 'there was something unconsciously gladiatorial and threatening about him . . . in many ways he was an actor from the nineteenth century, strangely ridiculous, often riveting, and unpredictably raw.' He had also acquired a reputation as an overpowering drinker and a man full of mischief. Unlike that other drinker, Burton, however, he loved the fun of it. His drinking, like his character, was puckish and expansive.

After a successful period in film – including *Lawrence of Arabia* (1962), during which he learned how to ride a camel, to do without water and indeed to speak Arabic – O'Toole returned to the stage in February 1963 with the lead role in Bertolt Brecht's *Baal*; it was not a success, but Brecht's biographer Martin Esslin believed that O'Toole was 'the greatest potential force among all English-speaking actors'. In October that year he took on the role of Hamlet under the direction of Olivier, who insisted on the uncut version, which lasted for almost five hours. This was the first production of the National Theatre Company at the Old Vic, but it received mixed reviews. *Plays and Players*, however, commented of O'Toole that 'this is not the poetic aesthete nor the babbling neurotic. It is a man of sufficient nobility and complexity to give the performance tragic stature.' He went back to film, but still felt the attraction of the stage. His first wife, Siân Phillips, recalled that it became his habit to refuse any fee for his stage work. He wanted, she said, 'to give something back'. In June 1965 he played Peter in David Mercer's *Ride a Cock Horse*, of which the critic Charles Marowitz wrote that 'O'Toole, once again the self-destructive hero, is now well versed in moral and physical deterioration. He plays the comedy like a music-hall veteran, and suggests that the serious stuff is still there on sufferance.'

In 1973–4 O'Toole was back at the Bristol Old Vic, where he appeared in the lead role of Chekhov's *Uncle Vanya* as well as in

Ben Travers's *Plunder* and Shaw's *The Apple Cart*. In 1980, having neglected the stage for film and television dramas, he returned to the Old Vic in London to play Macbeth. A young actor involved in the production, Kevin Quarmby, recalled that O'Toole's 'sole purpose for being in the play was to be *the* star. There wasn't a vision of the play, there was a concept of Peter O'Toole is a great star and everything must be done to ensure that all focus is on him at every moment.' It was a disaster, or what its director, Bryan Forbes, called 'a tragi-comedy of good intentions'; the critics were scathing, but the theatre was packed with people who had come to watch the supposed fiasco. Farce and fury surrounded the production and even saturated it. The famous actors' superstition of an 'unlucky' play seems to have been well founded in this case.

O'Toole survived the disaster, however, and returned to the English stage in 1983 with *Man and Superman* at the Haymarket, followed in 1984 by *Pygmalion*. The critics had toned down their abuse, and he came through unscathed. In 1986 he was back at the Haymarket and back with Shaw in *The Apple Cart*. In the autumn of 1989 he managed one of his best performances in Keith Waterhouse's *Jeffrey Bernard Is Unwell* at the Apollo. Here was a shaggy, knock-kneed spectre, a benign, incredulous grin plastered across his face. His voice was perfectly clear even as he slurred, his tongue always stirring in his mouth as if to check that his teeth were still present and correct. He caught the drunkard's habitual expression in the sideways leer, dark, smug and challenging. He would cough and cough, and the cough turned into a forced metallic laugh, like that of a fairground mannequin. There was also something of the music-hall clown as he toyed with the vodka or failed to set up an ironing board. His habitual intonation, here as elsewhere, was a high, strong tattoo upon the words, followed by a rich baritone purr. But he also exhibited those qualities that had been famous in his youth. The eyes were wandering and amused, the eyebrows raised in a partly ironic plea for mitigation, like a boy caught out by his nanny but who knows full well he can charm his way out of trouble. He might as well have been batting his eyelashes.

The slow grind from drunkenness to sobriety and back again was perfectly modulated. Towards the end of the play, O'Toole caressed the names of his drinking companions of Soho as if they were made of marble; when he mused on death it was with a drawl full of pathos, the pathos of a man bored of the sky and tired of the air. He quoted the old dictum that 'life is no laughing matter,' before replying, 'you could have fooled me.' And the remarkable quality he lent this unremarkable line lay in the emphasis on 'fooled' – as if it were part of a sentence such as, 'You could have fooled me, but you didn't; I fooled you.' It is, again, altogether unorthodox: the cool, disenchanted observation of one who has seen it all. This was a fundamentally melancholic character filtered through the technicolour prism of Peter O'Toole – cackling, giggling, commanding, a prince in his pots. O'Toole died, after a multitude of illnesses, on 14 December 2013. His preferred mode was the flamboyant, the excessive, even the bedizened. Among the wild, unsafe actors, he remains the unchallenged Dionysus, the true 'Master of the Revels'.

Twenty-two

A new breed

Alan Bates was a contemporary of Peter O'Toole and Albert Finney at RADA, and part of a new generation of actors that included Nicol Williamson and Tom Courtenay. He was born in Derbyshire on 17 February 1934, and was brought up close to the town of Belper. While attending Herbert Strutt Grammar School there, he became involved in school productions and often visited the Derby Little Theatre Club; Bates declared later that he 'became infatuated – I *had* to go every week.' In 1949 he joined the Derby Shakespeare Society, where he appeared in the role of Prince Arthur in *King John*. 'I'd found what I wanted to do,' he said, 'and what I thought I could do. It just hit me, and then it became an absolute obsession. I didn't care about anything else.' His early talent was such that he won a scholarship to RADA, but in 1952, at the end of his first year, he was called up for national service at RAF Newton. On his return to civilian life he joined the Midland Theatre Company in Coventry, where he made his first appearance on stage in 1955 in a now forgotten play entitled *You and Your Wife*.

Bates moved to London the following year and became one of the first members of the English Stage Company at the Royal Court Theatre, under the direction of George Devine. There in 1956 he first acted in Angus Wilson's *The Mulberry Bush* and Arthur Miller's *The Crucible*. Bates's third play was also the most challenging and influential; in March that year he played Cliff in the first production of *Look Back in Anger*. John Osborne's play caused a fissure in the theatrical landscape and became known as the earliest 'kitchen sink' drama, while its author became one of the 'angry young men' who dominated the late 1950s. Bates himself benefited from the controversy and publicity, playing the same part in Moscow and Edinburgh as well as on Broadway. On the back of that success he performed Edmund Tyrone in Eugene O'Neill's *Long Day's Journey into Night* at the Globe Theatre in 1957 and then, three years later, Mick in Harold Pinter's *The Caretaker*, which was transferred to Broadway the following year. He asserted later that 'you can't really get to the same depth of feeling every night, and I think you have to trust the fact that once you have found something, even if you don't feel it the next time, you have *been* there, and you will be convincing to an audience.' Bates's default expression in Pinter's play is one of simmering calm, appraising and very slightly amused, but his persona is a lair of latent horrors, awaiting their hour, invisible. The audience cannot be sure what he is going to do next, or which monster he might release, which is in some ways the test of good acting.

Bates once said, 'I've never really been typed in a recognisable way. I want every part to cut across the previous one, so people won't know what to expect next.' In that respect he resembled his most successful characters. He returned to the Royal Court in 1967 for David Storey's *In Celebration*, of which *Plays and Players* wrote that Bates 'has it in his nature to play tormented and self-divided characters with emotional truth and technical finesse'.

Bates had already moved into film, with productions such as *Whistle Down the Wind* (1961) and *A Kind of Loving* (1962), before returning to the English stage. In the title role of Simon Gray's *Butley* at the Criterion in 1971 he won the *Evening Standard*'s Best Actor award; this, too, went on to New York. He played a university lecturer who loses his wife and male lover on the same day.

Pinter, who directed it, noted that the character 'courts death by remaining ruthlessly – even dementedly – alive. It's a remarkable creation and Alan Bates as Butley gave the performance of a lifetime.' Bates was indeed at his most expansive. Sardonic, witty, desperate, mocking, he became a bourgeois King Lear, berating everyone in sight. He later said of the part that 'this man is literally on a self-destruct. But in a brilliant way. So that you are absolutely fascinated by this man who is just really sort of crumbling in front of you. Destroying everything around him. Every relationship.'

Either side of Butley, Bates played Hamlet at the Nottingham Playhouse and Petruchio with the Royal Shakespeare Company in Stratford. Of Hamlet he declared that 'he believes himself capable of doing something, but he does not trust himself to do it. That's true of me.' His association with Gray continued with *Otherwise Engaged* at the Queen's Theatre in 1975 and *Stage Struck* at the Vaudeville in 1979. Of the former, one critic wrote that 'Mr Bates maintains his unvarying cool with superb imperturbability, handling his debonair conversation with great skill.' 'You've got to be driven,' Bates once said, '*driven*.' He died of pancreatic cancer in December 2003. A kind of wounded innocence was his demesne, softening the contours of many otherwise brutal roles. He could, however, play any character, even if he could not play every mode.

Another of Bates's contemporaries at RADA, Albert Finney, shared a similar trajectory in his career, from the provinces to London and from stage to film. He was born on 9 May 1936 in Salford, Lancashire, where his father was a bookmaker, and he attended grammar school in that city before going on a scholarship to RADA in 1953. 'I grew up secure,' he once said. But that was not his inclination. 'Part of the reason I became an actor is that I like my life insecure.' He was unhappy during his first terms at RADA; it seems the teachers tried to train him to talk 'posh', as he called it, but he resisted. 'It wasn't until I realised that there was music in my voice and that the voice belonged to only me that I began to settle there. I simply refused to let RADA wipe my personality clean.' Some might assert that this is an operation that drama schools are almost obliged to perform. But that was not Finney's way.

On leaving RADA Finney joined the Birmingham Rep, where in April 1956 he first appeared on stage in minor roles, in plays such as Donagh MacDonagh's *Happy as Larry*; then he was ripped untimely from the womb of apprenticeship by being given the leading roles in *Henry V*, *Hamlet* and *Macbeth*. There must have been a rapid pace of production, since at the end of July 1956 he first came to London when the Birmingham company moved to the Old Vic for a season; there he played Belzanor in Shaw's *Caesar and Cleopatra*.

At some point Finney caught the attention of Charles Laughton, who, despite describing him as 'bloody terrible' in *Macbeth*, invited the younger actor to join him and his wife, Elsa Lanchester, in a production of Jane Arden's *The Party*, which opened at the New Theatre on St Martin's Lane in May 1958. Kenneth Tynan wrote that Finney 'brought to London from Birmingham those qualities of technical assurance and latent power that are the fruits of hard training and the buds of great acting'. The following year Finney moved with Laughton to the Shakespeare Memorial Theatre at Stratford, where he played Cassio opposite Paul Robeson's Othello and Lysander in Peter Hall's production of *A Midsummer Night's Dream*. He was also the understudy for Laurence Olivier in *Coriolanus*, in which, he reported, 'I started to get cocky and imitate Olivier and make the company laugh.'

In January 1960 Finney returned to London and starred in Lindsay Anderson's production of Harry Cookson's musical *The Lily-White Boys* at the Royal Court. Anderson recalled that Finney, although young, was able to 'get away with it by brilliant naturalism'. Finney himself called it 'naturalistic minimalism'. This was overshadowed by his successful performance as Billy Liar at the Cambridge Theatre in September of that year. Tynan wrote,

'Mr Finney is a true fascinator, as Richard Burton was at his age.' In his diary, John Gielgud described him as 'superb'. Finney left the production after eight months in order to take up the lead in Osborne's *Luther* at the Royal Court in 1961; it was transferred to the Phoenix, where it ran until March 1962. Caryl Brahms wrote that Finney, 'at all times a compulsive actor, is more than compelling as Luther. He is Luther . . . This was the most convincing performance that I can remember ever to have seen.' Tynan, again an enthusiast, described the actor as 'a reincarnation of the young Irving'. Finney confessed in an interview, 'My danger is that I can do it [acting] too easily. I need the neurosis of making my work more complicated and more difficult than it need be in order to avoid this facility – that I'm not just getting away with it.'

With the actor and producer Michael Medwin, Finney established Memorial Productions, which was primarily concerned with film but brought to the stage Peter Nichols's *A Day in the Death of Joe Egg*, in the New York production of which Finney also starred. He returned to the London stage in 1972, after an absence of six years, with Ted Whitehead's *Alpha Beta* at the Royal Court. The critic for *The Guardian* noted that 'through conscious application of outer detail he gave one a complete chart of the man's inner life.' He gave up acting for a while in order to become associate artistic director of that theatre, where he directed, among other plays, Joe Orton's *Loot*, *Krapp's Last Tape* by Samuel Beckett, and Victor Hugo's *Cromwell*. He returned to the stage in 1974 with a black comedy by Nichols, *Chez Nous*, at the Globe Theatre.

Finney moved to the National Theatre in December 1975 in order to recover his sense of classical acting:

I felt that it needed commitment. When you're making movies all the time, you stop breathing. You literally don't breathe in the same way that you do when you're playing the classics. When you have to deliver those long, complex speeches on stage, you can't heave your shoulders after every sentence. The set of muscles required for that kind of acting need to be trained.

He played Hamlet at the Lyttelton in March 1976, and Tamburlaine the Great at the Olivier in October. This version of Hamlet was no better received than his attempt at the part as a young actor twenty years before in Birmingham. But one critic noted that 'Finney has never had to banish sentimentality from his acting – it just doesn't figure in his technique . . . Finney is a gloriously physical performer. He is engaging, sexy, mischievous, witty and merciless.' His Tamburlaine was more warmly received, perhaps because he was playing an active warrior rather than a thinker.

It could be said that Finney passed from angry young man to grand old patriarch without any intervening period. We can describe two distinct styles in the early Finney and the late Finney, then, but both share the same quality of weight. This is weight in terms not of mass but of rhythm. He can be deliberate, but he is never monotonous. He has the power of emphasis that seems to have come from a strong will. That is perhaps why he was more fitted for Tamburlaine than for Hamlet.

When he elected to play Macbeth in 1978, it was not a success. Finney said that in the Olivier Theatre 'the energy going out of me didn't come back. Instead of being recharged like a dynamo, I felt like a battery running down.' He never acted again in Shakespeare or, indeed, at the National. This was a great loss, but the Olivier, with its unforgiving and unresponsive acoustics, has proved to be the mausoleum of many Shakespearean aspirations.

In 1983 Finney played as 'Sir' against Tom Courtenay's dresser in *The Dresser*. This is the most theatrical of all his films and is clearly, even ostentatiously, derived from the stage. It is also paradigmatic of Finney's 'late' style. Based on the career of Donald Wolfit, it shows Finney becoming a grand old man before his time.

That is why the role suited him admirably. By turns sweet, pitiful, magnificent and repulsive, Finney plays 'Sir' as if that character and Lear, the role that dominates the film, were inextricable. Here is a martinet who can crouch like Shylock, pleading for pity. When he stands, he swells, flinging his arms out as if to wring the necks of seagulls. Furious at the pitiful sound effects backstage, he roars, 'I wanted a STORM!' He reaches out to poor, long-suffering, long-loving Tom Courtenay, and gasps, on the brink of tears but still reliably histrionic, that 'I have nothing more to give.' When he cries that he is 'a man more sinned against than sinning', we believe him, despite all his vanity, his callousness and his impregnable self-absorption.

Childishness and vulnerability are attributes that Finney could bring even to the mightiest parts. In 1984 he directed, and played the lead role in, *The Biko Inquest* at the Riverside and a revival of John Arden's *Serjeant Musgrave's Dance* at the Old Vic. He then took on the role of Harold in Lyle Kessler's *Orphans* at the Hampstead Theatre. It was described by one critic as his 'best performance in years', and the play went into the West End, at the Apollo. The playwright himself agreed that Finney 'was absolutely wonderful in the production . . . I cherish what Albert brought to the role.' His acting is self-evidently internal, nourished by deep springs within him. He was soon back in the West End with three plays by Ronald Harwood, *J. J. Farr*, *Another Time* and *Reflected Glory*. They enjoyed respectful and respectable reviews, but there was a feeling that Finney was dissipating his talent. His last stage performance, with Courtenay and Ken Stott, was in the first production of Yasmina Reza's *'Art'* at Wyndham's in 1996. When asked once how he prepared for his parts, he replied that 'I try to rely on the part itself telling me how to approach it.' If a player of Shakespeare's time were alive, he would no doubt say exactly the same. As far as the English actor is concerned, the text itself is all the tutor and all the trainer he needs. Finney died after kidney cancer and a chest infection in 2019, at the age of eighty-two.

Ian Richardson, although of the same generation as Finney and O'Toole, was more reserved, and superficially more orthodox. He was Scottish rather than English by birth and training, but in Richardson's case it was a distinction without a difference. He was born in Edinburgh on 7 April 1934, and went to primary and high schools in the city. He was first on stage in an amateur production of *A Tale of Two Cities*, during the course of which the director advised him to change or modify his accent. As a result his mother paid for him to attend elocution lessons, a process that he continued when he became an announcer for the British Forces Broadcasting Service during his period of national service, and he was known in later years for his impeccably pronounced English accent. He had already made a connection with the theatre, however, by taking on the duties of stage management at the Edinburgh People's Theatre before being called up.

On being discharged from the army, Richardson enrolled at the College of Dramatic Art in Glasgow with the avowed intention of becoming a professional actor. He was materially assisted in that ambition by being awarded the James Bridie Gold Medal before leaving the college in 1957. The following year he joined the Birmingham Repertory Theatre and, as always in repertory, played many parts and assumed many faces. He was Jack Worthing in Wilde's *The Importance of Being Earnest*, and even took on the title role in *Hamlet*. The critic of the *Daily Telegraph* wrote of the play that Richardson was 'a slight, sad-eyed figure of settled melancholy, earnest, sweet and boyish, who could suggest heartbreak in an inflection, a twist of the lip'.

This success led to Richardson's engagement with the Shakespeare Festival under the direction of Peter Hall; it soon became the Royal Shakespeare Company, and although his original contract was for three years, he remained with the company for fifteen. He began with relatively small roles, such as the Prince of Aragon in *The Merchant of Venice* in 1960, but soon rose in the hierarchy of tried and trusted actors. In the same year he played Malatesti to Peggy Ashcroft in *The Duchess of Malfi* by John Webster at the RSC's new venue at the Aldwych. By the following year he was playing Oberon to Judi Dench's Titania; his king of the fairies is intense and inscrutable, with a hint of menace. When he stares out at us, we succumb. We cannot take our eyes from him, yet he barely moves a feature. After his intense effort to remove his native accent, his voice is that of an immaculately English necromancer. His vowels swell out from far back in his throat, sonorous and tickling.

In 1964 Richardson was Antipholus in *The Comedy of Errors*, as well as Ford in *The Merry Wives of Windsor*, which *The Independent* described as 'a study of obsessional jealousy as frightening as it was funny'. This was also the year in which the company toured Eastern Europe, as well as the United States; Richardson played Edmund in Peter Brook's production of *King Lear* and the Herald in the same director's *Marat/Sade* by Peter Weiss. When that play reached Broadway the following year, Richardson played Marat, and was the first actor to appear naked on the stage. These roles were followed by those of Coriolanus and Cassius. He was always excellent with cold or manipulative characters. His default, perhaps, is a hypnotic immobility of feature. When he breaks this, everything necessary is conveyed with complete economy.

Richardson rejoined the RSC for a number of striking roles, including Berowne and Richard II, the latter of which was described by Michael Billington as 'a performance of infinite sweetness, bruising irony and thunderous scorn'. Berowne was a favourite with him, and that warm, sceptical and witty worldling of *Love's Labour's Lost* was a perfect match for his particular skill. But when he played Robespierre in a BBC feature, *Danton's Death*, in 1978, he brought to the role great stillness and sensitivity combined with a manic and pitiless cerebrality. All this is conveyed in his face. He stares out, pondering what to do with his rival, and the eyes are hard and cold. In a cameo role as Hamlet, also on television, he holds Yorick's skull as his stern manner dissolves and he blinks rapidly; he will not and must not let those tears out. But then he becomes as hard as Savonarola again.

Richardson was a comic actor of great variety and range, but he excelled in what might be called 'straight' parts without the interventions of comedy. They include his most famous screen interpretation, that of Francis Urquhart in *House of Cards* (1990). His characteristic expressions here are more liquid, and his long face resembles that of a duchess obliged to spend a disagreeable amount of time in a hotel lobby. But he was more than an embodied voice. His movements, in every part, are strong, precise and expansive. His gestures also seem to have the grace of a classical orator, sweeping up and pummelling down. He might be the heir to Johnston Forbes-Robertson. The *New Yorker* reported that he 'is a master of the raised eyebrow, and he carries his head as if it belonged on a coin. His nose gleams like a dagger. His narcissism is cut so fine that he seems to be peeling off a personal supply of thin smiles.' It is not surprising, or even unusual, that his most memorable roles were confined to the small screen. As his career progressed, the urbane persona of stratospheric eyebrows and languorous eyes – one quite at odds with Richardson's native good humour and modesty – began to occupy the camera's attention to the exclusion of all else. In short, he became type-cast. As the century progressed, together with the influence of film and television, that fate would become the fate of many; the odd or unusual actor was more and more trammelled into roles that suited their quirks rather than their gifts. Many actors were obliged to hone their art in front of a camera rather than an audience, and there, too often, they stayed. Ian Richardson died of heart failure in 2007.

Glenda May Jackson was born on 9 May 1936 in Birkenhead, where her father was a bricklayer or hod-carrier and her mother a cleaner, and so part of the same social ambiance as many of her contemporaries. This was a period of what might be called real working-class theatre. While only a few months old she was taken with her family to the coastal village of Hoylake on the Wirral peninsula, where she was brought up. She was educated at Hoylake Holy Trinity Church of England School close by, before moving on to West Kirby Grammar School for Girls, some 13 kilometres (8 mi.) from her home town. While there she was involved in the YMCA Players in Hoylake. She left school with only a modicum of qualifications and worked behind the medicine counter of Boots the chemist for two years, while spending her private time in amateur theatricals and elocution lessons.

Jackson's commitment was rewarded in 1954 with a scholarship to RADA, and while still there she made her professional stage debut in 1955 with a walk-on part in *Doctor in the House* at the Connaught Theatre in Worthing. She moved on to fortnightly rep at the Queen's in Hornchurch, Essex, where she played a waitress in Terence Rattigan's *Separate Tables*. She was then taken on by the Arts Theatre Club in Soho and played Ruby in Alex Samuels's *All Kinds of Men*; for the next six years she was either out of work or with various repertory companies. She began at the New Theatre in Crewe before spending thirty months without a job.

Yet in 1964 Jackson's talent was clear enough that she was able to join the RSC, where she worked in the Theatre of Cruelty Season arranged at LAMDA by Peter Brook; in that capacity she played Charlotte Corday in *Marat/Sade* at the Aldwych, a production that eventually moved on to New York, where it ran for 144 performances. When she is ardent for Marat's blood her voice deepens into the familiar Jackson tone of a hard purr. Something dark scrabbles upwards through her body, something that warps her features and twists her lips. It is remarkable, not simply as a bravura performance but for her insight into the difference between hatred as an event in the mind and hatred that has purpose. Jackson was now being noticed, and the same year she was Bellamira in Christopher Marlowe's *The Jew of Malta*, a role as far from Charlotte as can be imagined. That Jackson could shift so swiftly from unbalanced ingénue to calculating courtesan is a striking tribute to her versatility.

In 1965 Jackson played the Princess of France in *Love's Labour's Lost* at Stratford, of which one critic reported that 'there is a certain hard, almost metallic, edge to her delivery of the verse which at first seems uncalled for but which it is soon evident is an essential quality of her stage personality and which distinguishes her from twenty other actresses.' Many actors play the princess as knowing and urbane, but perhaps only Jackson could have identified her essential toughness. This distinctive quality has survived. In July of the same year she was back at the Aldwych as Eva in Brecht's *Puntila*. The following month she was Ophelia at the Aldwych; her performance was striking enough that one critic, Penelope Gilliatt, commented that she was the only Ophelia who could also have played Hamlet.

In April 1973 Jackson played Katherine Winter in John Mortimer's *Collaborators* at the Duchess, a role she followed in early 1974 with that of Solange in Jean Genet's *The Maids* at the Greenwich Theatre. She was again at the Aldwych in February 1975 with the title role in *Hedda Gabler*, in a fine performance that was later translated on to the screen. Her body is lithe, her gestures smooth, but her face shows all. The sighs, the snorts, the glimpses of self-created agony in her eyes, all evoke a sense of frustrated entitlement and fettered yearning.

This was followed by a number of outstanding roles: Vittoria in Webster's *The White Devil* in 1976 at the Old Vic; Stevie Smith in Hugh Whitemore's *Stevie* at the Vaudeville the following year; and Cleopatra at the Aldwych in 1978. She then played the title role in *Rose* by Andrew Davies at the Duke of York's, a production that moved to Broadway in 1981. Of this performance the reviewer in the *Evening News* commented that 'this extraordinary actress so lights up the stage that once again she is going to dim the brightest adjectives in my armoury.' Jackson's acting is almost aggressively unsentimental. Where some actors might be tender, she is possessive; where some might weep, she tends to rage; where others rage, she will roar. This preference, or tendency, suggests an eschewing of glamour all the more admirable in a performer of undoubted personal appeal. She will not woo, or court, her audience. Her acting is like stripped wood, with all its splinters on display.

Jackson's last roles before leaving the stage for politics in 1992 were that of the eponymous heroine in Brecht's *Mother Courage* and Christine Mannon in O'Neill's *Mourning Becomes Electra*. It was a fitting transition to Westminster, having just played two roles for which her talents were supremely suited: one a cunning but vulnerable working-class survivor and the other an intense, driven obsessive. She came back to the stage in 2016 in the title role of *King Lear*, a feat that *The Telegraph* described as 'tremendous . . . No ifs, no buts. In returning to the stage at the age of eighty, twenty-five years after her last performance, she has performed one of those eleventh-hour feats of human endeavour that will surely be talked about for years to come by those who see it.' Facing the storm she stands, stiff-armed and stiff-legged, her chin thrust forwards, her eyes shattered mirrors. Like Richard Burton's, her voice is so distinctive as to be inimitable; it is precise and sharp, with a rich golden buzz at the back of the mouth. In common with many of her generation, she began her career speaking in the smooth, genial accents of Chelsea, and only when she returned to the stage did her native gruffness return. She is, supremely, a proud actor, commanding and uncompromising.

Twenty-three

Quiet flows the style

There are some actors who hide their light under several bushels. Nicol Williamson, for example, might be considered the most neglected actor of his generation. He was born in Hamilton, South Lanarkshire, on 14 September 1936, but his family moved to Birmingham before the Second World War. He attended the Central Grammar School in that city from the age of eleven to seventeen, and even in this early period he was engaged in amateur theatricals. Immediately on leaving school he enrolled at the Birmingham School of Speech and Drama, which he attended from 1953 to 1956. He then spent two years in national service, after which he joined the Dundee Repertory Theatre. He played there for two seasons, and appeared in thirty-three productions. That was the formidable range of most such companies, but it provided the best possible training for young actors. In October 1961 he travelled down to the Arts Theatre in Cambridge, where he played in Henry Chapman's *That's Us*; it transferred for a week to the Royal Court, where Williamson made his London debut. Later that month he played a murderous criminal, Black Will, in a tour of the sixteenth-century domestic tragedy *Arden of Faversham*; this was a role that was well suited to his own demon-haunted nature. In January 1962 he returned to the Royal Court to play Flute, the bellows mender, in *A Midsummer Night's Dream*, and the following month he played Malvolio in the same theatre.

In April of that year Williamson joined the Royal Shakespeare Company, where he first took on the role of an aircraft man in Henry Livings's *Nil Carborundum* at the New Arts Theatre in London; his spell of national service helped to bring conviction to his performance, which was described by one critic as 'faultless . . . in the regional post-Theatre Workshop manner so much in demand at the moment'. This was a reference to a training programme devised by Joan Littlewood, and its partly dismissive tone is telling. Here was a new style for a new kind of actor, unmasked and unmannered. Some more orthodox players had difficulty adjusting to a world in which actors did not rehearse in evening dress. Williamson next played, with the same company, Satin in Maxim Gorky's *The Lower Depths* and Leantio in Thomas Middleton's *Women Beware Women*. Of the former, one critic wrote that 'Nicol Williamson as Satin (Stanislavski's original role and the best part in the play) is as hungry and as generous as a lion, handling the final resolution of Gorky's play with a sort of impassioned tact . . . it carried utter conviction.'

Williamson returned to the Royal Court in April 1963, and starred in Frank Wedekind's *Spring Awakening* and Livings's *Kelly's Eye*. The critic John Russell Taylor wrote that 'the whole weight of the production falls on Nicol Williamson as Kelly . . . elsewhere he has looked in lesser roles like one of our more interesting young actors; here he effortlessly puts himself in the front rank.' In this play he appeared with Sarah Miles, who said later that 'the chip on his shoulder was so vast it dug right down into a great inner cavern.' Such a 'chip' can be the actor's greatest asset, however, for the English stage is not a realm in which complacency can thrive.

Williamson next appeared at the Royal Court in J. P. Donleavy's *The Ginger Man*, but that role was overshadowed by his most significant part to date, as the solicitor Bill Maitland in John Osborne's *Inadmissible Evidence*. Martin Esslin, a critic best known for coining the term 'theatre of the absurd', reported that 'Nicol Williamson is the anti-hero. He gives a memorable performance, eloquent, varied, full of memorable touches. A mammoth achievement.' Osborne himself described Williamson as 'the greatest actor since Marlon Brando'. The following month he played in a Ben Travers farce at the same theatre, and in December 1963 he was Vladimir in Samuel Beckett's *Waiting for Godot*. *Plays and Players* observed that Williamson had been subtly disparaged by comments to the effect that he 'has been widely praised by these clever Royal Court audiences', but in fact his performance of Vladimir 'is of a quality rarely seen on the London stage . . . Not your Cult of the Personality stardom, but the stardom of pure acting'.

We need not suppose for a moment that the reference to 'clever Royal Court audiences' is entirely complimentary. The first and greatest theatre for new writing has always stirred mixed feelings among critics. Since its subsidized status has allowed it to take risks that are denied to commercial theatres, some have felt its productions to be obscure or oppressively ideological. Whatever the truth of this, it was an ideal cradle for Williamson's fierce and unpredictable style. Beckett himself said that Williamson was 'touched by genius'. In his occasional Beckett monologues the dialogue is often furious and despairing, a gun-rattle torn and tearing. The fear of death, which Williamson felt so acutely and which Beckett presented so lyrically, can become a pot of blood hurled at the wall, splattering everywhere. Sometimes that hysteria spilled over into Williamson's own life, and he was well known for his sudden outbursts of temper, on occasion inflamed by alcohol. It is as well to remember that he believed strongly in using his own experience to inform that of his characters. It might seem that his and Beckett's visions elided perfectly.

Williamson, like others, was given the title of 'the Hamlet of his generation', by which was meant not necessarily the best actor but the most difficult, the most sensitive and the most troubled.

He is an actor with no filter, a naked soul, shivering and raging in the wind. As with most great actors, his eyes are always alive, telling their own story.

On his return from an American tour, Williamson took up an engagement in October 1973 with the RSC, where he played the leading role in a number of productions, including *Coriolanus* and *Macbeth*; he was also Malvolio in *Twelfth Night*. He had become accustomed to playing isolated and damaged characters, often close to the border of madness. He believed that his Macbeth 'was the best and truest thing I've been involved in in seven years', although he declared that 'there was no way that London would accept it.' Indeed it did not please all, but it was still compelling. His Macbeth was a warrior with the eyes of an abused innocent. He had the look of a man who has lost everything through no fault of his own, and is asking the world for reasons. His voice dives, shudders and whistles. He can roar as he whispers. Williamson then played in, and directed, Chekhov's *Uncle Vanya* at the Other Place in Stratford. That he also directed is of significance, since it gave him his pick of the roles. An actor who sought only praise and plaudits would have chosen to play Astrov, the self-assured and charismatic doctor who dominates the play, but Williamson was not such an actor. He chose Vanya himself, the tragicomic failure whose talents long ago withered in provincial obscurity.

Perhaps in an effort to remind himself of success, Williamson went back to the Royal Court in 1978 for another production of *Inadmissible Evidence*. *The Times* noted his 'technical virtuosity' and reported that his best effects 'are a product of the inner turmoil; and the most powerful of them verge on the inarticulate, and reveal his contradictory need to drive people away while suffering panic when anybody threatens to desert him'. One of his last theatrical performances was in a touring one-man show on the life and career of the American actor John Barrymore, with whom he seemed to identify.

Williamson then detached himself from England and took up living in New York, Amsterdam and Rhodes. His was always a restless spirit. In this context, it is noteworthy that towards the end of his life he preferred to play the piano and sing. It was in the Netherlands that he died of oesophageal cancer in 2011, at the age of seventy-five. Given his constant and almost frenetic tobacco use, such a death was not unexpected, yet it was somehow unfitting. Someone so frightened of his own mortality yet so courageous in all other respects perhaps deserved a wilder end.

Tom Courtenay is a quite different actor of the same generation. A gentle and unassuming man, he was attracted to characters of a similar disposition. He was born on 25 February 1937 in Hull, and went to Kingston High School before attending University College, London, where he felt unhappy and out of place except when performing with the Drama Society there. He also began attending the London theatres, where he saw Edith Evans, Peggy Ashcroft and Paul Scofield, among others. But he moved on to RADA, just down the road from the College, where he had been awarded a scholarship. 'So there I was,' he recalled, 'with a RADA scholarship, a good loud voice, reasonable health, and that was about it.' He was considered one of the most prominent of his contemporaries, although 'I hated the idea of learning technique for its own sake. You have to start with the character and then work outwards.'

Courtenay's first experience of the professional stage came at the Lyceum, Edinburgh, in August 1960, with the Old Vic company in a production of Chekhov's *The Seagull*; he played Konstantin Treplev, who has been described as 'a dreamer and compassionate soul who fills the void of his affection in his life with self-doubt'. Caryl Brahms, in *Plays and Players*, wrote that 'in many ways he is the truest Konstantin I have ever seen.' Certainly it became the kind of role at which he excelled. The production came to the Old Vic in London the following month, and received generally favourable notices.

In 1961 Courtenay replaced Albert Finney as Billy Liar at the Cambridge Theatre, where he played the mild but incorrigible fantasist with true conviction. 'I didn't need to imagine Billy's fantasy world,' he wrote in his exemplary memoir, *Dear Tom* (2000); 'it was in every molecule of my body and I had been practising it since childhood.' He was chosen to play the lead in a film version of the play two years later.

When young, Courtenay had the manner of a playful and imaginative schoolboy under a feckless or wandering star. He has always possessed a most particular energy or rhythm, at once sinuous and spiky, and his naturally flat and slightly harsh voice can turn as soft as a cushion. In *Billy Liar* we can see something of his range. Like Alec Guinness in *Kind Hearts and Coronets*, he plays many parts, but with a different intent; Billy imagines himself in great and mighty roles. His voice turns upper class in the company of his family, stays northern for his workmates, and becomes soft and wheedling whenever he needs some outward echo to his inner fantasies. So the voice and boy change, but the rhythm of his performance remains the same.

Other films, such as *The Loneliness of the Long Distance Runner* (1962), consolidated Courtenay's reputation, but from the mid-1960s he tended to concentrate on stage work. After the success of these first films, he said, 'people wanted me to go on playing that sort of part forever, but I couldn't see how I could advance at all, so I turned down a whole lot of parts, in which other actors then made their names.'

In early 1964 he joined the National Theatre Company and took the part of Andri in Max Frisch's *Andorra*, a strange Brechtian compilation in which Andri believes himself to be Jewish when he is not so. It was the first venture of the company into foreign drama. Martin Esslin wrote, 'Tom Courtenay plays the hero, the boy who is made into a Jew by being treated like a Jew, with subtlety and delicate understanding.' He played a very different role as Pasha Antipov in David Lean's film of *Doctor Zhivago* (1965); here he has an icy intensity borne on the soft tones of a poet. His wonderfully plastic face is impassive, the eyes like windows with the shutters closed. He manages to convey both iron will and deep doubt.

In 1966 Courtenay was enrolled in the Chichester Festival Theatre, where he played Trofimov in Chekhov's *The Cherry Orchard* and Malcolm in *Macbeth*. He then travelled to Manchester to play in that city's university production of J. M. Synge's *The Playboy of the Western World*, before joining the Manchester 69 Company for the lead role in *Hamlet*. 'Plays used to come in between films for me,' he said. 'Now it's the other way round. Manchester has given me confidence in myself.'

Courtenay returned to London for a Manchester 69 production of Oliver Goldsmith's *She Stoops to Conquer* at the Garrick in 1969, in which he played the principal male character, Marlow. Michael Billington wrote in *The Guardian* that 'London audiences can now see for themselves how Tom Courtenay has for some time been quietly nurturing his talent in the north and astutely widening his range.' He also noted that Courtenay 'conclusively gives the lie to the still current notion that the new generation of actors cannot play stylish period comedy.'

In 1972 Courtenay played Leonard in Alan Ayckbourn's Time and Time Again at the Comedy. By May 1973 he had returned to the Manchester stage with Shaw's *Arms and the Man*, but he came back to London in 1974 to take on the title role in Ayckbourn's trilogy *The Norman Conquests* at the Globe. He stayed in that production for more than a year. At the end of 1975 he was at the Royal Court to play the poet John Clare in Edward Bond's *The Fool*. This was also a demonstration of the actor's range and ambition, burrowing beneath the distractions and difficulties of the troubled poet. Courtenay seems best when he can advance the claims of a pure soul.

When the University Theatre in Manchester changed its identity to become the Royal Exchange Theatre in 1976, Courtenay
played the lead roles in its first productions of Richard Brinsley
Sheridan's *The Rivals* and Heinrich von Kleist's *The Prince of
Homburg*. From then the Royal Exchange became his theatrical
home, where he played, among many parts, Malvolio, Raskolnikov,
Andy Capp, Uncle Vanya and King Lear. Like so many great
actors, he could shift register in a moment. In *The Dresser*, opening
in 1980, Courtenay, even when he bellows in frustration, is as light
as a sandpiper, busy as a hummingbird but, by the end, mighty
and moving in his turn. He could be petulant or wilful, but these
characteristics are balanced by swift movement, both physical and
emotional. He also tested himself with Molière in *The Misanthrope*
and *The Miser* at the Royal Exchange as well as *The Hypochondriac*
at the Lyric, Hammersmith. He continued working through the
1980s and 1990s and into the present century, and shows no sign
of ending a remarkable career.

Anthony Hopkins was born in 1937, the same year as
Courtenay, but on New Year's Eve. He was raised in Margam, a
suburb of Port Talbot in Wales. His early education was not particularly inspiring, but his working-class parents dispatched him
in 1949 to West Monmouth Boys' School in Pontypool, where he
lasted for five terms before moving on to Cowbridge Grammar
School in the Vale of Glamorgan. He recalled in an interview,
'I was a poor learner, which left me open to ridicule and gave
me an inferiority complex. I grew up absolutely convinced I was
stupid.' Nevertheless, when he left school at the age of seventeen he entered the Royal Welsh College of Music and Drama in
Cardiff, from which he graduated in 1957 only to be called up for
national service, which lasted for two years.

But his theatrical ambition survived, and Hopkins first
appeared on the stage at the Palace Theatre, Swansea, in 1960
with a now forgotten play, *Have a Cigarette*. He was inspired to

act, especially after a chance encounter with Richard Burton, and briefly joined the Arts Theatre in Manchester before being accepted at the Nottingham Playhouse. In the summer of 1961 he was invited to audition at RADA. He was accepted, and graduated in the summer of 1963.

Hopkins worked for a while at the Phoenix in Leicester, where among other dramas he performed in Arnold Wesker's *Chips with Everything* and Christopher Marlowe's *Edward II*; he then joined the Liverpool Playhouse, a period that he once described as the happiest of his career. The manager there, David Scase, recalled that 'although he had the image of being strong and masculine he also had – still has – a lovely feminine delicacy which makes him a really complete actor.' He was also very ambitious, which augured well for his future.

Hopkins then spent a while at a repertory company in Hornchurch, Essex, before being summoned for an audition at the National Theatre. There he played a scene from *Othello* under the gaze of Laurence Olivier, and in 1965 he joined that august company. At first he began in such relatively small roles as a sailor in William Congreve's *Love for Love*, an Inca general in Peter Shaffer's *Royal Hunt of the Sun* and Borachio in *Much Ado About Nothing*. But then he was obliged, as the understudy, to take on Olivier's part as Edgar in Strindberg's *The Dance of Death* when the older actor contracted appendicitis. Olivier wrote in his memoir that 'a new young actor in the company of exceptional promise named Anthony Hopkins was understudying me and walked away with the part of Edgar like a cat with a mouse between its teeth.'

Perhaps as a result of this, Hopkins played Andrei in Olivier's production of Chekhov's *Three Sisters* in 1967, in which he received good notices, followed by the part of Audrey in an all-male *As You Like It*. Irving Wardle of *The Times* described Hopkins's part as 'the funniest of all the performances'. In 1971 and 1972 Hopkins remained with the National at the Old Vic with Fernando Arrabal's

The Architect and the Emperor of Assyria, in which he played the emperor, together with Thomas Heywood's *A Woman Killed with Kindness*. The director John Dexter noted that in this play 'one could see the emergence of a potential classical actor of some authority.' Hopkins's style is sometimes described as reserved, but that is not accurate. Instead he keeps something in reserve, something intense and almost chthonic. That is what gives his acting its extraordinary power. His own description is more cogent when he says that he 'acts like a submarine . . . I think the less one shows the better.' His voice is exceptional, at once rich and dry, lilting and sonorous: a talon under brocade. It is attendant upon his complete fluency; he never seems to be 'saying his lines'.

In 1985 Hopkins returned to the Old Vic for the part of Fichtner in Arthur Schnitzler's *The Lonely Road*, but he renewed his association with the Royal National Theatre in the same year as Lambert Le Roux in *Pravda* by David Hare and Howard Brenton; Hare recalled that 'when Tony walked on to the stage in the preview there was a great ovation, which moved him. He went on to give a sublime performance.' The critics tended to agree. And how could they not? The role of the charming predator was one that Hopkins made his own. In 1986 he was Lear and the following year Antony. He belongs in the company of those actors – such as Ralph Richardson or Antony Sher – in whose hands one is never quite safe. They are not reliably 'good', even when they are unquestionably 'great'. Hopkins himself has a latent ox-like energy beneath the almost Trappist silence he often shows. At this point in his career, however, it had become clear to him that 'for me, working in the theatre was an exercise in futility . . . After all, I only came into the theatre in the first place to do films.' That may have been a genuine explanation, but it does not really account for the length of time he laboured on the stage.

Hopkins moved to the Shaftesbury two years later to play René Gallimard in David Henry Hwang's *M. Butterfly*. This was to be his last appearance on the West End stage, as the ever-widening maw of film and television celebrity obscured him from theatre audiences. He seems to be one of those actors who grew bored or tired with nightly performances, and decided to tread the no less dangerous path of cinematic fame, which he has acquired with overwhelming success. His talent was, perhaps, better suited to the screen, since his intensity – his greatest gift – was easily smothered or diluted on the stage. Hopkins knows what the Elizabethan actors also knew: that power is best shown in stillness.

Twenty-four

All together now

While Albert Finney and Tom Courtenay may be considered part of the 'new wave' of actors who came to prominence in the 1960s, Derek Jacobi has continued the tradition of great classical acting. He was born in Leytonstone, Essex, in October 1938, to working-class parents. He attended Leyton County High School for Boys, where he became part of the drama club, then secured a scholarship to St John's College, Cambridge; this in itself, given the circumstances, was a remarkable achievement.

Jacobi had already enrolled at the National Youth Theatre, where he had been given prominent roles, and at university he acted with the Marlowe Society and the Cambridge University Amateur Dramatic Club. 'The list is virtually endless,' he wrote, 'as were the number of parts I performed as part of the Cambridge student rep.' At the Marlowe Society his director, George Rylands, told him, 'I'm going to drill my Mayflower players to *think* while they are speaking, think what the Elizabethan or Jacobean blank verses mean instead of ranting or throwing away the lines.' It was a lesson Jacobi did not forget. He played Hamlet, Prince Hal and Edward II, among other roles, at the Arts Theatre, and on graduating in 1960 he was offered employment by the Birmingham Repertory Theatre, where he made his first professional appearance in N. F. Simpson's comedy *One Way Pendulum*. He went on to play Troilus, Aaron the Moor in *Titus Andronicus* and Henry

VIII. He once said that 'the Birmingham rep gave me the biggest transfusion of theatrical blood that I needed to carry me through the life of a theatrical career.' But we must bear in mind what he has often said about the nature of his talent, quite without boasting (of which he is incapable); it came instinctively to him. This is a rare gift. One of the principal techniques of drama school is to weed out mannerisms, while rep, as several actors admit, allows them to flourish. But Jacobi, who has often said that his experience of rep obviated the need for such a school, reminds us that mannerisms need not be signs of affectation. Quite the opposite.

Jacobi had the good fortune to catch the attention of Laurence Olivier, who in 1963 invited him to join the newly established National Theatre in Chichester and at the Old Vic. He remained there for eight years. It was a form of security. 'Actors are vulnerable people,' he wrote in his memoir. 'We have raw nerves. We lay ourselves on the line, we have to be emotionally vulnerable – open.' He first played Brother Martin in John Dexter's production of George Bernard Shaw's *Saint Joan* at the Chichester Festival Theatre in June 1963, which transferred to the Old Vic four months later, before taking on the role of Laertes opposite Peter O'Toole's Hamlet, and then that of Cassio in *Othello*, with Olivier in the title role. In the filmed version of that performance, released in 1965, he dominates even more than Olivier's Othello. His Cassio is magnificently persuasive as a kind of courtier poet, but revealingly fragile as a man of action; it is a remarkable creation, which contains many elements that would recur in later performances. He has the power of a Johnston Forbes-Robertson, but with far greater speed; the gestures are flowing and expansive, although at times deliberately 'camp'. His verse-speaking is at once muscular and lyrical, while the head is typically held high. The prose passages he makes completely his own, or perhaps it would be truer to say that he is at ease in both modes, recognizing and obeying their respective demands.

Jacobi's popular reputation as an actor, however, was immeasurably increased by his role of the Roman emperor in the television series *I, Claudius* of 1976, in which he was obliged to age as the series progressed. An increasingly doddery, drunken and heartbroken Claudius, he could touch the heart even as he intended to quicken some contempt. Television fame did not prevent him from rejoining the Prospect Company as its leading man for the rest of the 1970s. He took the main roles in a number of productions, some of which stayed at the Albery Theatre and the Old Vic before taking to the road. He then played Hamlet, Caesar in *Antony and Cleopatra*, Rakitin in Ivan Turgenev's *A Month in the Country* and the title role in Chekhov's *Ivanov*. It was during one performance of *Hamlet* that he suffered a crippling bout of stage fright that kept him out of the theatre for two years. In 1978 he took Richard II to the television screen, a role in which, uniquely, he carried both authority and depth. His Richard is someone actually recognizable, by turns high-handed, witty, self-pitying, self-critical, compassionate and reflective. Jacobi appears genuinely to think matters through. His Richard, unlike that of many other actors, is not some figure lifted from a tapestry and obliged to speak. This is the legacy of the stage.

In 1982 Jacobi joined the Royal Shakespeare Company at the Barbican in London to play four leading roles; he was Benedick in *Much Ado About Nothing*, Prospero in *The Tempest*, as well as Peer Gynt and Cyrano de Bergerac. He recalled that 'before my stage fright my performances had been purely instinctive and intuitive, but now I had become more self-aware . . . It is my capacity for dreamy wonderment, combined with a terrible insecurity about who I am, where I am going and why and how, that gives me a craving, an absolute need to act . . . I can uninhabit myself at will.' It has been said that he 'has to have everything prepared beforehand, so everything he does is solid and securely worked out. He is the perfect craftsman.'

In 1990 Jacobi proved his range and versatility with Sartre's *Kean* at the Old Vic, Anouilh's *Becket* at the Haymarket, and *Macbeth* at the RSC at Stratford and London. By 1995 he was artistic director of the Chichester Festival Theatre, where he also took the lead role in Chekhov's *Uncle Vanya*. Vanya itself is a very difficult part to play, since his elaborate sense of merit can make him seem, on occasions, merely ridiculous. But Jacobi brought pathos and dignity to this unforgiving role, qualities that were somehow enhanced by perverse torrents of giggling. Bryan Appleyard noted, in an interview, that he is 'verbose, and a touch grandiloquent, touched by self-doubt'.

In this period Jacobi continued to work in film and on television, but he was back on stage to perform Prospero at the Old Vic in 2002. In early 2005 he played at the Crucible, Sheffield, in Friedrich Schiller's *Don Carlos*, which transferred to the Gielgud in London. Four years later he returned to the theatre with Malvolio at the Donmar Warehouse and at Wyndham's; the part won him the Olivier Award for Best Actor. In 2010 he played Lear in Michael Grandage's production at the Donmar, which the *New Yorker* described as 'one of the finest performances of his distinguished career'. Jacobi himself wrote that this part 'has undoubtedly been the peak of my theatrical career'. This was followed in 2016 by his Mercutio at the Garrick. Some actors have such natural presence that they play the same variety of temperament or character in each of their parts; Richard Burton and Peter O'Toole spring to mind. But Jacobi does not. He is one of those actors who seem able to transcend his personality; he is himself mild and modest, but he can transform himself into something extraordinary. He wrote in his memoir, *As Luck Would Have It* (2013), about 'the actor in me, the dressing-up part of me, which I never could understand, right from the beginning – and that still remains the case today'. He adds that 'audiences or viewers want to believe that they have been in the presence of a real person.' That is perhaps the definition of a great actor.

Diana Rigg was born in Doncaster, South Yorkshire, in 1938, but when she was two months old the Rigg family moved to Bikaner in India, where her father was employed as a railway engineer. As a result, her second language was Hindi. She was dispatched to England for her education, however, and attended the Fulneck Girls' School in Pudsey, West Yorkshire. She did not seem to enjoy her spell at this boarding school, except for the encouragement afforded her by her elocution teacher, who admired her speaking of verse.

In 1955 Rigg began three years at RADA, where her first appearance on the professional stage was in the Academy's production of *The Caucasian Chalk Circle* at the Theatre Royal, York, in 1957. For a while she earned her living as a model, until she became assistant stage manager at the Chesterfield Repertory Company in Derbyshire; there she was given a variety of tasks, including lighting and prompting as well as the occasional walk-on part. It was what the army might have called 'basic training'. In the summer of 1958 she joined the Scarborough Rep, where parts were more plentiful.

The following year Rigg took a step forward with the Shakespeare Memorial Company, which later became the RSC, in which she played a variety of roles until 1966. She returned with the company in 1962 to Stratford, where her Helena in *A Midsummer Night's Dream* was described by one critic as 'the most outrageously comic invention, and she makes the most of it. This girl is rapidly proving herself one of our best Shakespearian actresses.' In this role she was not the poor, constant, abused waif of earlier productions. Only Rigg seems to understand that Helena is a minx; she pouts, and preens, arguing an actress who approaches her roles critically, making no concession to received judgements. There is often a price for such boldness, but it is one worth paying.

At the RSC in 1962 and 1963 Rigg played Lady Macduff in *Macbeth* and Adriana in *The Comedy of Errors*, of which part *Plays and Players* reported that 'Diana Rigg, whose work with the company has consistently become more interesting this season, contributes a delightful study in wayward femininity.' Of her Cordelia with the same company, the novelist and critic R. B. Marriott wrote that 'Diana Rigg is the best Cordelia I have ever seen; entirely believable, a princess of mind and spirit, as well as utter truthfulness and compassion.'

Rigg moved to the Aldwych in 1964 as Adriana and Cordelia before embarking on a British Council tour; this was followed by an intermittent but significant break while she played Emma Peel in the television series *The Avengers* (1965–8), with which she made her popular reputation. This meant that, like Ian Richardson, she sometimes fell victim to type-casting. Her habitual glance, seductive rather than flirtatious, appraising rather than inviting, could not but attract certain roles at the expense of others. Her salient quality, a certain cool and amused command, was deployed again and again. But her range was far broader and deeper.

In 1966 Rigg was back at the RSC briefly in order once more to play Viola, of which Harold Hobson noted that 'of the whole company she speaks the verse as it should be spoken with a proper appreciation of its music and its pathos.' She came back to the London stage in 1970 playing the female lead in Ronald Millar's *Abelard and Héloïse* at Wyndham's; she then joined the National Theatre Company and in 1972 played Dottie in Tom Stoppard's *Jumpers*. In the same season she once more played Lady Macbeth, and in 1974 she played the young, witty and mischievous Célimène in Molière's *The Misanthrope*. Rigg described this last character as 'a fluid woman, very sexual, incapable of deep commitment, afraid of being alone'. A critic wrote that Rigg 'turned her back on the big money to join the National and gain the chance to tackle roles that demanded all her intelligence and that forced her to acquire new skills'.

After a period at the National Theatre and on other London stages, Rigg started working for the Almeida in Islington, and began by playing Cleopatra in John Dryden's *All for Love* in 1990. She said, 'Dryden is good to act in the sense that it's so glorious, but all the verse form is quite hard. It has to be in your bones. I love this sort of hard work. It drags you up by the scruff of your neck.' This was followed two years later by Euripides' *Medea* in the same theatre, which transferred to Wyndham's and then Broadway. One reviewer noted that 'Diana Rigg, returning to the limelight after too many years away, turns in the kind of searing performance that leaves an indelible impression on the memory.' She could play obsession with chilling clarity. It is precisely in such roles that she appears to excel. One searches in vain for the small, humdrum parts that Peggy Ashcroft, Edith Evans or Sybil Thorndike could make divine. Rigg, a big woman with strong features and the voice of Boudicca, was meant primarily for might. She said once that 'the memory of what you've done eventually gets eclipsed by the coming generation.' This is, perhaps, the ultimate fate of even the greatest actors. Diana Rigg died of lung cancer in 2020.

Ian McKellen is essentially of the same generation as Jacobi, and they performed a double act in a television series entitled *Vicious* in 2013. McKellen was born on 25 May 1939 in Burnley, Lancashire, and his family moved to Wigan just before the beginning of the Second World War; when he was twelve they moved again to Bolton and he attended an independent day school, Bolton School, where, as he once said, 'they encouraged drama with the same enthusiasm as they trained us for sport or self-sufficiency.' His appetite for theatre was in any case evident at an early age when he attended *Twelfth Night* and *Macbeth* when they were performed by Wigan's Little Theatre, an enterprise run by enthusiastic amateurs. While at school he performed in three sixth-form plays, and made yearly visits to Stratford to see whatever plays were available. He watched John Gielgud, Laurence Olivier and Vivien Leigh. The early death of his mother, according to his biographer, 'became a driver towards endless achievement and ambition'.

In 1958, at the age of eighteen, McKellen gained a scholarship to St Catharine's College, Cambridge, and while there he joined the Marlowe Society of players; in that company he acted in twenty-three plays over the next three years. He was Justice Shallow in *Henry IV*, Posthumus in *Cymbeline* and Doctor Faustus. Shallow elicited many favourable reviews, which confirmed McKellen's decision to become an actor. During this period he was directed by Peter Hall and John Barton, among others, who played an important role in his burgeoning career.

After leaving university McKellen enjoyed his first professional experience at the Belgrade Theatre in Coventry, where he played William Roper in Robert Bolt's *A Man for All Seasons*. For the next four years he did the rounds of regional repertory companies from the Arts Theatre, Ipswich, to the Nottingham Playhouse Company. He entered the West End in September 1964, where he was cast in James Saunders's *A Scent of Flowers*, a black comedy in which he played the leading role of Godfrey. It was an instant success, and on the first night earned fifteen curtain calls. The following year, partly as a result of his early success, he was asked to join Olivier's National Theatre Company at the Old Vic, where he took on the role of Claudio in *Much Ado About Nothing*. He remained there for eight months.

In the summer of 1965 McKellen was at the Chichester Festival Theatre playing the Protestant Evangelist in John Arden's *Armstrong's Last Goodnight* and Captain de Foenix in Arthur Wing Pinero's *Trelawney of the 'Wells'*. His family was in part made up of Protestant evangelists, so he knew intimately that which he performed. It is valuable, perhaps, to recall the manuals of sermons that his Elizabethan predecessors consulted so avidly. This was followed by the part of Alvin Hanker in Donald Howarth's comedy *A Lily in Little India*, which moved from the Hampstead Theatre Club to St Martin's in 1966. His was described as 'a disciplined and satisfying performance, some of its best moments silent'. Another critic commented that he 'endows the voluble Alvin with a tousled charm and plays him with obvious insight'. He had already proved his worth as a young actor.

McKellen was a formidable actor by the time he played Richard II and Edward II with the Prospect Company, in 1969, both of which demonstrated to one critic his 'combination of sheer animal magnetism and interpretative intelligence. McKellen shows that rage and almost indescribable relish for acting, as if the stage were both a natural stomping ground and a spiritual gymnasium for the exploration of personality.' He had become a 'classical actor'. This distinction between the modern and classical approaches is not always apparent to the audience, but it exists nevertheless. McKellen himself may be said to straddle the divide with no discomfort.

He tried his hand at directing plays by Stoppard and Joe Orton before in 1972 becoming one of the founders of the Actors' Company, a co-operative assembly in which parts great and small were shared equally. When the Company arrived at the Brooklyn Academy in New York, the critic Clive Barnes reported that McKellen played Edgar 'as if it were a star role . . . he is that rare bird, an intellectual actor with incandescence.' McKellen seems to have tired of playing with a co-operative, however, and he backed into the limelight when he joined the RSC in 1974. His first performance was the leading role in Christopher Marlowe's *Doctor Faustus*. It opened at the Edinburgh Festival and then came to the Aldwych in London.

In 1976 Trevor Nunn directed McKellen at Stratford as Face in Ben Jonson's *The Alchemist*, and then in another production of *Macbeth*, which once again enthused audiences and critics. The filmed version of the stage production of *Macbeth* is exceptional. McKellen fully serves the richness and power of the language, even if one does not always completely understand what he is saying. Nevertheless it is utterly compelling. When he comes to the 'tomorrow' speech, he neither rants nor weeps. He moves from indifference to reflection; then genius stirs. He begins at once talking to himself and to us. The voice is rich and flat as he delivers what may be called a nihilist's sermon. It shows collapse without surrender, and it is another reminder that he comes from a family of preachers. Of his other role, as Face, the critic of the *Daily Telegraph* noted, 'Ian McKellen is mercurial, switching impersonations like a magician. His final reversal to the servant, Jeremy, carries total conviction. The actor's energy and sharpness of definition are astonishing to behold.'

In 1988, after a period of performances in support of AIDS relief, McKellen returned to the conventional stage at the Vaudeville as Jerome in Alan Ayckbourn's *Henceforward*. The following year he played Iago at the Other Place in Stratford, before transferring to the Young Vic. In 1990 he was in one of Alan Bennett's monologues, *Chip in the Sugar*, at the Haymarket; later that year he played Richard III and Edgar in *King Lear* at the National's Lyttelton Theatre, which then went on a national and, in the case of the former, a world tour. 'Acting', he once said, 'is all to do with being conscious of what you are doing as well as being unconscious. It's being possessed but not possessive. Subjective and objective.'

Steven Berkoff noted in his autobiography that 'there is a quest in [McKellen's] face, a hunger which, like the wolf, will never be satisfied; his eyes reveal nothing to tell you what he will be.' There are certain actors who stub their toes, drop the ball or forget to feed the fire. But this is not McKellen's way; the fluency and confidence are complete. Watching him, you are lifted up and carried. You are in the hands of a master. Whither you are borne is another question. Antony Sher wrote of him that 'he's an actor to his fingertips, he lives, breathes and loves it . . . From day one, he's there performing, needing to entertain the director, the other actors, stage management, anyone who's watching.'

In 2007 McKellen began a world tour of *King Lear*, in repertory with Chekhov's *The Seagull*, which earned him much acclaim and some awards. Charles Spencer of the *Daily Telegraph* noted that it was 'one of the most lucid, powerful and moving productions of this great tragedy I have ever seen'. McKellen is nothing if not a shape-shifter, and his technique varies according to his part. But one continuity is clear, in the sense that he sketches the character quickly, vividly and boldly. Then he sits back, as it were, and lets this sketch do the work. Unlike Richardson or Laughton, his performances establish a general character; they are not, as a rule, punctuated by salient moments. His sheer talent allows him to get away with this.

He is not without his mannerisms. There is that feline smile, the sudden glottal stop he inserts to indicate crisis or fear. Despite these, however, he can truthfully be called the second Olivier. Like Olivier, he reliably elicits applause, and like Olivier he moves us most when he seems least to be trying. He is also part of the long and venerable tradition of activism in English theatre. A lifelong champion of gay rights, he has never ceased to fight for 'legal and social equality' for gay people everywhere. This tradition of dissent is one to which, perhaps moved by his example, more and more English actors subscribe.

Michael Gambon was born in Dublin in October 1940, and when he was six his family moved to Mornington Crescent in London so that his father could assist in the reconstruction of the city after the war. In common with many actors he became an altar boy, in his case at the Roman Catholic St Aloysius' College for boys in Highgate; he moved on to Crayford Secondary School, which he left at the minimum age of fifteen without any qualifications. He found employment at Vickers-Armstrongs as an apprentice toolmaker, and by the age of twenty-one he was a qualified technician. A less likely beginning for an actor can hardly be imagined, although working-class actors had already vaulted the parapets around the English stage. But that training is the reason Gambon first worked in the theatre as a carpenter rather than a player; he had passed the Erith Playhouse in Bexley, where there was an advertisement for backstage help, and he managed by some means to secure a walk-on part in Philip Johnson's *Orange Blossom*.

Gambon was stage-struck at once, and recalled, 'I thought, Jesus, this is for me. I want to be an actor.' From what depths this desire came is unclear, but it was genuine. Without any background at RADA, Central School or in rep, he invented an imaginary theatrical career in order to write to Micheál Mac Liammóir, who managed the Gate Theatre in Dublin. The gesture was in any case delightfully suitable, for had not Mac Liammóir (born Alfred Lee Willmore in London) reinvented himself as an Irishman? Gambon was accepted. His second appearance on stage was at that theatre in 1962, where he played the Second Gentleman in *Othello*. Mac Liammóir's company eventually came to London with Spike Milligan's *The Bed Sitting Room* at the Duke of York's, where in 1963 Gambon, as an understudy, was paid a pound to take over the actor's part for one night only.

Sensing his vocation, Gambon took part in an acting class organized by William Gaskill and George Devine. When Gaskill then took a post at the Old Vic, he was able to persuade Olivier to see the young actor, and Olivier agreed to let him join the National Theatre that was in the process of being born. Gambon was not of course given major characters, and for three years he took on a variety of small parts in *Hamlet*, Bertolt Brecht's *Mother Courage*, George Farquhar's *The Recruiting Officer* and Arthur Miller's *The Crucible*. But he was not happy playing servants or extras or spear-carriers. The leading roles still eluded him, and in 1967 Olivier suggested that he join the Birmingham Rep for more experience. He was accepted and, as a result, given more challenging roles, including the title role in *Othello* and, in 1968, *Macbeth*. In 1970 he was enlisted in the Royal Shakespeare

Company, where his range was further extended in Shaw's *Major Barbara* and in *Henry VIII*. Peter Hall said of him that 'fate gave him genius, but he uses it like a craftsman. He can switch off different areas of his personality and remake himself. Most actors bring the part to themselves. In some curious way, Michael takes himself to the part.' Gambon's own assessment, as we shall see, is subtly different.

In 1973 he played in Leonard Webb's *Not Drowning but Waving* at the Greenwich Theatre, where the next year he also played Tom in Ayckbourn's *The Norman Conquests*, a part he reprised at the Globe. He once said of acting to his biographer Mel Gussow, 'I don't really like it. I have to do it . . . It's a release – something inside you that has to come out.' He is sometimes slow in his movements, but always alive on his feet; he can become awkward and cumbersome, the perfect body language for a no-nonsense cockney boy. His voice may be deep and rough but varied and expressive, as are his facial expressions, which range from raised eyebrows to a slight shake of the head. In many instances he manages to convey the ordinariness or the sheer matter-of-factness of the character, together with an extraordinary sensitivity to the individual style. He is somehow more emphatic than those who perform with him. 'Charisma' is the term most frequently encountered in relation to Gambon's acting, but it is not altogether accurate. He does not compel our attention, for example, in the manner of Olivier. Perhaps it is more appropriate to suggest that there is a nimbus around him; he is, as it were, larger than himself. The actor Pete Postlethwaite once complained that acting beside him was like trying to act 'next to a cinema screen'.

Gambon migrated from the Globe to the Queen's Theatre in Simon Gray's *Otherwise Engaged* and Ayckbourn's *Just Between Ourselves*. In 1978 he returned to the National Theatre, where he spent some years garnering the roles he had previously been denied. He was now a formidable and popular actor. At the Olivier he played Benedick, Roderigo and, most significantly, the title role in Brecht's *Life of Galileo*. He once described this as 'the most important part in my life'. Certainly this was the play that bolstered and defined his reputation. It must be a matter of speculation what aspect of that stubborn and irritable outsider in Brecht's play, always dissatisfied with what he has achieved, most appealed to Gambon's sensibility.

Simon Callow wrote of his success at the Olivier that 'Gambon's iron lungs and overwhelming charisma are able to command a sort of operatic full-throatedness which triumphs over hard walls and long distances.' The response from the other actors was equally enthusiastic. As Gussow puts it in his biography, 'the applause grew to a roar of approval. All the actors – and there were more than forty in the company – came to their windows [their dressing rooms are aligned around a quadrangle] and gave him a long and thunderous ovation.' Gambon recalled, 'I stood at the window and wept my eyes out.' He could receive no greater confirmation of his excellence.

By now he had worked successfully in film and television, but he remained true to his first passion. In 1982 he played King Lear at Stratford with Antony Sher as the Fool; there is no recording of his performance, but some hints of its power can be gleaned from his own remark on the part that 'you stand, you reach out, and you draw the elements to you.' Sher wrote later:

we had watched a great Lear. I've never seen it bettered. What is it about Gambon? His scale is gigantic . . . there's something about him, a broadness – something about his features, his bone structure, and his soul – which makes his on-stage presence quite colossal . . . the very things that we seek to quell in real life – our appetites, our childishness, our fear – these things make for the best acting.

Gambon moved on in 1985 to the Theatre Royal for Pinter's *Old Times*, but he returned to the National in 1985–8 for works including Miller's *A View from the Bridge* and Pinter's *Mountain Language*. He was then Uncle Vanya at the Vaudeville, where he became a wistful, and rather timid, bear. His eyes were sad and long, his body habitually huddled on a chair or swing. He caught Vanya's self-pity perhaps better than his rage. This is often the way with Gambon; we expect thud and crash from that rough voice and those boulder-like features, but instead we are offered tenderness and subtlety.

Among subsequent parts, Gambon was Othello at the Stephen Joseph Theatre in Scarborough. He returned to the National in 1995 to play the lead in Jonson's *Volpone*, and at the Cottesloe in the same year he took the leading role of Tom Sergeant in David Hare's *Skylight*, which moved on to Wyndham's before transferring to Broadway. After productions at the Aldwych and Barbican, in 2000 he played John Shank in Nicholas Wright's *Cressida* at the Almeida, where he became an instructor of Elizabethan boy actors; Sheridan Morley noted that 'Gambon's eccentricity on stage now begins to rival that of his great mentor Ralph Richardson.'

Gambon went on to play the title role of Davies in a revival of Pinter's *The Caretaker* at the Comedy in the following year. In the play there is an interior coolness and detachment within the character which are chilling, but are required by the script. In fact Gambon performed in several Pinter plays as the proper context for his home-grown talents. 'I never ease into a part,' he once said. 'Every part I play is just a variant of my personality. I'm not really a character actor at all.' That is perhaps why one of his most formidable roles was that of Falstaff in the two parts of *Henry IV* at the National in 2005. 'I've been doing it so long,' he said, 'it's part of me. I think I was born to be an actor. I think it's what I was made to be. I'm sure of that . . . Acting is very sophisticated lying, isn't it? Highly skilled lying.' He retired from the stage in 2015.

Ben Kingsley was born Krishna Pandit Bhanji at the end of December 1943 in Snainton, a village in North Yorkshire, with an English mother and an Indian father of Gujarati descent. He was raised in Pendlebury, Lancashire, part of Greater Manchester, and attended the formidable Manchester Grammar School. After leaving, he attended the De La Salle College in Salford while becoming involved in dramatic productions in Manchester itself. He has said that 'thanks to Salford Players, where I stayed a year and learned my craft, I got my first job in professional theatre working in theatre-in-round.'

In 1965 Kingsley came to the West End with Alan Plater's *A Smashing Day* at the Arts; his success prompted Brian Epstein to offer him a career as a pop singer, but instead he wisely decided to join the RSC after a successful audition with Trevor Nunn. At the Chichester Festival Theatre in 1966 he played in *Macbeth* and Chekhov's *The Cherry Orchard*. In 1967 he performed in *The Merry Wives of Windsor* and as Amiens in *As You Like It*, as well as the wig-maker in John Vanbrugh's *The Relapse*; the following year he played Oswald in *King Lear* as well as Aeneas in *Troilus and Cressida* and Conrade in *Much Ado About Nothing*. But there may be something that binds these performances other than the actor himself. He is best at playing the role of an outsider or, perhaps, an *éminence grise*.

In 1969 Kingsley was again in *Troilus and Cressida*, but he then veered away from Shakespeare to play the Croucher in Sean O'Casey's *The Silver Tassie* and Winwife in Jonson's *Bartholomew Fair*. In 1970 he managed four Shakespearean dramas: *The Tempest*, *Richard III*, *Measure for Measure* and *A Midsummer Night's Dream*. He is an actor whose performances are difficult to describe, since his great gift is to find and evoke the hinterland of his character; watching him, we can imagine years and years of experience, of conditioning, frustration and dreaming. He can evoke a variety of moods, including the saintly, the petulant, the wily and the puckish. He manages to be at once sprightly and still. But Kingsley's skill lies at a deeper level, that of manifesting power and the rhythm that power confers. He once said in an interview, 'I love playing brave, fearless, tribal father figures.' He is capable of rage, but also of vulnerability. He can find in the hardest character some touch of tenderness or pain. His natural voice is lighter and less nasal than the one he habitually uses for his roles. Despite his bird-like physique, he is capable of great stillness, even heaviness, when the part requires it.

A run of Shakespearean performances culminated in the lead role in *Hamlet* in 1975 at the Other Place in Stratford. In the same year Kingsley appeared in both parts of *Henry IV* and *Henry V* at the Aldwych and the Royal Shakespeare Theatre. He once said that 'performing Shakespeare is a lot like galloping on a horse you love at full speed. If the horse feels insecure with you on its back it will throw you and break your neck. You will lose your voice, your lines, and you won't know how to breathe. But in the end it will be absolutely thrilling.' The image of the galloping horse is one that other actors have used in connection with Shakespeare. Simon Callow went so far as to contrast the 'galloping horse' of Shakespeare's verse with the comparatively severe, script-like idiom of the Restoration. English actors are as grateful now to be 'carried' by Shakespeare's rhythms and imagery as they were in Jacobean times. It ought to be mentioned, too, that Kingsley has an aptitude for research; he learns all he can in order to bring his characters to life. Yet crucially he knows when to stop. There might come a point when, if he tried to absorb any more, he would be unable to assimilate it. The final word may go to him. 'As an actor,' he said, 'I can put my hand on somebody else's shoulder and say, "I know". That's all that really counts.'

Jonathan Pryce was born at the beginning of June 1947 in Holywell, Flintshire, where his parents were grocers. He attended the Holywell Grammar School in North Wales, but at sixteen he enrolled in an art school before training as a teacher at Edgehill College in Ormskirk, Lancashire. (Despite the protestations to the contrary, most actors have dallied with alternative vocations that tend to be in the arts and, in particular, in those arts that involve making rather than reproducing.) At Ormskirk he took part in a college production and his tutor, suitably impressed, advised him to take up acting. His aptitude and inclination worked in his favour and he was granted a scholarship at RADA in London. Despite sometimes critical comments from the tutors, and what he considered to be the 'strait-laced' atmosphere of the academy, he pressed on, and at graduation he joined the Everyman Theatre in Liverpool, where he played Richard III. Sher described him as a 'natural born' Richard, perhaps because there is some extravagant fertility at work in his performances; he is the least *contained* of actors. And yet there is a paradox: he has been described as 'the quiet man of theatre'. But there is no necessary clash. Pryce is an essentially unorthodox actor who, for some reason, often finds himself in correct or restrained roles. As a result he works best under those directors who give him permission to expand.

Pryce recalled of the Everyman that 'it was a very free, anarchic unpretentious theatre and that appealed to me. I was young. I wasn't very ambitious or aware of anything I really wanted to do. I just kept falling into things because I enjoyed them.' He slowly made his way forward and was employed as artistic director at the Everyman while also performing in travelling productions of the RSC and the Nottingham Playhouse. After leaving the Everyman he decided to work with Richard Eyre at the Nottingham theatre, where in 1975 he played the lead character, Gethin Price, in Trevor Griffiths's *Comedians*; his was a vigorous and exhilarating performance that confirmed him as one of the leading actors of his generation.

In 1980 Pryce played Hamlet at the Royal Court, directed by Eyre, a performance that was greeted with much acclaim and won him the Olivier Award for Best Actor; it was perhaps best remembered for the novel effect of Hamlet being literally possessed by his father's ghost. Although this was Eyre's idea, Pryce makes the interpretation entirely his own. As the ghost speaks through him, the actor's naturally lyrical voice deepens horribly; now it rasps, grating and implacable. If it were not understood that this was indeed the spirit of his father, we would suspect that Hamlet had been infested by something altogether more malevolent than a mere ghost. It is an extraordinary performance, and it won him the familiar but convincing plaudit of 'the Hamlet of his generation'.

In 1981 Pryce played the unsympathetic Mick in Pinter's *The Caretaker*. He spent some years primarily in film but returned to the stage as Trigorin in Chekhov's *The Seagull* at the Queen's Theatre, in which one critic noted that 'Pryce's absolute honesty suffuses the production.' In 1988 he played Chekhov once again, at the Vaudeville, as Astrov in *Uncle Vanya*. To convey both intensity and elegance is a difficult feat, but he managed it here. He could switch modes with a speed that was not so much impressive as now entirely characteristic. His voice, as with many of Welsh descent, is startling in its distinctiveness. It seems jerked from the larynx in short spasms, lending everything he says a passionate and pleading quality. It is as if he is perpetually reassuring himself that all is well, even as he tries to reassure others.

Pryce was Henry Higgins in 2001 in the National Theatre's production of *My Fair Lady*, of which one critic wrote that 'Pryce uses his gentle vibrato to good effect on "I'm an Ordinary Man", the number pitched not far from a breakdown. His self-protection cracking, the actor later delivers an unusually revealing "I've Grown Accustomed to Her Face".' It was noted that 'Jonathan Pryce starts off, like everybody else playing Higgins, with the apparent disadvantage that he is not Rex Harrison. Pryce knows this cannot be helped and turns it brilliantly to his advantage. The result is a deeply sophisticated and entertaining performance.'

Decades after his training ended, Pryce remains intensely grateful to RADA. Indeed, he is as convinced of the virtues of drama school as Derek Jacobi is of the virtues of rep. We should perhaps pause to consider the influence of these different but often complementary arenas.

The training Pryce received would have been very different from that now available. In an interview, he mentioned mime and improvisation classes, movement and voice classes, and diction classes, but made no reference to *acting* classes. In one sense, this is scarcely surprising, since it was not until 1965, when the Drama Centre was founded, that such a course was thought to be necessary. But it is nonetheless revealing, for it shows how even the most committed and talented theatre practitioners still lay in thrall to the notion that, ultimately, acting could not be taught. Joan Littlewood herself, sometimes called 'the mother of modern theatre', believed that you could act or you couldn't. She was dismayed when East 15, the school founded on the very principles she had always espoused, became a training school for actors. Thus, until the 1960s at least, a drama school could teach you how to project your voice, alter your physicality, dance, sing, fence, articulate and even transform; what it did not teach was the work of rooting your performance in psychological reality. The acting class, the spine of every modern drama school, did not exist.

Antony Sher was born on 14 June 1949 in Cape Town, to a Lithuanian-Jewish family, and was educated at the Sea Point High School in the suburbs of that city. After nine months of compulsory national service he travelled to London in order to find a place at the Central School or RADA; he was not successful in either institution and instead enrolled at the Webber Douglas Academy of Dramatic Art in South Kensington from 1969 to 1971. He was to say of the experience that 'anarchy ruled', and that he left 'with no prospects'. Yet on graduating he joined the Everyman Theatre in Liverpool, where he worked with such actors as Trevor Eve and

Jonathan Pryce. His first role was the Fool to Pryce in *King Lear*. He wrote in his memoir, *Beside Myself* (2002), that 'the Everyman was one of the few places where, as a twenty-four-year-old, I could get to play leading parts.' In 1974 he played Ringo Starr in Willy Russell's musical *John, Paul, George, Ringo . . . and Bert*. The Fool and Ringo – quirky outsiders who make their way by virtue of wit and a certain cultivated harmlessness – were characteristic of his early period. It would not be strange if they reflected his own experience at that time.

The musical was a great success, and London managers came up to see it. Sher joined the theatre company Gay Sweatshop in 1975 and 1976, during which time he performed in *Thinking Straight* by Laurence Collinson, and later Ian Brown's *The Fork* and Edward Bond's *Stone*. The following year he made his first appearance at the Royal Court in David Hare's *Teeth 'n' Smiles*, which transferred to Wyndham's the following year. This was succeeded by the lead in Nikolay Gogol's *The Government Inspector* at the Royal Lyceum in Edinburgh. In this role, audiences saw a very different side to Sher: understated, ironic and, above all, menacing. In 1982 he was at the Garrick for Mike Leigh's *Goosepimples*; the part of the bewildered Muhammad was, according to one critic, 'brilliantly played by Antony Sher'. It was while working with Leigh that Sher – like Kingsley – acquired his formidable capacity for research. Having assembled what he thought the character required, he asked an amused and incredulous Leigh when work could begin. It soon became clear that far more was needed than a sheaf of paperwork. Sher and the other actors had to improvise and invent, and then improvise again, until a script could be established. From that point, any deviation was forbidden. 'Research', it transpired, was a matter of action, not speculation. Sher took the lesson to heart.

In the same year Sher became part of the RSC. While in that company he slowly graduated from minor to major roles, such as the Fool to Michael Gambon's Lear and, in the same year, the leading role in Molière's *Tartuffe* in the Pit (the Barbican's studio space), together with Mikhail Bulgakov's play about Molière, *The Cabal of Hypocrites*. In 1984 he played the title role in *Richard III*, for which he won the Laurence Olivier Award; the production was then transferred to the Barbican. This was the play that transformed the image of the errant king: Sher played him on crutches and in a tight black costume, so that his Richard resembled indeed the 'bottled spider' invoked by one of his enemies. It was a tremendous popular success. But the novelty of a Richard on crutches did not account for this alone. Sher chose crutches because he had already decided that his Richard should be severely disabled, not just 'politely crippled', as he put it, and that crutches would help with the massive hump he had already planned. For Sher, a supremely physical actor, conception of character tends to begin with the body.

The actor's memoir is at least as old as Thomas Betterton, but Sher's *Year of the King* (1985), his record of the rehearsal period for *Richard III*, is one of the most revealing. As usual, Sher devoted every spare hour to research. This entailed time spent in contemplation of serial killers, tyrants, and people crippled or traumatized. Throughout he illustrated his notes with remarkably vivid and skilful drawings. There was, however, an omission: Shakespeare's own text. Sher came to it obliquely and even warily. From the *Henry VI* plays he learned that Richard has a 'depressing amount' of running around to do (which would have made those famous crutches yet more problematic), but he somehow missed the fact that Richard was devoted to his father and became a monster only after his murder. Only in the final weeks did Sher accept the 'new Richard', one who was 'funny, even sexy'.

According to Sher himself, 'audiences flocked, queued overnight, bartered for black market tickets'. It worked so well, in fact, that his Richard has displaced even that created by Olivier, at least for those lucky enough to have seen it. It moved to the Barbican, and Sher eventually followed it with the part of Father Flore in Peter Barnes's *Red Roses*. But he was more enthusiastic about playing the role of Arnold Breckoff in Harvey Fierstein's *Torch Song Trilogy*, for which he also won an Olivier Award. For this project, he found that research, in the conventional sense, was of no use. In his own words, that performance had to be 'all heart'. Sher was, above all, a *vivid* actor; each of his characters lives and each is different with its own colours, textures and rhythms. He was one of the great transformers and, as a result, he was always surprising. Like most great actors, he dared to get it wrong.

Sher played Astrov with Ian McKellen as Uncle Vanya at the Cottesloe in 1992, and the following year he played the title role in Marlowe's *Tamburlaine the Great* at the Barbican, in one of the greatest of all stage performances. Here the Scythian shepherd becomes a Turkic warrior, a braggart with everything to brag of, a vicious robber who paces around his prey, a boorish seducer who becomes the most persuasive and tender of lovers. All the virtues of Sher's early style are present and triumphant, with his physical agility, his light, strong whip-like voice, and the extraordinary sense of ease that he brings to his script. This quality is all the more impressive given his avowed discomfort with the demands of verse-speaking. It really does seem that he has just thought of what he is about to say, as his eyes appear to be lit by helium. By some extraordinary feat of physical imagination he offers us a man who truly ages. The fencer's leap is replaced by a heavy stomp.

Sher went back to Shakespeare as Leontes in *The Winter's Tale* at Stratford and the Barbican in 1998–9. In that season he also played Macbeth at the Swan, before taking this production on tour to the Young Vic, Bath, Brighton, Tokyo and the United States. 'To play Shakespeare,' he wrote in his autobiography, 'you need a variety of resources. You need enormous technical ease to phrase, shape and finally breathe the language like normal speech. You need great curiosity about human beings. You need to be fascinated by our strange behaviour that you believe you're perceiving for the first time.' Many actors have discovered different aspects of Macbeth, but Sher perhaps covered most of them. He was tough, lean, a soldier with a predatory walk; but he could also be tender and manic, and even, when his character was most dead in heart, witty. More than most actors Sher preferred to work on stage. In his memoir *Beside Myself* (2002) he comments that there is no greater 'fix' than live acting. He was in fact an actor for all seasons, with a remarkable grasp of the essence of each character. He died of cancer in December 2021.

Sher once said of Simon Callow that 'I wasn't prepared for the sheer joyfulness of the man, apparently quite at peace with the world.' Callow was born in Streatham, south London, on 16 June 1949, and was educated as a Roman Catholic at the London Oratory School, which he left in 1967. He has said that he wanted to be a writer, rather than an actor, but on leaving school he sent a three-page letter to Laurence Olivier, who was then artistic director of the National Theatre. Olivier replied with an invitation to join the box-office staff, which may not have been the offer Callow had in mind; yet to watch actors in rehearsal is one of the best educations he could have enjoyed. He was enrolled at the Queen's University, Belfast, ostensibly to study French but really to engage in his own passion. Here he was employed for a time as Micheál Mac Liammóir's dresser, which was at the very least an exotic as well as instructive introduction to the stage.

Callow went on to train at the Drama Centre in London, where his appetite for the theatre was quickened. He once said:

The first eighteen months were very tough, because I was so resistant to revealing myself. I saw acting as a mask that you put on, this brilliant exterior. The real breakthrough was when each of us had to present a show about a moment in history, and I chose fourth-century BC Athens. My approach was essentially comic. I did it through the medium of this Greek Everyman, whom I called Testicles, in a moment of rare brilliant wit. Somehow playing Testicles really liberated me; I had this sudden surge of energy at my disposal. I was effective in the world, and I'd never really felt myself to be effective up to that point.

He wrote in his memoir, *Being an Actor* (1984), that 'it was then, in the moment, that acting became second nature to me.' He left the Centre at the age of twenty-four.

Callow's first appearance on stage was in 1973 at the Assembly Rooms theatre in Edinburgh, performing in *Ane Pleasant Satyre of the Thrie Estaitis*, and was then invited to join the Lincoln Repertory Company; in that company he played in, among other dramas, *Measure for Measure*, Shelagh Delaney's *A Taste of Honey* and Stoppard's *The Real Inspector Hound*. There are difficulties with the repertory season, as we have observed, but, as Callow wrote, it also 'sharpens memory, demands discipline, encourages decisions and makes for boldness'. These are not lessons he could have acquired elsewhere.

The following year Callow returned to Edinburgh to join the Traverse Theatre, where he performed in Strindberg's *Dream Play* and then in Carl Sternheim's *Schippel*, which moved to Belfast and then to London. Soon afterwards Callow joined Gay Sweatshop, where in 1975 he performed one of the leading roles in Martin Sherman's *Passing By*. In this play, about two gay men completely at ease in their sexuality, he had his first experience of what might be termed apolitical political theatre. In the same year he performed in C. P. Taylor's *The Plumber's Progress* at the Prince of Wales Theatre. In 1976 he acted in three little-known dramas (one of them a monologue), but the following year he moved on to

Joint Stock Company, where he played in Tony Bicât's *Devil's Island* at the Royal Court, Thomas Middleton's *A Mad World, My Masters* at the Young Vic, and Howard Brenton's *Epsom Downs* at the Round House. Despite his growing disillusion with the Joint Stock enterprise, Callow was at first deeply attracted by its promise of a new way of working, where all were responsible for the performance, for the administration and even, to an extent, for the writing. What sank the project, as far as Callow was concerned, was the uncovenanted authority of the director, which was still very much in place.

Callow has sometimes been described as 'fruity', but the better and more accurate word is 'fleshy'; he is an actor who gives flesh to whatever he speaks. Every nuance in the text, every shade of meaning, every hint or clue is coaxed into the light and given substance. It is interpreted through that extraordinarily supple voice, sometimes sweet as a clarinet and sometimes rich as a cello. The musical metaphors are, in his case, appropriate. His well-attested love of classical music undoubtedly feeds his style.

In 1977 Callow played the title role in *Titus Andronicus* at the Bristol Old Vic, in which he said that 'I lost my voice immediately.' But he recalled that in this part 'I discovered a rule: it is only necessary to establish the essential nature of a character once, very clearly, at the beginning of the play, and then you can play every variation you like.' It is a rumbustious part, but Callow soon got the measure of these irrepressible and boisterous roles. This was not always to his advantage. He admitted, 'I am always being asked for less: less noise, less energy, less laughter, less talking, less feeling, less trouble.' But 'less' is not in his vocabulary. He is always 'more'. As a result, he is given 'large' roles that encourage him to be, as the cliché has it, 'larger than life'. This booming, generous quality is evident in many different styles and shades of character. The extraordinary energy always remains, as if he were all oxygen, needing only a candle to burst into flame.

Callow once confessed, however, that 'the kind of characters I'm very uncomfortable playing are heroes. I hate to play heroic characters.' In 1977 he took on four further roles, from Anne Boyd's *Flying Blind* at the Royal Court to David Edgar's *Mary Barnes* at the same theatre. In 1979 he appeared at the Soho Poly in Snoo Wilson's *The Soul of the White Ant*, a powerful play of racial murder and police cover-up; he also played two roles at the Olivier, one of them being Orlando, but this was partly obscured by Callow's most illustrious performance to date, as Mozart in Shaffer's *Amadeus* to Paul Scofield's Salieri.

In 1983 Callow played Lord Foppington in Vanbrugh's *The Relapse* at the Lyric; he is always good at playing the dandy who displays what might be called 'butch camp'. He was at the Bush in 1985 as Luis Molina in Manuel Puig's *Kiss of the Spider Woman*, which he considered to be one of his best performances since 'in playing the character I had drawn on things in myself which enabled me to interpret and not merely play him.' The remark is revealing, for Molina, camp, dreamy and timid, is a figure who never acquires heroism yet somehow becomes heroic. And 'heroism' is precisely the quality with which Callow has always struggled. Here he could explore courage without its familiar associations. In 1988 he played the leading role in *Faust* at the Lyric, Hammersmith. For this production Callow, the supremely energetic actor, was required to cavort and leap around a vast net suspended over the stage. As Count Fosco in the musical version of *The Woman in White*, at the Palace Theatre in 2005, he was superbly himself as the irresistible and often charismatic villain of the piece. It is a role he has frequently been asked to assume.

In recent years Callow has also engaged in one-man impersonations of famous writers, including Wilde, Dickens and Shakespeare. His gifts of mimicry, and his range of voices, do justice to their subjects. Callow's body can turn lithe, or sensuous, or slow; every word gloats, coaxes or taunts. In his work with

Shakespeare he lingers on 'we are such stuff as dreams are made on' as if, at that moment, he himself had created those 'cloud-capped palaces' and he himself was doomed to disperse them. There is no trace of self-pity in that now gentle voice, and only the slightest breath of irony. It is an exquisite interpretation. He has also been a constant presence in film and on television, but they are quite different disciplines; 'stage acting', he once wrote, 'is always an art of projection, and movie-acting is always an art of introjection.' Callow seems to have mastered both.

Twenty-five

Acting essentials

Harriet Mary Walter was born in London on 24 September 1950 and, after an unhappy period in one boarding school, she moved at the age of thirteen to Cranborne Chase School, near Tisbury in Wiltshire. She seemed already half aware of her ultimate destiny, and after school she became, for a brief spell, assistant stage manager at the Ambiance Lunch Hour Theatre Club, beneath a restaurant in Queensway, west London. As a result she turned down the offer of a place at Newnham College, Cambridge, before being admitted to LAMDA in Hammersmith. One of her teachers there was Frank Whitten, whom she described as

> easily the most influential teacher in my life. He created the atmosphere and parameters within which we could experiment and learn things for ourselves. He didn't over-explain or over-analyse. He understood that the best way to learn was for us to allow a strong experience to imprint itself on our personal memories. Some of the improvisations he set up I still recall on a regular basis whenever I need reminding what the essence of acting is.

She trained there for three years before following Whitten in 1973 to the company he had established, the Common Stock Theatre in Fulham. She then moved on to the Duke's Playhouse in Lancaster, where she remained for two years; there she played one of the ugly sisters in *Beauty and the Beast* by David Pownall, as well as the title role in an adaptation of *Huckleberry Finn* and Elizabeth Proctor in Arthur Miller's *The Crucible*. Between 1975 and 1977 she toured with 7:84, a Scottish theatre group with a radical agenda.

Walter toured in 1977 with the Paines Plough company, based near Waterloo in the London borough of Lambeth, and then in the following year with the Joint Stock company. In 1979 she ceased touring for a while in order to play Jane in *A Fair Quarrel* by Thomas Middleton and William Rowley at the National; this was succeeded by a variety of roles in Bertolt Brecht's *Fears and Miseries of the Third Reich* at the Open Space on the Euston Road. In 1980 she became involved with the Royal Court, beginning with Ophelia opposite Jonathan Pryce's Hamlet. She wrote later that 'the remedy for me was to find a method in Ophelia's madness, so that I could root her actions in her motivations (however insane and disordered), just as I would with any other character I was playing.'

Soon afterwards Walter began a season with the Royal Shakespeare Company, which went from Stratford to Newcastle and then, in 1982, to the newly created Barbican Centre; she performed in five dramas including the roles of Helena in *A Midsummer Night's Dream* and Lady Percy in the two parts of *Henry IV*. Between 1987 and 1990 she was again part of the RSC, during which period she took on a number of roles, including the lead in John Webster's *The Duchess of Malfi*. In an interview about this production, she described Webster's verse as being

at times more contrived than Shakespeare's, more ornate than organic. I don't want to sound pretentious, but it's like the difference between the atmosphere when you listen to Mozart, and the atmosphere when you listen to Schubert. Actors tune into that on a non-intellectual level: rhythms and music and textures and colours in language, that aren't just about why am I here and what am I doing, and why am I saying it?

A critic observed that 'Walter's Duchess – proud and imperious when facing her murderers; tender, loving and even coy with Antonio – exhilaratingly drew forth the human and humane from the extraordinary.' She herself once said, 'there is nothing more frightening for an actor than being themselves.' So she can seem like a sphinx, carrying a secret that she will never fully divulge. She has a cool, gentle and slightly sad gaze, huge eyes in a raw-boned face, her smile inescapably wry. She is a deeply cerebral actor, and she often brings this quality to her acting in the form of gentle or indulgent irony.

In 1999 Walter played Lady Macbeth for the RSC at the Swan in Stratford. She wrote of this part that

> I had already scoured the text for any insights into Lady Macbeth as an individual, separate from her husband, but except for the odd 'most kind hostess' or 'fair and noble hostess' from the King, no one comments on her or throws any light on her character. Nobody seems to know her. She has no confidante . . . It was as though she had visited Shakespeare's imagination fully formed, giving away no secrets, and therein lies a lot of her power.

When Walter delivers the speech in the first act that includes 'Come to my woman's breasts,' her eyes turn in an instant from commanding complacency to wide-eyed horror. In itself this is a shift that any good actor should be able to accomplish, but there is something else. One sees, in those eyes, in that change, two people – not two moods or states, but two people, inhabiting the same body. It is as if her 'true' self reappears briefly, only to be suffocated by her 'real' heartless self. This ability to switch from one character to another is one of Walter's characteristic gifts. That was the power she conveyed to the audience.

From 2012 to 2016 Walter embarked on a bold and exhilarating enterprise by playing male roles in Phyllida Lloyd's all-female Shakespearean trilogy as though staged in a women's prison; she was Brutus in 2012, Henry IV in 2014 and Prospero in 2016. As *The Guardian* put it, the three plays were

> a glorious reminder that genuine diversity on stage offers astonishing creative benefits . . . Harriet Walter is mesmerising in one play after another, bringing her classical training to bear as a conflicted Brutus, then a Henry IV who wears his crown heavily, and finally a Prospero who knows that the steel bars of prison are resistant to all magic . . . this is genuinely art to enchant.

As Brutus in *Julius Caesar* she gave us, above all, an injured heart. In this she showed herself willing to reject certain elements in the text, with results as provocative as they are refreshing. She downplayed the spiteful relish in Brutus's insults, even his ordinate anger, where male actors would bring them to the fore. Similarly, when she justified the slaying of Caesar before the citizens, she offered a Brutus impassioned and pleading, not serene and authoritative. 'As he was ambitious, I *slew* him!' she cried in agony, her hands clenched above her head. This eschewing of humbug yielded a startlingly poignant performance but one, again, at an angle to the text. Like Ian McKellen, she is alert, not passive, and such actors will often dare to defy even Shakespeare himself. Her remarks on studying others could come quite easily from a Jacobean or Elizabethan actor. 'Sometimes', she wrote, 'if you look at somebody you can extrapolate from their exterior what might be happening in their interior.' There is, however, a final statement that sums up not only her approach to acting but also that of many modern English actors: 'Acting is what I do with who I am.'

If there is an actress who seems to make those words flesh, it is Juliet Stevenson. Juliet Anne Virginia Stevenson was born on 30 October 1956 in Kelvedon, Essex, and at the age of nine attended a primary school in Berkshire; Hurst Lodge School in Ascot was run by a Miss Stainer, who had previously been a dance teacher. Stevenson said of her that she was 'a progressively educational woman who had been a prima ballerina and who believed the arts were fundamental to a child's education'. From primary school she went on to another independent school, St Catherine's in Bramley, where she first became enamoured of acting after a recital of *King Lear* by some of the pupils. 'I walked out an hour later,' she once said, 'transformed by the language and the scale of feeling and thinking.' At the age of eighteen she won a place at RADA, where she won the Bancroft Gold Medal. She recalled, 'I can't imagine having had a career without RADA. It's inseparable from who I am as an actress.'

In 1978, a year after graduating, Stevenson joined the RSC, where she remained for the next eight years. In that first year she appeared in nine separate roles in necessarily small parts, from Iras and Octavia in *Antony and Cleopatra* to Yeliena in Mikhail Bulgakov's *The White Guard*; other actors were praised in this production but 'Juliet Stevenson [is] even better as the outwardly composed but inwardly seething Yeliena.'

In 1980 Stevenson was Lady Percy in *Henry IV*, and the following year she took on four different roles, as Hippolyta and Titania in *A Midsummer Night's Dream*, Susan in the *Witch of Edmonton* by Thomas Dekker, and Clara Douglas in Edward Bulwer-Lytton's *Money*. In 1983 she appeared at the Royal Court as Emma in Robert Holman's *Other Worlds*. She was back at the RSC for the next three years with Isabella, Cressida and Rosalind, as well as

Polya in Stephen Poliakoff's *Breaking the Silence*. She said of the first two roles that 'the fascination for me was taking away the judgements about her – like Cressida's a whore and Isabella is frigid because she won't sleep with Angelo – let's look at why these women are making these choices. What power do they have? What do they not have? The interesting question is always why.' She enlarged on this point in an interview in *The Guardian* where she remarked that

Very often the interesting things happen to the man. The woman is there as wife, mother, daughter, PA. A lot of writers won't give you your own narrative because it isn't deemed necessary. So much in our culture about women's identities relates to their sexual value. When that is no longer of interest they, as individuals, are past the point of being of any interest either. It's a source of frustration. As you get older, you get more experience, you have more to say, more layers. And at exactly the same time that's happening in your life, the roles are narrowing down. It's like you're on the up escalator but the parts are on the down escalator. You're waving to your actress self: 'Byeee!'

In a televised production of Henrik Ibsen's *A Doll's House* in 1992 Stevenson played Nora Helmer; there is an unformed quality that is just as it should be, and at the end her voice is light, rapid and breathless. These qualities paradoxically evince determination. She has spoken of how grief may be the hardest emotion to replicate, partly because of its essentially fugitive and plastic quality. Yet she is perhaps best known for the conviction she brings to the physical expression of sorrow. Tears, she tells us, cannot be called up on cue, so one can only wonder what reserves she is calling on when she weeps on stage. They come with the halting voice, the mucus, the clenched fists. She cries as humans cry, be they nuns, duchesses or middle-class women, facing the betrayal of all their hopes.

Perhaps the greatest miracle is that Stevenson never loses dignity. In 1995 she played the title role in *The Duchess of Malfi*, which began at the Greenwich Theatre before moving to Wyndham's. *The Independent* noted that 'Stevenson brings sensuality, fun, commanding authority, and guile to her role.' She also brings an authority, at once moral and completely human, to whomever she plays. She follows the thought as well as the feeling. The great characteristic of Stevenson's style is porousness: she is in the chair opposite you, listening as much as speaking. She is not the same in every role, but she brings the same 'feel' in a blend of openness and intimacy. There are very few actors who leave quite so strong an impression of a personality informing the player; it is a personality vulnerable, warm, determined, cerebral, sensitive and playful. But she is the least passive of actors. Where a more histrionic artist would take pains to emphasize heroism or suffering, Stevenson gives us the character's trajectory and tells us the character's story. She gives the appearance of finding out and sharing her discoveries with us.

A similar judgement might be made of Daniel Day-Lewis, who was born Daniel Michael Blake Day-Lewis on 29 April 1957 in the London district of Kensington. He was the son of the poet laureate, Cecil Day-Lewis, and the actress Jill Balcon. When he was two his family moved south to Greenwich, where he attended Invicta and Sherington primary schools. In 1968 he was sent by his parents to Sevenoaks School, an independent boarding school in Kent. According to one press interview, 'he felt himself an outsider, laughed at because he sounded posh, because he was Jewish [his mother had come from a Jewish family], and just because of his need to be something of an outcast.' But in one of the first of his experiments in creative imitation he learned the vocabulary, accent and mannerisms of his tougher contemporaries. This may have been his first exercise in acting. He was then dispatched to the more congenial atmosphere of Bedales in Hampshire, where he adopted what might be called his twin passions for woodwork and acting. There he performed in amateur dramatics, and was given the leading role of Florizel in *The Winter's Tale*, and in the summer of 1973 he was enrolled with the National Youth Theatre. But he did not leave Bedales for another two years.

Day-Lewis's first proper or rigorous training began at the Bristol Old Vic Drama School, where he remained for three years. His tutor in acting, John Hartoch, recalled that 'he was clearly focused on his acting – he had a burning quality.' Day-Lewis himself has said that he became an actor 'out of necessity'; he made that decision at the age of twelve. He graduated to the Bristol Old Vic repertory company itself, based in the Theatre Royal in that city, where he first appeared as a soldier in George Farquhar's *The Recruiting Officer* in 1979. Small parts naturally followed in 1980 with Nigel Williams's *Class Enemy* and Christopher Marlowe's *Edward II*. He was back at the Theatre Royal with *A Midsummer Night's Dream* and Joan Littlewood's *Oh, What a Lovely War!* He observed, 'I had the right nose for classical theatre.' Given the warm, mellifluous, inviting register native to him, his capacity to deepen and coarsen it is striking. He can bellow in brogue, whine like a New Yorker or coax in the accents of a Czech.

In 1981 Day-Lewis attracted more attention at the Little Theatre in Bristol with the role of Jimmy Porter in John Osborne's *Look Back in Anger*, and this was followed by the title part in the Christmas treat of *Count Dracula*. In 1982 he moved from Bristol to London, where at the Queen's Theatre he played the lead in Julian Mitchell's *Another Country*, in which his own experiences of boarding school might have magnified or even magnetized his performance.

Day-Lewis then joined the Royal Shakespeare Company, for which in 1983 and 1984 he played Flute in *A Midsummer Night's*

Dream and then Romeo during a regional tour. His unstinting and unwavering eagerness to submerge himself in each role has attracted as much bafflement as admiration, but no one questions the power of the result. He was a creator rather than an amanuensis; he did not interpret roles, but fashioned characters. 'The things that most interest me', he once said, 'tend to be at some distance from my own life, and they tend to be at some distance from the characters that have interested me before as well.' He does not see himself so much as hard-working as curious, and he follows the promptings of that curiosity wherever they might lead.

In 1984 Day-Lewis reprised the part of Dracula at the Half Moon Theatre in London before moving to the National Theatre to play Mayakovsky in Dusty Hughes's *Futurists* and finally, in 1989, the title role in *Hamlet*. This was the part he had to abandon as a result of nervous exhaustion, and he has never since appeared on stage. As an actor Day-Lewis had tremendous weight, with a poise, lyricism and grace all of his own. He could not help but convey something of his soul, intense, questioning and nomadic. As an admirer of pioneers he was something of a pioneer himself. He was not afraid to go 'where there be lions'.

Miranda Richardson was born on 3 March 1958 in Southport, a seaside town in Lancashire. She attended Southport High School for Girls as well as Southport Dramatic Club, where she performed in amateur productions such as *Cinderella* and the more sensational adaptation of *Lord Arthur Savile's Crime* by Oscar Wilde. After she left school at the age of seventeen she considered becoming a vet, but her real instincts intervened and she enrolled at the Bristol Old Vic Theatre School, one of the best training grounds in the country. She has referred to acting as 'an emotional fusion; you think yourself into the character'.

The year after graduating Richardson started work in repertory. She was enrolled at the Library Theatre in Manchester, where she became assistant stage manager and where she played

Philippa in Alan Ayckbourn's *Ten Times Table*, Kay in Brian Clark's *Whose Life Is It Anyway?*, Linda in Woody Allen's *Play It Again, Sam*, and Sophia Western in an adaptation of *Tom Jones*. They were all respectable parts, and Richardson moved on to the Derby Playhouse, where she also performed in four productions, including Ann in Arthur Miller's *All My Sons*.

Richardson made her London debut at the Queen's Theatre in 1981 with Lindsay Price's *Moving*. She did not remain in the West End, however, but moved on to Bristol, then to Lancaster and Newcastle. Like so many actors before, although not so much since, she has eagerly embraced the demands of the tour. For all the commonplaces about the English homing instinct, the English actor is a natural nomad.

It was in the West End, however, that Richardson flourished. She won an Olivier Award nomination in 1987 for her leading role as Beth in Sam Shepard's *A Lie of the Mind* at the Royal Court. In 1988 she moved on to the National Theatre, where at the Lyttelton she played in Thomas Middleton and William Rowley's *The Changeling* and Harold Pinter's *Mountain Language*. Of her performance in the former, *The Observer* remarked that

> in this setting Miranda Richardson is perfect as Beatrice-Joanna. She appears gilded herself and her face has an incandescent quality. De Flores says she smells of amber. She looks like a piece of amber. And when she talks it is as if talking itself were a revelation . . . Throughout, there is no embrace without fear, and passion is acted with an ardour that makes you feel you have never seen an embrace on stage before.

She was at the Royal Court in 1990 for the title role in *Etta Jenks* by Marlane Meyer, then in 1996 at the National once more in Wallace Shawn's *The Designated Mourner*, followed by the title role in the adaptation of Virginia Woolf's *Orlando* at the Edinburgh Festival that prompted one reviewer to call her 'the greatest actress of our time in any medium'. Her lips are always alive and always active; they purse, and wrestle, and grimace; her voice, however deeply she adjusts it to suit her character, tends to fall back into a cool, crisp rattle or leap upwards in a mocking singsong. It can be caressing, lazily assured, seductive or vulnerable.

As a comic actor, Richardson is in many respects unsurpassed. Although she is often obliged to play the fierce, the obsessive or the unhinged, she has confessed that her greatest love is for comedy. This slight, subtle actor has all the bravura and bonhomie of a pantomime dame, but she still allows the child within her to flourish. She has a talent for making the mad seem sensible, and the sane seem to be on the edge of collapse. In her serious roles she can be at once chirpy and chilly, a sparrow with the soul of an owl. This cannot but remind us of the twin, sometimes contending, imperatives that direct the modern English actor: they must bring themselves to the part and yet they must become something quite other. In this instance, we may say that if Juliet Stevenson has all the warmth of her characters, Miranda Richardson has none of the shrillness of hers. In person, she is less of an owl than a mother hen. 'Kind,' says one admirer, 'though kind doesn't cover it.'

Leonard Gary Oldman was born in New Cross, southeast London, on 21 March 1958. He was educated at West Greenwich Secondary School in Deptford, but left at the age of fifteen to work in a sports shop. On listening to Liberace he conceived a passion for the piano, and taught himself to play. He also became interested in boxing and football, but all of this activity may have been a form of creative improvisation, or part of a desire to leave New Cross. It was, perhaps, both. His real ambition to act was fired at the age of thirteen by seeing Malcolm McDowell in a film entitled *The Raging Moon* (1971), in which McDowell himself is confined to a wheelchair. Oldman confessed that he said to himself, 'I wanna do that.' True to his ambition, he joined the Greenwich and Lewisham Young People's Theatre in Woolwich in the mid-1970s while supporting himself in a variety of jobs. He then applied to RADA, but was not accepted.

Oldman was not to be diverted, however, and he was able to win a scholarship to the Rose Bruford College of Speech and Drama in Sidcup, Kent, from which he graduated with a BA in theatre arts in 1979. He learned what most learn in drama school, primarily the Stanislavski system, although, as he has mentioned, he came 'off the book' by exploring other methods and other approaches. The influence of Stanislavski, however, is clear. He is an actor who is prepared to toil and to take pains over the smallest detail.

Oldman seems to have made an impression as Puck at college in Sidcup, and indeed there is something of the elf about him. In 1979 he was taken on by the Theatre Royal in York to take part in repertory. One of his first parts was the leading role in *Thark*, a farce by Ben Travers, which was followed by a medley of favourites including *Cabaret*, Peter Nichols's *Privates on Parade*, and *Romeo and Juliet*. In the Christmas season he played Puss in *Dick Whittington and His Wonderful Cat*. To bring progress and variety to his new career, Oldman also studied mime and the techniques of *commedia dell'arte*. He was ambitious, diligent and hard-working. His fellow actor in *Dick Whittington*, Michael Simkins, recalled 'a bruising schedule of fifty performances in seven weeks, not to mention the drunken and relentless partying in various digs and rented bed-sits after curtain-down'. But Oldman's intensity seems to have been his abiding characteristic. He once said, 'I test positive for the theatre,' and it was this, combined with an unerring instinct, that sent him forward.

In 1980 Oldman joined the Glasgow Citizens' Theatre and played in Marlowe's *Massacre at Paris*, R. D. MacDonald's *Chinchilla* and *A Waste of Time*, and Shaun Lawton's *Desperado*

Corner; one of his contemporaries there was Mark Rylance. The company also toured Europe and South America. After his return in 1981 he went to the Mercury Theatre, Colchester, for *Oh, What a Lovely War!* In July 1982 Oldman joined with Glenda Jackson at the Lyric Theatre in MacDonald's *Summit Conference*, which ran for six months. He then moved on to the Pomegranate Theatre in Chesterfield to play the title role in Joe Orton's *Entertaining Mr Sloane*, before going on to the Palace Theatre in Westcliff to play Len in Edward Bond's *Saved*. He is perhaps best known for playing liminal characters, those who exist outside the gates and far from the comforting fireside. At one level he is all 'outer', a trickster and a master of transformation or disguise; at another, he is all 'inner', his most moving portrayals those of characters who carry a secret wound. In pursuit of psychological accuracy, he is delving into matters too personal to be spoken of.

Max Stafford-Clark, then artistic director of the Royal Court, saw Oldman's performance in *Saved* and asked him to take on the part of Scopey in the 1984 revival of Bond's *The Pope's Wedding*. For this part he won a Best Newcomer award from *Time Out* and the London Critics' Circle award for Best Actor. This success inaugurated a number of engagements at the Royal Court over two years, including Ron Hutchinson's *Rat in the Skull* and Nicholas Wright's *The Desert Air*, as well as Middleton's *Women Beware Women* and Trevor Griffiths's *Real Dreams*. Oldman is a supremely theatrical actor. He has a taste for 'ham', which should not be surprising in a Londoner. But that is balanced by his delicacy and restraint when he chooses to deploy them. Perhaps the influence of his working-class parents is also visible; acting might be fun, but it is above all work.

Oldman became a member of the RSC in 1985, in which year he played in seven different productions, beginning with Francis Wyndham's *Abel and Cain* at the Almeida and ending with Bond's *The Tin Can People* at the Pit. In 1987 he was Mr Homer in William Wycherley's *The Country Wife* at the Royal Exchange Theatre in Manchester. He then returned to the Royal Court for Caryl Churchill's *Serious Money*, which seems to have been his last appearance on the stage. An effervescent energy, ragged and fierce, lay at the heart of Oldman's acting for the theatre. Sometimes it was contained, and was transmuted into intensity; sometimes it was suppressed in favour of gentleness and warmth. But it was often released, and then it emerged as a force of nature. Clearly, then, he loved the stage, and it is said that even now he feels a 'misty-eyed' pang when he remembers it. The tale of the actor who would prefer to work on stage, but is obliged to work in film, is not an uncommon one.

Twenty-six

A new style

The 'new wave' is an expression often used to denote the working-class actors who broke upon the stage, and later the cinema, during the 1950s and 1960s. Albert Finney, Tom Courtenay, Richard Burton and Alan Bates were closely allied to the new 'kitchen sink' plays, and their style had the bite and rasp, the subversive vitality, required by that drama.

Yet soon after this generation a second 'wave' rolled and broke. From RADA emerged Juliet Stevenson, Jonathan Pryce, Alan Rickman and Anton Lesser. Unlike the previous 'wave', they were not united by any particular style or even approach; indeed, if anything a determined eccentricity, a waywardness and even whimsy, characterized their acting. In true English fashion, they were less rebels than wanderers. If they lacked the weight and size of their predecessors, they had perhaps more subtlety, more suppleness and more polish.

Kenneth Branagh was born in the area of Tigers Bay in Belfast on 10 December 1960. He was first educated at a primary school in that city, but when he was nine he and his family moved to Reading in Berkshire in order to avoid the Troubles that invaded the area and perhaps inculcated a certain steeliness in his character. He attended the local Meadway comprehensive in the suburb of Tilehurst, where he took part in school productions and also participated in elocution lessons to remove his Belfast accent. In the late 1970s he also joined Progress Theatre in Reading, which specialized in innovative productions; he performed in Tom Stoppard as well as Shakespeare. It was at this juncture that the desire to be an actor was confirmed. In 1978 he auditioned for a place at RADA, where he stayed for three years; towards the end of this period he played Hamlet, and Billy in Graham Reid's television drama *Too Late to Talk to Billy* (1982). He concluded his career at the Academy with John Webster's *The White Devil*.

In 1982 Branagh won the Society of West End Theatres award for Best Newcomer as well as RADA's Bancroft Gold Medal for his role as Judd in Julian Mitchell's *Another Country*. The *Financial Times* concluded that 'his technique is assured and flawless', a judgement that his severest critics would not dispute. The following year was spent in television work. In 1984 he joined the Royal Shakespeare Company, where he took the title role in *Henry V*, which played to capacity audiences before moving to the Barbican. Michael Billington of *The Guardian* wrote that Branagh acted 'as if he owned the stage, as if the stage was his by right'. This was a performance that seemed to some to eclipse that of Olivier.

While both are compelling, one difference is clear. Olivier, although more varied in tone, is not at ease with the verse and therefore its meaning is sometimes lost. Branagh, more confident, follows one tone throughout, but it is the right tone and conveys an almost mystical plangency. Yet his Henry is no moral monolith. When the plans for war are presented to him, he invokes his conscience in the dead, cool tones of one who has already decided to drop his conscience into the nearest oubliette.

This bravura was always part of Branagh's performances. He appeared in three other RSC productions, as Laertes in *Hamlet*, as Mike Bassett in *Golden Girls* and as the King of Navarre in *Love's Labour's Lost*, all of which earned commendatory reviews. Never one to waste time or opportunity, he then returned to film and television. In 1986 he performed opposite Samantha Bond in *Romeo and Juliet* at the Lyric, a production that Bond herself described as 'the hottest ticket in town – you couldn't get a seat', although it was not altogether a critical success.

The following year Branagh established, with David Parfitt, the Renaissance Theatre Company; it was a bold enterprise, exhibiting what one critic called 'his practicality, self-determination and entrepreneurial spirit'. The company began with Branagh's own *Public Enemy* and John Sessions's *The Life of Napoleon*. These were followed by *Twelfth Night* in 1987 and continued with touring productions of *Much Ado About Nothing*, *As You Like It* and *Hamlet*. The last play, directed by Derek Jacobi in 1988, had Branagh in the title role, of which Milton Shulman in the *Evening Standard* wrote that 'Branagh has the vitality of Olivier, the passion of Gielgud, the assurance of Guinness.'

In the autumn of 1992 Branagh was Hamlet in a production by the RSC; his biographer Mark White commented that 'what was striking about his performance was its technical proficiency: his diction and phrasing, the clarity, power and suppleness of his voice.' The *Daily Mail* echoed this praise by declaring that 'he is undoubtedly the great Hamlet of our time. I have seen none to match him in many a season.' In this production, more than in any other, he treated Shakespeare's soliloquies as if they were arias. If not all would agree with that approach, none would deny that he has brought it to something like perfection. For above all else he is a supremely accomplished actor who gives the sense of complete self-control.

After a long absence from the stage, Branagh returned to the Crucible in Sheffield in 2002 for the part of Richard III; it was genuinely and generously applauded, with the *Financial Times* affirming that 'I don't know that I've ever heard an actor who can project fast Shakespearian diction without it seeming at all period or mannered. I was amazed how modern a lot of the lines seemed.' The following year he played the leading role in David Mamet's

Edmond at the Olivier Theatre. Billington noted 'Branagh's mesmerising performance. [He] invests Edmond with a chunky ordinariness concealing a bottled rage.' It was generally considered to be a tour de force of anger and prejudice, and it revealed a very different aspect of Branagh's playing. Here was a character at war with life, an embittered, savage bigot who is also a thinker and a dreamer, who endures prison rape and ends up almost in love with his abuser. Nothing could be further from the roles usually associated with this most polished of actors. In this period he was also engaged in film and, just as he can often slip into a theatrical style for his performances on screen, so he seems to favour a cinematic style for his stage productions.

In 2013 Branagh co-directed and starred in *Macbeth* at the Manchester International Festival, a production that was sold out for its entire run, and which he then took to Broadway, where he made his acting debut. This was another part in which he was entirely convincing; despite his tendency to bring the same texture to every part, velvety and sleek, he has the ability to transform himself, adopting the physical rhythms and even the voice of the character. He has always spoken the verse 'trippingly', with full respect for its rhythms and avoiding, above all, excessive emphasis. His body, although thickset, was lithe and athletic, his voice harsher and deeper than usual. After the murder of Duncan he lets out a wail. He does not want to go back to the corpse. He cannot go back to the corpse. It becomes plausible, for one agonizing moment, that if he did, then he might, just might, repent.

Two years later he established the Kenneth Branagh Theatre Company, in which he would play the once traditional role of actor-manager. In that capacity he presented five plays at the Garrick between October 2015 and November 2016. He played the leading role in the first and last of them, *The Winter's Tale* and John Osborne's *The Entertainer*. In the former play his 'cuddly' charisma was the perfect carapace for menace. His very gentleness makes the insane jealousy of Leontes all the more chilling and incomprehensible. He extended his scope by publicizing the fact that *The Winter's Tale*, *Romeo and Juliet* and *The Entertainer* would be released in cinemas. He is perhaps still best known for his work in film and television, but he must be congratulated for his ambition and bravery in attempting to bring to life the older traditions of the theatre.

Mark Rylance is of the same generation as Branagh; he was born Mark Waters on 18 January 1960 in Ashford, Kent, and in 1962 his family moved to the United States. There his father taught English at the University School of Milwaukee, where Rylance was enrolled. He came back to England in 1978 and, to the astonishment of his parents in America, entered RADA. 'When I got into RADA, my parents were incredibly surprised. I was intensely shy; I couldn't speak until I was six.' He also changed his name to Rylance, since there was already a Mark Waters on the books of the theatre union Equity. Having been brought up in the United States, he had some difficulty in adjusting to British student life. 'I did love being a student,' he said in an interview, 'but I was very lonely and intense . . . I had this idea: no pain, no gain.' That intensity is still with him, all the more striking for the elaborate ease in which it is often couched.

Rylance stayed at RADA for the traditional three years, but in 1980 he joined the Chrysalis Theatre School in Balham, run by two dedicated actors. That year he found work with the Glasgow Citizens' Theatre, where he made his first professional appearances as a soldier in Carlo Goldoni's *The Battlefield*, as Michael in Bertolt Brecht's *The Caucasian Chalk Circle*, and most prominently as Bazza in Shaun Lawton's *Desperado Corner* in 1981. The Citizens' Theatre had a fine reputation, and it was a suitable beginning. In 1982 he was accepted into the RSC, at first playing comparatively minor roles.

Rylance was soon given more prominent parts, and in 1983 he played the lead in *Peter Pan*. In 1985 he played Rocca in Malcolm McKay's *Airbase* at the Oxford Playhouse, and the following year he was Puck in Britten's opera at the Royal Opera House. These in turn led him back to the RSC, where he played Hamlet and Romeo in 1989. He established a new company, Phoebus' Cart, in 1990 with Claire van Kampen, whom he later married, but it managed to perform only *Macbeth* and *The Tempest*, and was not an overwhelming success.

In 1995 Rylance was Macbeth at the Greenwich Theatre, and that year he was appointed the first artistic director of Shakespeare's Globe Theatre, a post he held for some ten years. During this period he acted and directed in every season. His first production in the new theatre was *Two Gentlemen of Verona*, performed in modern dress, in which he played Proteus; this was a part in which, according to a critic, 'Rylance's natural sweetness and miraculous audience rapport convince you that he is a good person gone astray.' This was followed by Thomas Middleton's *A Chaste Maid in Cheapside* and the title role in *Henry V*.

Henry, the hero of Agincourt, was a light presence in this version. Here he was a kind of man-child, well-meaning, awkward and kindly. As he wooed the princess, he managed, beautifully, to convey the absurdity of their position. Henry is, after all, seeking to conclude a political match as gracefully as possible, and to do so he must talk of love. Rylance ambled about her and ambled back, smiling ruefully, tripping over the straw as he tripped through his French. He seemed to be saying, 'I know it seems ridiculous, but I really do love you. I'm surprised myself!' Gentle waves of warmth rolled from his creased eyes, his awkward grin. Small wonder she gave in. It was the most improbable interpretation, but as so often, Rylance illumined aspects of the character that had hitherto been ignored or not even imagined. There is no doubt that he is a contemporary actor, but it is hard to decipher what that contemporaneity consists of; it may be his lack of pomposity and grandeur in the familiar Shakespearean mode, or his conversational tone and the natural projection of his voice, or his employment of pauses and silences. His acting is, above all, human in the sense that it is vulnerable, fallible and recognizable.

Henry v was followed by *The Merchant of Venice* and Dekker and Middleton's *The Honest Whore*, but they were perhaps outdone by Rylance's next role, as Cleopatra. Stephen Fay described him in *The Independent* as resembling Elizabeth Taylor: 'He makes his entrance wearing a wig of black hair drawn tightly back from a high forehead, and falling in curls down his back; his eyebrows are black . . . There are moments when he nearly goes over the top, but he manages to stay just the right side of excess.' Dishevelled, in rags, Rylance acted the final scenes in a heart-rending monotone, squatting amid a pile of candles, shaking with grief. But he also knew precisely when to exploit the incongruity of his appearance for comic effect, just as the players would have done in the sixteenth century.

One performance was notable for an incident that, with a less steady hand on the helm, could have proved disastrous. In dealing with it, Rylance showed charm as well as flair – not to mention some courage. Halfway through the play, a very large heckler cried out that he had paid to see actresses and not 'a bunch of poofs'. Rylance did not break stride for a moment. Clearly feeling that the man's political education would have to wait, he opened his arms in the most regal of gestures and invited the heckler, if he was quite serious and indeed felt defrauded, to go to the box office, where his money would be refunded. All was said in the sweet, deep voice of Cleopatra. The heckler growled a little more, but eventually left. Rylance gave a great sigh and smiled, to general laughter and applause. This was the only moment when he broke with his character. Shakespeare's own company, well used to barracking, would have approved.

Rylance was Hamlet in 2000 and Cloten in *Cymbeline* in 2001, then in the following year Olivia in an all-male version of *Twelfth Night* that the critics, despite their initial misgivings, applauded; *The Independent* wrote that 'Rylance, startlingly, turns her into a revelation. As no one has ever done before, he brings out the unexpected comedy of Olivia's barricaded predicament.' With the assistance of the director, Tim Carroll, he helped to rejuvenate the theatrical practice of the sixteenth century. In 2003 he played the title role of *Richard II*, where, characteristically, he slipped humour into the most unlikely scenes. The doomed king invited his courtiers to 'tell sad stories of the death of kings' with a light laugh and a puckish, self-deprecating smile. Richard might be guilty of hubris, callousness or fecklessness, but not of self-pity. It was an interpretation both bold and completely true to the text.

Rylance was Duke Vincentio in *Measure for Measure* in 2004, and Prospero in 2005 in a *Tempest* with all the parts divided between just three actors. In the words of the director, Matthew Warchus, 'he was born with the ability to lie in an astonishingly convincing way. It's supernatural. Add to that his showmanship, and his psychological truth – which are usually mutually exclusive – and you have something virtually unique.' Most of Rylance's characters have in common what might be called a wounded quality, however well disguised by cunning or strength. But if he is an open soul he does not display, like Nicol Williamson, an open sore: there is nothing extravagantly agonized or self-flagellating to his acting. The audience sees in that crumpled face and hears in that soft and rich but almost lugubrious voice the elements of 'unaccommodated man' and 'a poor bare, forked animal'. After giving up his role as artistic director, he returned to the Globe in 2012 as Richard III, where he managed to bring soul to this most wonderfully soulless of villains. Unlike most of the actors who play the role, he understood that Richard is, after all, a human being.

Rylance had already performed outside the purlieus of the Globe. In 2000 he played Henry in Yasmina Reza's *Life × 3* at the Royal National Theatre. In 2007 he was Robert in Marc Camoletti's French farce *Boeing Boeing*, at the Comedy and then on Broadway. But one of his greatest successes was as Johnny 'Rooster' Byron in Jez Butterworth's *Jerusalem* at the Royal Court in 2009. His was an overwhelming success as the philosopher, poet, drug-pusher, waster, bard and lord of the wood; he boomed even when he whispered, and the critic of *The Independent* reported that 'Rylance is magnificent in a hugely demanding role, and restores one's faith in the power of theatre to make a really beautiful noise and on a scale that is both epic and potentially popular.' It was a colossal performance in every sense; the wounded soul was still there, but now it had a body of brass encasing it. As one critic put it, 'there's no explanation forthcoming of how he does what he does.' He just does it.

Simon Russell Beale was born on 12 January 1961 in Penang, then part of British Malaya, where his father was stationed with the Army Medical Services. He was enrolled as a chorister at St Paul's Cathedral at the age of eight, and was admitted to the cathedral school, where he was introduced to the stage in *A Midsummer Night's Dream*. He moved on to Clifton College in Bristol, where in the sixth form he played Desdemona and also performed in Stoppard's *Rosencrantz and Guildenstern Are Dead*. From Clifton he made the successful transition to Gonville and Caius College, Cambridge, where he gained a first-class degree in English and was offered the chance to study for a doctorate. Instead he applied to the Guildhall School of Music and Drama, from which he graduated in 1983. In 1986 he joined the Swan Theatre of the RSC, where in his first year he performed small roles in *The Winter's Tale*, Ben Jonson's *Every Man in His Humour*, Nick Dear's *The Art of Success* (which transferred to the Pit) and Thomas Heywood's *The Fair Maid of the West* (which moved to the Mermaid the following year).

In 1988 Beale performed Sir Fopling Flutter in George Etherege's *The Man of Mode*, and played in Bond's *Restoration* as well as in *Macbeth*. The following year he acted in five different plays at the Pit. In 1990 he was back at the Swan as Thersites in *Troilus and Cressida*, and he played the title role in *Edward II* at the same venue. He was also the King of Navarre in the RSC production of *Love's Labour's Lost*, and Konstantin in Anton Chekhov's *The Seagull*. Clearly he was not the kind of actor who could be trusted to carry a spear or, for that matter, a briefcase; with the exception of Ferdinand, the list already shows an actor whose natural realm was the echoing cave, the desolate heath or the padded cell. He was meant to be great and he was meant to be odd. As his range widened so his characters became more significant.

It was a slow but perhaps necessary, even if occasionally frustrating, progress. Beale played Edward II at the Pit in the following year, together with the King of Navarre and Konstantin in the main house at the Barbican. In 1992 he played Richard III in a performance that was described as 'electrifying'. The next year he was Edgar in *King Lear* and Ariel in *The Tempest*, giving strong evidence of his range and versatility. His Edgar was an almost excessively gentle man so harried by misfortune and heartbreak that he becomes by the end a ferocious, even sadistic, force of nemesis. As his treacherous half-brother reels on the ground, Beale springs forwards to claw at his eyes. In 1994 he was back in *The Tempest*, and played Oswald in Henrik Ibsen's *Ghosts* as well as Edgar in *King Lear*. One critic remarked, 'Simon Russell Beale almost always has an introspective, vulnerable quality. All actors do more than speak the words, but he finds the humanity of the part and finds a way of conveying it without speaking.'

In 1995 Beale played Ferdinand in Webster's *The Duchess of Malfi* at Wyndham's, where, according to the *Financial Times*, he 'presents another of his gifted studies in self-conscious, horrified loathing . . . Beale's melancholy lycanthropia reminds us that Angela Carter's line about some wolves being hairy on the inside derives directly from this play.' That year he also joined the National Theatre, where he proved his eminence with Mosca in Jonson's *Volpone*, in which the *Sunday Times* noted that 'Beale sends each word winging across the stage like poisoned darts . . . Jonson's dark masterpiece is delivered with just the right intemperate energy.' In 2000, at the Lyttelton, he played Hamlet at last, to great and enduring success. His ability to seem natural, or 'normal', while touching the pinnacle of lyrical grandeur is one of Beale's most important characteristics. His speech to the players is earnest, slightly camp, rather breathless, and with touches of placatory humour. This Hamlet, prince though he be, cannot help but blush and giggle slightly in the presence of artists. Effervescent vulnerability, sometimes hidden beneath bravado, sometimes deferred by success, is one of the characteristics of his acting style.

In his earlier years he had laboured in small or minor roles, eschewing the delights of instant celebrity on film or television, but his reward for hard work had arrived. He had earned the title, now often bestowed on him, of 'the greatest actor of his generation'. In 2001 he took the lead in Charlotte Jones's *Humble Boy* at the Cottesloe, which transferred to the Gielgud; it was reported that 'the ever dependable extraordinary Simon Russell Beale has again produced a stupendous performance as an angry, child-like, hapless man who stutters when under pressure. He delivers his sharp witty lines with precision timing.' Another critic remarked that 'for me, it is Russell Beale who stands out in this cast. This is truly a brilliant piece of acting, demonstrating the range from comic timing to more solemn and thought-provoking playing.'

In 2012 Beale was Timon of Athens at the Olivier; his malediction on Athens in that role is all on one note, but it is the monotony not of a hectoring demagogue but of a monk at Compline. It cannot be incidental that Beale loves sacred music. His verse-speaking, so fluent and rapid, argues a continuity with the Elizabethan theatre.

One of his stage characteristics is verse spoken at an unsparing velocity, halted by a sudden hiatus. This is very close to 'reality'. His voice itself is thin, nasal, but marvellously expressive, stretching the diphthongs, stamping on the consonants and wringing the vowels for every drop of sound.

Beale took a turn with the Michael Grandage Company between December 2012 and March 2014 in a revival of Peter Nichols's *Privates on Parade* at the Noël Coward Theatre. It was as camp as a hairnet, wall-to-wall ham, and Michael Billington wrote in *The Guardian*, 'I suspect the big draw will be the prospect of Russell Beale impersonating Marlene Dietrich, Vera Lynn and Carmen Miranda. Good as he is in the drag numbers, he is at his best in a song which harpoons exactly Noël Coward's sour, anti-socialist acerbity.' Of course he also manages to convey the tribulations of a 'real person'. That has become second nature to him.

From January 2014 he played Lear, under the direction of Sam Mendes, at the National. His was a compelling interpretation from an actor whose next leap you can never foresee; his voice has a cold, rattling rasp; but then, when challenged by Cordelia, all the purely human rage rushes out. When the full extent of his other daughters' perfidy is revealed, his mouth works, his eyes stare. He can say nothing because he knows he can do nothing. In the sixth scene of the fourth act, when the mad Lear meets the blind Gloucester, the long, sustained note gives way to a mode that is musing and even conversational; he does not rail against injustice but points it out, calmly if vigorously. The only token of his inner turbulence is an obsessive scratching of his arms.

In the spring of 2015 Beale starred at the Donmar Warehouse in Steve Waters's *Temple*, in which he played the Dean of St Paul's during the Occupy London protest. In the autumn of that year he played the title role in Ian Kelly's *Mr Foote's Other Leg* at the Hampstead Theatre and then at the Haymarket. In November

2016 he returned to the Royal Shakespeare Company to play Prospero; the play migrated from Stratford to the Barbican in the summer of 2017. His performance was one of the fullest and richest on the modern stage; his movements are quick and nervous, while his gestures are perfectly assimilated and perfectly suited to his speaking of the verse. It seemed that he was only a few, tremulous footsteps ahead of his own inner tempest. Just occasionally, this storm raged out, as when Ariel asked, 'Do you love me, master?' Beale paused, for an age almost, then wept, his hand over his face, before bursting out, 'Dearly, my delicate Ariel.' There was a tic we saw in his Lear: a wide-eyed, upward gaze, at once challenging and pleading, like a wounded bear's as it heaves itself up from a pit. It has been said that Beale uses his parts to investigate his own consciousness. This may contain a truth, but it misses the point; if he journeys inwards, he draws you after him. Wherever he goes, into whatever dark crevices or on to what whirring carousels he ventures, he makes you his companion. Indeed, where so many actors are spoken of as the heirs to Laurence Olivier, Beale holds perhaps a still greater honour: he bears the torch first lit by Charles Laughton.

Ralph Nathaniel Twisleton-Wykeham-Fiennes was born in the village of Wangford, outside Ipswich, on 22 December 1962 into, as the name suggests, a distinguished family. In the early 1970s the family moved to Ireland, where they lived for some time in West Cork and County Kilkenny. Fiennes was educated first at St Kieran's College, a Catholic school in Kilkenny, and then at the independent Newtown School in County Waterford established by the Society of Friends or Quakers. The family moved back to England later in the decade and settled in Salisbury, where Fiennes was sent to Bishop Wordsworth's School, which has a high reputation for academic excellence. But that was not the path he chose to follow. In 1979 the family moved to London, although Fiennes stayed on in Salisbury to complete his A level examinations; this was a wise decision, since it helped him to enrol at the Chelsea School of Art in 1981. He remained there until 1983, when he was accepted at RADA, at which he was known by his contemporaries as 'The Voice Beautiful' and where he won a number of awards.

Fiennes's first engagement was with the Theatr Clwyd in north-eastern Wales, where he performed in Stoppard's *Night and Day*. In 1985 he joined the New Shakespeare Company, which performed at the Open Air Theatre in Regent's Park. He began by playing relatively small parts, such as Curio in *Twelfth Night* and Cobweb in *A Midsummer Night's Dream*. Early in 1986 he was hired by the Oldham Coliseum Theatre, where he appeared in Barry Heath's *Me Mam Sez*, followed by *The Mad Adventures of a Knight* and *Cloud Nine*. He once said that 'doing rep toughens you up. You go through the mill and you can't be precious about it.'

Fiennes returned to Regent's Park in 1986 as Lysander in *A Midsummer Night's Dream*, in which he was described as 'pale and interesting'; then, at last, he was Romeo. In 1987 he was enlisted in the National Theatre, where he performed in Luigi Pirandello's *Six Characters in Search of an Author* at the Olivier, as well as Brian Friel's version of Ivan Turgenev's *Fathers and Sons* at the Lyttelton. He then played in Nick Darke's *Ting Tang Mine* at the Cottesloe. For several months of 1987 he remained in repertory at the National, with parts from *Macbeth* to *Waiting for Godot*.

In 1988 Fiennes moved on to the Royal Shakespeare Company, where he remained until 1991, taking on roles in *Much Ado About Nothing* and *King John* before embarking on a compilation entitled *The Plantagenets*, in which he was much admired; his biographer York Membery relates that 'infallibly audible, Ralph brought his trademarks of dignity and intelligence to the role.' He also took on larger parts as his confidence and experience grew, such as Troilus and Edmund in 1990, and concluded his time at the RSC with Berowne in *Love's Labour's Lost*.

In 1991 the RSC decided that there was nothing 'suitable' for Fiennes's particular talents, but he assuaged any disappointment with two screen roles: the title part of *A Dangerous Man: Lawrence after Arabia* and Heathcliff in *Wuthering Heights* (both 1992). They also added an entirely different dimension to his stage career. As Heathcliff in particular, Fiennes gave the world a foretaste, or rather foreshadowing, of his peculiar quality as an actor. His was not the petulant, passionate Heathcliff offered by Olivier, a human being who has made some unfortunate choices, but rather a wildling who has died and risen again as a demon. He is granite, implacable, unearthly to the corners of his faint, mirthless smile.

But in 1993 Fiennes prepared himself to play Hamlet at the Hackney Empire, a long way from Hollywood. One journalist remarked of his performance that 'Fiennes is a proven master at portraying souls in flux . . . Fiennes plays lost souls so effectively that you wonder if he must be one himself.' Jonathan Kent, joint artistic director of the Almeida, commented that Fiennes possessed 'phenomenal classical technique. He can speak in heightened verse as if that were the only way he *could* express himself.' His command of Shakespearean character is as remarkable as his mastery of the verse; they are, perhaps, inseparable. His performance is available only in vignettes, but it is clear that Fiennes was unafraid to bring 'the antic disposition' to the fore. He has the sullen stare, the wild movements and wilder rage. Yet humility is the keynote to his Shakespearean acting. He does not impose upon the text. He observes and respects Shakespeare's silences, which are not the formal pauses at the ends of the line but the negative space in which real meaning can be discerned. It is as if he recognizes the actor's true role as a channel rather than a fountainhead, a conduit both of sense and of sensibility. When anger is called for, he darts straight to the real emotion behind it – whether it be hostility, resentment, hatred or anguish.

At the Almeida itself, Fiennes played in David Hare's translation of Chekhov's *Ivanov*, succeeded by Coriolanus and Richard II. Of his role in Chekhov it was reported that 'Fiennes has become England's leading avatar of angst, possessed of eyes that seem to bear silent witness to unspeakable pain.' The *Daily Telegraph* joined in the general enthusiasm for his performance when its critic wrote that 'anyone who has had any experience of clinical depression will recognise the listlessness of his voice, the sudden bursts of pettish temper, the restlessness and self-contempt.' He researches, as other contemporary actors do or attempt to do. But research has its limits. He said, 'a lot of the time I feel things intuitively . . . People ask about research. There is research, but actually a lot of it is intuition and imagination.'

Fiennes changed direction in 2001 when he made a guest appearance in Hamish McColl, Sean Foley and Eddie Braben's *The Play What I Wrote* at Wyndham's, and in 2003 he played Carl Jung in Christopher Hampton's *The Talking Cure*; of the latter role, one review noted that 'As played by Fiennes with watchful unease, Jung is a man being torn apart by emotions he is trying to keep in check as he finds himself falling in love with the first patient he attempts to treat.' Fiennes was back at the RSC the same year with the title role of Ibsen's *Brand* at Stratford and the Haymarket. 'I don't *mimic*,' he once said, 'but I suppose I'm aware of this person's energy and demeanour, that I've taken it on board.'

In more recent years Fiennes played Jack Tanner in George Bernard Shaw's *Man and Superman* at the National in 2015, which the critic of *The Observer* described as a 'towering' performance. Solness in Ibsen's *The Master Builder*, at the Old Vic the following year, was described as a 'superb performance' in which 'Solness becomes a tragic figure haunted by hubris.' In 2016 Fiennes also played the title role of Richard III at the Almeida, in which part he was again remarkable. The lips barely move, the eyes are steady and dark. His Richard is understated, grave, embittered, utterly recognizable as a loyal but undervalued courtier who has for too long been forced to watch while others take the credit. It is a formidable interpretation. In 2018 he played Antony at the National, a warm and deeply human performance that won him the title of Best Actor at the *Evening Standard* awards. He is now perhaps better known for his film work, but, in common with most actors, he is most in thrall to the theatre. 'I keep going back,' he once said, 'because I miss it. I miss *that thing*.'

Don Williams was born in Trinidad on 23 May 1951, and as a small boy he was inspired by watching Marlon Brando in the filmed version of *On the Waterfront* (1954). 'I loved how expressive everyone was,' he said. 'You really understood their lives. I thought, I'd rather like to do that when I grow up.' But growing up brought other challenges. Following the death of his father, Don – then aged six – was brought with his brother to England by his mother to renew their lives. It took three weeks to cross the Atlantic, but their first experience of the unknown country was not favourable. 'England was a real disappointment if I'm honest,' he said. 'It was painted in the colonies as this beautiful, golden, bright place and it was absolutely the opposite.' His family settled in Newcastle upon Tyne, by which he was similarly unimpressed: 'I remember thinking, "This is so dull, just so dull." And the world is anyway a frightening place for a child. One had to adapt to survive, and I did. I just got on with it.' He said, 'My mother's generation had protection their children didn't have because they were adults when they left. We didn't have a map, we had to make a new one, a new map of how to exist.' That sense of loss and displacement has stayed with him, and may have helped to create the depth and resonance of his acting. He has also said, 'I've been thinking about my identity a lot as I've got older. I'll always be an immigrant, a foreigner.'

Don and his brother attended school in Newcastle, where, as he remembered, they were the only black children in the school:

'I got called rude names but I'd stand up for myself. I became a Geordie and got nicknamed the Young Pele because I was good at football. The teachers were worse. One teacher thought he should stop me being left-handed and asked if I'd learned to write up a tree.' But a chance encounter helped to shape his future. He was acting in a school play, during which he had to shake and shudder at the sight of a ghost (shades of Hamlet?), when a local bishop in the audience came up to him afterwards and told him, 'I jolly well believed you.' That seems to have been the moment when he fitfully caught a glimpse of himself as an actor.

So, although Don attended Harris College in Newcastle for his further education, at the age of seventeen he applied for a job at the Flora Robson Playhouse in that city; he became an assistant stage manager, learning some of his future trade by keen observation. Soon he moved on to the Drama Centre in Chalk Hill, northwest London, where, as far as he was concerned, his training was perhaps more theoretical than practical. But there was one practical benefit. He discovered that there was another actor called Don Williams and so he renamed himself after Newcastle's Warrington Road, where he had grown up.

In 1973 Warrington was offered his first substantial role, in Eric Chappell's *The Banana Box*, when it opened at the Apollo Theatre in London. In this he played a student, Philip Smith, who lodged in a boarding house managed by one Mr Rigsby, the racist landlord played by Leonard Rossiter. If this sounds familiar, that's because it is. It became the foundation of the television series *Rising Damp*, which gave Warrington his first national audience. In this he might be considered fortunate since, as he said of his black contemporaries, 'the good young actors are there; what's not there is any imagination on the part of the powers that be about the parts they can play. Young black actors' careers do not run on the same tram-lines as their white contemporaries, who have the classic canon and can progress in television and film. For black actors, it's much more stop-go.' In his case the light has been green rather than red, and he has performed with the National Theatre, the RSC, the Bristol Old Vic and the Royal Exchange in Manchester. One of his principal roles came in 1985 as the Angel Gabriel in *The Mysteries* at the National Theatre. In 1997 he played Antonio in *The Merchant of Venice* at the Birmingham Repertory Theatre, which proved beyond doubt that he could climb the final rung to theatrical success.

Warrington's stage credits include Kwame Kwei-Armah's *Elmina's Kitchen* at the Garrick in 2005 and, two years later, the same dramatist's *A Statement of Regret* at the Cottesloe, a play in which Warrington was reported by *The Guardian* to have given a fine performance as a man 'full of ruined grandeur, as the disintegrating hero'. In 2013 he played the lead role of Joe Keller in the Talawa Theatre Company's production of Arthur Miller's *All My Sons* at the Manchester Royal Exchange; the Talawa company is a black theatrical venture founded in 1986. Its production was described by *The Guardian* as 'flawless'. One critic noted that 'When Don Warrington's Joe is finally forced to acknowledge that the strangers destroyed by his self-protective self-interest are "all my sons", the production reaches an intensity that fuses his statement into a declaration that is both emotionally wrenching and rationally convincing.' The *British Theatre Guide* remarked that 'he creates a beautifully nuanced portrayal of this proud man who has built strong barriers to protect himself and his family from what others may think of him.'

Three years later, with the same company and in the same theatre, Warrington took on his most commanding performance as Lear. The *Daily Telegraph* applauded his interpretation and added that 'he ascends the cliff face with magnificent authority. He rages around his daughters like a hulking thunder cloud in human form, not just the incarnation of absolute rule but of something more ancient and of the earth.' The critic added, 'his Lear combines a compulsive self-destructive streak with a heartbreaking self-awareness – and although his unmooring from himself is complete, Warrington invests Lear's madness with a spark of humane vitality that can't be vanquished.'

This was a fleshy, gravelly portrayal within a production referred to by *The Telegraph* as 'a heartbreaking tour de force'. Warrington himself said of the part that 'It's like looking at Mount Everest and thinking, "I'm going to try and climb that – and it's snowing."' It is therefore no surprise that his Lear begins as a moss-eaten mountain, vast, monolithic but almost imperceptibly crumbling. But this mode shifts, and in the most surprising ways. When passion breaks out, it is the passion of a child, petulant but unignorable. Here is a man who has never truly grown up. This is a commonplace of Shakespearean exegesis, but Warrington's interpretation gives it new life precisely because the man we see at the beginning is so very grand, so very great and so very kingly. He has moments of simple humanity, as in his fond, fatherly cackle, like a fizzing squib, and in his warm embrace. When at last he sees the true nature of his relations with Goneril and Regan, and the fact that he is indeed a helpless old man, he changes completely.

Warrington's voice is his glory: rich, precise, cultivated, and with a suggestion of a lisp. It has a dusty, cracked feel, as if someone had caught the voice of a great Shakespearean actor of former times. It has, too, a certain elegant weariness, as of someone who has seen the circle of time in its endless revolutions and can fetch only a sigh in response. His face is his other glory. As a young man in *Rising Damp*, he was positively beautiful.

Like Antony Sher or Albert Finney, Warrington somehow skipped the middle age of acting. The remarkable grace of his youth settled into the gravity of his later years with no apparent intermission. Age has brought a certain solemnity, even sulkiness, to his expression, which makes the sudden, wolfish smile on stage all the more engaging and unsettling. In 2018 he took on the part

of Willie Loman in Miller's *Death of a Salesman*, which he invested
with such physical presence that one critic noted,

> It's piercingly painful to see Willy lectured and called
> 'kid' by his arrogant young white boss – a devastating
> double-whammy of crass insensitivity and racist condes-
> cension. Warrington's patriarch is sometimes a bully,
> sometimes childlike, always frightened. His body, drained
> of vigour, seems almost to have a bulk that he can no longer
> bear; at one point he collapses to the floor in a hunched
> heap, head drawn in like a tortoise.

This is an actor who grows in strength and purpose with every part
he plays. He is of an older generation than many other celebrated
black actors, so it is perhaps unsurprising that he is more politicized in his approach. He approves of racial quotas in the acting
profession, for example, on the principle that 'we're not all starting
from the same place.' He is reliably phlegmatic on the question of
what actors should do with the opportunities offered. 'There was
no plan,' he has said of his own career. 'There's never a plan. It's
just you do what's in front of you and you end up where you end
up.' Setting aside his particular circumstances, this seems like good
advice for any actor.

Sophie Okonedo was born on 11 August 1968 in London, and
was raised on a large council estate (since demolished) in Wembley
Park. Then, for a while, she lived above a fish-and-chip shop. Her
mother was Jewish, and her father was the son of a Nigerian, so
she was blessed with the mixed ancestry of which she is proud.
An actor must understand many worlds. Her father left the family
when Okonedo was young, and she recollected that

> what interests me is that I've been brought up in a white
> family, and, being black myself, I can really relate to that

side of it – questioning your heritage and where you're from; asking, 'Is this really my parent?' Particularly when you're young, and everyone says, 'That can't be your mum.' Nowadays everyone's mixed race, it's not such a big deal, but in the 70s when I was growing up it was more unusual. I used to say, 'Mum, am I adopted?'

Okonedo's maternal grandmother used to take her to the Wembley Liberal synagogue, but she did not feel entirely happy there. She has said, 'I certainly felt that, as a teenager, a lot of the parents of [Jewish] children would have been unhappy if they came home with me. I certainly felt stared at when I went to synagogue.' Questions of identity are always implicated in the actor's art. 'I have a sense of those things inside me, which is very handy for acting,' she remarked. 'There are a lot of things I can draw on.'

The first intimation of Okonedo's later professional life came when she watched a young black girl playing an orphan in a televised Royal Variety Performance excerpt from the musical *Annie*, and told her mother, 'That's what I want to do.' She said later that 'literally, from that moment on that was just what I decided to do. That was that. No deviating.' Her mother, then a teacher of Pilates, took her to the musical itself, but the black girl was no longer in the cast. There may be much here to ponder, on the black orphan and the absence. She did not perform at school, unlike many young actors, but 'it was always in my mind.' She was neither encouraged nor discouraged in her young ambition and, having finished school at the age of sixteen, she started work on a clothing stall in Portobello Market, as well as with the Sanctuary health club in Covent Garden. While there she came upon an advertisement in *Time Out* for a writing school at the Royal Court, organized by Hanif Kureishi, which in turn led to her enlisting in the youth theatre group and a small part in the Royal Court's *Serious Money*, Caryl Churchill's 'city comedy' of 1987. At this point she applied for three drama schools before securing a scholarship at RADA. She thoroughly enjoyed her training there: 'So I thought, "Wow, this acting game is really easy. So easy!"'

It may not have been as easy as she anticipated. Some of Okonedo's earliest theatrical appearances were in conjunction with the RSC, in which she played succeeding roles in four non-Shakespearean plays: Richard Brome's *A Jovial Crew*, *The Odyssey*, Christopher Marlowe's *Tamburlaine the Great* and Middleton and Rowley's *The Changeling*. But she did not achieve true recognition until she was cast as the female lead in Trevor Nunn's production of *Troilus and Cressida* at the National in 1999, for which she was rewarded with glowing reviews. The critic of the *Sunday Times* observed that 'Sophie Okonedo's Cressida is one of the very few I have seen to come close to the character's tragic ambiguity.' *Variety* reported that 'Okonedo – in the more difficult role – moves from (somewhat excessive) girlish flirtation to a benumbed fearfulness and beyond. Realizing that the brutishness of the Greeks demands its own guileful, pragmatic response, Okonedo's Cressida emerges all too fully as all things to men, at mournful cost to her own identity.'

Okonedo said later, 'I had a fantastic experience there. I was part of a company of actors and I really grieved when I left because I felt very much a part of the whole building . . . It was a real privilege to be waiting in the wings to go on.' Hers was the first black Cressida on the English stage, but she has said of such roles in general that 'it might cross my mind that this is interesting because it was written white, but that is secondary. It may surprise you, but I actually don't think about being black most days. So I don't think about it when I'm acting. I'm not thinking: "Is this person black or white?"' That sentiment is common to black actors of her generation.

Okonedo's next major stage part came as the mother in Joe Penhall's *Haunted Child* at the Royal Court in 2011. *The Guardian* observed that 'Sophie Okonedo as Julie is the very pattern of maternal anxiety while making an overwhelming case for the pleasures of domestic stability and daily normality,' while *The Observer* noted, 'Sophie Okonedo brings to the part of the mother all her considerable ability for suggesting pent-up, about-to-brim-over emotion: she looks sodden with unspent tears.' She travelled to Broadway for her next two significant dramas, *A Raisin in the Sun* by Lorraine Hansberry in 2014 and as Elizabeth Proctor in Arthur Miller's *The Crucible* two years later, although the latter left her exhausted. 'It was intense,' she recalled. 'I found it very tough. It was a very long run of a play that really has no light in it. I was so affected by the part, it was just so gloomy, the play . . . it left a little cloud over me.' She also said, 'it is just so dark and I found that tiring. There's a lot of anger in the play. That was a show I probably shouldn't have done for 16 weeks; it was a bit too long.'

Okonedo returned to the London stage in 2017 with Edward Albee's *The Goat, or Who Is Sylvia?* at the Haymarket. It was in certain respects another difficult play, and Okonedo herself said,

> I found it quite shocking. But everything I do is based on instinct, so when people say 'Why did you do that?' I don't really know . . . my gut just told me to. My body is my barometer. The minute I go into my head to try to work something out, that muddles me a little bit – my instincts are always very physical. It might be that I start shaking when I read the script or break out in a sweat.

She works from her feelings outwards to her performance, and that may account for her emotional perceptiveness and her capacity for concentrated and controlled power. That level of intensity must be extended for the length of the play. So *The Stage* said of *The Goat* that 'her performance is rich, her emotional responses to the situation convincing,' and *WhatsOnStage* added that it was she 'who most perfectly catches the emotional tug that gives the play its impact'.

Okonedo's most recent role was that of Cleopatra in Shakespeare's play at the National in 2018, for which she was awarded the Natasha Richardson Award for Best Actress. The *Evening Standard* commented that she 'revels in Cleopatra's contradictory nature, her disarming mix of regal pride and playful charm'. Another critic noted that 'Okonedo is a delight as the petulant mistress, regaling her attendants with fickle attention-seeking flirtations. But, as much as she demurs and depends on her Antony's devotion, Okonedo's Cleopatra radiates poise and self-assurance.' Michael Billington wrote in *The Guardian* that, 'like all good Cleopatras, she is also quick-witted: she assumes a self-mocking majesty with the messenger who comes with news of Antony's marriage before ducking him in the palace pool. Okonedo is fiery, funny, mercurial.' Speaking of this role, Okonedo reflected, 'I work at the words deeply, for months and months, then somehow she is past me and I can't think of anything else other than the way she feels. Although it is me as well, and I use myself in all of it.' This might serve as a template for all English actors, or at least for the most accomplished. The text, as ever, is the teacher. But it evinces too the influence of modern drama training, in which it is recognized that the actor must begin with the self or there can be no reality to their performance.

It may be argued that the role of Cleopatra does not offer the actor the latitude allowed, even demanded, by that of Hamlet. There are only so many interpretations available. Okonedo chose to emphasize the sheer size of Cleopatra's personality. She shows a queen who feels she should have been an empress, although she has no empire. Her lithe, quick movements, far too emphatic for someone whose little finger should be able to direct armies, her hot commands, which should be little more than murmurs if all obeyed as they should, show one whose gilded canopy is shrinking.

She has presence without power, at least without human power. For, as ever, there is something ethereal or preternatural about Okonedo's acting.

Suppleness is here the master theme. Some actors 'switch' from feeling to feeling; Okonedo darts. There is no 'join', no seam, in her acting. A quiet, heavy, bored cast of expression might leap into tigerish rage, her neck and face becoming all sinew and teeth. Then, as pain intrudes, the pillars under her cheeks collapse, the blazing eyes dim. She begins – and there is no other word for this – to *vibrate* with grief.

She might be called the mistress of stress. 'Emotional physical resonance' is the keynote of all acting, and Okonedo offers it in abundance. You might be watching an entire play performed within one human body, with every organ, even the tiniest, stretched until it sings. Given Okonedo's avowed inability to sing, this image might seem wayward, but she might perhaps approve of it. Her voice, naturally warm, usually retains the soft consonants and languorous vowels of her native city. In this, too, she is unusual. Even when playing the aristocrat or the queen, she makes little concession to received pronunciation. She will be herself, come what may.

All artists tend to lay emphasis upon what they wish they could do, rather than what they do, and Okonedo is no exception. In common with so many actors who have found themselves guided, or coerced, into film, she feels always the pang of the first longing. 'I don't think I'd be an actor,' she said, 'unless I did theatre as well.' And then she offers us the unanswerable thrill, which both Burbage and Alleyn also knew: 'There's something about the energy that happens between the playwright, yourself as the actor, the other actors on stage, the audience, and this thing, this energy, is going through all those voices, and you can feel it.'

It has been the fate of many English actors to see their love of theatre atrophy after the blandishments of the screen. Like Glenda

Jackson, her only obvious antecedent, Okonedo seems a prophet crying in the wilderness, at home amid the rocks, feeding on the locusts and wild honey of humanity at its most desperate. But she gives no hint of this in interviews. There we see a figure whose thoughtfulness is tempered by human warmth and an almost girlish enthusiasm. She sometimes seems almost unaware of her fame, and does not conform to any theatrical stereotype of vanity or envy. That gift of ordinariness (for it is a gift) may come from her modest childhood or from her unassuming character. It may also derive from her mixed identity, which allows her to see the world from a variety of perspectives, English, Nigerian and Jewish among them. But perhaps she is just herself, and in fact she seems most adept at playing unremarkable people thrust into remarkable situations: 'I don't like going for more than a year without doing theatre. I don't mind falling flat on my face so long as I feel I'm open to the possibility of something extraordinary happening . . . My preference is for stories about how we get through this life, what it is to be human, because I'm always struggling with it myself.'

Adrian Anthony Lester was born Anthony Harvey on 14 August 1968 in Birmingham. He was the son of Jamaican immigrants, his mother a medical secretary and his father the manager of a cleaning company. From an early age he sang as a treble in the choir of St Chad's Cathedral in the city. He attended Archbishop Masterson Roman Catholic School, and later admitted that he was 'crap at school. Just didn't apply myself'. But he applied himself in a different manner and at the age of fourteen he began to act in small parts with the Birmingham Youth Theatre, where he proved himself to be a good dancer and, having been trained in a choir, an excellent singer. When he left school at sixteen he attended Joseph Chamberlain Sixth Form College for one year, while also performing in an opera at the Midlands Art Centre in Birmingham. The following year he applied to RADA, and was accepted. His path was now set. 'I really felt like this kid from the small city coming to this massive one,' he said. 'I used to walk around the centre of London when I had a day off. I didn't know anyone. No one knew me.' That was about to change.

Lester first came to public attention as Rosalind in Cheek by Jowl's all-male production of *As You Like It*, which toured from July 1991, touched the Lyric, Hammersmith, over Christmas and then continued worldwide, finishing at the Albery in January and February 1995. Declan Donnellan, the co-founder and director of the company, noted that Lester 'gave a performance that managed to be both mesmerising and humble at the same time. He wore his breathtaking range so lightly, never telling you "I am a great actor" – which of course he was and is.' His voice in this production was light, soft and fluent, as if every surface in the face and mouth were gently vibrating, with only a slight burr to hint at its Birmingham origin. It could belong to one of Jane Austen's more cerebral heroines.

At the end of each performance, as Donnellan also recalled, 'when Adrian took off his headband, smiled at the audience, and said "If I were a woman . . ." you could often hear people gasp – because of their own personal miracle of belief, because they had theatrically "forgotten" that the young woman they had spent the evening with was a 6ft black guy.' Given that the production notes left no doubt of the show's central feature, and that the audience knew quite well that he was a man, Lester's success as a woman represents an achievement indeed. A blend of reflectiveness and femininity is apparent in everything he does, underlying, although never undercutting, even his most virile roles. Recalling how he was first drawn to acting, he mentions the transformative miracle before anything else. 'I was profoundly affected by this process of shape shifting,' he said. 'I remember thinking, "How do you do that?" To me, it was the alchemy, creating something precious out of nothing.' The production itself was a great success in part because of Lester's performance.

During a break in the tour Lester played Anthony Hope in the National Theatre's production of Stephen Sondheim and Hugh Wheeler's *Sweeney Todd: The Demon Barber of Fleet Street*. He also appeared at the Albery in 1996 as Robert in Sondheim's *Company*, of which *The Times* wrote that 'Lester brings an open-faced guilelessness and charm to a part that can be a blank. Small wonder that his director, Sam Mendes, calls Lester's performance "sensational".' Lester won the Olivier Award for Best Actor in a Musical, and it is easy to grasp the reason. Here he plays a man on the brink of divorce. As he sings the ballad 'Being Alive', we see the full force of the poet Sappho's description of love as 'the limb-loosener'. As he reaches out to the world, or perhaps to his wife, Lester's hands hang loose, his body out of joint, his face racked and babyish in grief. Like too many English actors, he was obliged to adopt a rather strained, rather generalized New York accent for the part, but this brittle casque cracks under the force of his feeling. His voice turns thick, always just about to break into a sob, but always – just about – recovering.

In 2002 Lester played Hamlet in a production at the Young Vic, directed by Peter Brook. His sweet prince wore dreadlocks that he grew against the advice of another black actor. 'He said to me,' Lester recalled, '"Your skin colour does half the work. But if you put dreads on as well, then you're helping them not to see the character." I went, "Do you know what? I'm going to go for it."' From the first, Lester shows himself entirely at ease in the verse. When he smiles, it is with a breadth and warmth suggestive of a young girl invited to a dance. Somehow, then, he contrives to make Hamlet *likeable*. It is as if he has considered and rejected the notion that cerebrality precludes warmth. In his dealings with his mother and uncle, however, he is just barely polite. A jeer and a snarl are implicit throughout. Above all, he seems to command them; so powerful is his sense of injustice that the king himself, played with wonderful authority, is rebuked and diminished in his presence.

It is hard to reconcile Hamlet's seemingly remorseless murder of Polonius with the popular view of the prince, but Lester offers at least a suggestion of remorse. He cries out in anguish as well as with the more familiar contempt and exasperation. It does not last long. After all the fury in his confrontation with his mother, he returns to a state of complete self-control, voice and body slowing to a quiet pulse of rage. The voice resumes its soft burr. We recall his tenderness to the murdered Polonius and feel that after all, in spite of all, he is a man of spiritual and moral weight. For a moment. Then, as he lifts the corpse, he dandles its hands in mockery, grinning.

Hamlet was followed by the equally formidable roles of the king in *Henry v* at the National Theatre in 2003 and Othello in 2013. Like all male actors of colour, Lester had to scale the mountain of the 'Moor'. Earlier – usually white – interpretations of Othello have tended to place him centre stage and at a remove to the other characters, magnificent but desperately alone. Partly at Lester's urging, this was eschewed in his version. His Othello is a military commander, at ease in society and at ease with his men. And were it not for Rory Kinnear's Iago glowering in the background, we would find it impossible to imagine any division between Othello and his wife, joyfully and playfully in love. There is not the slightest hint of later collapse, and so, when it comes, it is all the more violent and unsettling. Lester can be a very physical actor. He seizes Iago by the throat, jamming him against the wall. When he slaps his once-beloved wife, it is with a blow so stunning that she reels. It was in this period that Lester celebrated the role of the theatre:

> I'll never leave it. The intellectual and emotional power of the material has always been greater in the theatre for me; it's always a new conversation, because every audience is different. I know some actors don't want to see faces out there; they prefer to perform to a black wall. But

I like knowing I'm talking to people. I look out and I find someone to perform for: that person at the back, I'll do it for him. It really helps, especially with darker material.

In 2012 Lester appeared as Ira Aldridge in the play *Red Velvet* by his wife, Lolita Chakrabarti, at the Tricycle Theatre. It was a well-chosen role, since Aldridge himself was the first black actor of stature in nineteenth-century England. Aldridge was born in 1807 in New York, where he first began to act, but he came to England in his teens and there acquired the distinction of becoming the first black Shakespearean actor. So Lester performs double homage – to his great predecessor (who also performed Othello) and to the rich heritage of nineteenth-century acting that still exerts an influence on the contemporary stage. *The Telegraph* noted that he 'thrillingly radiates the charisma of the young Aldridge' and gave 'a strong impression of the heft of Aldridge's playing'. So, in a sense, he went back to his theatrical and imaginative roots.

It is perhaps not accidental that three black actors – Warrington, Okonedo and Lester – should emerge like a starburst in one period. Actors of colour had previously been marginalized or neglected, underused or misused, but the influence of American cinema and cultural changes in British television have changed that unhappy situation. It is quite possible, however, that the players described here would question the title of 'black actors' and prefer to be known as actors who just happened to be black.

BENEDICT TIMOTHY CARLTON CUMBERBATCH was born in Hammersmith on 19 July 1976 and brought up in the London borough of Kensington and Chelsea. His parents are both established actors. From the age of eight he was sent to boarding schools, the first of them being Brambletye in East Grinstead, Sussex, from which he graduated in 1990 as an arts scholar to Harrow School.

It might be said that he belongs to the new crop of public-school actors. At Harrow he became a member of the Rattigan Society, devoted to amateur dramatics, in which his first role was that of Titania. After leaving Harrow in 1995 he took a 'gap year' in West Bengal, India, before beginning at the University of Manchester in the autumn of 1996, where he studied drama. After graduating he attended the Edinburgh Festival, where he played in Albee's *The Zoo Story* before spending a further year training at LAMDA, where he obtained an MA in classical acting. In the period after LAMDA he was largely unemployed, and was obliged to earn his living as a waiter. It is always salutary to remember that most young actors spend much of their time doing anything but acting.

Cumberbatch returned to the Edinburgh Festival in 2001 to play Anton Schill in Friedrich Dürrenmatt's *The Visit*. In the spring of 2001, however, he was employed by the Open Air Theatre in Regent's Park, where he played Demetrius in *A Midsummer Night's Dream* and Ferdinand in *Love's Labour's Lost*. The following year, at the same theatre, he played Orlando in *As You Like It* and Benvolio in *Romeo and Juliet*. Intriguingly, these characters are all of the stolid, worthy type. It may be that Cumberbatch had not yet found his vision, although it is equally plausible that he had not yet found his audience. However that may be, in the years to come he was to be celebrated for qualities quite opposite to those of worthiness and stolidity.

In 2004 Cumberbatch began working at the Almeida, where he played Lyngstrand, an inanely cheerful invalid, in Ibsen's *The Lady from the Sea* and the following year George Tesman in the same playwright's *Hedda Gabler*. The latter, *The Stage* wrote, was 'a beautifully turned performance as a serious youthful scholar'. He was at the Almeida in 2006, when he played George in Tennessee Williams's *Period of Adjustment*. *Variety* recorded, 'Cumberbatch is good at indicating male fear of failure, and he in particular handles the added vowel sounds of the Texan drawl with serious aplomb.'

He then moved on to the Royal Court for two years with Eugène Ionesco's *Rhinoceros*, Max Frisch's *The Arsonists* and, in 2008, Martin Crimp's *The City*. A shift in casting becomes apparent: the last three parts are altogether darker and more surreal than those he had attempted before. It could be said that he had found his pedestal and was beginning to inch his way up its sides.

In 2010 Cumberbatch played the leading role of David Scott-Fowler in Terence Rattigan's *After the Dance* at the National Theatre. The *Daily Telegraph* commented that he was 'compelling as the alcoholic husband who sees a chance of a better life but realises he cannot bring it to fruition'. *The Guardian* added to the praise: 'Benedict Cumberbatch conveys not just the surface smoothness of the self-destructive David but also the intelligence of a man who realises he is a wastrel.' The *Evening Standard* may complete the trio of congratulations with its remark that 'while Cumberbatch's physical pose is remarkable, it's his voice that is the real marvel: dense as treacle, but unerringly precise.' He had much to offer as an actor, in other words, with lightness of touch and true sensitivity. He is one of the more 'soulful' English actors, delicate in address and earnest in intent. He possesses great charm and vulnerability, but he also has an inner sophistication that he can never quite suppress; he could not demonstrate the simplicity, for example, of Gary Oldman.

The following year Cumberbatch alternated with Jonny Lee Miller as Frankenstein and 'the creature' at the National Theatre. That dual role was, by definition, an impossible task. Cumberbatch had to move, smell, speak, see and above all react in a body that was not his own. We encounter him already fully grown, but composed of contending limbs and animated by a mind that does not know itself. Such was the task he set himself to accomplish. His carriage is chaos; awakening, he flings about his arms and legs, or perhaps they fling him about. It is not as if he is testing his limbs so much as trying to overcome them. It is a superb study, with all the sense of toil attendant on that word. For this portrayal of the creature, he received the Olivier Best Actor Award.

Cumberbatch's range is far greater than was originally thought, but nevertheless he tends to be given those parts that fit his unconventional good looks – that of the loner, the tortured genius, the soul haunted or hounded. Indeed, he might be said to have invented a new type with the 'omega male', a man in bitter and perpetual conflict with those smug and gleaming 'alphas' who so reliably win the crown or the girl. His gifts lie, moreover, in a realm that has only recently – which is to say, over the past hundred years – come to be regarded as the actor's true arena, that of transformation. Cumberbatch is a shape-shifter, extravagantly so on stage, more subtly on celluloid. And he manages a feat that perhaps only an Englishman could make plausible: to act so politely while terrifying the horses.

Chiwetel Umeadi Ejiofor was born on 10 July 1977 in Forest Gate, east London, to Nigerian parents. His father was a doctor, and his mother a pharmacist. He began his schooling at the Dulwich College Preparatory School, where he played the grave-digger in *Hamlet*. The first taste of acting seems to have stayed with him since, on moving to Dulwich College itself, he took the part of Angelo in *Measure for Measure*. It was while studying *Henry IV*, however, that he decided to become a theatre actor. He was drawn to the stage for another reason, too, since while growing up in London he never had any sense of community 'apart from in the theatre – it was the only communal activity I was engaged with.' To become a film actor was never the aim. It is a familiar story.

At the age of eighteen Ejiofor enrolled at the National Youth Theatre, where 'I was a kid with this funny name. And people were like, "It's going to be quite difficult for you to make any money as an actor."' But nothing could stop him now. For great or dedicated actors, there is only one star to follow. He subsequently gained a scholarship to LAMDA, but left after a year when offered a part in Steven Spielberg's film *Amistad*. For the NYT in 1995–6 he played Othello at the Bloomsbury Theatre and repeated the part at the Theatre Royal, Glasgow, later in 1996. For his performance as a mental patient, Christopher, in Penhall's *Blue/Orange* at the Cottesloe, he received the 2000 *Evening Standard* Theatre Award for Outstanding Newcomer. In 2007 he played Trigorin in Chekhov's *The Seagull* at the Royal Court, but the same year he again played his formative and most formidable role as Othello at the Donmar Warehouse, and with his exemplary performance he was awarded the Laurence Olivier Award for Best Actor.

As Othello, Ejiofor was very much 'the Moor', an African, a foreigner in Venice. But, explaining himself before the Senate, he is brisk, urgent, unapologetic. Ejiofor concedes nothing to the received notion that this speech is somehow prepared. He is in haste, impatient with his accusers. Here is no defence: there is none needed. It is a torrent of storytelling, unfiltered. From every word hangs a fruit: it is perhaps the richest rendition of that central moment. His last speech is 'wrought, perplex'd' indeed. The verse gushes, a torrent of pain and bewilderment and self-reproach. *The Times* noted that he was 'wonderfully warm when he's embracing a Desdemona he clearly adores, agonisingly bewildered when he's convinced that she is adulterous and genuinely tragic when he's wailing with grief over her deathbed'. Ejiofor also possesses a fine ear for Shakespeare's cadences and in particular for the music of Othello's speech patterns, together with the combined weight of phrases and pauses.

It is said of some actors that they are 'all soul'. Chiwetel Ejiofor seems to be all spirit. His eyes alone compel attention; set far apart, they resemble pools of light. In roles that demand villainy, he gives us ambiguity. At drama school, actors are told to doff their knowledge and park their minds. Like other great actors, however, Ejiofor gives us acting that is at once visceral and cerebral. But like other actors, too, he does not seem altogether at ease when called upon to reveal the secrets of his craft. An interviewer for *The Guardian* noted that 'he is convinced of one thing: what makes him a good actor is that we know nothing about him. And he is determined to keep it that way.' Of his identity he is not in the least self-conscious. 'I don't spend that much time think-ing about race in the context of the industry,' he has said. 'I just don't. I can't speak on those things, because I haven't thought about it that much.' He has explained that 'I'm not positioning myself. I'm not running for office. I'm an actor . . . Put it this way, I don't want to be known as Chiwetel, I want to be known as the actor-who-is-Chiwetel, if you follow my distinction there. Doesn't everybody want that, to be known by reputation, rather than the fact of X, Y or Z?'

Ejiofor's fellow actors speak warmly of him, and recognize his possession of professional rigour combined with personal tender-ness. Benedict Cumberbatch remarked that 'Chiwetel conjures up the most profound empathy . . . There's something about him and what he transmits as an actor that's very earnest, very vul-nerable, very sharp – and you really care for him.' Sarah Paulson observed that working with him proved 'a masterclass in subtlety and in nuance'. The British film director Steve McQueen speaks of Ejiofor's 'nobility'. This seems to be a fitting summary of his career so far. Few have a natural aristocracy of carriage and address, but Ejiofor has it in abundance.

Epilogue

What is the state of play and the state of playing? How will the future mould it? Overall, English actors are more persuasive, more accurate and more naturalistic than they were at the end of the last century. They are, to be blunt, 'better', although not necessarily greater. This is only partly owing to actors' training. If anything, they are more influenced by working in a 'post-Method' period. It is possible, for example, to conflate styles – even in the same production – that would not normally blend, from the flamboyant to the intimate.

The perennial allure of the actor is now linked with the culture of the celebrity, although this is only a new variation on an ancient theme. For centuries the audience has yearned to resemble the players or to have what they have; they have also wished that the characters on stage might be real, and truly part of the human world. To the fascination of the shaman, or simply of the transformer, is now added the nimbus of fame. This carries with it certain new and perhaps uncovenanted responsibilities. The English actor, for example, seems to be a far more politicized creature than his or her forerunners.

Over the past half-century, sporadic attempts have been made to reinstate the great civic Mystery cycles. At the beginning of one production in York, the actor playing God paused to sip at a cup of tea: creating the universe, he explained, was thirsty work. A small gaggle of onlookers smiled indulgently from the pavement. There was no vast, rapt audience. God was not summoned in a blaze of verse. The cup of tea set the tone. Perhaps this is as it should be; actors will reflect the age, whether they wish it or not.

Even as provincial rep has declined, the urban fringe has flourished. There are more than fifty fringe venues in London alone. No one, the actor least of all, expects any remuneration from this, but it is an encouraging development nonetheless. For the actor, it has an added benefit in the frisson of knowing that you are engaged in acting purely for the joy of it.

A fringe theatre is usually found above a pub, with all the restrictions that that entails. Space is limited, and may be reserved for the next performance, so actors must often rehearse somewhere else, such as in a community centre or even a church. Speed is of the essence, as the actor changes costume or assembles and dismantles the set. Above all, actors in performance must overcome formidable competition from the public house below in the roar of laughter, the pulse of music or the frenetic yells of support for a favourite team. In some respects, therefore, the actor in the fringe is closer to an Elizabethan counterpart than is the actor in the West End. The pro bono nature of acting in fringe inevitably means, however, that not all can participate, or not for very long. While it can sometimes lead to greater things, the fringe sooner or later proves an expensive indulgence.

Bridging the gap between the pre-modern and modern ages is the Elizabethan actor; he wore the livery of the courtier and was as close as most would get to an aristocrat. The groundlings, after all, went to *Henry V* not to be reminded of their lodgings in Cheapside, but rather to forget them. History thus gives the lie to the notion that 'relevance' is the only consideration that theatre practitioners should bear in mind.

Does any artist have a niche, or their own particular hollow, in history's temple? Perhaps some do, but actors do not. Increasingly, in a world where most are talented and all are skilled, the only gift that makes an actor exceptional is his or her appearance. So it is little wonder that many have decided to take matters into their own hands. Perhaps the most vivid and vital theatre troupe now working, Complicité, was founded, in the words of its artistic director, as 'a project between a group of people who wanted to work and weren't prepared to wait around and have work given to them'. This leads us to the English actor's current predicament and the solution that many have adopted.

The master theme appears to be *autarkeia*: do it yourself. You create a company. You form collectives. You write your own plays, direct them and produce them. Everyone participates, in a manner familiar from centuries ago. One young actor observed that 'when you've created it, you're giving some of that power back to yourself.' Another expanded on this by remarking that 'gone are the days of sitting by your phone, waiting for your agent to call: "come on, come on – where's that part at the National?" It's never going to happen. You've got to put yourself out there in whatever way you can.' All this is heartening. Since the post-war rise of the director, actors have tended to passivity; now, perhaps, they are beginning to remember that they are, after all, artists and not simply hired workers. But there are less encouraging signs, for example the fact that few young actors nowadays want to play in classical theatre.

For those who do succeed, and succeed early, unexpected dangers await. Imelda Staunton observed that the young actor can be 'very highly exposed very early on'. This is a thought echoed by many of an older acting generation. What happens next? What happens when you fail, as fail you sometimes will? You are swept aside. In contrast, the Liverpool Everyman – nurse and tutor to so many great actors – is now reinstating a repertory theatre company after a hiatus of twenty-five years. Other considerations aside, the company wanted to give young actors who could not afford drama school the chance to audition and to show what they could achieve.

The actor now lives in a world of many media, and multi-disciplinary theatre is one result. There is also devised theatre, in which actors, not necessarily guided by a director, create their own drama. Street theatre can still be seen and may, in time, prove the actor's best hope. But the question cannot be deferred. Will theatre survive in its present state? This question was compounded by the threat of ever-recurring lockdown during the COVID-19 pandemic. It may be that, after the great collapse of 2020, a new kind of theatre will be born, one that relies far less on subsidy, a theatre in the open, which is spontaneous and which returns to its ancient roots. Perhaps the English actor will re-mount the pageant waggon and rattle off for the provinces. Or it may be that players will find new and ancient spaces in the crumbling tenement, the stone circle, the disused village pavilion. Come what may, they will once more need their optimism and their recognition that they are part of a tradition that has lasted more than a thousand years.

Further reading

Archer, William, *Eminent Actors* (London, 1890)

—, *Henry Irving, Actor and Manager: A Critical Study* (London, 1885)

—, *William Charles Macready* (London, 1890)

Astington, John, *Actors and Acting in Shakespeare's Time: The Art of Stage Playing* (Cambridge, 2010)

Auerbach, Nina, *Ellen Terry: Player in Her Time* (Philadelphia, PA, 1987)

Baker, Henry Barton, *History of the London Stage and Its Famous Players (1576–1903)* (London and New York, 1904)

—, *Our Old Actors* (London, 1881)

Barker, Clive, and Maggie B. Gale, eds, *British Theatre Between the Wars, 1918–1939* (Cambridge, 2000)

Barratt, Mark, *Ian McKellen: An Unofficial Biography* (London, 2006)

Beadle, Richard, and Alan J. Fletcher, eds, *The Cambridge Companion to Medieval English Theatre* (Cambridge, 2008)

Benedetti, Jean, *David Garrick and the Birth of Modern Theatre* (London, 2001)

Billington, Michael, *One Night Stands: A Critic's View of Modern British Theatre* (London, 2002)

Brown, John Russell, ed., *The Oxford Illustrated History of Theatre* (Oxford, 2001)

Callow, Simon, *Being an Actor* (London, 2004)

—, *Charles Laughton: A Difficult Actor* (London, 1987)

Cibber, Colley, *An Apology for the Life of Mr Colley Cibber* (London, 1966)

Clough, Valerie, *Sir Ralph Richardson: A Life in the Theatre* (London, 1989)

Cordner, Michael, and Peter Holland, eds, *Players, Playwrights, Playhouses: Investigating Performance, 1660–1800* (New York, 2007)

Coveney, Michael, *Maggie Smith: A Biography* (London, 2015)

Curry, Julian, *Shakespeare on Stage: Thirteen Leading Actors on Thirteen Key Roles* (London, 2010)

Desmet, Christy, ed., *Lives of Shakespearian Actors*, part IV, vol. I: *Helen Faucit, Lucia Elizabeth Vestris and Fanny Kemble by Their Contemporaries* (London and New York, 2011)

Dillon, Janette, *The Cambridge Introduction to Early English Theatre* (Cambridge, 2006)

Donohue, Joseph, ed., *The Cambridge History of British Theatre*, vol. II: *1660 to 1895* (Cambridge, 2004)

Emeljanow, Victor, ed., *Lives of Shakespearian Actors*, Part V: *Herbert Beerbohm Tree, Henry Irving and Ellen Terry by Their Contemporaries* (London and New York, 2013)

Findlater, Richard, *These Our Actors: A Celebration of the Theatre Acting of Peggy Ashcroft, John Gielgud, Laurence Olivier, Ralph Richardson* (London, 1983)

Fisk, Deborah Payne, ed., *The Cambridge Companion to English Restoration Theatre* (Cambridge, 2000)

Freeman, Lisa A., ed., *Lives of Shakespearian Actors*, part II: *Edmund Kean, Sarah Siddons and Harriet Smithson by Their Contemporaries* (London and New York, 2009)

Gielgud, John, *An Actor and His Time* (London, 1979)

Goring, Paul, ed., *Lives of Shakespearian Actors*, part I: *David Garrick, Charles Macklin and Margaret Woffington by Their Contemporaries* (London and New York, 2008)

Gurr, Andrew, *The Shakespearean Stage, 1574–1642* (Cambridge, 1992)

Hartnoll, Phyllis, *The Oxford Companion to the Theatre* (Oxford, 1983)

Hazlitt, William, *Dramatic Essays* (London, 1895)

Highfill, Jr, Philip H., Kalman A. Burnim and Edward A. Langhans, *A Biographical Dictionary of Actors, Actresses, Musicians, Dancers, Managers and Other Stage Personnel in London, 1660–1800* (Carbondale and Edwardsville, IL, 1991)

Hillebrand, Harold Newcomb, *Edmund Kean* (New York, 1933)

Holland, Peter, and Stephen Orgel, eds, *From Script to Stage in Early Modern England* (Basingstoke, 2004)

Holroyd, Michael, *A Strange Eventful History: The Dramatic Lives of Ellen Terry, Henry Irving and Their Remarkable Families* (London, 2009)

Howe, Elizabeth, *The First English Actresses: Women and Drama, 1660–1700* (Cambridge, 1992)

Irving, Laurence, *Henry Irving: The Actor and His World* (London, 1989)

Kendall, Alan, *David Garrick: A Biography* (London, 1985)

Leach, Robert, *An Illustrated History of British Theatre and Performance* (London and New York, 2020)

Lewes, George Henry, *On Actors and the Art of Acting* (London, 1875)

Marston, Westland, *Our Recent Actors: Being Recollections Critical, and, in Many Instances, Personal, of Late Distinguished Performers of Both Sexes* (London, 1890)

Miller, John, ed., *Darling Judi: A Celebration of Judi Dench* (London, 2004)

Milling, Jane, Peter Thomson, Baz Kershaw and Joseph Donohue, eds, *The Cambridge History of British Theatre* (Cambridge, 2004)

Moody, Jane, and Daniel O'Quinn, eds, *The Cambridge Companion to British Theatre, 1730–1830* (Cambridge, 2007)

Morley, Sheridan, *John G: The Authorised Biography of John Gielgud* (London, 2001)

Nungezer, Edwin, *A Dictionary of Actors and of Other Persons Associated with the Public Representation of Plays in England before 1642* (New Haven, CT, and London, 1929)

Olivier, Laurence, *On Acting* (London, 1987)

Oya, Reiko, *Representing Shakespearean Tragedy: Garrick, the Kembles, and Kean* (Cambridge, 2007)

Redgrave, Michael, *In My Mind's I: An Actor's Autobiography* (New York, 1983)

Redgrave, Vanessa, *Vanessa Redgrave: An Autobiography* (London, 1991)

Sawyer, Robert, ed., *Lives of Shakespearian Actors*, part III, vol. I: *Charles Kean, Samuel Phelps and William Charles Macready by Their Contemporaries* (London and New York, 2010)

Shepherd, Simon, *The Cambridge Introduction to Modern British Theatre* (Cambridge, 2009)

Styan, J. L., *The English Stage: A History of Drama and Performance* (Cambridge, 2008)

Swanson, Alan, *David Garrick and the Development of English Comedy: A Study of Adaptation on the Eighteenth-Century Stage* (Lewiston, NY, 2013)

Tomalin, Claire, *Mrs Jordan's Profession: The Story of a Great Actress and a Future King* (London, 2012)

Trussler, Simon, *The Cambridge Illustrated History of British Theatre* (Cambridge, 2000)

Tynan, Kenneth, *Tynan on Theatre* (Harmondsworth, 1964)

Walter, Harriet, *Other People's Shoes: Thoughts on Acting* (London, 2003)

Wells, Stanley, *Great Shakespeare Actors: Burbage to Branagh* (Oxford, 2015)

White, Mark, *Kenneth Branagh* (London, 2005)

Wiles, David, *Shakespeare's Clown: Actor and Text in the Elizabethan Playhouse* (Cambridge, 1987)

Williams, Carolyn, ed., *The Cambridge Companion to English Melodrama* (Cambridge, 2018)

Acknowledgements

I would like to thank my two research assistants, Murrough O'Brien and Thomas Wright, for their invaluable assistance in preparing this volume. I would also like to thank Dr John Gayner for allowing me access to his important theatrical collection.

Index